THE NEW INTIFADA

THE NEW INTIFADA
RESISTING ISRAEL'S APARTHEID

◆

EDITED BY ROANE CAREY

INTRODUCTION BY NOAM CHOMSKY

VERSO

LONDON • NEW YORK

First published by Verso 2001
© The contributors 2001

The moral rights of the authors have been asserted

Verso
UK: 6 Meard Street, London W1F 0EG
USA: 180 Varick Street, New York, NY 10014-4606

Verso is the imprint of New Left Books

ISBN 1-85984-377-8

British Library Cataloguing in Publication Data
A catalogue for this book is available from the British Library

Library of Congress Cataloging-in-Publication Data
A catalog record for this book is available from the Library of Congress

Typeset and designed by Steven Mosier
All photographs ©Ron Wurzer, unless otherwise noted
Printed and bound in the UK by Biddles Ltd, Guildford and King's Lynn

CONTENTS

FOREWORD

When Ariel Sharon's visit to the Haram al-Sharif/Temple Mount in September 2000 led to the eruption of rioting, few could have predicted the extent and duration of the violence that followed. But Palestinian frustration had been mounting for years. As the contributors to this volume demonstrate, in various ways, the plight of Palestinians only grew worse during the "peace process," as the series of Oslo agreements became known. Their lands continued to be expropriated, their groves and orchards plowed under, the territories under their nominal control criss-crossed by several hundred miles of Jewish-only bypass roads, whose purpose was to further their dispossession.

The American people have a particular responsibility in this conflict, since our government provides Israel with several billion dollars in military and economic aid every year. The US government has for decades enabled Israel's brutal repression and continued illegal occupation. No less crucial has been US diplomatic backing—at the United Nations and elsewhere, Washington has ensured carte blanche for its favorite client state at every turn.

The original inspiration for *The New Intifada* arose out of disgust at the mainstream media's consistent misrepresentation of the basic facts of this uprising, merely the latest installment in a long history of fabrication. This book attempts to correct the balance, in part by analyzing the origins of the conflict, particularly the structural flaws in the Oslo agreements, and in part simply by giving voice to the Palestinian side of the conflict and to those Israelis and Americans who abhor the repression carried out in their name—voices rarely tolerated in the US media. Some critics will no doubt accuse the book of bias; in fact, the contributors have in every case applied universal principles of justice and human rights to the Israel-Palestine conflict. Those who expect such a volume to be uncritically supportive of the Palestinian leadership or strategy will be disappointed, but we have no intention of substituting one fairy tale for another.

The New Intifada attempts to further an understanding of the conflict by addressing not only the struggle in the territories and the media distortions attendant upon them, but also the continuing crisis of the Palestinian refugees, especially those in Lebanon. Through an interview with Azmi Bishara, a Palestinian Member of the Knesset, the book examines the problems facing the Palestinian citizens of Israel, a constituency of which much of the world is entirely ignorant. We also discuss strategies for achieving justice for Palestinians, without which there can be no peace for Israel.

As the repression intensified, Palestinians increasingly resorted to suicide bombings. In late May a series of attacks in Israel culminated in the June 1 bombing of a disco in Tel Aviv, with twenty-two dead and some 100 injured. It was followed by a cease-fire, which was broken immediately by both sides. As this book goes to press, Israeli Prime Minister Ariel Sharon is demanding a complete cessation of Palestinian resistance to the occupation while offering nothing substantive in return, clearly a recipe for more violence. At the same time, his long career as a war criminal began to attract renewed attention after a June BBC documentary highlighted his role in the 1982 Sabra and Shatila massacre in Beirut, Lebanon. The following day an official criminal investigation was opened in Belgium, whose laws allow for the prosecution even of heads of state for war crimes, crimes against humanity and genocide. Human Rights Watch subsequently joined the call for a criminal investigation.

There are frequent references in this volume to the *Nakba*, or "catastrophe," the common term by which Palestinians remember the mass expulsions and massacres that accompanied the 1948 war. After the disco bombing, there were increasingly open discussions in Israel—in the Cabinet, the military high command and the media—of another such "solution" to the question of Palestine. Both the authoritative Jane's Information Group and UPI reported that Israel had completed detailed plans for a massive invasion of Palestinian areas that would include jet fighter and helicopter gunship attacks, artillery bombardment, and at least two divisions of infantry and paratroopers. Israeli deaths were expected to be in the low hundreds, with Palestinian deaths in the thousands. A possible foreshadowing of how this might be carried out could be seen in the area south of Hebron: after the murder of an Israeli settler in early July, the Israeli army closed off the entire area to outsiders, including human rights observers, journalists and Red Cross workers, and began a days-long scorched-earth campaign, evicting hundreds of inhabitants, demolishing dozens of houses and destroying wells, reservoirs and farmlands. We may choose to ignore the portents; we will be less able to evade the consequences.

Several people provided invaluable assistance at various stages of the book's production. Verso publisher Colin Robinson originally conceived the idea, and he has been consistently supportive throughout. Ali Abunimah and Nader Hashemi gave helpful advice in the selection of some contributors. Shifra Stern has been a font of information and an immensely resourceful media guide since well before I began work on this volume. Nina Nazionale read the text at several stages and suggested numerous improvements. Any oversights or mistakes are, however, entirely my own responsibility. And finally, I owe a debt of gratitude to Ashraf El Amreeti, Qassem Ali, and their colleagues at Ramattan Studios; Omar Barghouti; Nidal and Issa Barham; Moussa and Afaf Hashhash; and Mouin Rabbani and Abdel-Rahman El Burai (Abu Hussein) for their gracious hospitality.

Roane Carey, July 2001

INTRODUCTION

NOAM CHOMSKY

The latest phase of the Israel-Palestine conflict opened on September 29, 2000, the Muslim day of prayer, when Prime Minister Ehud Barak dispatched a massive and intimidating police and military presence to the Al-Aqsa compound. Predictably, that led to clashes as thousands of people streamed out of the mosque, leaving several Palestinians dead and about 200 wounded.[1] Whatever Barak may have intended, there could hardly have been a more effective way to set the stage for the shocking sequel, particularly after the visit of Ariel Sharon and his military entourage to the compound the day before, which might have passed without such serious consequences.

The opening events established the pattern for what followed. "During these crucial days there was no evidence of Palestinian gunfire," an important UN inquiry found. In the following months, as far as they could determine, "the IDF [Israeli army], operating behind fortifications with superior weaponry, endured not a single serious casualty as a result of Palestinian demonstrations and, further, their soldiers seemed to be in no life-threatening danger during the course of these events," as they killed hundreds of Palestinians and imposed an even more brutal regime than before, subjecting the population to harsh collective punishment and humiliation, the hallmark of the occupation for many years. (The UN report found that "the majority of Israeli casualties resulted from incidents on settlement roads and at relatively isolated checkpoints…as a consequence of the settlements, and irritations resulting indirectly therefrom. In this regard, account must be taken of settler violence against Palestinian civilians in areas adjoining settlements, and of IDF complicity in such violence.") The current practices, along with earlier ones, have been reviewed in extensive detail and bitterly condemned by international human rights organizations. Like the report of the been virtually ignored in the United States.[2]

Reports of human rights organizations receive wide attention wh otherwise; the Al-Aqsa Intifada breaks no new ground in that reg illustration as I write, in April 2001 Human Rights Watch published a to Israeli atrocities in the Hebron district, where tens of thousands imprisoned for months while a few hundred settlers are free to abu their property under military protection. The study was immediately r (and perhaps only) mention in the United States was in paragraph 1 days later.[3]

Left: Palestinians cover their faces to evade Israeli army tear gas in Ramallah

The pattern of events underscores a fact of crucial importance. It is highly misleading to use the phrase "Israel-Palestine conflict," as I did at the outset: it should be termed the "US/Israel-Palestine" conflict. For similar reasons, it is improper—particularly in the United States—to condemn "Israeli atrocities," just as such practice would have been improper in the case of Russian-backed crimes in Eastern Europe, US-backed crimes in Central America, and innumerable other such examples.

These conclusions are illustrated graphically by the events in the first days of the Al-Aqsa Intifada. On September 30, the IDF killed 12-year-old Muhammad al-Durra in response to rock-throwing (in which he was not involved) near the small Israeli settlement at Netzarim, which is hardly more than an excuse for a major military base and road system that has cut the Gaza Strip in two, one of several barriers separating Gaza City from the south (and Egypt). "IDF soldiers in a heavily protected bunker fired repeatedly upon Palestinian Red Crescent Society (PRCS) ambulances attempting to evacuate" the severely wounded boy and other casualties, Human Rights Watch reported. "The firing from the IDF outpost continued for at least forty-five minutes, although during this time there was no apparent return fire from Palestinian demonstrators or police." Ambulances sought in vain to "evacuate large numbers of Palestinians wounded by heavy IDF fire from the bunker and possibly from sniper towers in the Netzarim settlement"; earthen berms were constructed "to provide people with some protection from sniper fire from the Netzarim settlement." Amnesty International found that the IDF "apparently even targeted people helping to remove the wounded," reporting that a PRCS ambulance driver "died after Israeli troops shot him in the chest" as he sought to evacuate casualties.[4]

All of this proceeds thanks to direct US support, tolerance, and evasion.

The next day, October 1, "Israeli special forces firing from and around a well-protected rooftop position" killed two Palestinians, facing no apparent threat themselves. On the same day, Israel escalated the level of violence when "an IDF helicopter gunship fired recklessly and repeatedly on areas immediately adjacent to the [PRCS] field hospital at Netzarim, disrupting operations there," at least 400 meters from any clashes; and on the Egypt-Gaza border, helicopters fired missiles that killed two Palestinians and wounded dozens. The next day, October 2, helicopters firing missiles at buildings and cars in the Netzarim area killed ten Palestinians and wounded thirty-five.[5]

IDF helicopters are US helicopters with Israeli pilots. American supply is critical because "it is impractical to think that we can manufacture helicopters or major weapons systems of this type in Israel," the Ministry of Defense reported.[6]

On October 3, the defense correspondent of Israel's most prestigious newspaper reported the signing agreement with the Clinton Administration for "the largest purchase of military helicopters by Air Force in a decade," along with spare parts for Apache attack helicopters for which an been signed in mid-September. Also in mid-September, the Israeli press reported, US a joint exercise with the IDF in the Negev aimed at reconquest of the territories that had been transferred to the Palestinian Authority. The Marines provided training with weapons that the IDF still lacked, and in "American fighting techniques."[7]

On October 4, the world's leading military journal reported that Washington had approved a request for Apache helicopters along with more advanced attack equipment. The same day, the US press reported that Apaches were attacking apartment complexes with rockets at Netzarim. In response to queries from European journalists, US officials said that "US weapons sales do not carry a stipulation that the weapons can't be used against civilians. We cannot second-guess an Israeli commander who calls in helicopter gunships." White House national security spokesman P.J. Crowley added, "We are not in a position to pass judgment on decisions made on either side," calling on both sides to exercise restraint. A few weeks later, the local Palestinian leader Hussein Abayat was killed by a missile launched from an Apache helicopter (along with two women standing nearby), as the assassination campaign against the indigenous leadership was initiated.[8]

Rushing new military helicopters to Israel under these circumstances and with such authorization for use is surely newsworthy. There was no news report or editorial comment. The sole mention in the United States was in an opinion piece in the Raleigh, North Carolina, *News and Observer*.[9] An Amnesty International condemnation of the sale of US helicopters also passed unnoticed. That remained true in the months that followed, including the most recent announced shipment in February 2001, a $500 million deal for Boeing Apache Longbow helicopters, the most advanced in the US arsenal, noted marginally in the United States as business news. In a similar style, a major news story (May 17) reported the reluctance of President Bush to become more "directly involved" in the Israel-Palestine conflict, and his Administration's inability to support the Mitchell committee report by asking Israel for a settlement freeze because Prime Minister Sharon is "philosophically opposed to such a proposal." On the same day, a few lines under "World Briefing" reported that the US Army Corp of Engineers began construction of a $266 million Israeli military base (paid for by the United States) in the Negev, a symbol "of America's continuing commitment to Israel's security," Ambassador Martin Indyk declared.[10]

Well reported, however, are stern US admonitions to Palestinians to end their terror, because "we do not believe in rewarding violence" (US Ambassador Indyk)[11]; and regular official statements deploring violence and expressing tempered disapproval of Israel's assassination program. Washington's actual attitudes are revealed by its actions; the coverage speaks for itself.

None of this is unusual. With regard to Israel-Palestine specifically, the pattern has been routine for over thirty years, ever since the United States separated itself from the international consensus on the conflict. Though the most significant facts are missing from mainstream commentary, and often ignored or misrepresented even in scholarly work, they are not controversial. They provide the indispensable background for any serious understanding of what is happening now.

US-Israel relations improved dramatically after Israel's military victory in 1967. In the background, as always with regard to this region, lie its incomparable energy resources. Emerging from World War II as the overwhelmingly dominant global power, the United States undertook careful and sophisticated planning to organize the world system in its interests. That included effective control over the region's oil, previously shared with France and Britain. France was removed, and the British gradually declined to the status of a "junior partner," in the rueful words of a British Foreign Officer. Though there was much talk about the Russians, and there is no doubt that the possibility of global war was the major element in strategic planning, the immediate problem throughout was the threat of independent nationalism—a fact now largely conceded, even in official documents.[12]

In essentials, the United States took over the framework of control of the Middle East that was established by Britain after World War I. The states of the region were to be administered by what Britain called an "Arab Facade," weak and pliable; Britain's "absorption" of the colonies would be "veiled by constitutional fictions as a protectorate, a sphere of influence, a buffer State, and so on," a device more cost-effective than direct rule. When needed, British muscle would be available. The United States modified the system by incorporating a second tier of "local cops on the beat," as the Nixon Administration called them: local gendarmes to ensure order, preferably non-Arab, with police HQ in Washington, and US-UK force in reserve.

Throughout this period, Turkey has been considered a base for US power in the region. Iran was another, after the effort by its conservative nationalist government to gain control over Iran's resources was thwarted by a UK-US military coup in 1953. By 1948, the US Joint Chiefs of Staff were already impressed with Israel's military prowess, describing the new state as the major regional military power after Turkey. Israel could offer the United States means to "gain strategic advantage in the Middle East that would offset the effects of the decline of British power in that area."

In 1958, the CIA advised that "a logical corollary" of opposition to Arab nationalism "would be to support Israel as the only reliable pro-Western power left in the Middle East."[13] The reasoning was implemented only after 1967, when Israel performed a highly valued service to the United States by destroying Nasser, the symbol of Arab nationalism, feared and detested as a "virus" who might "infect others," a "rotten apple" who might "spoil the barrel," in the conventional terminology of planners, commonly reshaped for public purposes as the "domino theory."

By the early 1970s, a tacit tripartite alliance of "local cops" had taken shape under the US aegis: Iran, Saudi Arabia, and Israel (Turkey is taken for granted; Pakistan was an associate for a time). With by far the largest petroleum reserves, Saudi Arabia is the central component of the Facade; any serious departure from obedience would doubtless bring harsh penalties. The arrangements were publicly explained by US intelligence specialists and by political figures, notably Henry Jackson, the Senate's leading specialist on the Middle East and oil. Jackson observed that thanks to the "strength and Western orientation" of Israel and Iran, these two "reliable friends of the United States," along with

Saudi Arabia, "have served to inhibit and contain those irresponsible and radical elements in certain Arab States…who, were they free to do so, would pose a grave threat indeed to our principal sources of petroleum in the Persian Gulf" (meaning primarily profit flow and a lever of world control; the United States was not dependent on Middle East oil for its own use).

US domination of the Gulf region had already come under threat in 1958, when the Iraqi military overthrew the main British client regime. Internal US-UK records provide a revealing account of their concerns and plans, essential background for understanding the Gulf War in 1991.[14] Nasser's Egypt, as noted, was considered the major threat until Israel's 1967 victory; US aid to Israel increased rapidly, even more so in 1970 when Israel performed another important service, blocking potential Syrian support for Palestinians being massacred in Jordan.

The fall of the Shah in 1979 was a serious blow. President Carter at once sent a NATO general to try to instigate a military coup. When this failed, the two remaining pillars—Saudi Arabia and Israel—joined the United States in an effort to overthrow the regime by providing military aid; that is the conventional device to overthrow a civilian government, which had been employed with great success in Indonesia and Chile. Exploiting its intimate relations with the Shah's regime, Israel re-established military contacts and sent US arms, funded by Saudi Arabia. The goals of the operation were explained clearly and publicly at once,[15] but largely ignored in the United States; later, they were reframed in the more acceptable terms of an "arms for hostages" deal, though that could not have been the initial motivation, since there were no hostages. The US-Israeli-Saudi project was an entirely natural reaction to the downfall of the Shah, given the basic structure of the system of control. When Washington's friend and ally Saddam Hussein fell out of favor for disobeying orders (his huge crimes and programs to develop weapons of mass destruction were of little consequence, as the record of US-UK support for him demonstrates), the United States turned to the "dual containment policy," aimed at Iran and Iraq.

It is within this general context that US-Israel relations have evolved over the years, though Israel also became a valued contributor to Washington's operations in Latin America and elsewhere.[16] The cold war was always in the background, primarily because of the ever-present threat of major war. But as has been true rather generally, it was a secondary factor, as the historical and documentary record reveals; as mentioned, the conclusion has been pretty much conceded. The disappearance of the Russian deterrent led to important tactical modifications, but no essential change in basic policies, or in the US-Israel relationship. An assessment that seems to me realistic was given in April 1992 by General (res.) Shlomo Gazit, former head of Israeli military intelligence, later a high official of the Jewish Agency and president of Ben-Gurion University, a highly respected strategic analyst and planner, considered a dove. With the collapse of the Soviet Union, he wrote,

Israel's main task has not changed at all, and it remains of crucial importance. Its location at the center of the Arab Muslim Middle East predestines Israel to be a devoted guardian of stability in all the countries surrounding it. Its [role] is to protect the existing regimes: to prevent or halt the processes of radicalization and to block the expansion of fundamentalist religious zealotry.[17]

Though welcomed in Washington as a major victory, Israel's military success in 1967 posed serious threats. Then–Defense Secretary Robert McNamara later reported that "we damn near had war" when the US fleet "turned around a [Soviet] carrier in the Mediterranean"; he gave no details, but it may have been when Israel conquered the Golan Heights after the cease-fire, eliciting severe warnings from the USSR, including ominous hot-line communications. Recognizing that military confrontation is too dangerous, the great powers proposed a diplomatic settlement, formalized as UN Security Council Resolution 242, passed in November 1967. The resolution called for Israeli withdrawal from the territories it had conquered and for a full peace treaty that would recognize every state's right to live in peace and security within recognized boundaries: in brief, full peace in return for full withdrawal, with at most marginal and mutual adjustments, such as straightening a crooked border. It is important to bear in mind that 242 was strictly rejectionist—using the term here in a neutral sense to refer to rejection of the national rights of *one or the other* of the contending national groups in the former Palestine, not just rejection of the rights of Jews, as in the conventional racist usage. Resolution 242 called for a settlement among existing *states*: Palestinians were unmentioned, apart from oblique reference to "a just settlement of the refugee problem."

Resolution 242 remains a cornerstone of international diplomacy on the Israel-Arab conflict, but with two major changes. The first was a crucial shift in the international consensus, which, by the mid-1970s, had abandoned the rejectionist principles of the resolution and called for a Palestinian state in the occupied territories; the United States retained its rejectionist stand, but now in international isolation. The second change had to do with the US interpretation of 242. That change dates from February 1971, when newly elected President Sadat of Egypt accepted Washington's official policy, in fact went beyond it by offering a full peace treaty in return for Israeli withdrawal only from Egyptian territory. Israel officially welcomed this as a genuine peace offer; it was a "famous…milestone" on the path to peace, Yitzhak Rabin, then Ambassador to Washington, recounts in his memoirs. But while officially welcoming Egypt's expression "of its readiness to enter into a peace agreement with Israel," Israel rejected the offer, stating that it "will not withdraw to the pre-June 5, 1967 lines," a position that it maintains to the present.

The United States faced a dilemma: Should it maintain its official position, thus joining Egypt in a confrontation with Israel? Or should it change the interpretation of 242, opting for Kissinger's call for "stalemate": no negotiations, only force? Kissinger prevailed. Since then the United States has interpreted 242 to mean withdrawal only insofar as the United States and Israel determine. The earlier interpretation continued to be reiterated officially until the Clinton Administration, which argued at the December 1993 UN session that past UN resolutions are "obsolete and anachronistic" in the light of the September 1993 Israel-PLO agreement, to which we return.[18] But the official endorsement of 242 was meaningless, because Washington continued to provide military, diplomatic, and financial support for Israel's gradual integration of the territories. President Carter, for example, forcefully reiterated the official position,[19] while increasing US aid to Israel to about half of total US foreign aid, as part of the Camp David settlement.

After the 1971 rebuff, Sadat warned that if his efforts to reach peace continued to be rejected he would have to go to war. He was dismissed with contempt; recall that this was a period of triumphalist and racist arrogance in both Israel and the United States, later bitterly denounced in Israel. The 1973 war turned out to be a near disaster for Israel—and the world; there was again a threat of nuclear confrontation. Even Kissinger understood that force alone is not enough. He turned to the natural backup strategy: since Egypt could not be ignored, the major Arab deterrent would have to be removed from the conflict. The result, achieved by Carter at Camp David, freed Israel "to sustain military operations against the PLO in Lebanon as well as settlement activity on the West Bank," as Israeli strategic analyst Avner Yaniv put it.[20] Israel proceeded on this course at once, with massive support from the Carter Administration and its successors.

Sadat became a greatly admired "man of peace" in 1977, though his heroic stance was far less forthcoming than in 1971; by 1977 he had joined the international consensus calling for Palestinian rights. The crucial difference is that by 1977 the United States had reluctantly adopted Sadat's 1971 proposal, in the wake of the 1973 war ("Kissinger's war," it should be called). The events of 1971 have been excised from general commentary and review.

American isolation became still more extreme as the international consensus abandoned its rejectionism. Matters came to a head in January 1976, when the UN Security Council debated a resolution, introduced by the Arab "confrontation states" (Egypt, Jordan, and Syria) and publicly backed by the PLO, calling for a two-state settlement incorporating UN 242 but now supplemented with a Palestinian state in the occupied territories. Israel refused to attend the session, instead bombing Lebanon, killing fifty civilians, with no pretext other than retaliation against the UN. The resolution was supported by Europe, the Soviet Union (which was in the mainstream of diplomacy throughout the period), the Islamic world—in fact near-unanimously. The United States vetoed the resolution, and did so again in 1980. At the General Assembly, the United States regularly voted alone (with Israel, occasionally some other client state) against resolutions with a similar thrust. Technically, there are no vetoes at the General Assembly, but a US vote against, even in isolation (as is common, on a wide range of issues), is effectively a veto. In fact, it's a double veto, since such occasions are typically vetoed from commentary and even from history, as the events just reviewed have been. The United States also blocked all other diplomatic initiatives: from Europe, the Arab states, the PLO. The press commonly did not even mention them.

The record is instructive. To select one example among many, on December 10, 1986, *New York Times* Middle East correspondent Thomas Friedman wrote that the Israeli group Peace Now has "never been more distressed" because of "the absence of any Arab negotiating partner." A few months later, he quoted Shimon Peres as deploring the lack of a "peace movement among the Arab people" such as "we have among the Jewish people," and saying that there can be no PLO participation in negotiations "as long as it is remaining a shooting organization and refuses to negotiate." He was speaking almost three years after Israel had rejected another one of Arafat's offers for negotiations leading to mutual recognition, which the *Times* had refused to report; NB: *refused*. Six days before Friedman's article on the distress of Peace Now, a headline in the mass-circulation Israeli journal *Ma'ariv* read: "Arafat indicates to Israel that he is ready to enter into direct negotiations." The offer was made during Peres's tenure as Prime Minister. Peres's press adviser confirmed the report, commenting that "there is a principled objection to any contact with the PLO, which flows from the doctrine that the PLO cannot be a partner to negotiations." Yossi Beilin, at the dovish extreme of Peres's Labor coalition, observed that "the proposal…was dismissed because it appeared to be a tricky attempt to establish direct contacts when we are not prepared for any negotiations with any PLO factor." Other high officials took a much harsher stance. None of this was reported in the mainstream US media, though Friedman was alone in using the occasion to issue one of his periodic laments over the bitter fate of the only peace forces in the Middle East, which lack any Arab negotiating partner. Soon after, he received a Pulitzer Prize for "balanced and informed coverage" of the Middle East, of which this is a representative sample, and was appointed *Times* chief diplomatic correspondent.[21]

There is a conventional term for Washington's success in blocking any diplomatic settlement, in international isolation: it is "the peace process," a choice of terminology that would not have surprised Orwell. The peace process in this sense has been bipartisan. There is an illusion that the (first) Bush Administration took a harsh line toward Israel.[22] The truth is closer to the opposite. An illustration is the official Administration position of December 1989 (the Baker Plan), which endorsed without reservations the May 1989 plan of Israel's Peres-Shamir coalition government. That plan in turn declared that there can be no "additional Palestinian state…" (Jordan already being a "Palestinian state"), and that "there will be no change in the status of Judea, Samaria and Gaza [the occupied territories] other than in accordance with the basic guidelines of the [Israeli] Government." Israel would conduct no negotiations with the PLO. But Israel would permit "free elections," to be conducted under Israeli military rule, with much of the Palestinian leadership either in prison without charge or expelled. The plan was unreported in the United States apart from the last provision, which was praised as a positive and forthcoming offer. What one does read is that Baker strongly reiterated US support for "total withdrawal from territory in exchange for peaceful relations"—while he was quietly lending decisive support to programs to ensure that nothing of the sort would happen.[23]

Through the first months (1988) of the first intifada, Washington's increasingly desperate efforts to pretend that Arafat was not willing to consider a diplomatic settlement were beginning to elicit international ridicule. The Reagan Administration therefore agreed to accept Arafat's longstanding offers and to enter into negotiations; the standard interpretation was that Arafat had at last capitulated to Washington's steadfast advocacy of peace and diplomacy. Washington's actual reaction, unreported in the United States, was made explicit in the first session of the negotiations: US Ambassador Robert Pelletreau informed Arafat that he must abandon any thought of an international conference—unacceptable, because of the international consensus—and call off the "riots" in the occupied territories (the intifada), "which we view as terrorist acts against Israel." In short, the PLO must ensure a return to the pre-intifada status quo, so that Israel would be able to continue its expansion and repression in the territories with US support. This was well understood in Israel. In February 1989 Prime Minister Rabin assured a Peace Now delegation that the negotiations were only "low-level discussions" that avoided any serious issue and granted Israel "at least a year" to resolve the problem by force. "The inhabitants of the territories are subject to harsh military and economic pressure," Rabin explained, and "in the end, they will be broken," and will accept Israel's terms. The version for the US public was quite different.

The last of the regular UN General Assembly resolutions supplementing Resolution 242 with an affirmation of Palestinian national rights was in December 1990, 144-2. A few weeks later, the United States went to war with Iraq, and George Bush triumphantly announced the New World Order in four simple words: "What We Say Goes," surely in the Middle East. The world understood, and withdrew. The United States was finally in a position to impose its own unilateral rejectionist stand, and did so, first at Madrid in late 1991, then in the successive Israel-PLO agreements from 1993. With these measures, the "peace process" has advanced toward the bantustan-style arrangements that the United States and Israel intended, as is clear in the documentary record and, more important, the record on the ground.

Surely it was clear on September 13, 1993, when Rabin and Arafat formally accepted the Declaration of Principles with much fanfare in Washington. The DOP outlines with little ambiguity what was to come.[24] There have been few surprises since.

The DOP states that the "permanent status," the ultimate settlement down the road, is to be based on UN Resolution 242 alone. The suppressed historical record makes it very clear what that means. First, the operative meaning of 242 is the US version: partial withdrawal, as the United States and Israel determine. Second, the primary issue of diplomacy since the mid-1970s had been whether a diplomatic settlement should be based on 242 alone, as the United States insisted, or 242 supplemented with the resolutions, which the United States had blocked, calling for recognition of Palestinian national rights, the position of the rest of the world. The DOP kept explicitly to Washington's unilateral rejectionism.

One could choose to be deluded—many did so. But that was a choice, and an unwise one, particularly for the victims.

Arafat was compelled to "renounce terror," once again. The sole purpose was humiliation. As Secretary of State George Shultz informed President Reagan in December 1988, Arafat had said "Unc, unc, unc" and "cle, cle, cle," but he had not yet said "Uncle" in properly servile tones. The importance of this further renunciation of the right to resist was unnoticed, because no such right exists in the US doctrinal framework. That was made clear in the (unreported) US-PLO negotiations of 1989, as just reviewed; and before that, in December 1987, when the UN General Assembly debated its major resolution on international terrorism, condemning the plague in the strongest terms and calling on all nations to act forcefully to prevent it. The resolution passed 153-2, with the United States and Israel voting against and Honduras alone abstaining. The offending passage states "that nothing in the present resolution could in any way prejudice the right to self-determination, freedom and independence, as derived from the Charter of the United Nations, of peoples forcibly deprived of that right…, particularly peoples under colonial and racist regimes and foreign occupation or other forms of colonial domination, nor…the right of these peoples to struggle to this end and to seek and receive support [in accordance with the Charter and other principles of international law]." These rights are not accepted by the United States and Israel; or at the time, their South African ally. Given the vote, the resolution was (routinely) unreported and vetoed from history. That US victory has been highly significant for Lebanon and the occupied territories.

In return for Arafat's capitulation, the United States and Israel conceded nothing.

The DOP incorporates the US version of the peace process in all essential respects. One cannot really accuse Israel of violating the Oslo agreements, except in detail. Without violating the wording of the DOP (or the carefully constructed subsequent agreements), Israel continued to settle and integrate the occupied territories with US support and assistance.[25] Intentions were not concealed. They were announced openly by Rabin and Peres and implemented by them and their successors.

The exact scale of the US-Israel settlement programs is not entirely clear because of the devices that are used to conceal them. Settler leaders allege that the settler population has doubled to 210,000 since Oslo (not counting 180,000 in Arab East Jerusalem, effectively annexed in violation of Security Council orders, but with tacit US support). They report further that 10 percent of the settlers keep addresses within Israel, hence are not counted. Construction in the settlements for the year 2000 was reported to be more than three times as high as in Tel Aviv, more than ten times as high as in Jerusalem and in general far higher relative to population than within the Green Line (Israel proper). Population growth and public expenditures have also been much higher: 60 percent of construction in the territories is state-funded, compared with 25 percent in Israel, and all the governments have employed a variety of inducements to encourage settlement.[26]

The "Rabin-Bush formula," adopted also by Barak, was that settlement would be limited to "natural growth," under a policy of "freezing settlements." But "there is freezing and there is reality," the Israeli press reports, adding that the far right is "happy to adopt the Rabin formula," grateful for the "massive increase in building authorization" under Barak, initiated under Rabin shortly after he had accepted the DOP. Israel's most prominent diplomatic correspondent, Akiva Eldar, writes that "according to official statistics, full compliance with the Rabin-Bush formula would mean that Israel announces a total freeze—plus demolishes 500 apartments. Right now, there are 9,844 new (and empty) apartments either finished, or under construction.... Thus the Israelis made a mockery of the American deal, and the Americans stayed silent"—and forked over the cash. Eldar adds that plans of religious extremists (mostly American) for Hebron include construction on valuable archeological sites, over the strong protest of the Archeological Council. Thirty-eight senior Israeli archeologists called on Barak to cancel the construction plans (which proceed). The Council chairman condemned the plans as "in grave violation of the law and custom that enables archeological digging and research to be conducted in the ancient sites in our land," destroying "the Hebron of our forefathers and King David, and the historical and archeological infrastructure of the Land of Israel and the People of Israel's past in our land." And, of course, continuing the dispossession and torture of the Palestinians, the vast majority.[27]

In late 2000, as Barak's term was drawing to a close, his Ministry of Construction announced that 10,000 units were under construction in the occupied territories, two-thirds in urban settlements; the Ministry of Housing announced $25 million to subsidize construction and infrastructure for 2001, in addition to a similar sum announced in April for twenty-five "bypass roads"—an extensive highway system designed to integrate the settler population within Israel, while leaving the Palestinian population invisible and isolated. "The Barak government is leaving Sharon's government a surprising legacy," the press reported as the transition took place a few months later: "the highest number of housing starts in the territories since the time when Ariel Sharon was Minister of Construction and Settlement in 1992, before the Oslo agreements." Figures of the Barak Ministry reveal that the rate of new construction increased steadily from 1993 to 2000, when it reached five times the level of 1993, three and a half times 1994, to be increased further under the Sharon-Peres government.[28] In July 2000, contracts were awarded for 522 new dwellings in Israel's Har Homa, a project on land expropriated from an Arab enclave in southeast Jerusalem that has lost 90 percent of its land since Israel's takeover in 1967 through "town planning" (a euphemism for replacing Arabs by Jews, reminiscent of some uses of "urban planning" in the United States).

The Har Homa project, on Jabal Abu Ghneim, completes Israel's encirclement of the vastly expanded "Jerusalem" region. The project was initiated in the last months of Shimon Peres's Labor government, put on hold after strong domestic and international protest during Benjamin Netanyahu's Likud administration, resumed energetically (and without protest) under Barak. For the Israeli far right, however, Labor's Har Homa project was much less significant than its E-1 program, which received much less publicity. This involved new housing and road construction to extend Greater Jerusalem to the city of Ma'ale Adumim to the east, virtually splitting the West Bank in two. Michael Kleiner, a Member of the Knesset and head of the expansionist Land of Israel Front (Hazit Eretz Yisrael), greeted the announcement of the project with much appreciation, observing that this plan, which "was the initiative of the former [Peres] Housing Minister Benjamin Ben-Eliezer [now Minister of Defense in the Sharon-Peres government] with the authorization of Yitzhak Rabin," is "the most important" of the Front's demands, he explained, more so than Har Homa.[29]

In the Sharon-Peres government, the task of concealing the ongoing programs and rejecting international protests is assigned to Foreign Minister Peres. A report on the government programs for more extensive settlement is headlined "Peres rejects international objections to settlements." Peres repeated the "natural growth" formula designed to quiet protest, a traditional contribution of the doves.[30]

The basic principle was described in 1996, during the last months of Peres's administration, by Housing Minister Ben-Eliezer, as he announced the plans for Har Homa and for carrying further the Rabin-Peres programs to expand Greater Jerusalem in all directions, to include Ma'ale Adumim (east), Givat Ze'ev (north), Betar (south), and beyond. Labor "does everything quietly," Ben-Eliezer explained, with "the complete protection of the Prime Minister [Peres]," using such terms as "natural growth" instead of "new settlements." Labor dove Yossi Beilin censured the incoming Netanyahu government for its inflammatory rhetoric. The Rabin government, he wrote, "increased settlements by 50%" in "Judea and Samaria" (the West Bank) after Oslo, but "we did it quietly and with wisdom," whereas you foolishly "proclaim your intentions every morning, frighten the Palestinians and transform the topic of Jerusalem as the unified capital of Israel—a matter which all Israelis agree upon—into a subject of world-wide debate."

Beilin's statement is only partially accurate; the "quiet wisdom" extends well beyond Jerusalem. The differences of style can presumably be traced to the constituencies of the two political groupings. Labor, the party of educated professionals and Westernized elites, is more attuned to Western norms and understands that the sponsors prefer "not to see" what they are doing. Likud's crude methods of achieving basically the same results are an embarrassment to Western humanists, and sometimes lead to conflict and annoyance (see note 22).

Ma'ale Adumim is described as one of the "neighborhoods of Jerusalem" in US reporting. Accordingly, Clinton's final offer could not have been more reasonable and generous when he said that "what is Jewish should be Israeli"—"failing to mention," the foreign press observed, "that this would entail Israel annexing settlements it built in occupied East Jerusalem," in fact far beyond in all directions. But that is an irrelevance. The great virtue of Clinton's "creative compromise…is that at least we now know what the only realistic final deal looks like," Thomas Friedman explained. The President has spoken. What more can there be to say?[31]

Those who stubbornly remain unsatisfied will discover that Ma'ale Adumim uses 1/16 of the 50,000 dunams allotted to it in Israeli planning, a standard percentage, designed to permit "natural growth." The story of Ma'ale Adumim is recounted by Israel's leading human rights organization, B'tselem.[32] The settlement was established under the Labor government in the mid-1970s, and grew rapidly "with the help of a massive flow of resources from the government," the town website reports. The official Metropolitan Jerusalem Plan anticipates expansion by 285 percent from 1994 to 2010, to 60,000 residents. Its lands were expropriated from several Palestinian villages, including Abu Dis, which, according to the plans of the doves, is to become the Palestinian Al-Quds (that is, Jerusalem) by linguistic sleight-of-hand. But Abu Dis is deprived of its lands, in contrast to Israeli "Jerusalem," which will occupy a fair chunk of the West Bank. The state authorities found that there had been "widespread illegal building" by Jewish settlers. The "solution" was simple, as in other settlements: "to provide retroactive permits rather than to demolish the structures." The solution is demolition, often brutal, when Arabs build illegally, as they must to survive because of the stringent conditions imposed on Arab construction.

The expulsion of the Jahalin Bedouin from 1993 to allow further expansion of Ma'ale Adumim was carried out in a particularly cruel fashion. They sought "to avert their terrible fate"—and terrible it was, very visibly so—"by petitioning the High Court of Justice," which lived up to its tradition of meekly obeying state authorities, though it did express the hope that the IDF would ease the expulsion "as an act of grace." In November 1999, the High Court rejected another Palestinian petition opposing further expansion of Ma'ale Adumim, suggesting that "some good for the residents of neighboring [Palestinian villages] might spring from the economic and cultural development" of the all-Jewish city.

The end result, B'tselem concludes, is that here, as throughout the territories, "the helpless local population is totally subject to regulations set by the military force of the occupation in order to promote its political interests," increasingly so during the Oslo peace process.

The Ma'ale Adumim Municipality explains that "the political objective in establishing the town was settlement of the area east of Israel's capital along the Jerusalem-Jericho route," thus separating Ramallah and the northern Palestinian enclave from Bethlehem and the southern one. Every US-Israeli peace plan includes some version of this condition, along with expansion of "Jerusalem" to the north and south. As before, the final Clinton-Barak proposals of January 2001 include another salient to the north, effectively partitioning the northern sector. The three enclaves are separated from the former Jerusalem, the traditional center of Palestinian life. They are hemmed in by extensive infrastructure construction, including "a vast road system, running for some 400km, which bypasses Palestinian population centres and enables settlers and military forces protecting them to move speedily and safely through the West Bank."[33] Constructed on 160,000 dunams of expropriated land, the bypass road system also prevents expansion and development of Palestinian villages and impedes the flow of commerce and people, though Arabs can travel on what are officially called "Palestinian roads," many of them quite hazardous, for example the Bethlehem-Ramallah road (perhaps to be closed entirely if the Clinton-Barak formula, or something like it, is implemented). In addition, "access roads" lead to Jewish settlements, with their swimming pools and well-watered gardens (Palestinian villages and towns have little water, often none during the dry season). If a single settler passes on an access road, all Palestinian traffic is stopped, "causing long delays and much resentment." Regular Israeli closures imprison the population further, "often preventing or greatly detaining even emergency traffic, such as ambulances."[34] The Israeli press has reported many examples of the kind of brutality and purposeful humiliation one expects of an occupying army that can act without restraint.

Every step of the way, this proceeds with US authorization and subsidy, funneled through various channels, along with critical military and diplomatic support. The United States has also taken pains to ensure that the escalating state terror during the current confrontations will be free from observation, let alone inhibition. UN initiatives have been blocked throughout. On March 27, 2001, the United States vetoed a Security Council resolution calling for international observers. According to European sources cited in the Israeli press, the proposal was "scuttled" by Washington's "four no's," which "shocked the representatives of the four European countries that put together the resolution—Ireland, Britain, Norway and France." The United States rejected any mention of the word "siege," of the principle of land-for-peace, of settlements, or of international law and the Geneva Conventions. Arabs and their allies had already abandoned their own resolution, hoping that Europe could "negotiate with the Americans over the formula." A US diplomat explained that "the United States believes the UN should stay out of the settlement debate" and that "the Geneva Convention issue" should be resolved between Israel and the Palestinians, without "prejudgment" through UN involvement.[35]

The matter of the Geneva Conventions is particularly significant.[36] These were adopted after World War II to bar the practices of the Nazis, including transfer of population of the conqueror to occupied territory or any actions that harm the civilian population.[37] Responsibility for monitoring observance of the Conventions was assigned to the International Committee of the Red Cross, which has determined that Israel's settlement programs violate the Fourth Convention. The ICRC position has been endorsed by numerous resolutions of the UN Security Council and General Assembly. The United States has been unwilling to take a public stand on such blatant violation of a central part of international law, particularly in light of the circumstances of the establishment of the Conventions. It therefore abstains from otherwise unanimous endorsement, leaving Israel alone in declaring that it is exempt.

Under the Conventions, it is the responsibility of the High Contracting Parties, including Washington, "to respect and to ensure respect" for the Conventions "in all circumstances." They "should do everything in their power to ensure that the humanitarian principles underlying the Conventions are applied universally," the ICRC has determined. It is therefore Washington's responsibility to prevent settlement and expropriation, along with collective punishment and all other measures of repression and violence. The ICRC has also determined (February 2001) that Israel's closures and blockades violate its Convention obligations, not to speak of the excessive and unlawful use of force repeatedly condemned by every significant human rights organization in Israel, the United States, and elsewhere—and the UN, in an EU-sponsored resolution, passed unanimously apart from the United States.[38]

It follows that the United States is in express and extreme violation of its obligations as a High Contracting Party. Not only is it not acting to ensure respect for the Conventions, as it is obligated to do, but it has been actively engaged in violating them. All significant US-Israel activities in the territories are in flat violation of international law. The "concessions" offered by Clinton and Barak, which are defined as the only "realistic" plan and have gained such acclaim for their magnanimity and generous spirit, do not exist, any more than Russia could make "generous concessions" when it withdrew from Afghanistan, or Germany when it was driven from occupied France. It is hardly necessary even to discuss the specific arrangements, repugnant as they are on elementary moral grounds.

There is a good reason why Washington wants any reference to the Geneva Conventions suppressed, and why the media cooperate so fully—even to the extent of informing readers that the "disputed" territories are "considered" to be occupied territories by the Palestinians, which is true enough: the Palestinians and everyone else apart from Israel and its superpower patron.

There are substantial forces in Israel that have long been in favor of some kind of Palestinian state in the occupied territories. Prominent among them are Israeli industrialists, who were calling for a Palestinian state even before the Oslo agreements. The president of the Israeli Industrialists' Association, Dov Lautman, recommended the NAFTA model that was then under negotiation—"a transition from colonialism to neo-colonialism," the labor correspondent of the journal of the Labor Party commented, "a situation similar to the relations between France and many of its former colonies in Africa." The Israeli coordinator of operations in the territories explained that the goal of his work is to "integrate the economy of the territories into the Israeli economy."[39] A bantustan-style statelet would allow Israeli firms to place assembly plants on the Palestinian side of the border, providing cheap labor with no need for concern about environmental or other constraints on profit-making. It would also relieve concerns that some of those derided as "beautiful souls" might see the way workers are treated and call for minimally decent conditions and wages.

Again on the NAFTA model, a separate state would provide a useful weapon against the Israeli working class, offering ways to limit wages and benefits and undermine unions—much as in the United States, where manufacturers develop excess capacity abroad that can be used to break strikes, and threaten "transfer" to Mexico to disrupt union organizing, a significant consequence of NAFTA that has probably impressed Israeli manufacturers.[40] Poor Israeli workers in "development towns" and the Arab sector would be particularly affected, as has already happened. During the neoliberal onslaught of the 1990s, Israeli workers struggled against privatization of the ports and dismantling of collective-bargaining agreements endorsing rights they had won. Employer associations tried to break strikes by diverting cargo ships to Egypt and Cyprus, but that still leaves transportation costs. A port in Gaza would be ideal. With the collaboration of local authorities in the standard neocolonial fashion, port operations could be transferred there, strikes broken, and the ports transferred to unaccountable private hands.[41]

It is not surprising that Israel is coming to resemble the United States, with very high inequality and levels of poverty, stagnating wages and deteriorating working conditions, and erosion of its formerly well-functioning social systems. As in the United States, the economy is based heavily on the dynamic state sector, sometimes concealed under the rubric of military industry. It is also not surprising that the United States should favor arrangements that make its outpost look pretty much like the sponsor itself.

There are, however, also nationalist reasons to oppose territorial expansion. One growing concern is the "demographic crisis" resulting from the differential Jewish and Arab birth rates (and among the Jewish population, the difference between the secular and religious populations). Projections indicate that before too long Israeli Arabs and ultra-religious Jews, many non-Zionist, will become a major part of the population. A conference of prominent figures on the problem in March 2001 received considerable media attention, as did a call from the respected analyst Shlomo Gazit for establishment of a temporary dictatorship to implement stern internal measures to deal with "the demographic danger," which he regards as "the most serious threat that Israel faces." For the same reason, he issued a strong call for total withdrawal from the territories, unlike the Clinton-Barak or other plans.[42]

The essential meaning of the Oslo peace process is well understood by prominent Israeli doves. Just before he joined the Barak government as Minister of Internal Security, historian Shlomo Ben-Ami observed in an academic study that "in practice, the Oslo agreements were founded on a neo-colonialist basis, on a life of dependence of one on the other forever." With these goals, the Clinton-Rabin-Peres agreements were designed to impose on the Palestinians "almost total dependence on Israel," creating "an extended colonial situation," which is expected to be the "permanent basis" for "a situation of dependence." Ben-Ami went on to become the chief negotiator and architect of the Barak proposals.[43]

Step by step, the United States and Israel have labored for thirty years to construct a system of permanent neocolonial dependency. The project took new forms as the "peace process" was put in place, along lines projected in the DOP and spelled out in close detail in the interim agreements. The plans have been implemented in the settlement and construction programs carried out regardless of who is in office, often most effectively under the Labor doves, who tend to be more immune from criticism. Throughout, they have relied crucially on the military, diplomatic, and financial support of the United States, and not least, the ideological support of articulate educated opinion.

Notes

1. Graham Usher, "The Al-Aqsa Intifada," *Middle East International*, October 13, 2000.

2. John Dugard (South Africa), Kamal Hossain (Bangladesh), and Richard Falk (USA), *Question of the Violation of Human Rights in the Occupied Arab Territories, including Palestine*, UN Economic and Social Council, Commission on Human Rights, E/CN.4/2001/121, March 16, 2001. Israel refused to cooperate, but a wide range of Israeli sources were consulted. For some early reports on the Al-Aqsa Intifada, see Human Rights Watch, *Israel, the Occupied West Bank and Gaza Strip, and the Palestinian Authority Territories*, Vol. 1.3 (E), October 2000; Amnesty International, *Israel and the Occupied Territories: Excessive Use of Lethal Force*, October 19, 2000. See Adam Leigh, "Human rights groups condemn the use of 'excessive and deadly force,'" *Independent* (London), October 18, 2000.

3. Human Rights Watch, *Center of the Storm*, April 11, 2001. Daniel Williams, *Washington Post*, April 16, 2001.

4. Human Rights Watch, Amnesty International, October 2000, *op. cit.* In an eyewitness report from Netzarim, the outstanding Israeli journalist Amira Hass describes the failure to report gunfire from the settlement and IDF submachine-gun fire from "distant surveillance towers…against thousands of unarmed demonstrators" to prevent them from approaching fortified positions where soldiers were not in danger. Hass, "Media Omissions, Army Lies," *Le Monde diplomatique*, November 2000.

5. Human Rights Watch, October 2000, *op. cit. Report on Israeli Settlement* (Washington, DC), November-December 2000, noting the confirmation by IDF deputy chief of staff Moshe Ya'alon.

6. General Amos Yaron, deputy director, *Globes* (journal of Israel's Business Arena), December 21, 2000.

7. Amnon Barzilai, *Ha'aretz*, October 3, 2000; also Avi Hoffmann, *Jerusalem Post*, September 8, 2000. Uri Blau, *Kol Ha'ir*, January 26, 2001, with a photograph of "Marine forces in an exercise in the Negev."

8. Robin Hughes, *Jane's Defence Weekly*, October 4; Charles Sennott, *Boston Globe*, October 4; Dave McIntyre (Washington), Deutsche Presse-Agentur, October 3, 2000. Gideon Levy, *Ha'aretz*, December 24, 2000, and Graham Usher, *Middle East Report*, Winter 2000, on the murders in Beit Sahour on November 9.

9. Ann Thompson Cary, "Arming Israel…," *News and Observer* (Raleigh, NC), October 12. Database searches here and below by David Peterson.

10. "Amnesty International USA Calls for Cessation of all Attack Helicopter Transfers to Israel," AI release, October 19, 2000. *Aviation Week & Space Technology*, February 26, *Jane's Defence Weekly*, February 28, 2001, and other military journals. *International Defense Review*, April 1, 2001. Reuters, AFP, February 19; AP, February 20, financial pages; *Wall Street Journal*, February 20, 2001, a sentence in section B, p. 10, in business announcements. *America*, March 5, 2001. Jane Perlez, "U.S. Gingerly Discusses Taking More Active Role," *NYT*, May 17, 2001; William Orme, "World Briefing," May 17, 2001. See also Robert Fisk, "Death in Bethlehem, Made in America," *Sunday Independent*, April 15, 2001, and the National Lawyers Guild report, *The Al Aqsa Intifada and Israel's Apartheid: The U.S. Military and Economic Role in the Violation of Palestinian Human Rights* (www.nlg.org).

11. Laurie Copans, *Boston Globe*, March 3, 2001.

12. See, e.g., *National Security Strategy of the United States*, the White House, March 1990, the first White House submission to Congress on the Pentagon budget after the fall of the Berlin wall, hence particularly revealing. For extensive quotes, see my *Deterring Democracy* (New York, 1991), chapter 1. For sources not given below, see my *World Orders Old and New* (New York, 1994; updated 1996).

13. "Issues Arising Out of the Situation in the Near East," comments on NSC 5901/1, Jan. 24, 1958.

14. For a review of these records, see *Deterring Democracy*, chapter 6.

15. See my *Fateful Triangle* (Cambridge, MA, 1983).

16. See Israel Shahak, *Israel's Global Role* (Association of Arab-American University Graduates [AAUG], 1982); Benjamin Beit-Hallahmi, *The Israeli Connection* (New York, 1987); Jane Hunter, *Israel's Foreign Policy* (Cambridge, MA, 1987). More generally, Jonathan Marshall, Peter Dale Scott, and Jane Hunter, *The Iran-Contra Connection: Secret Teams and Covert Operations in the Reagan Era* (Cambridge, MA, 1987).

17. *Yediot Ahronot*, April 1992, cited by Israel Shahak, *Middle East International*, March 19, 1993.

18. The Clinton Administration also called for abolition of the special committee on Palestinian rights, which it termed "biased, superfluous and unnecessary," and refused to condemn Israel's settlement activity because it is "unproductive to debate the legalities of the issue." Clinton also reversed longstanding official US support for UN Resolution 194 of December 11, 1948, which affirms the right of return for Palestinian refugees. Jules Kagian, *Middle East International*, December 17, 1993; *Middle East Justice Network*, February-March 1994. See *World Orders*, chapter 3.

19. See Jimmy Carter, reviewing official declarations through 1991, *Washington Post*, November 26, 2000.

20. Yaniv, *Dilemmas of Security* (Oxford, 1987), p. 70.

21. For extensive review, see my *Necessary Illusions* (Cambridge, MA, 1989), App. 5.2.

22. The basis is US annoyance at the brazen manner of settlement under Prime Minister Yitzhak Shamir. When the style returned to the norm, with no significant change in substance, cordiality returned.

23. Baker cited by Carter, *op. cit.* Note Baker's use of the word "territory," not "the territory" or "the territories." In US diplomacy, that has been the device for claiming that UN Resolution 242 meant only partial withdrawal, contrary to the international interpretation, including the United States until 1971.

24. For what it's worth, I don't say this in retrospect. See my article in *Z* magazine, October 1993 (dated September 2), discussing the draft of the DOP. See *World Orders*, chapter 3 (1994) on the document.

25. The agreements were carefully crafted by Israeli negotiators (with US backing) with unclear and sometimes conflicting provisions, escape hatches, vague reciprocity conditions, etc., in such a way as to make it possible for supporters of the occupation to argue that Israel is not violating the agreements. In contrast, the concessions by the Palestinians are far-reaching and, given the relations of power, are in effect. For review of the crucial Oslo II Interim agreement, see *World Orders* (1996 edition, epilogue).

26. Shlomo Tsezna, "The Building in the Territories Was Frozen, and Continues at Full Speed," *Ma'ariv*, August 18, 2000; Akiva Eldar, *Ha'aretz*, May 1, 2001. See also *The Economist*, April 26, 2001, and innumerable reports in the foreign and particularly the mainstream Israeli press, many reviewed in *World Orders* and the updated 1999 edition of my *Fateful Triangle*.

27. Tsezna, Eldar, *op. cit.*

28. *Report on Israeli Settlement*, November-December 2000. Shlomo Tsezna, *Ma'ariv*, February 27, 2001. Sharon is often condemned as a war criminal; Peres is as well. Among his accomplishments are the murderous Iron Fist operations in Lebanon in the mid-1980s and the 1996 invasion of Lebanon, supported by Clinton until international protest over the bombardment of the UN refugee camp at Qana, killing over 100 civilians who had fled there, became so strong that Clinton had to withdraw support and instruct Israel to terminate the aggression, as it did.

29. Baruch Kra, *Ha'aretz*, February 6, 2000, translated in *Report on Israeli Settlement*, March-April 2000. On all these matters, see again *World Orders*. On Har Homa, see my article in Haim Gordon, ed., *Looking Back at the June 1967 War* (Praeger, 1999), papers from a 1997 conference at Ben Gurion University, Beersheva; excerpts in the extended 1999 edition of *Fateful Triangle*.

30. Ziv Maor and Aluf Benn, *Ha'aretz*, April 10, 2001.

31. Jane Perlez, *New York Times*, December 26, 2000, and January 8, 2001; Judy Dempsey, *Financial Times*, January 9, 2001; Friedman, January 2, 2001.

32. Nadav Shragai, *Ha'aretz*, February 16, 2000. Yuval Ginbar, *On the Way to Annexation: Human Rights Violations Resulting from the Establishment and Expansion of the Ma'aleh Adumim Settlement* (B'tselem, July 1999). *Report on Israeli Settlement*, January-February 2000.

33. Dugard et al., *op. cit.*

34. Ibid.

35. Amira Hass, "Four U.S. Rejections Scuttled Security Council Resolution," *Ha'aretz*, April 13, 2001. Washington's frequent opposition to human rights, not only in this case, may have been a factor in the selection of Sweden, France, and Austria rather than the United States for the three Western seats at the UN Human Rights Commission shortly after. Many other hypotheses were entertained. Barbara Crossette, Christopher Marquis, *New York Times*, May 4, 2001. Secretary of State Colin Powell is quoted as saying that the vote on the Palestinians angered countries that sought to retaliate. David Sanger, *New York Times*, May 9, 2001. Powell may have been referring to the Security Council veto, or perhaps to the EU-sponsored resolution of April 18; see note 38 below.

36. For a careful review, see the ignored Human Rights Watch study *Center of the Storm*. See also Allegra Pacheco's article in this volume.

37. There are reservations concerning military necessity that are inapplicable in the present case.

38. Agence France-Presse, "UN Human Rights Commission Condemns Israel on Three Counts," April 18, 2001. The vote was 50–1; Costa Rica abstained and one country was absent. There were a few scattered mentions in the US press (April 19), none in the national press.

39. Asher Davidi, *Davar*, February 17, 1993; translated by Zachary Lockman in *Middle East Report* (MERIP), September-October 1993.

40. See Kate Bronfenbrenner, *Uneasy Terrain: The Impact of Capital Mobility on Workers, Wages, and Union Organizing* (Cornell, September 6, 2000), under contract with the US Trade Deficit Review Commission, updating a 1997 study, also undertaken under NAFTA rules. Such studies are routinely ignored in public commentary, but not by workers (or, presumably, employers).

41. See economic correspondent Efraim Davidi, "Globalization and Economy in the Middle East," *Palestine-Israel Journal*, Vol. 7, Nos. 1-2, 2000.

42. Ya'ir Sheleg, *Ha'aretz*, March 24, 2001, on the conference and reactions. Shlomo Gazit, Amir Rappoport, *Yediot Ahronot*, March 26, 2001; also Reuven Weiss, reviewing Gazit's distinguished background. See text at note 17.

43. Ben-Ami, *A Place for All* (Hebrew) (Hakibbutz Hameuchad, 1998). Cited by Efraim Davidi, *op. cit.*

PART I

REPRESSION AND RESISTANCE

1. PALESTINIANS UNDER SIEGE

EDWARD W. SAID

November 2000

On September 29, the day after Ariel Sharon, guarded by about a thousand Israeli police and soldiers, strode into Jerusalem's Haram al-Sharif (the "Noble Sanctuary") in a gesture designed to assert his right as an Israeli to visit the Muslim holy place, a conflagration started which continues as I write in late November. Sharon himself is unrepentant, blaming the Palestinian Authority for "deliberate incitement" against Israel "as a strong democracy" whose "Jewish and democratic character" the Palestinians wish to change. He went to Haram al-Sharif, he wrote in the *Wall Street Journal* a few days later, "to inspect and ascertain that freedom of worship and free access to the Temple Mount is granted to everyone," but he didn't mention his huge armed entourage or the fact that the area was sealed off before, during and after his visit, which scarcely ensures freedom of access. He also neglected to say anything about the consequence of his visit: on the 29th, the Israeli Army shot at least five Palestinians dead. What everyone ignored, moreover, is that the natives of a place under military occupation—which East Jerusalem has been since it was annexed by Israel in 1967—are entitled by international law to resist by any means possible. Besides, two of the oldest and greatest Muslim shrines in the world, dating back a millennium and a half, are supposed by archeologists to have been built on the site of the Temple Mount—a convergence of religious topoi that a provocative visit by an extremist Israeli general was never going to help to sort out. A general, it's as well to recall, who had played a role in a number of atrocities dating back to the 1950s, and including Sabra, Shatila, Qibya and Gaza.

According to the Union of Palestinian Medical Relief Committees, as of early November, 170 people had been killed, 6,000 wounded: these figures do not include fourteen Israeli deaths (eight of them soldiers) and a slightly larger number of wounded. The Palestinian deaths include at least twenty-two boys under the age of 15 and, says the Israeli human rights organization B'tselem, thirteen Palestinian citizens of Israel, killed by the Israeli police in demonstrations inside Israel.[1] Both Amnesty International and Human Rights Watch have issued stern condemnations of Israel for the disproportionate use of force against civilians; Amnesty has published a report detailing the harassment, torture and illegal arrest of Arab children in Israel and Jerusalem. Parts of the Israeli press have been considerably more forthcoming and straightforward in their reporting and commentary on what has been taking place than the US and European media. Writing in *Ha'aretz* on November 12, Gideon Levy noted with alarm that most of the handful of Arab members of the Knesset have been punished for objecting to Israel's policy toward Palestinians: some have been relieved of committee work, others are facing trial, still others are undergoing police interrogation. All this, he concludes, is part of "the process of demonization and delegitimization being conducted against the Palestinians" inside Israel as well as those in the occupied territories.

"Normal life," such as it was, for Palestinians living in the occupied West Bank and the Gaza Strip is now impossible. Even the 300 or so Palestinians allowed freedom of movement and other VIP privileges under the terms of the peace process have now lost these advantages, and like the rest of the 3 million or so people who endure the double burden of life under the Palestinian Authority and the Israeli occupation regime—to say nothing of the brutality of thousands of Israeli settlers, some of whom act as vigilantes terrorizing Palestinian villages and large towns like Hebron—they are subject to the closures, encirclements and barricaded roads that have made movement impossible. Even Yasir Arafat has to ask permission to leave or enter the West Bank or Gaza, where his airport is opened and closed at will by the Israelis, and his headquarters have been bombed punitively by missiles fired from helicopter gunships. As for the flow of goods into and out of the territories, it has come to a standstill. According to the UN Special Co-Ordinator's Office in the Occupied Territories, trade with Israel accounts for 79.8 percent of Palestinian commercial transactions; trade with Jordan, which comes next, accounts for 2.39 percent. That this figure is so low is directly ascribable to Israel's control of the Palestine-Jordan frontier (in addition to the Syrian, Lebanese and Egyptian borders). With Israel closed off, therefore, the Palestinian economy is losing $19.5 million a day on average—this already amounts to three times the total aid received from donor sources during the first six months of 2000. For a population that continues to depend on the Israeli economy—thanks to the economic agreements signed by the PLO under Oslo—this is a severe hardship.

What hasn't slowed down is the rate of Israeli settlement building. On the contrary, according to the authoritative Report on Israeli Settlement in the Occupied Territories (RISOT), it has almost doubled over the past few years. The Report adds that "1,924 settlement units have been started" since the start of the "pro-peace" regime of Ehud Barak in July 1999—and there is in addition the continuing program of road-building and the expropriation of property for that purpose, as well as the degradation of Palestinian agricultural land both by the army and the   settlers. The Gaza-based Palestinian Center for Human Rights has documented the "sweepings" of olive groves and vegetable farms by the Israeli army (or, as it prefers to be known, Israel Defense Force) near the Rafah border, for example, and on either side of the Gush Katif settlement block. Gush Katif is an area of Gaza—about 40 percent—occupied by a few thousand settlers, who can water their lawns and fill their swimming pools, while the 1 million Palestinian inhabitants of the Strip (800,000 of them refugees from former Palestine) live in a parched, water-free zone. In fact, Israel controls the whole water supply of the occupied territories and assigns 80 percent of it for the personal use of its Jewish citizens, rationing the rest for the Palestinian population; this issue was never seriously discussed during the Oslo peace process.

What of this vaunted peace process? What has it achieved and why, if indeed it was a peace process, has themiserable condition of the Palestinians and the loss of life become so much worse than before the Oslo Accords were signed in September 1993? And why is it, as the *New York Times* noted on November 5, that "the Palestinian landscape is now decorated with the ruins of projects that were predicated on peaceful integration"? And what does it mean to speak of peace if Israeli troops and settlements are still present in such large numbers? Again, according to RISOT, 110,000 Jews lived in illegal settlements in Gaza and the West Bank before Oslo; the number has since increased to 195,000, a figure that doesn't include those Jews—more than 150,000—who have taken up residence in Arab East Jerusalem. Has the world been deluded or has the rhetoric of "peace" been in essence a gigantic fraud?

Some of the answers to these questions lie buried in reams of documents signed by the two parties under American auspices, unread except by the small handful of people who negotiated them. Others are simply ignored by the media and the governments whose job, it now appears, was to press on with disastrous information, investment and enforcement policies, regardless of the horrors taking place on the ground. A few people, myself included, have tried to chronicle what has been going on, from the initial Palestinian surrender at Oslo until the present, but in comparison with the mainstream media and governments, not to mention the status reports and recommendations circulated by huge funding agencies like the World Bank, the European Union and many private foundations—notably the Ford Foundation—who have played along with the deception, our voices have had a negligible effect except, sadly, as prophecy.

The disturbances of the past few weeks have not been confined to Palestine and Israel. The displays of anti-American and anti-Israeli sentiment in the Arab and Islamic worlds are comparable to those of 1967. Angry street demonstrations are a daily occurrence in Cairo, Damascus, Casablanca, Tunis, Beirut, Baghdad and Kuwait. Millions of people have expressed their support for the Al-Aqsa Intifada, as it has become known, as well as their outrage at the submissiveness of their governments. The Arab Summit in Cairo in October produced the usual ringing denunciations of Israel and a few more dollars for Arafat's Authority, but even the minimum diplomatic protest—the recall of ambassadors—was not made by any of the participants. On the day after the summit, the American-educated Abdullah of Jordan, whose knowledge of Arabic is reported to have progressed to secondary school level, flew off to Washington to sign a trade agreement with the United States, Israel's chief supporter. After six weeks of turbulence, Hosni Mubarak reluctantly withdrew his ambassador from Tel Aviv, but he depends greatly on the $2 billion Egypt receives in annual US aid and is unlikely to go any further. Like other leaders in the Arab world, he also needs the United States to protect him from his people. Meanwhile, Arab anger, humiliation and frustration continue to build up, whether because their regimes are so undemocratic and unpopular or because the basics—employment, income, nutrition, health, education, infrastructure—have fallen below tolerable levels. Appeals to Islam and generalized expressions of outrage stand in for a sense of citizenship and participatory democracy. This bodes ill for the future, of the Arabs as well as of Israel.

In foreign affairs circles during the last twenty-five years, the word has been that the cause of Palestine is dead, that pan-Arabism is a mirage, and that Arab leaders, mostly discredited, have accepted Israel and the United States as partners, and in the process of shedding their nationalism have settled for the panacea of deregulation in a global economy, whose early prophet in the Arab world was Anwar al-Sadat and whose influential drummer-boy has been the *New York Times* columnist and Middle East expert Thomas Friedman. In October 2000, after seven years of writing columns in praise of the Oslo peace process, Friedman found himself in Ramallah, under siege by the Israeli army (and under fire). "Israeli propaganda that the Palestinians mostly rule themselves in the West Bank is fatuous nonsense," he announced. "Sure, the Palestinians control their own towns, but the Israelis control all the roads connecting these towns and therefore all their movements. Israeli confiscation of Palestinian land for more settlements is going on to this day—seven years into Oslo." He concludes that only "a Palestinian state in Gaza and the West Bank" can bring peace, but says nothing about what kind of state it would be. Nor does he say anything about ending military occupation, but neither do the Oslo documents. Why Friedman never discussed this in the thousands of column inches he has published since September 1993, and why even now he doesn't say that today's events are the logical outcome of Oslo, defies common sense, but it is typical of the disingenuousness that surrounds the subject.

The optimism of those who took it on themselves to ensure that the misery of the Palestinians was kept out of the news seems to have disappeared in a cloud of dust, along with the "peace" that the United States and Israel have worked so hard to consolidate in their own narrow interests. At the same time, the old framework that survived the cold war is slowly crumbling as the Arab leaderships age, without viable successors in sight. Mubarak has refused even to appoint a vice president, and Arafat has no clear successor; in Iraq and Syria's "democratic socialist" Ba'ath republics, as in the Kingdom of Jordan, the sons have taken over—or will take over—from the fathers, covering the process of dynastic autocracy with the merest fig leaf of legitimacy.

A turning point has been reached, however, and for this the Palestinian intifada is a significant marker. For not only is it an anticolonial rebellion of the kind that has been seen periodically in Setif, Sharpeville, Soweto and elsewhere, it is another example of the general discontent with the post–cold war order (economic and political) displayed in the events of Seattle and Prague. Most of the world's Muslims see the uprising as part of a broader picture that includes Sarajevo, Mogadishu, Baghdad under US-led sanctions, and Chechnya. What must be clear to every ruler, including Clinton and Barak, is that the period of stability guaranteed by the tripartite dominance of Israel, the United States and local Arab regimes is now threatened by popular forces of uncertain magnitude, unknown direction, unclear vision. Whatever shape they eventually take, theirs will be an unofficial culture of the dispossessed, the silenced and the scorned. Very likely, too, it will bear in itself the distortions of years of past official policy.

Meanwhile, it is correct to say that most people hearing phrases like "the parties are negotiating," or "let's get back to the negotiating table," or "you are my peace partner," have assumed that there is parity between Palestinians and Israelis and that, thanks to the brave souls from each side who met secretly in Oslo, the two parties have at last been settling the questions that "divide" them, as if each had a piece of land, a territory from which to face the other. This is seriously, indeed mischievously misleading. In fact, the disproportion between the two antagonists is immense, in terms of the territory they control and the weapons at their disposal. Biased reporting disguises the extent of the disparity. Consider the following: citing an Anti-Defamation League survey of editorials published in the mainstream US press, *Ha'aretz* on October 25 found "a pattern of support" for Israel, with nineteen newspapers expressing sympathy for Israel in sixty-seven editorials, seventeen giving "balanced analysis," and only nine "voicing criticism against Israeli leaders (particularly Ariel Sharon), whom they accused of responsibility for the conflagration." In November, FAIR (Fairness & Accuracy in Reporting) noted that of the ninety-nine intifada stories broadcast by the three major US networks between September 28 and November 2, only four made reference to the "occupied territories." The same report drew attention to phrases such as "Israel…again feeling isolated and under siege," "Israeli soldiers under daily attack," and, in a confrontation where its soldiers were forced back, "Israelis have surrendered territory to Palestinian violence." Highly partial formulations of this kind are threaded through network news commentary, obscuring the facts of occupation and military imbalance: the Israel Defense Forces have been using tanks, American and British-supplied Cobra and Apache attack helicopters, missiles, and heavy machine guns; the Palestinians have none of these things.

The *New York Times* has run only one Op-Ed piece by a Palestinian or an Arab (and he happens to be a supporter of Oslo) in a blizzard of editorial comment that favors the US and Israeli positions; the *Wall Street Journal* has not run any such articles; nor has the *Washington Post*. On November 12 one of the most popular US television programs, CBS's *60 Minutes*, broadcast a sequence that seemed to be designed to let the Israeli army "prove" that the killing of the 12-year-old Muhammad al-Durra, the icon of Palestinian suffering, was stage-managed by the Palestinian Authority. The Authority, it was said, had planted the boy's father in front of Israeli gun positions and moved the French TV crew that recorded the killing into position nearby—all to prove an ideological point.

Misrepresentation has made it almost impossible for the American public to understand the geographical basis of the events, in this, the most geographical of contests. No one can be expected to follow and, more important, retain a cumulatively accurate picture of the arcane provisions that obtain on the ground, the result of mostly secret negotiations between Israel and a disorganized, premodern and tragically incompetent Palestinian team, under Arafat's thumb. Crucially, the relevant UN Security Council Resolutions—242 and 338—are now forgotten, having been marginalized by Israel and the United States. Both resolutions stipulate unequivocally that the land acquired by Israel as a result of the war of 1967 must be given back in return for peace. The Oslo process began by effectively consigning those resolutions to the rubbish bin—and so it was a great deal easier, after the failure of the Camp David summit in July 2000, to claim, as Clinton and Barak have done, that the Palestinians were to blame for the impasse rather than the Israelis, whose position remains that the 1967 territories are not to be returned. The US press has referred again and again to Israel's "generous" offer and Barak's willingness to concede part of East Jerusalem plus anything between 90 and 94 percent of the West Bank to the Palestinians. Yet no one writing in the US or European press has established precisely what was to be "conceded" or quite what territory on the West Bank he was "offering" 90 percent of. The whole thing was chimerical nonsense, as Tanya Reinhart showed in *Yediot Ahronot*, Israel's largest daily. In "The Camp David Fraud" (July 13), she writes that the Palestinians were offered 50 percent of the West Bank in separated cantons; 10 percent was to be annexed by Israel and no less than 40 percent was to be left "under debate," to use the euphemism for continued Israeli control. If you annex 10 percent, decline (as Barak did) to dismantle or stop settlements, refuse over and over again to return to the 1967 lines or give back East Jerusalem, deciding at the same time to hold on to whole areas like the Jordan Valley, and so completely encircle the Palestinian territories as to let them have no borders with any state except Israel, in addition to retaining the notorious "bypass" roads and their adjacent areas, the famous "90 percent" is rapidly reduced to something like 50–60 percent, the greater part of which is only up for discussion some time in the very distant future. After all, even the last Israeli redeployment, agreed at the Wye River Plantation meetings of 1998 and reconfirmed at Sharm el Sheik in 1999, has still not occurred. It bears repeating, of course, that Israel is still the only state in the world with no officially declared borders. And when we look at that 50–60 percent in terms of the former Palestine, it amounts to about 12 percent of the land from which the Palestinians were driven in 1948. The Israelis talk of "conceding" these territories. But they were taken by conquest and, in a strict sense, Barak's offer would only mean that they were being returned, by no means in their entirety.

To begin with, some facts. In 1948 Israel took over most of what was historical or Mandatory Palestine, destroying and depopulating 531 Arab villages in the process. Two-thirds of the population were driven out: they are the 4 million refugees of today. The West Bank and Gaza, however, went to Jordan and Egypt, respectively. Both were subsequently lost to Israel in 1967 and remain under its control to this day, except for a few areas that operate under a highly circumscribed Palestinian "autonomy"—the size and contours of these areas was decided unilaterally by Israel, as the Oslo process specifies. Few people realize that even under the terms of Oslo, the Palestinian areas that have this autonomy or self-rule do not enjoy sovereignty: that can only be decided as part of the final-status negotiations. In other words,

Israel took 78 percent of Palestine in 1948 and the remaining 22 percent in 1967. Only that 22 percent is in question now, and it excludes West Jerusalem (of 19,000 dunams there, Jews owned 4,830 and Arabs 11,190, the rest was state land),[2] all of which Arafat conceded in advance to Israel at Camp David.

What land, then, has Israel returned so far? It is impossible to detail in any straightforward way—impossible by design. It is part of Oslo's malign genius that even Israel's "concessions" were so heavily encumbered with conditions, qualifications and entailments—like one of the endlessly deferred and physically unobtainable estates in a Jane Austen novel—that the Palestinians could not feel that they enjoyed any semblance of self-determination. On the other hand, they could be described as concessions, making it possible for everyone (including the Palestinian leadership) to say that certain areas of land were now (mostly) under Palestinian control. It is the geographical map of the peace process that most dramatically shows the distortions that have been building up and have been systematically disguised by the measured discourse of peace and bilateral negotiations. Ironically, in none of the many dozens of news reports published or broadcast since the present crisis began has a map been provided to help explain why the conflict has reached such a pitch.

The Oslo strategy was to redivide and subdivide an already divided Palestinian territory into three subzones, A, B and C, in ways entirely devised and controlled by the Israeli side since, as I have been pointing out for several years, the Palestinians themselves have until recently been mapless. They had no detailed maps of their own at Oslo; nor, unbelievably, were there any individuals on the negotiating team familiar enough with the geography of the occupied territories to contest decisions or to provide alternative plans. Whence the bizarre arrangements for subdividing Hebron after the 1994 massacre of twenty-nine Palestinians at the Ibrahimi Mosque by Baruch Goldstein—measures undertaken to "protect" the settlers, not the Palestinians. Figure I on the following page shows how the core of the Arab town (120,000 inhabitants)—20 percent of it, in fact—is under the control of roughly 400 Jewish settlers, about 0.03 percent of the total protected by the Israeli Army.

Figure II shows the series of Israeli pullbacks made in widely separated—that is, noncontiguous—areas. In the first, Gaza is separated from Jericho by miles and miles of Israeli-held land, but both belong to an autonomous Area A that, in the West Bank, was limited to 1.1 percent of the territory. The Gaza component of Area A is much larger mainly because, with its arid land and overpopulated and rebellious masses, Gaza was always considered a net liability for the Israeli occupation, which was happy to be rid of all but the choice agricultural land at its heart and the various settlements, retained until now by Israel, along with the harbor, borders, entrances and exits. The other maps in Figure II (Figure III was presented by Israel as an optimal withdrawal map at the Camp David summit, though announced earlier) show the snail's pace at which the hapless Palestinian Authority has been allowed to take over the large population centers (Area A); in Area B, Israel allowed the Authority to help police the main village areas, near where settlements were constantly under construction. Despite joint

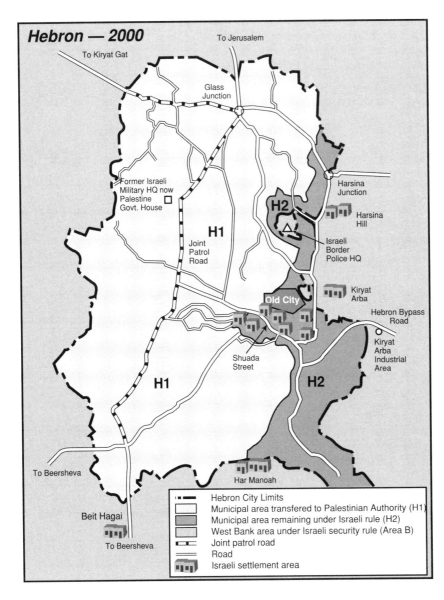

Hebron — 2000

To Kiryat Gat

To Jerusalem

Glass Junction

Former Israeli Military HQ now Palestine Govt. House

Harsina Junction

H2

Harsina Hill

H1

Joint Patrol Road

Israeli Border Police HQ

Old City

Kiryat Arba

Hebron Bypass Road

Kiryat Arba Industrial Area

Shuada Street

H1

H2

To Beersheva

Har Manoah

Beit Hagai

To Beersheva

▪━▪━	Hebron City Limits
	Municipal area transferred to Palestinian Authority (H1)
	Municipal area remaining under Israeli rule (H2)
	West Bank area under Israeli security rule (Area B)
▭▬▭	Joint patrol road
	Road
🏘	Israeli settlement area

Figure I shows the situation in Hebron now, with the Arab town dominated by Israeli settlements.

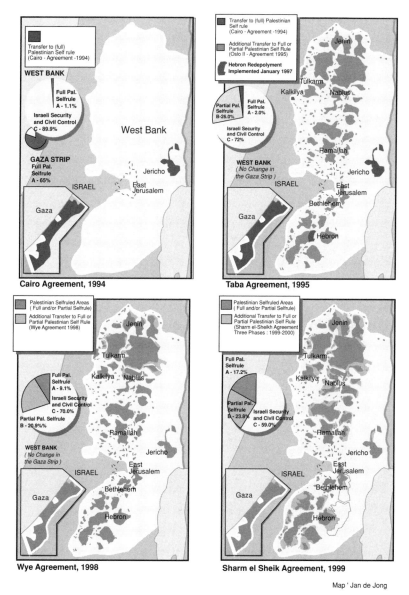

Cairo Agreement, 1994

Taba Agreement, 1995

Wye Agreement, 1998

Sharm el Sheik Agreement, 1999

Map ' Jan de Jong

Figure II follows the sequence of Israeli transfers of West Bank territory to Palestinian self-rule between 1994 and 1999.

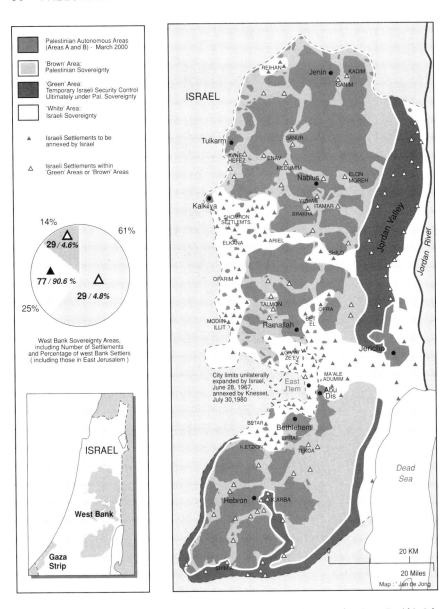

Figure III shows Israel's final-status map, put forward in May 2000 and presented at Camp David in July.

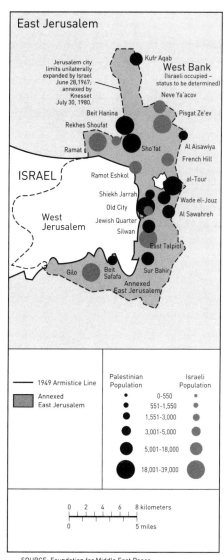

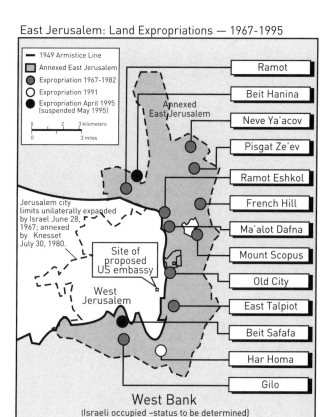

Figure IV: The map on the left shows the current demographic status of annexed East Jerusalem.
The map on the right gives a breakdown of land expropriations in the same part of the city between 1967 and 1999.
All maps by Jan de Jong and courtesy of the Foundation for Middle East Peace in Washington, DC.

patrols of Palestinian and Israeli officers, Israel held all the real security of Area B in its hands. In Area C it has kept all the territory for itself, 60 percent of the West Bank, in order to build more settlements, open up more roads and establish military areas, all of which—in Jeff Halper's words—were intended to set up a matrix of control from which the Palestinians would never be free.[3]

A glance at any of the maps reveals not only that the various parts of Area A are separated from each other, but that they are surrounded by Area B and, more important, Area C. In other words, the closures and encirclements that have turned the Palestinian areas into besieged spots on the map have been long in the making and, worse still, the Palestinian Authority has conspired in this: it has approved all the relevant documents since 1994. In October Amira Hass, the *Ha'aretz* correspondent in the Palestinian territories, wrote that in 1993 the two sides

> agreed on a period of five years for completion of the new deployment and the negotiations on a final agreement. The Palestinian leadership agreed again and again to extend its trial period, in the shadow of Hamas terrorist attacks and the Israeli elections. The "peace strategy" and the tactic of gradualism adopted by the leadership were at first supported by most of the Palestinian public, which craves normalcy

—and, I would have thought, a real ending of the occupation, which, to repeat, was nowhere mentioned in any of the Oslo documents. She goes on:

> Fatah (the main faction of the PLO) was the backbone of support for the concept of gradual release from the yoke of military occupation. Its members were the ones who kept track of the Palestinian opposition, arrested suspects whose names were given to them by Israel, imprisoned those who signed manifestos claiming that Israel did not intend to rescind its domination over the Palestinian nation. The personal advantage gained by some of these Fatah members is not enough to explain their support of the process: for a long time they really and truly believed that this was the way to independence.

By "advantage" Hass means the VIP privileges I mentioned earlier. But then, as she points out, these men, too, were members of "the Palestinian nation," with wives, children and siblings who suffered the consequences of Israeli occupation, and were bound, at some point, to ask whether support for the peace process did not also mean support for the occupation. She concludes:

> More than seven years have gone by, and Israel has security and administrative control of 61.2 percent of the West Bank and about 20 percent of the Gaza Strip (Area C), and security control over another 26.8 percent of the West Bank (Area B).

> This control is what has enabled Israel to double the number of settlers in ten years, to enlarge the settlements, to continue its discriminatory policy of cutting back water quotas for 3 million Palestinians, to prevent Palestinian development in most of the area of the West Bank, and to seal an entire nation into restricted areas, imprisoned in a network of bypass roads meant for Jews only. During these days of strict internal restriction of movement in the West Bank, one can see how carefully each road was planned: so that 200,000 Jews have freedom of movement and about 3 million Palestinians are locked into their bantustans until they submit to Israeli demands.

To which one should add, by way of clarification, that the main aquifers for Israel's water supply are on the West Bank; that the "entire nation" excludes the 4 million refugees who are categorically denied the right of return, even though any Jew anywhere still enjoys an absolute right of "return" at any time; that restriction of movement is as severe in Gaza as it is on the West Bank; and that Hass's figure of 200,000 Jews in Gaza and on the West Bank enjoying freedom of movement does not include the 150,000 new Israeli-Jewish inhabitants who have been brought in to "Judaize" East Jerusalem.

The Palestinian Authority is locked into this astonishingly ingenious, if in the long run fruitless, arrangement via security committees made up of Mossad, the CIA and the Palestinian security services. At the same time, Israel and high-ranking members of the Authority operate lucrative monopolies on building materials, tobacco, oil, etc. (profits are deposited in Israeli banks). Not only are Palestinians subject to harassment from Israeli troops, but their own men participate in this abuse of their rights, alongside hated non-Palestinian agencies. These largely secret security committees also have a mandate to censor anything that might be construed as "incitement" against Israel. Palestinians, of course, have no such right against American or Israeli incitements.

The slow pace of this unfolding process is justified by the United States and Israel in terms of safeguarding the latter's security; one hears nothing about Palestinian security. Clearly we must conclude, as Zionist discourse has always stipulated, that the very existence of Palestinians, no matter how confined or disempowered, constitutes a racial and religious threat to Israel's security. All the more remarkable that in the midst of such amazing unanimity, at the height of the present crisis, Danny Rabinowitz, an Israeli anthropologist, spoke bravely in *Ha'aretz* (October 17) of Israel's "original sin" in destroying Palestine in 1948, which with few exceptions Israelis have chosen either to deny or to forget completely.

If the geography of the West Bank has been altered to Israel's advantage, Jerusalem's has been changed entirely. The annexation of East Jerusalem in 1967 added seventy square kilometers to the state of Israel; another fifty-four square kilometers were filched from the West Bank and added to the metropolitan area ruled for so long by Mayor Teddy Kollek, the darling of Western liberals, who with his deputy, Meron Benvenisti, was responsible for the demolition of several hundred Palestinian homes in Harit al Magharibah to make way for the immense plaza in front of the Wailing Wall.[4] Since 1967 East Jerusalem has been systematically Judaized, its borders inflated, enormous housing projects built, new roads and bypasses constructed so as to make it unmistakably and virtually unreturnable and, for the dwindling, harassed Arab population of the city, all but uninhabitable. As Deputy Mayor Abraham Kehila said in July 1993, "I want to make the Palestinians open their eyes to reality and understand that the unification of Jerusalem under Israeli sovereignty is irreversible." (See Figure IV. Recent small-arms fire directed at the new Jerusalem settlement of Gilo from the neighboring Palestinian village of Beit Jala has been unanimously reported in the media without anyone mentioning that Gilo was built on land confiscated from Beit Jala. Few Palestinians will forget their past so easily.)

The Camp David summit in July broke down because Israel and the United States presented all the territorial arrangements I have been discussing here—only slightly modified to give Palestinians back two "nature areas," a euphemism for desert land, so as to increase their portion of the total land area—as the basis for the final settlement of the Palestinian-Israeli conflict. Reparations were, in effect, dismissed by the Israelis, although they are not an entirely alien idea to many Jews. I have seen no mention in the Western media of a long report on Camp David written by Akram Hanieh, editor of the Ramallah daily *Al-Ayyam* and a Fatah loyalist who, since his deportation by the Israelis in 1987, has been close to Arafat. Hanieh makes it clear that from the Palestinian point of view Clinton simply reinforced the Israeli position, and that, in order to save his career, Barak wanted a quick conclusion to critical issues such as the refugee problem and Jerusalem, as well as a formal declaration from Arafat ending the conflict definitively. (Barak has since called for early elections as a way of staving off a total parliamentary defeat.) Hanieh's gripping account of what took place is soon to appear in English translation in the Washington-based *Journal of Palestine Studies*.[*] It shows that the "unprecedented" Israeli position on Jerusalem was in fact tailored to that of the Israeli right wing—in other words, that Israel would retain conclusive sovereignty over even the Al-Aqsa mosque. "The Israeli position," Hanieh says, "was to reap everything"—and to give almost nothing in return. Israel would have got the "golden signature" from Arafat, final recognition and "the precious 'end of conflict' promise." All this without a complete return of occupied territory, an acknowledgment of full sovereignty or a recognition of the refugee issue.

Since 1967 the United States has disbursed more than $92 billion in unconditional financial and military aid to Israel, while offering blanket political support that allows Israel to do as it pleases. Britain, whose foreign policy is a carbon copy of Washington's, also supplies military hardware that goes directly to the West Bank and Gaza to facilitate the killing of Palestinians. No state has received anywhere near as much foreign aid as Israel and no state (aside from the United States itself) has defied the international community on so many issues for so long. Were Al Gore to become President this policy would remain unchanged. Gore is uncompromisingly pro-Israeli and a close associate of Martin Peretz, Israel's leading pro-rejectionist and anti-Arab rhetorician in the United States, and owner of *The New Republic*. At least George W. Bush made an effort during the campaign to address Arab-American concerns, but like most past Republican Presidents, he would be only sightly less pro-Israeli than Gore.

For seven years, Arafat had been signing peace process agreements with Israel. Camp David was obviously meant to be the last. He balked, no doubt, because he had woken up to the enormity of what he had already signed away (I'd like to think his nightmares are made up of unending rides on the bypasses of Area C); no doubt, too, because he was aware of how much popularity he had lost. Never mind the corruption, the despotism, the spiraling unemployment, now up to 25 percent, the sheer poverty of most of his people: he finally understood that, having been kept alive by Israel and the United States, he would be thrown back to his people without the Haram al-Sharif and without a real

* Barak was, of course, defeated by Ariel Sharon in the February 6, 2001, election. See Hanieh, "The Camp David Papers," *Journal of Palestine Studies*, Vol. 30, No. 2 (Winter 2001).

state, or even the prospect of viable statehood. Young Palestinians have had enough and, despite Arafat's feeble efforts to control them, have taken to the streets to throw stones and fire slingshots at Israeli Merkavas and Cobras.

What Israel has depended on in the past, the ignorance, complicity or laziness of journalists outside Israel, is now countered by the fantastic amount of alternative information available on the Internet. Cyber activists and hackers have opened a vast new reservoir of material that anyone with a minimum of literacy can tap into. There are reports not only by journalists from the British press (there aren't any equivalents in the US establishment media) but also from the Israeli and Europe-based Arab press; there is research by individual scholars and information gleaned from archives, international organizations and UN agencies, as well as from NGO collectives in Palestine, Israel, Europe, Australia and North America. Here, as in many other instances, reliable information is the greatest enemy of oppression and injustice.

The most demoralizing aspect of the Zionist-Palestinian conflict is the almost total opposition between mainstream Israeli and Palestinian points of view. We were dispossessed and uprooted in 1948; they think they won independence and that the means were just. We recall that the land we left and the territories we are trying to liberate from military occupation are all part of our national patrimony; they think it is theirs by biblical fiat and diasporic affiliation. Today, by any conceivable standards, we are the victims of the violence; they think they are. There is simply no common ground, no common narrative, no possible area for genuine reconciliation. Our claims are mutually exclusive. Even the notion of a common life shared in the same small piece of land is unthinkable. Each of us thinks of separation, perhaps even of isolating and forgetting the other.

The greater moral pressure to change is on the Israelis, whose military actions and unwise peace strategy derive from a preponderance of power on their side and an unwillingness to see that they are laying up years of resentment and hatred on the part of Muslims and Arabs. Ten years from now there will be demographic parity between Arabs and Jews in historical Palestine: what then? Can the tank deployments, roadblocks and house demolitions continue as before? Might it not make sense for a group of respected historians and intellectuals, composed equally of Palestinians and Israelis, to hold a series of meetings to try to agree to a modicum of truth about this conflict, to see whether the known sources can guide the two sides to agree on a body of facts—who took what from whom, who did what to whom, and so on—which in turn might reveal a way out of the present impasse? It is too early, perhaps, for a Truth and Reconciliation Commission, but something like a Historical Truth and Political Justice Committee would be appropriate.

It is clear to everyone on the ground that the old Oslo framework, which has done so much damage, is no longer workable (a recent poll conducted by Birzeit University shows that only 3 percent of the Palestinian population want to return to the old negotiations) and that the Palestinian negotiating team led by Arafat can no longer hold the center, much less the nation. Everyone feels that enough is enough: the occupation has gone on too long, the peace talks have dragged on with too little to show for them, the goal, if it was to have been independence, seems no closer (thank Yitzhak Rabin, Shimon Peres and their Palestinian counterparts for that particular failure), and the suffering of ordinary people has gone further than can be endured. Hence the stone-throwing in the streets, yet another futile activity with its own tragic consequences. The only hope is to keep trying to rely on an idea of coexistence between two peoples in one land. For now, though, the Palestinians are in desperate need of guidance and, above all, physical protection. Barak's plan to punish, contain and stifle them has already had calamitous results, but it cannot, as he and his American mentors suppose, bring them to heel. Why is it that more Israelis do not realize—as some already have—that a policy of brutality against Arabs in a part of the world containing 300 million Arabs and 1.2 billion Muslims will not make the Jewish state more secure?

This article was originally published in the London Review of Books *for December 14, 2000.*

Notes

1 The casualty figures as of July 5, 2001, as reported by the Union of Palestinian Medical Relief Committees, citing the Health, Development, Information, and Policy Institute, include 560 Palestinians killed and more than 16,000 wounded, 1,500 of them permanently disabled. Of these dead, eighty-three were under 16 and 174, almost one-third of the total, were 18 or younger. B'tselem reported that as of June 30, 115 Israelis had been killed, thirty-five of them members of the security forces. —Ed.

2 These figures are taken from *Jerusalem 1948: The Arab Neighbourhoods and Their Fate in the War*, edited by Salim Tamari (Jerusalem, 1998).

3 Halper has written the most impressive studies of Israeli territorial planning during the Oslo process; see, for instance, his study of the trans-Israel highway, "The Road to Apartheid," in *News from Within* (May 2000) and "The 94 Per Cent Solution: A Matrix of Control," in *Middle East Report* 216 (Fall 2000). The Dutch geographer Jan de Jong, who drew up two of the maps reprinted here, has also done important work in this area.

4 A sobering account of Kollek's golden era emerges from *Separate and Unequal: The Inside Story of Israeli Rule in East Jerusalem*, by Amir Cheshin, Bill Hutman and Avi Melamed (Cambridge, Massachusetts, 1999).

2. UNDER THE GUN: A PALESTINIAN JOURNEY
AHDAF SOUEIF

Autumn 2000

I have never, to my knowledge, seen an Israeli except on television. I have never spoken to one. I cannot say I have wanted to. My life, like the life of every Egyptian of my generation, has been overcast by the shadow of Israel. I have longed to go to Palestine, but have not wished to go to Israel. And now I am going there. I have not felt such anticipation or such fear since I was a child. For the past two months I have been following the news of the intifada. I have compared the images on the BBC and CNN with those on al-Jazira and other Arab channels. I have unspun stories, fumed at the American newspapers and been grateful for some of the reporting in some of the British press. I have started and ended my days reading appeals for help on the Internet. And over and again I have asked myself: "What is it that I can do?" Now at last I can do something; I can go see for myself, and write. But going means going there.

Monday

It is the first day of Ramadan and we are on the road from Amman to the bridge and I am staring out at the desert and thinking—as I always do—how much I miss it when I'm in England: ten minutes of rolling dunes, then rock formations rising like huge chocolate gateaux followed by dunes again—but this time rippling as though having a joke, then a bend in the road and a green valley opens up and suddenly a row of Bedouin women walking elegantly along a ridge, then sand again and we are at the Jordanian terminal which seems almost empty. We unload and our driver makes inquiries. The West Bank, al-Daffa, is closed. He points to a large, low building and through the windows we see that it is crammed with people. "But Jerusalem?" the woman with whom I've shared the taxi asks. Jerusalem, apparently, is open.

I know nothing of this woman except that the small daughter on the seat next to her is called Malak—Angel. An orthodox priest in black robes and a gray braid comes out of the room and takes a taxi back to Amman. We go to another part of the terminal. Buses are waiting, loaded with people. Angel's mother decides to go VIP for the sake of the child. I walk along behind her.

We hand over our passports and are ushered into a large room with sofas and Arabic newspapers. An exhausted woman comes in. She says she sat in this room yesterday from 2 pm till 8 pm, then was told Jerusalem was closed and had to go back to Amman. But an official comes in and waves us out. A van this time and when we get off—there it is: "al-Jisr," Umm Angel [Angel's mother] says—the bridge. A wooden construction, just like in the pictures, with wooden walls so you can't jump off and into the Jordan River. We walk across, two women and a red-haired child and there, above our heads, are Israeli soldiers just as I've seen them on television for four decades: their eyes behind shades, their faces behind machine guns and above them two crossed Israeli flags, one fluttering in the breeze, the other caught in some spike of machinery and lying limp. We stop at a kiosk and hand our passports in through a window to a young woman in army uniform. She waves us on. Another van and on to another terminal building. Had there been Jordanian soldiers and guns on the other side? I didn't see any, but maybe I just didn't notice.

We are sitting in a smallish, brightly lit room with vividly blue armchairs. Serious attempts at decor have been made: a cactus growing out of a half-coconut shell tilts on an Arab-style carved wooden table, rubber plants and plastic flowers droop from dusty glass shelves, an empty drinks dispenser glows coldly in the corner. On the walls are three reproductions: two are Kandinsky-like, but the third is a large close-up of the two forefingers of God and Adam just failing to meet.

A polite young Israeli comes in and asks me in broken Arabic to fill out some forms. Then he comes back to escort us to the passport window. I say: "I don't want my passport stamped." He says: "I know."

2:30 pm, Jerusalem

I head out of the hotel and start walking. Every car I pass I imagine exploding into flames. How far away does one have to be not to be killed by an exploding car? But the sun is shining as I head down Salah el-Din Street—and I am at home. The street is lined with bakeries, haberdasheries, shoeshops, small grocers, hairdressers. Girls in school uniform and headscarves walk in groups, chatting, laughing. Boys loiter and watch them. The names on the shops and the doctors' signs are the familiar mix of Muslim and Christian Arab, French and Armenian. The French cultural center has wide-open doors and an inviting garden; there is a smell of roasting coffee. It's like a smaller, cleaner, uncrowded Cairo. But two buildings look different from the others: they are modern, precise, their angles are sharp, they fly the Israeli flag, and they are the only ones with closed gates that are made of steel bars.

But then appearing in front of me are the walls of the Old City. Closer in I see the ancient gateway and beside it an Israeli army car and five soldiers armed with machine guns. I tie a scarf under my chin and walk past them, through al-Zahra Gate, and I am in a medieval Arab city: Orshalim al-Quds, Jerusalem the Sacred, a city made of rose-hued stone. The streets are paved with it; like cobbles, only larger, the stones are worn smooth and shine in the light. Down steps, round bends and another rosy alley stretches ahead. The houses seem to grow out of the street. Their green iron doors are closed and around many of them are the decorations that proclaim the resident has made the pilgrimage to Makkah.

You see these in any Egyptian village but here, instead of the representations of the pilgrim and his/her transport, you get delicate drawings of flowers and birds.

A small handwritten sign on the wall points to al-Aqsa. I walk down Mojahedin (Holy Warriors) Street. A small boy, maybe 4 years old, skips along chanting "ya Saddam, ya Saddam, come and blow up Tel Abeeb." A few steps behind him his mother smiles at me. And now I am in front of the gateway to al-Haram al-Sharif (the Noble Sanctuary). Inside the gateway, sitting at a wooden table, are three armed soldiers. One stands up and blocks my path: "Papers." I don't like the look of them. I'm one and they are three. My passport is British but it says born in Cairo. Egypt has just recalled its ambassador. But a couple of local men from the administration of the mosque are standing just inside the gateway. I hand over my passport. The soldier flicks through it. "In England, you live?" He has a heavy, East European accent.

"Yes."

I've been told don't explain, don't justify, don't be defensive. Minimal response.

"What town?"

"London."

"Why you are going in?"

I decide: "To pray."

"You are Muslim?"

"Yes."

The Israelis have closed the Haram to all Palestinian Muslims, except residents of Jerusalem. And the men have to be above 45. The soldier goes through my bag, which I have emptied of everything except purse, tissues and comb. His mates look into the bag, too. He motions me on with his head.

A few steps and I am in the vast enclosure of the Haram. Brown earth with shrubs, patches of grass, trees. To my left, the city walls; to my right, the Sanctuary wall is the back of houses and churches, and ahead of me the path rises to meet a wide set of white steps leading to a great stone terrace and out of that rises the golden Dome of the Rock. I sit on a low stone wall under the open sky surrounded by small Mameluke structures and sense utter peace.

Later the women come out of prayers. They look at me with open curiosity:

"*Salamu aleikum!*"

I return the greeting.

"From where, sister?"

"From Egypt."

They want to know if I have somewhere to stay, otherwise any one of them will take me home. They all live in the old city, the Dome of the Rock is their local mosque; they nip down every day to pray.

Two minutes takes me round a corner, up some stairs and into Umm Yaser's home. Her two young daughters-in-law are both students. They whisper and laugh together over their books.

"She got married three days ago," Umm Yaser says, pointing to one of the girls. "Just over a cup of coffee. Who can have a wedding now when people are being killed every day?"

"Does the situation affect you here, in the Old City?"

"Look!" Umm Yaser says taking me to her door, pointing at the shuttered house across the lane: "The settlers took it over. They put chairs out here in the lane and pick quarrels with the young people coming and going." But how did they take it over?

"Since Ariel Sharon bought two houses here he's made it easy for them."

But how? Who would sell to Sharon?

"Awwad Abu Sneina. Everybody knew he was a spy. He vanished from the neighborhood and next thing we knew the Israeli flag went up on the house and Sharon had bought it. But when Abu Sneina died there wasn't a burial ground that would take him. That day my son was playing football and the ball hit one of them [the settlers]; they grabbed him and said they'd call the police. We said call the police. But they called some other settlers instead. Two hundred of them came from Atarot Cohunim, hit us with everything they had—even their walkie-talkies. The people praying in the mosque heard the noise and came to our help and it was a battle. The police said we were the aggressors. At the Hadasa hospital they would not treat us under the insurance. They made us pay 450 shekels. Affect us? They do what they like to us."

She talks of tear gas pumped into houses, of rubber bullets which the Palestinian children peel to extract the steel marble within, which they then aim back at the soldiers with their slingshots. She talks of the threat to her mosque, of an ambulance bringing a 78-year-old neighbor back from hospital, how soldiers searched it and stripped it down to the cooling unit: "They've grown afraid of the air itself." I feel dizzy with the detail piling up in my head and leave before I can be made to stay and eat.

Through Bab el-Silsila I see several young Jewish men in black clothes hurrying along and into the tunnel that—I assume—leads to the Wailing Wall. Farther along a mild-looking man wearing a yarmulke and leading two children steps out of a building. From within I hear the sound of children chanting in Hebrew. The sun has set and it is time to break my fast.

In Bab el-Amoud a man at a stall fills me a pita bread with falafel, salad and tahini. He finds a chair for me and places a glass of water on the ground at my side. I sit inside the ancient gateway and eat—within sight of the army car and the soldiers and beyond them a beautiful, Indian-looking building standing alone. Two young men lean against a wall discussing what the Arab states can reasonably be expected to do. If only Egypt and Jordan would open the borders, they say, so we're not mice in a trap like this.

Back at the hotel I phone a journalist contact. An American, I think. I ask a few questions, then my enthusiasm for the city bursts forth—and is met with silence.

"What? You don't agree?"

"Well, yes," she says. "It's just that I think everything would be so much easier if it wasn't there."

I go out to the grocery next door. I want to buy some yoghurt and dates for my pre-dawn meal. The TV set on the wall is tuned in to a Palestinian channel showing the news. Every pot of yoghurt I pick up is labeled in Hebrew only. "Don't you have any Palestinian yoghurt?" I ask and the man ushers me to another refrigerator.

The news comes through of five workers killed by settlers. A sixth man had managed to get away. The ambulances had raced to the scene but been stopped by the army. Everybody in the shop has stopped in mid-motion and is watching the set. The tears roll down my face as someone's wife wails on the screen but everybody else is impassive. When the item is over they go back to what they were doing.

The key to my hotel room will not lock from the inside. From the outside it's fine, but not from the inside. I try and try. I feel uneasy about alerting people to the fact that my door does not lock. I decide that I'm safe enough here. I sit down to write today's notes.

Soon I will have to try to meet some Israelis.

Tuesday

Abraham, Ibrahim al-Khalil [Hebron], the Friend of God, father of the Arabs through Ismael son of Hagar, and of the Jews through Isaac son of Sarah. At midday I am in the city that bears his name and houses his magnificent mosque. We have circuited two roadblocks to get here, turning a journey of half an hour into one of an hour and a half. Our car has Israeli license plates and so—as we pass the Uruba refugee camp—my driver puts a large sign saying "Press" in Arabic against the windscreen to prevent us being pelted with stones. When we pass the giant settlement of Kiryat Arba, my driver turns the Arabic sign over to display the English. "They came in 1969. They pretended they were a group of Swedish tourists and stayed in a hotel. Their leader was Moshe Levinger. Then they started clashing with the people and they were backed by the military governor. They took the land and built the settlement."

Think of al-Khalil as two parts: the old city surrounding the mosque, and the new suburbs that have grown out of it. The main square of the new part is teeming with people. Vegetable and fruit stalls teeter on the edges of pavements and on traffic islands. The Israelis have expropriated the old marketplace and bulldozed it. Raise your eyes from the bustle and you see the evidence of shells and mortars on the building surrounding the square. A gaping hole where the offices of *al-Ayyam* (The Days) newspaper used to be. Doctors' clinics, toy shops, a hairdresser: rubble, soot, shattered glass and pockmarks. Raise your eyes further and you see the Israeli army sandbagged on people's rooftops, their guns trained on the throng below. "Twelve tons of equipment on my roof," a man tells me, "and they urinate in our water tanks."

Al-Shuhada (The Martyrs) Street leads into the old city. It is empty and the shops are shuttered. At its end I see concrete roadblocks and as I watch I see a soldier emerge from behind a building beyond the roadblocks; he surveys us, his machine-gun aimed. When he disappears I start walking down the road. My guide pulls me back: "No. There's already been shooting today." The soldier reappears, followed by another. There are maybe twenty meters between us. A young man comes out of a building and says: "You don't need to be scared of them. Look!" He runs a few paces toward them, jumps up and down, stamps his feet, waves his arms and yells out the Arabic equivalent of "Boo!" The soldiers duck behind the wall. "See! They're cowards!" he laughs and saunters off.

As we stand talking a tall man appears carrying a camera and wearing a white helmet and a white bullet-proof vest with "Press" written in black across it. Awad Awad works for Agence France-Presse. He stops to talk and my guide tells him I'm writing an article for the *Guardian*. "You want to go in?" he asks.

I follow him through the roadblock and round the corner. Now I can see the soldiers grouped behind the wall at the end of al-Shuhada Street. Behind a building at the other side of the street are a journalist and three more photographers. We walk past the soldiers, then Awad says "Run!" and we run across the street and join the posse of cameras on the other side. We introduce ourselves and shake hands. "What are they doing?" a man asks nodding toward the seven soldiers huddled behind the wall. "Making a plan," another laughs.

The soldiers break up and three of them run across the road toward us. They crouch behind the concrete blocks, their guns aimed at the empty street. If I stretch out my hand I can touch their back-packs. After a moment a stone crashes into one of the concrete blocks and splinters off. A boy dances across the street. A shot is fired. It is alarmingly loud. The same event is repeated six times in the next half hour. Twice, in the silence following a shot, a woman walks quickly across the street. Three people in blue dungarees and helmets with IPIF written in red across their bullet-proof vests [international observers] stand across the road. I cannot make out if they are men or women. They carry clipboards and timers and seem to be recording the times of the shots. The photographers tell me that when there is going to be any real action the soldiers simply shoo away the IPIF people. A mobile rings and it is my guide begging me to come back.

I want to go into the old city but my guide and driver are fearful and reluctant. As we argue in the street an imposing man in a gray cashmere overcoat appears. They seem awed by him. I later learn that he is a Palestinian journalist who has been shot in five separate incidents. He says, "Come on chaps. It's your duty to take her in. You've got Israeli license plates. She's got a British passport. Take her in."

Reluctantly they make a detour and try to drive into the old city. Forty thousand people live here under curfew. Twelve thousand children cannot go to school. Fifteen mosques are closed. In the center, armed, live what Israel says are 400 settlers and the Palestinians say are 100. All this is for their benefit.

"If the army were to go away," I ask, "and the settlers were content to live here among you, would you let them?"

"They would go away."

"But if they wanted to stay, could they?"

"But they've taken people's homes. If you could go into the center you would see families camped by their homes, refusing to leave, and the settlers throw rubbish on them and beat them up. They're not even proper settlers; they are religious students, mostly from the United States, volunteering to come for one or two years to do their religious duty by being here."

The city is beautiful. Like old Jerusalem, it is made of pink stone. The narrow streets wind up and down like the streets of an Etruscan town. The houses lean against each other, one house's roof forming the other's patio. Ornate stone balconies look out on to the empty street. The sun shines, the air is clean and fresh, the light is so perfect we could be on a film set. A dark green patrol car passes and does not stop us. The microphone blares out in accented Arabic: "O people of al-Khalil. Beware breaking the curfew." Round the next bend a yellow taxi is at a stop in the middle of the road, leaning to one side. A group of children has gathered round it watching, hushed and still. We pull in by a wall and park. A woman leans against the taxi with a baby in her arms. "I know it's a curfew," the driver says, "but she has just come out of hospital, and she had the baby, so I drove her. Look what they've done." A soldier had taken out a knife and slashed the two tires on the driver's side. Naturally he only has one spare tire. With the curfew how is he going to get another one? Two boys are helping him change one wheel. The other children look on in silence. The woman starts walking off slowly.

We carry on, on foot. Up some steps leading down to the center an old man is climbing. "Can we get to the center?"

"No. They've blocked it off."

"Is there somewhere from where I can at least see the center and the mosque?"

"Yes, from my house," and he turns back to lead the way.

Through a green iron door I step into paradise. Terrace after terrace of pink stone, green plants and flowers growing out of tin cans, trellises with vines, doorways that the old man opens with big keys and that lead into vaulted chambers where ancient Sufis meditated and prayed to be vouchsafed a vision. Some of the chambers have Mameluke niches where I imagine the Sufis kept their jars of water and bundles of dates. I emerge from a chamber to find myself looking at a wall with wire-mesh windows and above them the Israeli flag. "Yes. They are here," he says. They are looking at us and we keep our eyes averted. "They occupied the building next door and they tried to get me out of this. I said I would bring out my sword and kill the first man to step over my threshold."

"What happened?"

"They put iron doors on the street openings between my house and the mosque—and they set up this surveillance camera up there."

"And now they leave you alone?" as I take a photo of the camera.

"I have no children now or young men to make trouble. There is just me and my wife. The [Palestinian] Authority came and said: 'Give us the biggest vault. We'll make it into a museum.' " And?

"I threatened them too with my sword. They would have turned it over to the Israelis."

An old woman appears on a balcony and calls to him to bring the guests into the house. On the patio outside the house two very old Singer sewing machines sit side by side. "I just oiled them yesterday." He spins the wheel to prove that they work beautifully.

In the living room there is another sewing machine. "But this one can do embroidery," he says, and pulls out a rag to show us the different stitches. "I don't know what he wants with all these old machines," his wife says. On the wall there are the three young men. On each there is written a name prefaced by "The Martyr."

"My nephews," the old woman says. "Come, you can see the mosque from the kitchen window." I see the rose-pink walls of Ibrahim's Sanctuary and beyond them, in the central town square, the army camp with the sandbags, the guns, the soldiers and the white flag with blue star. My guide tells me that Saturday is the worst day here because the settlers have more time to walk around upturning vegetable stalls and kicking people. The army protects them, he says. My driver loses patience: "We've gone down the road of 'peace' as we were asked to. Meetings and summits without end. And what's the result? Is this right? That a wronged population should be punished? In '94 Baruch Goldstein murders the worshipers and this is what we get? The mosque is divided, and now with the curfew this old man who has prayed in it every day of his life cannot set foot in it?"

"The unjust will be visited with retribution," the old man says gently, "and I pray on my terrace within sight of the Sanctuary walls."

I think of the decisive battle, in 1517, when Mameluke Egypt fell to the Ottoman Turks. When the dashing Mameluke knights, until then the finest fighting force in the world, rode out to do battle, they found themselves with the modern technology of Ottoman guns in front of them and treachery at their backs.

Back on the road the taxi is still there. We drive out of al-Khalil, negotiate roadblocks and go on to the motorway. Ahead of us is an army truck. He drives slowly and we are not allowed to pass him. In the back three young soldiers watch us. It is getting near to sunset and breaking the fast. A roadblock near Bethlehem and we are pulled over. My driver opens his window and hands over his papers. I stare ahead but suddenly my door is flung open. A rather plump young soldier bends down, smiling:

"What did they thay today? The Tanthim? That they would thtop the shooting?"

Somehow the lisp reassures me.

"Who?" I ask.

"The Tanthim."

When I look blankly at him he says: "Fatah. What did they thay today?"

"I'm frightfully sorry," I say, speaking posh. "I don't know. I've been out all day and haven't seen the news."

"But you have a radio in the car?"

My driver leans over and speaks in Hebrew: "What would she know? Can't you see she's foreign?"

They wave us on. My driver is convinced the soldier's questions were a trap. "Son of a bitch," he laughs, "they don't miss a trick."

Maybe there are cafes in West Jerusalem or Tel Aviv where intellectuals, artists, people, sit around and debate the condition of the country and the "Palestinian problem." Maybe they debate the ethics of an army of occupation holding a population hostage, or the civil rights of an Arab population in a Zionist state, but these places—the places that are lit up at night—how do I find them? In the entertainment guide I look at the listings: films, recitals, cabarets. I consider taking a taxi and simply buying a ticket. But even the thought makes me uneasy.

Wednesday

Albert Agazerian teaches history at Birzeit University. He meets me just inside Bab el-Khalil gate and we walk toward the house where he lives with his family inside the Armenian convent grounds. He points out the first British consulate and the first British church: "Layers of history," he says. "Dig here and you come up with at least seventeen layers of history—and their stories are all woven together. Here in Jerusalem we have what the whole world today is headed for: plurality. But the Israelis want to cancel everybody's story except their own."

Madeleine, his wife, insists on giving me a jar of their olives. Her family has always got their olives from a particular farm near Nablus. Now the farmers are fighting not only the closures, she says, but the settlers, who set fire to the olive groves or take chainsaws to the trees. "The farmers," she tells me, "slip out on Friday night and gather their own harvest while the settlers keep the sabbath." It's as though they have to steal their own crop.

My attempts to reach the other side of all this have so far not been successful. Shlomo Shamir, sometime Israeli ambassador to Egypt, could not see me because he was investigating the killings of the thirteen Arab-Israelis in Israel.

Could we not talk about broader issues?

No. They are all related.

Gershon Baskin, who specializes in getting Arabs and Israelis together, has not returned my calls.

I am still trying to speak to someone from the Yesha council to arrange a meeting with a settler. It's not simple. From the first word it's not simple: I have often been asked whether I have a problem with English as the "language of my oppressor." I understand the question but I do not feel it; the British occupation was out of Egypt before I was born. English was the language of my first reading and I love it.

When the voice at the other end of the phone said "Shalom" I said "Shalom" back out of courtesy. I was left with a nasty feeling, a feeling that I had been somehow complicit. For the remaining seven calls I would respond with "Good morning/evening." When the Israeli army of occupation has been removed from the streets of Palestine I will say "Shalom" to a Jewish visitor to the Holy Land as I would join my hands and bow my head to an Indian one.

And if a meeting should be arranged, how would I get there? My Palestinian driver won't go near a settlement. And who will I get to go in with me? For there is no way I am going alone.

Last night I walked back to my hotel up Salah el-Din Street. I was still wearing the headscarf I wore at al-Aqsa, and my dress reached to just above my ankles. I passed the barred building which I now know is the Israeli court. In front of it was the armored car and four soldiers with the obligatory machine guns. They were laughing together and I also thought that in the space of two days my fear had disappeared, my heart did not lurch. I must have taken thirty paces or so and was about to turn the corner when I felt something hit my left shoulder hard and heard the crack as whatever it was ricocheted off me and hit—I suppose—the ground. What did I feel? I felt shock as I turned ice-cold then hot. I felt my throat block up and the tears rise to my eyes, and then I felt pure anger and I turned. As I looked at the ground to try to identify what had hit me one of the transits that carry people between towns screeched to a stop by my side. The door was pulled open and inside I saw women who looked like me, and children. The driver leaned over: "Are you all right?"

"Yes," I said. I found that I was feeling ashamed, ashamed of having been hit. "Did you see who hit me?" I looked around the street. It was deserted except for the soldiers.

"No, we just heard the sound. Do you need help? We're going to Ramallah."

"My hotel's just round the corner."

"Don't wait here. Get in. I'll take you to the hotel."

"I'm all right," I said.

"God will punish them," a woman said. They did not drive off until I was round the corner and out of sight.

When I got to my room I pushed the heavy table with my suitcase on it against the door. I took off my coat and dress. In the mirror I could see the purple bruise on my left shoulder. It did not hurt, but in my mind I kept walking back to the soldiers, challenging: "Did you see who hit me?"

Thursday, 4:30 pm

I am sitting in the lobby of the hotel when Judy Blanc walks in. Stylish and small with her gray hair worn short and close-fitting, she is unmistakably a New Yorker. Her husband got a job as professor of Arabic at the Hebrew University in 1954 and she came with him. I have been told by my Palestinian friends that she is "one in a million." I ask her if this is true and she laughs "not quite." She says that the recent events—terrible as they are—have been useful in clarifying the Palestinians' priorities. That the Israeli government can no longer manipulate the confusion between principles and negotiating positions.

I ask her—it seems necessary to ask basic questions—where the "good" Israelis are? How can people, people who are aware that their government is subduing an entire population, cutting off their water and electricity, beating them up—I feel embarrassed at listing the misdeeds of the Israeli government to her—how can people, people with souls, tolerate this?

"But they're not aware," she says. "It's so easy not to see it. You live in West Jerusalem or in Tel Aviv. You don't need to notice the Palestinians. If they're there they're in the background. And there is a fundamental racism in this society that makes it possible for people to delude themselves, to not see what's happening. If you want to know what's happening you have to go looking for it, to East Jerusalem or the West Bank. Not many Israelis will do that."

Are there any Israelis working with Palestinians now?

"No. The Palestinians saw that the liberal position of making contact one on one was corrupting the political process. Now they do what the University of Birzeit has always done: any joint activity between Palestinians and Israelis has to be based upon the Israelis' articulated commitment to the minimum demands of the Palestinians: 242 and the Right of Return."

What about Peace Now and similar organizations?

"They have a problem. They supported Ehud Barak and now they say he's gone as far as he can and the violence has to stop. The TV liberals are really hampered by the fact that they supported him. Do you know, one of my friends, a good liberal, said to me last week: 'I finally understood that Oslo was not the same for the Palestinians as it was for us.' It took her seven years."

2 am

I have been in my room for the last four hours, writing up my notes. There is so much to write. I have pushed the curtains wide open on my huge window; outside there are the massed houses and, above them, the tiny sliver of the four-night-old crescent of Ramadan. Fasting has never been as easy as it is here. From time to time I hear a quick series of explosions but I'm no expert and they could be kids playing, for all I know.

Since I have been here I seem to have lost all apprehension (apart, that is, from the table wedged against the door). The contempt in which the people hold the army is infectious. "They are cowards," one young man tells me. "Let them just come out from behind their barricades, their helmets, their machine guns and tanks and American technology. Let them meet us man to man, stone to stone."

I am shedding aspects of me that are superfluous to the situation. I do not wonder for a second whether I should or should not ask a question: I have no concern to be liked. Not once have I had to drag my usually unruly mind back to the business at hand. Every time I glance at it, it's working, completely focused, recording, recording. Maybe I'm shedding "me." And the bits of me that remain are the bits that cry as I write down the stories I hear. And the children look wonderingly at my tears and their mothers explain: "It's all new to her."

And were it not for my own children, back in London, I would stay. Stay in this city that brings out the cleanest and the clearest of me—and bear witness.

Thursday

For three nights now I have stayed up writing past 2 am, and yet I have not recorded all I have heard and seen. I have not even really thought about all I have heard and seen—that will come later. For now the present facts are all I can manage.

We start early for Ramallah and a couple of minutes from my hotel I see two Israeli flags fixed to the flat roof of a house. Next to them four boys in civilian clothes nurse machine guns. My driver, Abu Karim, says these are four houses that have recently been taken from their Arab residents.

Out of Jerusalem, major roads are being built to connect up with the settlements. The roadworks are guarded by Israeli army trucks.

The road north to Ramallah—the road that the Palestinians may use—will lead us through the town of Bira and the news is that Bira was shelled last night. Soon we see the concrete blocks, the waiting cars, the soldiers, and we swerve off to the right and drive through dirt roads. Abu Karim points to a rectangular crater in the middle of the road the size of a grave. The army, he says, does this just to make life more difficult. A bone-jolting twenty minutes later we rejoin the main road about one kilometer up from where we had left it.

An hour and a half later (and a distance equivalent to, say, Chelsea to Kingston) we are sitting in Rita Haniyya's living room listening to her and her friend Layla Qasim. The women, one Christian, the other Muslim, are founders of the National Union of Palestinian Women (NUPW) and worked hard to establish the Center for the Support of the Family in Ramallah, a day-center where children were taught music and encouraged to draw. "The children are not allowed to see maps of Palestine or learn their own history," they tell me. Eighteen months ago the Israelis closed the center down for "inspiring sedition."

"Sedition!" snorts Layla Qasim. "We were trying to help the mothers give their children a 'normal' childhood. You know what the children sing? They sing: 'Papa bought me a trifle/A machine-gun and a rifle.'"

"We were struggling to get them to sing normal children's songs. But normal children's songs have nothing to do with the reality of their lives.

"When the children said, 'The Jews came and took my cousin/Mixed our rice with the flour and the sugar,' we would say don't say the Jews, it's the Israelis, the Zionists. We were battling with the ethics of language."

"The media in Britain," I say, "ask why mothers allow their children to go out and throw stones at the army."

"Allow?" says Rita Haniyya, "You should see the quantities of Valium we've dispensed to women in the camps simply to help them cope with their lives: when their children go out to play they're playing under the guns of the army observation post above them—these people have been living under 'temporary emergency' conditions for thirty-three years, and some since 1948. They don't go looking for the army, the army is right on their doorstep."

"There isn't a child," says Layla, "who doesn't have a father or a brother banished or jailed or killed. When the soldiers come in and beat up a father—the kids see it—all they've got is one room. They see their father being beaten. What do you think it does to them? They ask us if people in the whole world live like this. What can we tell them? A 3-year-old comes in and tells me: 'The Jews came and beat my father and his tummy fell out onto the floor but we got him to hospital and they're going to mend him.'"

The names come thick and fast, Jihad Badr, who was bringing up his kid sisters and brothers after their mother died of cancer, who survived an operation for a brain tumor but was killed in the al-Aqsa demonstrations; Hania, 13, who was shot in the leg, bundled into an army car and hit repeatedly on the same leg: "I didn't scream," they tell me she said, "not because I was feeling brave, just because I was afraid they'd kill me." The Hammouri twins, 19, shot on the same day. And on and on.

The NUPW now trains women in first aid and civil defense, it organizes vaccinations, it gives counseling and advises on home economics (this includes boycotting Israeli and American products). It is funded entirely by donations from its more well-off members—many of them abroad. There are 4 million Palestinians in Israel and the occupied territories, 5 million in the diaspora.

"We've compromised," Rita Haniyya says, "they have West Jerusalem, the Carmel, Jaffa and Haifa and so on. They have Israel. But they want everything; it's their nature. They attack us—physically—

in three ways: through the army, the settlers, and the Mustaribs [agents who pretend to be Arab]."

The Mustaribs, she says, mingle with the people during demonstrations: "They choose a child, grab him, throw their kaffiyehs over their faces (so they can mingle again without being identified), whip out their yarmulkes and a gun and rush with the child over to an army car."

"You know the worst of it is," they say, "that they keep you guessing. You never know if a road is to be open or closed. When they're going to shut off your water or turn off your electricity. Whether they're going to permit a burial. Whether they're going to give you a permit to travel. You can never ever plan. They create conditions to keep you spinning."

At Oslo, Israel agreed to hand over some major Arab towns to the Palestinian Authority. Israel, however, retained all the areas surrounding the towns, so that to get from one to another the Palestinians had to carry permits, which were checked at Israeli checkpoints. With the intifada the Israeli army simply encircled the towns, preventing the residents from leaving or entering. Critics of Oslo at the time said this was a blueprint for disaster. No one understands why the Palestinian Authority agreed to it. Some say they simply didn't have maps. It is at the soldiers encircling their towns that the youths and children of the intifada throw stones.

There are some good Israelis, Rita says, people of conscience. "Look at what Amira Hass writes in *Ha'aretz*. And Uri Avnery. But they're marginalized."

Are you in touch with them?

"Not any more. We realized they would go so far and no further. The best of them balks at the right of return for the refugees. Even Leah Rabin wanted East Jerusalem. At the beginning of the intifada when they got in touch we said you've been talking to us for years; now it's time for you to talk to your government."

Back in Jerusalem I break my fast at a small cafe outside al-Zahra Gate. On the street outside is the army car and the soldiers. At the table behind me three elderly men are extolling the days of Gamal Abdel Nasser and the idea of pan-Arabism. They end up singing popular Egyptian songs of the '60s: "Ya Gamal/Beloved of millions" and "We said we'd build and now we've built/the Hi-i-gh Dam."

The owner, recognizing my Egyptian dialect, gives me a tamarind juice and pudding on the house. He asks if I'm OK at my hotel. His family would have been glad to take me in but they're in al-Khalil (Hebron). He used to commute, it's only half an hour, but now with the closures he can only manage to sneak in to see them once a week.

A silent candle-lit demonstration outside the New Gate of the Old City. Sixty candles flickered in the hands of sixty Palestinian women just outside the gate. Opposite them, on the other side of the road, fifty Israeli women dressed in black held fifty candles.

Friday

This is the first Friday of Ramadan and Barak, in a move designed to "achieve quiet during the month of Ramadan," has repealed the ban on men under 45 praying at the al-Aqsa mosque.

Israeli mounted police, armed and dressed in riot gear, guard the gates of the Old City as though we were armed and dangerous football hooligans. We pass through al-Zahra Gate in single file between two rows of soldiers with machine guns. Each man has to stop and show his identity papers. The women, if they keep their heads bowed and their eyes on the ground, are left alone. At Bab Hutta, the actual gate to al-Haram al-Sharif, there are more soldiers with guns. Inside, the men head for al-Aqsa, the women for that choice jewel, the Dome of the Rock. Because the Israeli amnesty does not extend to the people of the West Bank, there are maybe 20,000–25,000 people here today instead of the 500,000 you would normally expect.

At the Dome I squeeze in through Bab al-Janna (the Gate of Paradise). In straight lines, shoulder to shoulder, we pray, then sit to listen to the sermon. The Imam preaches patience, steadfastness and opposition. He reminds us of the Prophet's saying that there are those who fast and gain nothing except hunger; to fast is to renounce falsehood, hypocrisy and all bad deeds. He lists the crimes of the Israeli military occupation against the people.

He lists the demands of the people: an end to the occupation, the implementation of UN Resolution 242 and the return to the borders of June 4, 1967, an independent and sovereign Palestinian state in the West Bank, Gaza and East Jerusalem, the release of Palestinian prisoners from Israeli jails, the right of return to the homeland of all Palestinian refugees. He repeats God's promise that the righteous shall prevail, then he prays for al-Aqsa itself. Again and again he implores God to protect it from the plots being woven against it, again and again the women's voices from the Dome and the men's voices from al-Aqsa rise: Amen.

The Al-Aqsa, where the men pray, is close to Bab el-Magharba (the Gate of the Moroccans) which is close to the Wailing Wall. As prayers end, groups of young men and boys start gathering there. But there the army and police are solidly waiting and everyone knows that if one stone hits that wall someone will be shot. But the *shabab* [youth] are in the grip of fervor, and a man who some say is a "Fatah element" starts yelling Hamas slogans and, playing Pied Piper, leads them away from the certain danger of Bab el-Magharba and through the terraces of al-Haram to the relative safety of Bab el-Sabbat. There they stop.

Outside the gateway is a police station that they had set fire to a while back. The administrators of the mosque rush to place wooden barriers between the *shabab* and the small army of soldiers and police taking up positions outside with guns aimed. The *shabab* chant of the Prophet's victory against the Jews at Khaybar in the seventh century, and some of them rush back into the Haram and try to break down the iron door leading to the stairs of the minaret. It will not break. One young man climbs a wall and tries to open a higher door into the minaret.

On the walls of the terraces hundreds of women and older men stand and watch. The atmosphere is almost one of carnival. Maybe a thousand *shabab* are facing the soldiers, but the gate is narrow so it's not too hard for the elders to hold them back. On the steps just opposite the gate, the steps leading up to the top of the city wall, the photographers stand with their cameras, helmets and bulletproof vests. Something happens outside and the *shabab* scatter for a moment, then regroup. A woman in an embroidered Bedouin dress pushes forward into their midst, yelling along with them and a man tries to hold her back: "They might shoot you!"

"Let them shoot me. Am I worth more than any of these youngsters?"

A woman in horn-rimmed spectacles waves her arms at the soldiers from the wall where she's standing: "Get out!" she shouts, "Get out! You've strangled us, may God strangle you."

One young man is ordering his little brother to go home. "Let me stay," the kid begs. "Just for a few minutes. Let me stay." It takes a cuff on the side of the head to send him home. A couple of smallish stones are pitched across the wall. "Bet that landed on our car," a very well-dressed, slim young man says to his companion.

A well-built youth picks up a large rock and throws it to the ground to smash it. It doesn't smash and he picks it up again. As he raises it a mosque caretaker runs up and takes it from him, quietly, without a word. He places it carefully under a tree and the young man walks away. An argument is breaking out on the side: "They shouldn't make trouble," a tall, fair man shouts. "The Israelis will close it down. Let people pray."

A bystander laughs: "You've been praying for fifty years. What good has it done you?"

A diminutive sheik in a very trim costume and brand-new red cleric's hat is marching measuredly up and down beside the yelling demonstrators with a megaphone: "Your presence here incites them. Disperse. Disperse."

No one pays any attention to him except one man who says to his neighbor: "He does this every Friday."

There are women and girls sitting chatting under the trees. Eventually the *shabab* start to drift away. It has taken two hours but this time, here, the Palestinians have no martyrs.

Saturday Noon, Ramallah

The great hall of Our Lady of the Gospels independent school in Ramallah is filling up with students. Hundreds of girls and boys crowd into the seats talking and laughing. On the stage the principal, Mrs. Samira, and the guest speaker, Dr. Mustafa Barghouti, are setting up the overhead projector. Dr Barghouti is one of the triumvirate heading the People's Party of Palestine, and—more important—he has been organizing all the medical aid work for the intifada.

This talk is part of the independent schools of Ramallah's joint initiative to "document the truth and demand our legitimate rights before the world." This group of kids is in economic band A; their parents can afford to educate them privately, can stop them going to the barricades. Their hair is glossy, their teeth are good. As Mrs. Samira lists the names of the participating schools they cheer and stamp and she outlaws whistling.

They all want to know how they can contribute. They ask, why has the Authority not declared Oslo dead? Why does it arrest members of Hamas? What is the Authority doing to protect civilians from the attacks of the settlers? Why does the Authority continue to try to coordinate security with the Israelis? They want a program to support the thousands of workers who've lost their jobs inside Israel. They want the leadership to pull together and an end to the factions. They want to talk to the world. They want independence and they want to know what they can do.

Dr. Barghouti tells them they can join the NGO across the road. They can be trained in first aid and primary care, in crisis management. They can do media work, monitor the Net, respond to articles. They crowd around to put their names down before they rush off to be picked up by parents at 2:30 pm sharp.

3 pm, Ramallah

Another Barghouti (it's a massive family), Marwan Barghouti, is mostly on the move. He is 41, the chief executive officer of Fatah. Since the intifada he's been on the streets with the *shabab* and he has formed the People's Watch, groups in each village that try to defend the villagers against the settlers. Everybody says he is targeted by the Israelis (*Ma'ariv* called him one of the "triangle of terror: Arafat, Barghouti and Rajoub, head of Palestinian intelligence"). Some say he's targeted by the Palestinian Authority—for being too popular.

In his office, against a huge poster of al-Aqsa, he repeats that the intifada and negotiations do not preclude each other; that the intifada is the only way the people have of projecting their own voice, their own will, into the negotiations. He points at a poster of Muhammad al-Durra and says: "We need to get away from the image of the Palestinian as a victim. This is a better poster," pointing at a poster of a child confronting a tank.

I say, "That kid was killed a few days later."

He says, "Yes."

I wonder whether there is space to get out of the "victim" frying pan without falling into the "fanatical Islamic terrorist" fire. The margin is terribly narrow. Then a man sitting with us—clearly an old friend—says: "But I hear Qassam [Barghouti's 16-year-old son] is down at the barricades. Why don't you stop him?" Barghouti waves the question away. The man insists: "You have to stop him." And for a moment the militia leader looks helpless: "I can't," he says. "How can I?"

3:45 pm

Abu Karim is getting restless. He wants to be home in Jerusalem before sunset, but I have asked to see the barricades and now we examine them. An area of desolation at the edge of the town—which means ten minutes from the center. After sunset this will turn into a battleground. Concrete blocks, stones, burn marks, some shattered glass. Two Israeli army cars on the other side of the concrete.

A woman appears from nowhere. Fortyish, poor, dressed in black, she is an Egyptian who has married a Palestinian and lived here for twenty-five years. Umm Basim, I have heard of her, heard that she lost her eldest son in the previous intifada and that she is in the thick of the action at the barricades every night.

Is it because of your son, I ask, that you come here?

"No. I have four more, and they are with me here. I come because this situation has to end. We can't live like this."

I ask if I may take her photo. She hesitates: "It won't appear in any Egyptian newspapers? I wouldn't want my mother to know what I'm doing. She'd worry." As I take the photo she turns to the man who brought us here: "I've seen Qassam here. Tell his father to keep him away."

Sunday, 10:30 am

Psagot. ("Bascot," the students at Birzeit University had said, "biscuits. Think American cookies.")

Psagot is a settlement built ten years ago on a hilltop just outside Ramallah and Birah. The Palestinians say it was built by the government (like other settlements) on land expropriated from Birah. They say it was positioned strategically to halt the natural expansion of the town and to control the Arab population. They say the settlers are armed and the army itself can move into the settlement at very short notice. For the past two months Birah and Ramallah have been shelled every night from Psagot.

My calls to the Yesha council have paid off and they have sent me here to meet Chaim Bloch.

A Western journalist connects me to a taxi driver who will go to a settlement (but charges triple), and from the start, the journey is unlike any other I've made here. Smooth, wide roads, speeding cars, no roadblocks. And Psagot, like almost every settlement, on the top of a hill like a lookout, like the spooky small town of *Edward Scissorhands*. Barak's proposed budget for the coming year would spend $300 million on settlements.

Chaim Bloch is courteously waiting for us outside his house. He is dressed in a suit with a buttoned-up shirt and no tie. He has a longish light-brown beard and speaks softly and carefully. His father, a textile engineer, was offered a job in Israel thirty-one years ago, and within two weeks the family had moved over from Baltimore. I work out that Mr. Bloch is 39. I had thought him older.

In Israel, if you choose to do religious studies you are exempt from military service. For the young men who want to do both, special yeshivas exist. There are thirty of them around the country. Bloch is a graduate of one and, until recently, he had always taught at another. Now he teaches Jewish law as it relates to monetary management as a kind of "continuing education" course. He has been in Psagot nine years.

Why Psagot?

"Because this is the land of Judea and Samaria. It is here that the Israeli destiny is to be decided."

The people across the valley, in Ramallah and Birah, say this land was expropriated from them. How do you feel about that?

"The government of Israel never takes land without paying for it. The Arabs tried to bring a court case against us and in the end they begged us to allow them to drop it because they were going to be ruined."

There are UN resolutions stating that the West Bank and Gaza are illegally occupied.

"Israel is a law-abiding nation but there can be differences in the interpretation of the law. What we are doing here is not against international law." Then, without pause: "Even if I was 100% sure that international law was against me it would not change my views. Just because international law says something does not make it so."

But if not the law, what is your reference?

"God promised us this land. The state of Israel was here 2,000 years ago and God promised this land to our forefathers 37,000 years ago. There was never a state of Palestine here."

The one thought that I have is that I am not afraid anymore, not even uneasy. I feel nothing. I am conducting an interview.

Well, I say, there was never Syria or Lebanon or Jordan or Iraq. As states. It was all part of the Ottoman Empire and was carved up by the British and the French.

"This is the land promised to us by God."

OK. You say this land is yours because you were here 2,000 years ago. Across the valley there is a man who says this land is his because he has been here for 2,000 years. If—just for a moment—you put yourself in his position…

"I do not put myself in his position. You do that for a friend, on a personal matter. This is a question of nations. And my business is to look after the interests of the Jewish nation."

So you have no individual moral responsibility in this matter?

"No."

Well, from your point of view, what should the Palestinians do?

"They can go on living here. No one will throw them out. But they have to understand that they are living in a Jewish state. If they do not like that there are many places where they can go."

But if they live here, in a Jewish state, they don't have the same rights as the Jews.

"Yes. It is a Jewish state and they live as a minority. Believe me, 90 percent of Palestinians admire us and want to live in the state of Israel."

I know that a poll among young Palestinians found that they admired Israeli democracy as it was applied to the Jews. But it is not applied to the Arabs.

"Ninety percent of Palestinians would be happy to live in the state of Israel. I know this."

You know that 90 percent of Palestinians would be happy to live as second-class citizens forever?

"This is what my Palestinian friends tell me."

You have Palestinian friends?

"Yes."

Forgive me but—who are they?

Silence.

I don't want to know their names, just—where did you meet them, for example?

"One is a mechanic. He had to fix something for my car. And the other—he knows him.

"Could I just ask you how life on the settlement works—economically?"

"How do you mean?"

Well, I've heard that settlements get government help.

"Barak's government has cut back on most of what we got from Netanyahu. We get hardly anything."

(My companion Judy Blanc ascertains that the house he lives in was bought for a fifth of the market value. For a settler to travel to and from his or her settlement the government provides an armored bus and two army car escorts. Water, the main resource under government control, is divided between the Arab population and the Israeli settlers: each settler is allocated 1,450 cubic meters of water per year. Each Palestinian is allowed to use eighty-three cubic meters. Electricity is regularly shut down in the Palestinian towns while the settlements are lit up.)

Mr. Bloch, you have Israel. If you do not allow the Palestinians their own state in the West Bank this conflict will never end.

"Not everything has to be solved now."

You are happy that your children should inherit this conflict?

"Happy?" His voice rises, but only slightly. "My sister was on the bus that they blew up. The woman sitting next to her was killed. Children had to have their limbs amputated. I am not happy."

But you believe your children should inherit this situation?

"Those children on the bus—I pray that God will never ask me to pay such a terrible price. But if He does, I shall pay it."

As we drive away from Psagot I feel empty. I look at my notes and realize that I have no impression of what the living room we had been in looked like—except that it was bare and functional and sunny—and looked out on Ramallah. The taxi driver (even with $100 in his pocket) is speeding and angry and has an argument with a speeding young Israeli. Through the window I hear: "*Kess ikhtak!*"

(Your sister's c***).

Is that the same in Hebrew? I ask.

No, that was Arabic, Judy says.

"I see a terrible fire," Mme. Haniyya had said to me, "a terrible fire coming to swallow us all, Israelis and Palestinians —unless the Palestinian people are freed from their bondage."

1:30 pm

On the way back to the bridge I see that the army has dug a brand-new trench between the road and the town of Ariha (Jericho).

After

Exhaustion hits me the minute I get to London. This conflict has been part of my life all my life. But seeing it there, on the ground, is different.

What can I do except bear witness?

I am angrier than before I went. And more incredulous that what is happening in Palestine—every day—to men, women and children, should be allowed by the world to continue.

The choices are in the hands of Israel. They can hand over the West Bank, Gaza and East Jerusalem and live within their borders as a nation among nations. There are no choices for the people of Palestine.

Ilan Halevi, a Jew who fought with the PLO, says it's a question of macho image: "Israel does not want to be seen as 'the fat boy of the Middle East.' "

Others say Israel does not want to be a "nation among nations." It wants the beleaguered, plucky image—and the moral indulgence and billions of dollars' worth of aid that goes with it. If that is so, then the Israeli government has joined others of the region who are not working in the interests of their own people.

Awad Awad [the photographer] says the Israelis have declared that they will not renew the licenses of any Palestinian photographers working with the international media.

What will you do?

"Just carry on taking photographs. I'm a photographer."

I have seen women pushing their sons behind them, shoving them to run away, screaming at the soldiers: "Get out of our faces! Stop baiting the kids!"

I have heard a man say: "I have four sons and no work. I cannot feed them. Let them go out and die if it will help our country, if it will end this state of things."

I have seen children calmly watch yet another shooting, another funeral. And when I have wept they've said, "She's new to this."

I have listened to everybody predict that the leadership would do a deal. "But if they don't bring us independence and the right of return the streets will catch fire."

Palestinian weddings are celebrated over coffee, but when a young man is killed his mother is held up over his grave. "Trill out your *zaghrouda* [ululation], mother," his friends say, the *shabab* who might die tomorrow. A mother says to me: "Our joy-cries now only ring out in the face of death. Our world is upside down."

This article was originally published in the Guardian *December 18–19, 2000.*

Some names have been changed.

3. A SMORGASBORD OF FAILURE:
OSLO AND THE AL-AQSA INTIFADA

MOUIN RABBANI

Peace on the Horizon

When Edward W. Said, the foremost and most forceful Palestinian critic of the Oslo agreement, published a collection of essays on the subject in mid-2000 under the title *The End of the Peace Process: Oslo and After,*[1] he appeared to betray not only an abiding hostility to the new Israeli-Palestinian reality, but a profound detachment from it as well. It had after all been less than a year earlier, in one of the most lopsided election results in Israel's brief history, that Labor Party leader and Yitzhak Rabin protégé Ehud Barak had brought an abrupt end to Benjamin Netanyahu's belligerent premiership. While Netanyahu's fate had been sealed by a host of political and personal failings, Barak's pledges to restore visible movement to the Palestinian and Syrian tracks of the peace process and put an end to Israel's disastrous involvement in Lebanon clearly weighted the scales further in his favor.

Barak was soon translating words into action; his September 1999 Sharm el Sheik agreement with the Palestinians provided for further Israeli redeployments in the West Bank, addressed a number of other outstanding interim issues and, most important, established clear deadlines for reaching a "framework agreement" on a permanent settlement (February 2000) and a comprehensive Israeli-Palestinian peace treaty (September 13, 2000).

As *The End of the Peace Process* went on sale, Barak reversed twenty-two years of Israeli policy toward Lebanon and, over the objections of senior military officers, in May 2000 implemented a unilateral withdrawal from southern Lebanon, which was certified as a fulfillment of UN Security Council Resolution 425 (1978) by UN Secretary General Kofi Annan. Soon thereafter, and primarily at Barak's urging, Clinton invited the Israeli and Palestinian leaders to a July summit at Camp David to cut the Gordian knots separating them from a permanent settlement and thus bring the central component of the Middle East conflict to a satisfactory conclusion. The collapse of the summit after fifteen grueling days and nights of negotiations did not appear to dampen Barak's enthusiasm for a peace treaty with Yasir Arafat. Indeed, praised unceasingly for his political courage by Clinton, and alternatively lauded and reviled at home for offering "unprecedented concessions" to the Palestinians, Barak's repeated claim not to have "left a single stone unturned" in the search for peace was reinforced by his continued diplomatic pursuit of Arafat, culminating in a September 25 dinner at his residence

Left: Palestinian newspaper office showered by Israeli gunfire in Ramallah

in honor of the Palestinian leader. In the world beyond, Israel's Camp David proposals impressed European leaders enough for them to inform Arafat that if he persisted in rejecting them and attempted to break the deadlock with a unilateral declaration of statehood, he would be considered a spoiler who had abandoned the peace process and would lose their support. And aside from a joint statement during Camp David by Egyptian President Hosni Mubarak and Saudi Crown Prince Abdallah bin Abd-al-Aziz supporting Palestinian claims to East Jerusalem, Arab support was decidedly tepid.[2]

As September 2000 drew to a close, participants and observers alike were all but unanimous in their prognosis that a comprehensive Israeli-Palestinian peace treaty, or at least a detailed framework agreement leading to the establishment of a Palestinian state and including mechanisms for resolving the outstanding issues, would soon be concluded. The prospect of renewed violence in the occupied territories was not considered particularly worrisome and had been factored into many such predictions. In this respect, a controlled confrontation was seen as serving the interests of both Arafat and Barak: improving a bargaining position here, establishing the outer limits of flexibility there, and poignantly reminding skeptical constituents everywhere of the terrible alternative to an imperfect peace.

Although Israeli military planning took into account the possibility of a general Palestinian uprising involving the extensive use of firearms against Israeli soldiers and settlers, such scenarios—detailed in the "Field of Thorns" operational plan completed in September 1996—were premised upon a short conflict lasting from several days to a few weeks, and which however sharp would from beginning to end be closely orchestrated by the Palestinian Authority (PA).[3] In other words, it was conceived as a confrontation that in character would not go beyond an extended replay of the Israeli-Palestinian clashes that engulfed the West Bank and Gaza Strip the same month "Field of Thorns" was completed, leaving more than seventy Palestinian and fifteen Israeli dead (the so-called Tunnel Intifada) in the space of one week.[4]

Despite increasing signs of popular unrest during the year preceding the Al-Aqsa Intifada, there was good reason to dismiss the possibility of a sustained rebellion, particularly one with important similarities to the 1987-93 uprising. Most crucially, it would challenge and potentially destroy the foundations of Israeli-Palestinian cooperation established at Oslo, and in so doing would challenge the PA's political hegemony and the Barak government's stability as well. Additionally, the political forces considered to have the greatest interest in fomenting such an uprising, the Palestinian leftist and Islamist oppositions, had since Oslo been effectively neutralized by the PA, in the first case through a process of political marginalization and fragmentation resulting in the left opposition's virtual irrelevance, and in the second through a skillful campaign of repression coordinated with Israel and the CIA that reduced the Islamic Resistance Movement (Hamas) and Islamic Jihad to a state of organizational and military paralysis. The mainstream Palestine National Liberation Movement (Fatah), which played a central role in the previous intifada, was typically written off as little more than a PA appendage preoccupied with obtaining sinecures for its members.

The Palestinian economy, whose development was considered critical to the success and legitimation of Oslo, was furthermore finally beginning to show signs of life after shrinking by more than a third relative to its already battered state at the end of the previous uprising. While it had by no means recovered to pre-Oslo—to say nothing of 1987—levels, it had at least ceased to deteriorate further and was, according to the World Bank and others, exhibiting encouraging signs of growth.

The general population, written off by many as apathetic and disillusioned in equal measure after seven years of PA rule governed by the strictures of Oslo, for its part appeared preoccupied with the struggle for survival and, in more fortunate cases, reaping the rewards of previous struggle. The generation that came of age after 1993, as good a barometer of the popular mood as any, seemed, to the chagrin of older activists, little different in its priorities, concerns, activities, and ambitions from youth elsewhere.[5] More broadly, opinion polls revealed consistently strong, if gradually declining, levels of support for the continuation of the peace process.[6] If the growing disillusionment reflected genuine anger at Israel's systematic prevarication with respect to signed agreements, the institutionalization of its blockade of the occupied territories, and its intransigence on emotional issues such as prisoner releases, the continued support suggested a determination to maintain the degree of normalcy PA rule had restored to daily life after the violent mayhem of the first intifada's final years, and the hope that the remaining impediments and larger political issues perpetuating them would eventually be resolved through the process.

Overall, the prospects for mass mobilization seemed remote. The global dimensions of the Oslo coalition's optimism, and consequent despair among critics of an impending *fait accompli* of regional proportions, extended even to Said: "With Ehud Barak's assumption of power in May 1999," he concluded in the introduction to *The End of the Peace Process*, "things have certainly speeded up, so much so that a comprehensive peace between Israel, the Palestinians, Syria, and Lebanon will very likely be signed, if not completely implemented, within a year or so."[7] Or so it seemed.

A Formula for Conflict

The affront to national and religious sensibilities represented by Ariel Sharon's September 28 forced entry into the Haram al-Sharif was certainly sufficient cause for mass protest, but even in combination with the shooting death of at least four Palestinians at the same site the following day, it does not account for the intensity and duration of the Al-Aqsa Intifada. In similar precedents, neither the 1990 Al-Aqsa massacre, in which fourteen were killed and more than a hundred wounded, nor the 1994 massacre of twenty-nine Muslim worshipers at Hebron's Ibrahimi Mosque by Baruch Goldstein during the month of Ramadan, nor the September 1996 opening of a tunnel alongside the Haram al-Sharif and onto the Via Dolorosa by the Netanyahu government produced a comparable reaction.[8]

The fact that Sharon was perceived by the Palestinian leadership as acting at the behest of the Barak government, belligerently flaunting Israeli control over East Jerusalem during the height of permanent-status negotiations on Jerusalem in a manner that demanded a response, also does not add enough fuel to the fire to account for the ensuing explosion. While both Israel and the Palestinian Authority expected the other to initiate a clash after the collapse of the Camp David negotiations and (particularly in Israel's case) prepared for such an eventuality, neither sought a protracted confrontation.[9] The unprecedented human, material, and economic cost borne by the Palestinian population during the uprising, under circumstances in which Palestinian security agencies did not (in contrast to the 1996 Tunnel Intifada) intervene as an organized force,[10] further suggests that however important the role of the PA, other factors were also clearly at work.

While the uprising's immediate context does much to explain its origins and initial development, an appreciation of its scope and objectives must take into account the framework for Israeli-Palestinian relations negotiated at Oslo in 1993, and particularly the manner in which its application during subsequent years affected the lives and aspirations of West Bank and Gaza Strip Palestinians, who in their majority initially did not oppose the agreement.[11] In this context, the fact that military occupation, settler colonization, and economic underdevelopment preceded Oslo is less significant than the reality that these have since 1993 been consolidated when most expected their removal.

In light of the above the debate between critics who, like Said, have consistently argued that Oslo was structurally doomed from the outset and those who share the Palestinian leadership's view that the process ran aground because Israel refused to abide by its commitments (i.e., problems of implementation) merits closer examination. Consideration of these conflicting perspectives is essential both to understanding the causes of the current uprising and evaluating proposals designed to resolve the crisis.

The Palestinian claim that Israel refuses to implement signed agreements and violates its commitments in various other ways is beyond dispute.[12] A simple comparison of the September 1993 Declaration of Principles ("Oslo"), the September 1995 Interim Agreement ("Oslo II"), the January 1997 Hebron Protocol, the October 1998 Wye River Memorandum, and the September 1999 Sharm el Sheik agreement reveals a clear pattern in which Israel first refuses to implement its own commitments, seeks and obtains their dilution in a new agreement, subsequently engages in systematic prevarication, and finally demands additional negotiations, leading to a yet further diluted agreement.

This pattern is most evident with respect to the removal of Israeli military forces from West Bank and Gaza Strip territory. Whereas Oslo specifies that "Israel will be guided by the principle that its military forces should be redeployed outside populated areas" and "to specified locations,"[13] it states nothing about the functional fragmentation of the West Bank into areas designated as "A" (Palestinian security control), "B" (Palestinian civil and Israeli security control), and "C" (continued full Israeli occupation), introduced in Oslo II,[14] nor about its phasing of the redeployment into three installments over a period of eighteen months for reasons not specifically related to the preparedness of the Palestinian police to assume responsibility in areas evacuated.

Similarly, whereas Oslo II's redeployment applied to the occupied territories in their entirety save those areas specifically excluded ("specified military locations," East Jerusalem and other West Bank territory annexed by Israel since 1967, Jewish settlements, and the center of Hebron), the Hebron agreement, which *inter alia* renegotiated Article VII of Annex I of Oslo II concerning redeployment in Hebron, reversed this principle. Henceforth, even territory not subject to the abovementioned exemptions from Israeli redeployment would, unless specified otherwise in additional agreements, remain under full Israeli control. Thus Israel would redeploy *from*, rather than *to*, specific locations.

Wye reinforced this principle and added several innovations of its own. Pursuant to its terms an area's change of status from C to B or B to A (and thus not necessarily from full Israeli to full Palestinian security control) was sufficient to meet the criteria for redeployment, such that the agreement required Israel to transfer only 1 percent of West Bank territory from C to A (an additional 12 percent would change from C to B, and 14.2 percent from B to A).[15] Furthermore, the PA was required to designate fully a quarter (3 percent) of the new B areas as "Green Areas and/or Nature Reserves," an entirely new category that committed the PA to enforce "standards that do not allow new construction."[16] Thus, despite the illegality of Jewish settlement expansion and repeated international demands for the immediate cessation of such activity (including UN Security Council resolutions calling for the dismantling of all settlements in the territories occupied in 1967), the only explicit prohibitions on construction in the entire corpus of Israeli-Palestinian agreements concern *Palestinian* building activity. (Indeed, Oslo is pointedly mute on the legal status of Jewish settlements and calls only for the negotiation of their permanent status, thus implicitly elevating them to parity with Palestinian towns and villages.)

Additionally, Wye parceled the implementation of Oslo II's second of three redeployments into three stages stretching over ten weeks.[17] And the scope and implementation of the final, third redeployment specified by Oslo II was in Wye made subject to agreement by a joint Israeli-Palestinian committee,[18] a development that gave Israel the formal right to revise commitments already entered into, restrained only by its interpretation of its own interests and Washington's automatic concurrence.

The Sharm el Sheik agreement, considered necessary to (re)negotiate the implementation of Wye's unfulfilled second and third stages of Oslo II's outstanding second redeployment, sought to terminate the interim transfer of territory altogether. Instead, Barak—who, as Chief of Staff of the Israeli army, had been publicly skeptical of Oslo and as a cabinet member abstained when Oslo II was brought to a vote—hoped to integrate further redeployments, and Oslo II's third and final one in particular, with the permanent-settlement negotiations—a move designed to substantially weaken the PA's bargaining position in these talks.

Only partially successful in this attempt, Israel insisted on calculating the redeployment percentages on the basis of a West Bank from which annexed East Jerusalem, No Man's Land (a narrow strip of territory running along the Green Line), the Latrun salient, and the portion of the Dead Sea located within the West Bank had already been subtracted. By not including these areas, which together total 315 square kilometers,[19] Israel reduced the surface area of the West Bank by some 5.4 percent, thereby reducing the physical scope of further redeployments, which were calculated as percentages of West Bank territory. After one such exercise in late 1999, Israel unilaterally brought the redeployment process to a halt.

Thus, seven years after Oslo was sealed with a handshake on the White House lawn, the PA was in full control of less than a fifth of the West Bank and scarcely two-thirds (65 percent) of the minuscule Gaza Strip. With an additional area comprising between a fifth and a quarter of the West Bank designated Area B,[20] Israel remained in full control of some 60-70 percent of the West Bank and 35 percent of the Gaza Strip, and furthermore retained the right to act as it saw fit (including settlement expansion and physical invasion) in much of the rest of the West Bank (Area B).

It should come as no surprise, then, that there was unanimity among Palestinians that Israel had shown itself to be an untrustworthy, and above all utterly recalcitrant, counterpart. A special fury was reserved for the United States, and particularly the professional Israel lobbyists in the State Department, such as Dennis Ross and Martin Indyk, who managed the process.[21] Loathed as unreconstructed advocates for the Israeli adversary, their sole, immutable tactic seemed to be to demand further Palestinian concessions irrespective of Israel's contractual obligations, on the pretext that further compromise was required to enable the Israeli government of the day to sell the agreement either to the Israeli public (as in the case of Rabin) or to the most extremist members of the governing coalition (as with Netanyahu).

If its experience of the interim agreements failed to do so, the permanent-status negotiations provided unmistakable evidence that Israel considered the Oslo agreement's recognition of the legitimacy of Israeli sovereignty over 78 percent of historical Palestine but one component of the compromise. As far as Israel was concerned, the final disposition of the remaining fifth of Palestine occupied in 1967, the full recovery of which Palestinians consider the irreducible minimum of their national claims and which UN Security Council Resolution 242 by international consensus obligates Israel to relinquish,[22] was also a legitimate subject for discussion. Israel's determination to negotiate rather than implement the terms of 242—to "compromise the compromise"—was strenuously denounced by the Palestinians. From the leadership's perspective, tactical surrender to keep Oslo's interim phase and thus the prospect of a permanent settlement alive was one thing; strategic capitulation on final-status issues quite another.

In sharp contrast to Oslo's faithful, its opponents consider the various Israeli abuses of Oslo par for the course; in their view it is the structure of the agreement that is the paramount issue and has determined the manner of its implementation. In other words, an agreement repeatedly violated with impunity is first and foremost a bad one.

Oslo's fatal flaw—as consistently argued from the outset by Said and others—is that it is neither an instrument of decolonization nor a mechanism to apply international legitimacy to the Israeli-Palestinian conflict, but rather a framework that changes the basis of Israeli control over the occupied territories in order to perpetuate it. As such, the process is constitutively incapable of producing a viable or durable settlement, and will ultimately result in further conflict.[23]

In fact, the relationship between Israel and the PLO forged in Oslo and consummated in the occupied territories is demonstrably not one based upon a reciprocal recognition of equal (or even comparable) rights; whereas the lion's share of Palestinian concessions historically demanded by Israel were made in the letters of recognition exchanged pursuant to Israel's demand prior to ratification of Oslo, the relevant agreements never refer to the West Bank and Gaza Strip as occupied territories; do not explicitly commit Israel to desist from illegal activities—such as settlement expansion or grave breaches of the 1949 Fourth Geneva Conventions—designed to further consolidate Israeli rule over Palestine and the Palestinians; and make no attempt either to resolve the core issues that collectively define the Israeli-Palestinian conflict (for example, borders, refugees, and Jerusalem) or establish unambiguous guidelines for their settlement. Instead, the latter are shunted aside under the heading "final-status issues" and postponed for negotiation at the end of the process.[24]

To quote from the record, PLO Chairman Yasir Arafat's August 1993 letter to Israeli Prime Minister Yitzhak Rabin explicitly "recognizes the right of the State of Israel to exist in peace and security" without even making an attempt to specify borders; "accepts" Resolutions 242 and 338 without reference to their substantive meaning; unconditionally "commits" the PLO to the "peaceful resolution" of the conflict and resolution of "outstanding issues through negotiations"; "renounces the use of terrorism and other acts of violence and will assume responsibility over all PLO elements and personnel in order to assure their compliance, prevent violations and discipline violators" without any qualification of any sort; "affirms that those articles of the Palestinian Covenant…inconsistent with the commitments of this letter are now inoperative and no longer valid" (and promises to "submit to the Palestinian National Council for formal approval the necessary changes" to the Covenant); and, in both this and a separate letter to Norwegian Foreign Minister Johan Jorgen Holst, all but explicitly commits the PLO to terminating the intifada. Rabin's response, all of one sentence, commits Israel, "in light of the PLO commitments included in your letter…to recognize the PLO as the representative of the Palestinian people and commence negotiations with the PLO within the Middle East process."[25] Full stop. The contrast between the above and the agreement's calculated silence on core Palestinian concerns (repackaged by Israeli, Palestinian, and American diplomats as "constructive ambiguity") could hardly be greater.

Thus the imbalance of power inherent in Oslo guaranteed its "distorted" outcome.[26] Through it an ascendant Israel seeking to end the tactical burden of direct military occupation forged a functional partnership with a weakened and exhausted PLO, in which the former would retain possession of the West Bank and Gaza Strip's strategic assets (land, water, borders, Jerusalem) and the latter would assume formal responsibility for the indigenous population in the framework of a recognized Palestinian entity.[27] It is a process whose foundation stone is Israel's own interpretation of its security interests, and to which all else, including individual and collective Palestinian rights, is subordinated.[28] It is a process that necessarily leads to separation within the occupied territories under continued Israeli hegemony, as opposed to the partition of Palestine through a comprehensive Israeli withdrawal from the West Bank and Gaza Strip. In doing so it formalizes arrangements tantamount to apartheid (the Dutch/Afrikaans word that literally translates as "separateness").[29]

Seen from this perspective, the massive acceleration of Israeli settler colonization since 1993; the parallel construction of a road network to connect the settlements to Israel and each other in a manner that bypasses Palestinian population centers; the deliberate fragmentation of PA areas into noncontiguous ethnic enclaves and detailed Israeli control of Palestinian movement into, out of, and between them; and the sustained effort to prevent the emergence of an independent Palestinian economy are only to be expected and faithfully reflect the true "spirit of Oslo." Moreover, in view of the bilateral character of the agreements (whose implementation was never guaranteed by the international community but rather sponsored by Israel's strategic ally, the United States, which defines the PLO as a terrorist organization on probation), it is entirely logical that the dynamic of the Israeli-Palestinian relationship is primarily governed by the huge imbalance of power between them and Israel's consequent ability—facilitated by Oslo—to impose its will upon the Palestinians. Because this dynamic makes it virtually impossible to correct either Oslo's studied neglect of the requirements for peace or Israel's additional distortions of Oslo, it effectively paves the way to further conflict.

The facts on the ground certainly bear the burden of such an interpretation. Between September 1993 and 2000, the total settler population (excluding Jerusalem and its environs) increased from 110,000 to 195,000, a staggering 77 percent. In absolute terms, the annual rate of implantation of Jewish settlers in illegal West Bank and Gaza Strip colonies averaged 4,200 between 1967 and 1993, 9,600 between 1986 and 1996, and over 12,000 between 1994 and 2000.[30] Land expropriations have also continued apace, amounting to 40,178 dunams in 1999 alone.[31] So insatiable (and largely uncontested) has been Israel's appetite for Palestinian land since 1993 that few could fault the observer who concludes that Oslo's actual achievement was to broker the end of the *Arab* occupation of "Judea and Samaria."

The relevant statistics also show Barak to have been a considerably more avid settler than Netanyahu. During Barak's first year in office, his "peace cabinet" authorized 1,924 housing starts across the Green Line, a full 65 percent more than the 1,160 approved by the Netanyahu government in 1997. Similarly, Barak permitted construction to resume in eleven of the seventeen unauthorized settlement outposts established immediately after the Wye agreement (in response to then-Foreign Minister Ariel Sharon's public appeal to settlers to "grab every hilltop") but frozen by Netanyahu in 1999.

And in order to connect these new homes and outposts, $198 million in road projects were under construction across the Green Line in 2000. Because every 100 kilometers of colonial road require 10,000 dunams of land, more than 40 percent of lands expropriated in 1999 (16,657 dunams) were dedicated to road construction, spelling a rootless end for approximately 15,000 trees.[32] (Such roads serve the additional purpose of bolstering and perpetuating the encirclement of the several dozen isolated Palestinian enclaves, a reality that has to be seen on a map in order to be properly appreciated.)[33] And on account of the systematic segmentation of the land, it became impossible to drive more than a few kilometers without entering Israeli-controlled territory and that unique world of military checkpoints manned by soldiers dedicated to the systematic brutalization and humiliation of anything Arab.

Meanwhile, in the economic sphere, Israel's continued control of the occupied territories' external borders and internal boundaries, and its institutionalized, permanent blockade of the West Bank and Gaza Strip, had taken a harsh toll on the population. According to a World Bank study completed before the outbreak of the Al-Aqsa Intifada, Yemen is now "the only country in the MENA region that has a lower average income than the [West Bank and Gaza Strip]."[34] Israel's systematic restrictions on labor flows, trade, and movement—well in excess of anything experienced prior to 1993—ensured that the pipe dream of a Palestinian "Singapore of the Middle East" trumpeted so often after the White House Handshake would give way to the reality of Soweto on the Mediterranean.

By September 28, 2000, life under Oslo had become an intolerable proposition. Although the PA had introduced genuine improvements in West Bank and Gaza Strip life—notably in the spheres of personal security and infrastructure—this garnered it and Oslo little credit. Addressing the worst depredations of Israeli rule was the least people expected of a Palestinian regime and a peace process, and the PA and Oslo's failures tended to leave an altogether more lasting impression. Viewed from the ground, the problem of Oslo was not so much that it failed to match the initial expectations, but rather that apart from some meager improvements here and there things kept getting worse. Settlements kept increasing in size and number, hundreds of prisoners incarcerated before 1993 continued to languish in Israeli jails, Jerusalem was placed off limits to all but a select few, and seven years on, people felt that the Israeli noose—that comprehensive system of bureaucratic controls that became more refined and detested as time wore on—was still tightening. Only the PA and the prospect of an acceptable permanent settlement stood between the growing popular anger and an explosion, and Camp David effectively removed these from the equation.

In this context, Barak's Camp David proposals offered conclusive proof of the apartheid-and-bantustan scenario that Oslo's critics had been condemning for the better part of a decade. Although full details have yet to emerge, it is common knowledge that in these negotiations Israel sought, among other objectives, to annex permanently strategically located Jewish settlement clusters and roads, to fragment the proposed Palestinian state into a series of enclaves, to maintain ultimate authority over the Gaza-Egyptian and West Bank–Jordanian border, and to retain overall control over a substantially expanded Jerusalem.[35] In other words, the Palestinian entity—in arrangements akin to the interwar mandates system established by the League of Nations—would be reduced to an Arab protectorate under Israeli domination and supervision.[36] Within these strictures, as Israeli leaders rather enjoyed pointing out, the Palestinians were free to define their entity as a state, an empire, or any other term of their choosing. They could even join their Israeli partners in claiming that the entity encompassed 90–95 percent of the West Bank, though in reality little more than 60 percent was on offer.[37] And the basis of any such settlement would be the "five no's" enunciated amid much fanfare by Barak on the eve of the Camp David summit: no withdrawal to the June 4, 1967, boundaries; no dismantling of (all) settlements; no division of Jerusalem; no Arab army west of the Jordan River; and no return of Palestinian refugees.

While Barak habitually claimed that he had "left no stone unturned" at Camp David in his search for peace, the Palestinians came to the conclusion that on account of his "five no's" he had disregarded rather too many, and began literally throwing them at Israel's soldiers and settlers to drive home their rejection of continued occupation. It certainly appeared to portend the end of Oslo. Even the Treaty of Versailles, to which Said compared it, lasted longer.

The Uprising

Although the Al-Aqsa Intifada did not begin as a revolt against Oslo, a refusal to return to the status quo ante is the main factor that unites all levels of Palestinian society and politics, and has thus been its driving force. Propelled by the bitter harvest of the 1987–93 uprising, and deeply impressed by the stark contrast between Israel's systematic disdain for its Palestinian "peace partner" and comparatively scrupulous respect for unwritten understandings with its sworn enemy Hezbollah (at least after 1996), those leading the current rebellion, like Fatah West Bank secretary general Marwan Barghouti, insist that this time around the struggle will continue until Israel both agrees to a genuine peace and actually implements it. As far as they are concerned, the days when Israel exploited the illusion of a peace process to camouflage its expansionist policies, simultaneously tying Palestinian hands with interminable negotiations over increasingly insignificant procedural questions, while US and European negotiators proposed ever-more convoluted and irrelevant measures to "build trust" and "enhance confidence" (while undermining its last vestiges with policies designed to accommodate rather than challenge the latest turn in Israeli policy), are history.

In its opening phases the current uprising seemed very much like the last one: spontaneous mass demonstrations resulting in clashes between armed Israeli soldiers and stone-throwing Palestinian youths; commercial and general strikes; the formation of a broad political coalition (the National and Islamic Forces, or NIF) to provide direction to the revolt and facilitate political coordination;[38] and its rapid expansion from one region to the next.

Within days, it also developed into a familiar recurrence of the 1996 Tunnel Intifada: exchanges of gunfire between Israelis and Palestinians; armed offensives against Israeli outposts located within Palestinian towns, such as the tomb of a sufi sheik in Nablus, which in the early 1970s Jewish settlers occupied on the utterly spurious pretext that it is the burial site of the prophet Joseph;[39] huge numbers of casualties resulting from the massive deployment of Israeli force; and frenzied US and Arab efforts to get the peace process back on track.

Very quickly, however, things began to deviate from their previous pattern. Instead of the armed intifada containing the popular one they reinforced each other, repeatedly being driven to new heights by each new Israeli outrage (the September 30 killing of 12-year-old Muhammad al-Durra being a particularly noteworthy example). Instead of the leadership intervening to impose order and put an end to the unrest, it withdrew the security forces and sent mixed messages to the street. Instead of the clashes being limited to the boundaries between Area A and territory under Israeli control, they spread throughout the occupied territories and subsequently across the Green Line as Palestinians within Israel rose up in a deliberate act of national solidarity. Perhaps most important, instead of the PA acting like Israel's gendarme, the South Lebanon Army, Fatah began acting like Hezbollah.

The active participation of Fatah as an organized force acting with relative autonomy was perhaps the single most important factor in transforming the initial clashes into a sustained rebellion. The militarization of the uprising has been another primary characteristic of the Al-Aqsa Intifada, which emerged in the context of Fatah's undisputed leadership of the struggle. At the same time, the uprising's failure to transcend the level of a prolonged outburst of resistance to the occupation and develop into a comprehensive strategy for national liberation, and as an integral part of such a strategy to nurture a civil rebellion by a mobilized population, must also be primarily ascribed to Fatah.

The explanation for these factors is in significant part to be found in Fatah's complex relationship with the PA. Although Fatah members form the backbone of the PA and the two are closely intertwined, the movement as such is not the party of government. Rather, Fatah has suffered an identity crisis of sorts since Oslo. One trend, generally identified with the senior echelons of the formerly exiled PLO bureaucracy, considers its mission all but accomplished and would like to see the organization gradually transformed into a bureaucratized ruling party whose main functions—like the Baath Party in Syria or, until recently, the Mexican PRI—are to legitimize the state, co-opt elites, dispense patronage, and check the opposition.

The other trend, primarily associated with Fatah's pre-Oslo organizational infrastructure within the West Bank and Gaza Strip, has on the whole taken a more skeptical approach to the peace process and has a more developed vision of the future Palestinian society. For both these reasons, and also because it is less influential within the PA than its rival wing, it has sought to maintain Fatah as an autonomous political movement neither subordinate nor in opposition to the PA. Rather, this wing of Fatah seeks to keep itself sufficiently connected with the popular base in order to mobilize it in pursuit of Palestinian national objectives and lead Palestinian society into a new era, while at the same time sufficiently involved with the PA to obtain the resources to fulfill this ambition.[40]

The problem for this more activist wing within Fatah is that the movement's close association with the PA in the popular mind led it to continually lose ground. Through the uprising, it has been able to demonstrate its distinct identity vis-à-vis the PA, outflank the opposition, and recoup its losses in spectacular fashion. Only Fatah, which has extended its tentacles throughout the security services and which the PA leadership will only confront under the most extreme of circumstances, was in a position to resume the armed struggle; had it been independently initiated by Hamas or the Popular Front for the Liberation of Palestine (PFLP) in a direct challenge to the PA, these organizations—and the rebellion—would have been immediately crushed by these same security services. Similarly, only Fatah has the clout to conduct operations such as the January 17 assassination of the notoriously corrupt and universally reviled Arafat confidant and head of the Palestinian Broadcasting Company, Hisham Makki.[41] Had it been Islamic Jihad, the shots that killed Makki could well have unleashed an internecine bloodbath. At the same time, it has been Fatah that has ensured the formal loyalty of the NIF to the PA, and that apart from itself no genuinely popular movement whose fury might be directed inward has emerged.

In view of these complexities it would be erroneously simplistic to reduce Fatah, as the movement led by Arafat and the one that supplies the security services with most of its cadres, to a flag of convenience utilized by the PA to prosecute the uprising while deflecting responsibility for it. At the same time, it would be equally mistaken to view the broader relationship between the PA and NIF as heading for an inevitable confrontation. While there is indeed a basic contradiction between the PA's approach to the Al-Aqsa Intifada as a tactic to bring Oslo to a successful conclusion and Fatah's as a strategy to transcend it, these can coexist so long as the uprising does not develop in ways that threaten the political survival of the current leadership, and the latter does not act to terminate the uprising without a *quid pro quo* that the movement can successfully market to both its constituents and NIF coalition partners as a clear road map to genuine independence.

On the ground, Fatah's strategy has primarily been to turn the tables on Israel's infrastructure of control; where Israel has established isolated settlements within or on the outskirts of Palestinian towns in order to strangulate them and interrupt Palestinian territorial continuity, these and the bypass roads that service them have been subject to almost daily attack to underscore their own vulnerability and the more general point that Israel's physical and infrastructural presence within the occupied territories, far from contributing to Israeli security, is in fact its Achilles' heel. (As a result, the total settler population appears to be in decline for the first time since 1967.) If Israel responds to this challenge with massive reinforcements, it only increases the number of potential targets. If it subsequently resorts to measures of collective punishment such as the escalation of the siege,[42] it only increases support for and participation in acts of armed resistance. And if Israel resorts to the aerial and naval bombardment of Palestinian cities and the assassination of Palestinian militants by airborne death squads to curtail these, it exposes itself to heightened international censure, regional isolation, and revenge attacks in kind. And should it decide to seek a definitive solution by eliminating the PA or substantially weakening its security services (whose existence and hegemony is—unlike that of the PLO—of strategic interest to the West, and whose destruction therefore also threatens the latter's interests), it need only remind itself who replaced Fatah in southern Lebanon after Israel expelled the PLO from Beirut in 1982.

By contrast, Israel's Field of Thorns operational plan is designed to force Palestinian activists to disabuse themselves of the notion that Israel can be compelled to adopt policies by external pressure, to drive a wedge between the proverbially militant fish and the popular sea that sustains them, and to pressure the PA to curtail unrest by threatening its vital interests and, if necessary, its very existence. An escalating combination of overwhelming firepower, wholesale sanctions, special operations, and outright encroachments upon Area A, Field of Thorns pits heavily armed soldiers against civilian demonstrators, and the widespread use of artillery, naval, and air power against what are essentially a police force and lightly armed guerrillas. Graduating through collective punishments, financial and other sanctions against the PA, and a comprehensive territorial siege involving widespread defoliation and the fragmentation of the occupied territories into dozens of isolated enclaves that can be socially and economically paralyzed at will, the plan involves the use of targeted and mass arrests, special operations, and the use of both traditional and aerial death squads to liquidate militia and eventually political leaders. If the combination of above measures proves insufficient, Field of Thorns calls for them to be supplemented by the ethnic cleansing of specified neighborhoods in Area A, culminating in the outright military invasion and (temporary or permanent) re-occupation of one, several, or all PA territories, and the outright destruction of the PA as a political entity, elimination of its government apparatus, and dismemberment of its security forces.[43] The higher up the ladder of escalation one goes, the more the confrontation acquires the character of a direct conflict with the PA.

The problem for Israel is that its approach is specifically designed to restore and secure the status quo ante. Yet for both the PA and Fatah, to say nothing of other Palestinian forces, the status quo is precisely the problem, and opposition to it is what unites them. In this respect Israel's claim that the uprising was planned and has been orchestrated to the last detail by the PA and specifically Yasir Arafat on account of the latter's rejection of the concept of peace with Israel is difficult to take seriously, in view of what is known about the political transformation of the Palestinian national movement since the mid-1970s, the record of the political process that began in Madrid in October 1991 and ended at Camp David in July 2000, and, not less important, the depth and breadth of Palestinian opposition to continued Israeli hegemony.[44]

The argument that the PA has a clear and unconditional obligation to incapacitate every individual and organization whom Israel chooses to identify as posing an actual or potential threat to its "security" is, within the framework of Oslo, basically sound. Similarly, the argument that the PA's passive attitude toward renewed resistance to the Israeli occupation is a flagrant violation of existing Palestinian commitments to cease and smother such resistance—irrespective of any Israeli refusal to uphold its own obligations—is simply unanswerable. The Palestinian riposte that they have a legitimate and inalienable right under international law to resist foreign military occupation and that this right takes obvious precedence over an expired political agreement that has furthermore only consolidated an illegal occupation is certainly no less correct. It is not, however, an assertion that can be put forward in good faith by the PA, which was established as a result of Oslo and pursuant to the previously cited 1993 letters of recognition.

The above notwithstanding, the PA's position has in practice been to neither oppose nor actively participate in the uprising, but to acquiesce in the involvement of individual PA personnel. Senior Palestinian security officers have doubtless been involved in the planning and execution of various operations, and it appears incontrovertible that various security forces have undertaken specific (for the most part demonstrative) activities. In pursuing this policy the PA leadership is basically providing retroactive blessing to actions that it correctly feels powerless to prevent, undertaking the minimum necessary to retain that level of political credibility with the Palestinian street and political factions required for the legitimation of its diplomatic activities, and providing Israel with the occasional pointed reminder of its residual military capacities. Characterized as a policy of "riding the tiger," it is one based more upon influence than control, with the constantly shifting degree of influence determined by the relative proximity between the leadership's positions and the mood of the street and the NIF factions at any particular time.

In sharp contrast to the September 1996 clashes, an integral component of the leadership's policy during the Al-Aqsa Intifada has (with the exceptions noted immediately above) been not to commit its own forces to the confrontation except in cases of self-defense, and more particularly the defense of Area A from direct Israeli encroachment or invasion. While there has certainly been cooperation between individual members of PA security agencies, Fatah cadres, and activists from other organizations, and while the direct involvement of senior PA officers or security agencies in specific instances of such cooperation is likely, the notion that the armed campaign is being led or coordinated by Presidential Security (Force 17) or other PA agencies and somehow could not be sustained without them doesn't hold water. To take the most obvious example, namely the Hamas suicide bombings within Israeli cities, for which the Sharon-Peres government held Arafat personally and all but solely responsible, there is simply no plausible explanation as to why Hamas would voluntarily expose its organizational infrastructure to a past adversary and potential rival for no discernible benefit. As was the case in 1994–96, when Hamas was in all but open conflict with the PA, it hardly needs access to the PA's armories to build bombs consisting of small amounts of homemade explosives and nails, nor is it dependent upon covering fire by PA security to infiltrate members into Israeli territory. It is an even safer bet that the bombers never listened to the daily rantings of Yusif al-Qazzaz on Voice of Palestine or took note of the various commentaries offered by the Palestine Broadcasting Corporation (PBC). Rather, it is the unprecedented siege and terror unleashed by the Israeli military that has their undivided attention and makes them receptive to the sermons of Sheik Ahmad Yasin.

Seen from the Palestinian perspective, the Al-Aqsa Intifada is not only a general response to the structural and procedural failures of Oslo, but also a specific one to a campaign of violence viewed as deliberately initiated by Israel in order to extract further and entirely unacceptable political concessions from the Palestinians. As a PFLP slogan expressed it in reference to the unalterable minimum demand for a Palestinian state in the entirety of the 1967 occupied territories and Israel's determination "to compromise the compromise," "95% of 65% < 22%" (the West Bank and Gaza Strip constitute 22 percent of historic Palestine).

Whereas the PA has responded to Israel's instrumental approach to the current confrontation in kind by seeking to utilize the uprising to improve its negotiating position (and which, in view of the January 2001 Taba negotiations offering the Palestinians up to 85 percent of the West Bank rather than Camp David's 65 percent, appears to have been rewarded), Fatah and more broadly the NIF have sought to recast the terms of the Israeli-Palestinian conflict in order to achieve a settlement based on the "red lines"of Palestinian legitimacy rather than the limits of Oslo.

For the latter approach to bear fruit it above all requires a strategy to transform what remains an uprising into a disciplined and sustained struggle for national liberation. Indeed, it can only succeed through the purposeful mobilization of the various sectors of Palestinian society, the promulgation of clear and achievable political objectives, and strict adherence to a sophisticated (and therefore sufficiently flexible) program to realize these objectives. It must be prosecuted in a manner that maximizes Arab and regional popular support and in so doing imposes a consensus of solidarity upon their regimes (including the Palestinian one); in word as well as deed persuades Israeli opinion that peace, security, and rights are indivisible commodities either forged or forsaken upon the altar of Israeli policy toward the Palestinians and the wider Arab world; and transforms Israeli hegemony into a painful liability for its international sponsors while building international coalitions to erode Israel's privileged position and once again condemn it to pariah status. It is a struggle in which the use of force must be subordinated to political objectives rather than permitted to become an end in itself, and in which civil disobedience campaigns properly conducted can achieve more against a fortified position than a crate of rocket-propelled grenades. In each of the above respects, and despite the obvious and important differences, there are volumes to be learned from the strategic and tactical decisions adopted with such evident success by the African National Congress/United Democratic Front in South Africa and Hezbollah in Lebanon.

The development of the NIF during the early phases of the Sharon-Peres government suggests that it is increasingly cognizant of the need to develop a sustainable program. It began to organize activities that encouraged the participation of wider sectors of the population (for example, popular marches against new Israeli barricades), invited leading civil society organizations to participate in its deliberations, and discussed problems relating to the provision of public services and other matters of germane interest to the civilian population that were being inadequately addressed (if at all) by the PA. When a number of NIF factions were invited by the latter to assume ministerial posts in an emergency government of national unity, they declined on the grounds that a common political and socioeconomic program needed to be agreed upon before proceeding to the allocation of posts.

Nevertheless, the NIF has so far proved unable to move to a higher level of political coordination, repeating the PLO's experience of permitting each of its constituent factions to conduct an independent military strategy with the resultant contradictions and confusions. In this respect, the escalation pursued by Hamas and Islamic Jihad in March 2001 through a series of bombings within Israel—just as a popular civil disobedience campaign against the tightening siege was taking shape and visibly throwing Israel off guard—played directly into Sharon's hands and facilitated his effort to resume and escalate Barak's campaign of bombardment and assassination, thus taking the wind out of the nonviolent campaign's sails and replacing the Palestinian war of attrition against the occupation with an Israeli war of attrition against the PA. It is an error Hezbollah would never have made. Similarly, the uprising has spawned a host of new and often localized militias and armed cells, which appear primarily accountable to themselves and their immediate political environment rather than a national political authority.

The historical record of the Palestinian national movement, the limited room for maneuver available to the leadership, the absence of strategic discipline within Fatah and more broadly the NIF, and the manner in which Oslo has facilitated Israel's ability to implement Field of Thorns[45] (and the Sharon-Peres government's "100-day plan" deriving from it and initiated in March 2001) does not augur well for the prospects of the Al-Aqsa Intifada. As the possibilities for either a permanent Israeli-Palestinian settlement or a resumption of interim arrangements continue to recede, a prolonged low-intensity conflict propelled by yet unable to rupture the political stalemate, punctuated by occasional bouts of intensified bloodletting, domestic chaos (whether Palestinian or Israeli), and futile diplomacy, remains the most likely scenario. The possibility of uncoordinated action precipitating an endgame, perhaps developing into a conflict of regional proportions, is also not to be excluded. Yet, it is premature to conclude that the uprising represents the definitive eclipse of an era in Palestinian politics or Israeli-Palestinian relations. For this to happen an alternative strategy formulated by alternative forces (whether Islamist, secular, or Israeli) would have to be implemented and achieve political hegemony.[46]

The Al-Aqsa Intifada is above all a rejection of all that has occurred during the previous seven years. The uprising itself serves as a poignant daily reminder that irrespective of the odds—and if necessary in direct opposition to political arrangements and commitments endorsed by their own leadership—Palestinians will not abandon their national struggle, and that Israel has yet to decide between a historic compromise with them and irreconcilable conflict with the entire Arab world. At the same time, Israel is not going to concede any of the Palestinians' basic demands anytime soon. In order to make its point, it has unleashed a level of violence unprecedented in the history of the occupation, and it has imposed a siege that has stopped normal life dead in its tracks. It is the test of wills all over again, but with a much higher price. This makes it all the more difficult to predict where it will end.

Notes

1. Edward W. Said, *The End of the Peace Process: Oslo and After* (New York, 2000).

2. Immediately after his return from Camp David, Arafat undertook a tour of every Arab state prepared to receive him in addition to Iran. His specific objective, to convene summit meetings of the League of Arab States and the Organization of the Islamic Conference (OIC) in order to bolster his position with Arab and Islamic resolutions demanding the restoration of East Jerusalem to Palestinian sovereignty, was a resounding failure. King Muhammad VI of Morocco, for example, failed to convene the OIC's Jerusalem Committee, over which he presides, stating instead that he would favorably consider any Palestinian request for such a meeting.

3. Shraga Elam, "'Peace' with Violence or Transfer," *Between the Lines* 2 (December 2000) and references cited therein, particularly Anthony Cordesman, *Peace and War: Israel versus the Palestinians. A Second Intifada?* (Washington, DC, 2000).

4. The September 1996 clashes had been the most violent the occupied territories experienced since 1967, and they demonstrated the ability of the lightly armed PA security forces to give their Israeli counterparts a bloody nose, even as the latter extracted a much higher price from the Palestinians. The Tunnel Intifada additionally demonstrated the residual capacity of the Palestinian leadership to marshal the Palestinian street and foment a crisis when left with no diplomatic alternative and, acting through its security forces, rapidly contain popular unrest and channel it back into the peace process—thus reconfirming the political arrangements against which the demonstrators were ostensibly protesting. The May 2000 *Nakba* clashes, which featured widespread demonstrations in support of the right of return of Palestinian refugees but derived their heightened intensity from the festering issue of political prisoners (who were at the time conducting a hunger strike), were similarly interpreted as a PA production staged for domestic and international political considerations. Reports that Palestinian gunmen fired at Israeli positions despite strict instructions to the contrary, and of an increasingly critical tone emanating from the Fatah movement, failed to impress those Israelis, Palestinians, and others who continued to reduce the sum total of Palestinian politics to the calculating mind of Arafat. For more on the September 1996 uprising see Mouin Rabbani, "Palestinian Authority, Israeli Rule: From Transitional to Permanent Arrangement," *Middle East Report* 26:4 (October-December 1996); Graham Usher, *Dispatches From Palestine: The Rise and Fall of the Oslo Peace Process* (London, 1999), pp. 117–21. On the May 2000 clashes, see Usher, "The Territories Erupt," *Middle East International* 625 (May 19, 2000).

5. I am indebted to Daoud Talhami, member of the political bureau of the Democratic Front for the Liberation of Palestine (DFLP), for this observation.

6. The most comprehensive and regular polling of West Bank and Gaza Strip Palestinian public opinion since 1993 has been conducted by the Jerusalem Media and Communications Center (www.jmcc.org).

7. Said, *The End of the Peace Process*, p. xi. The passage was written in late 1999.

8. It bears recollection that it was also a calculated, state-sponsored provocation by Ariel Sharon—his November 1987 acquisition of a house in Jerusalem's Old City in which he has yet to spend his first night—that helped set the stage for the 1987–93 intifada. Similarly, Israel has in both cases, and with considerable justification, claimed that Palestinians were emboldened on the eve of their uprisings by events in Lebanon; in 1987 by a daring hang-glider raid undertaken by the Popular Front for the Liberation of Palestine-General Command across the Lebanese-Israeli border, which left six Israeli soldiers dead, and in 2000 by the Hezbollah movement's expulsion of Israel from Lebanon.

9. For numerous such references in the Israeli and Palestinian press during July-September 2000, consult the English-language daily summary of the Middle Eastern press, *Middle East Monitor* (London), for the period concerned. Israel and the Palestinians typically accused each other of preparing and fomenting a confrontation.

10. The observation is valid as of late May 2001.

11. On the initial Palestinian reaction to Oslo in the occupied territories, see Usher, *Dispatches from Palestine*, pp. 12–17.

12. Israel does not deny that it has refused to implement key provisions of the Oslo agreements, but it claims that this has been because of Palestinian violations of the same agreements. The record, however, supports the conclusion that although there have been clear Palestinian violations of various provisions of the agreements, Israel's territorial ambitions and/or internal political constraints typically provide a more accurate explanation of its conduct. The bimonthly *Middle East International* (and particularly the contributions of Graham Usher) provides an excellent record of the Oslo era in this and many other respects, as do the "Peace Monitor" and "Settlement Monitor" regularly published in the *Journal of Palestine Studies*.

13. Declaration of Principles, Article XIII:3.

14. Israeli-Palestinian Interim Agreement, Article IX:2.

15. The Wye River Memorandum, articles I:A:1 and I:A:2. Whether these percentages apply to the total surface area of the West Bank (however calculated) or merely the sum total of territories within a particular designated category at the time of the agreement is left unspecified.

16. *Ibid.*, Article I:A:1. The passage cited speaks volumes about Israeli cynicism, Palestinian ineptitude, and American partiality.

17. *Ibid.*, Articles 2-4 of the appended "Time Line" defined in the agreement's preamble as an "integral attachment" to it.

18. *Ibid.*, Article I:B.

19. See "Monitoring Israeli Colonizing Activities in the Palestinian West Bank and Gaza," a joint project of the Applied Research Institute in Jerusalem and the Land Research Center in Jerusalem, available at www.poica.org.

20. Palestinian Academic Society for the Study of International Affairs (PASSIA), *Diary 2001* (Jerusalem, 2000), p. 258. See also Said's article and the accompanying maps in this volume.

21. The Israel lobby's direct penetration of the senior echelons of the US foreign policy establishment, a process that began during the second Reagan Administration and reached unprecedented heights during the Clinton years, has generally been

a taboo subject in the United States. Among the Clinton officials with a direct role in the formulation and implementation of US Middle East policy who were previously functionaries of the Israel lobby or held leadership positions in pro-Israel organizations are National Security Adviser Samuel Berger; National Security Council Middle East specialist (and subsequent US Ambassador to Israel) Martin Indyk (an Australian who was made a US citizen immediately after Clinton took office by a special act of Congress); State Department Special Coordinator for Middle East Affairs Dennis Ross, and his deputy Aaron David Miller. One can imagine the outcry in the US media if George W. Bush had appointed officials of the National Association of Arab Americans and the Arab American Institute to these same positions.

22. Ambiguities attributed to Resolution 242's withdrawal clause are in this respect resolved by the clarity of its preamble, which specifies "the inadmissibility of the acquisition of territory by force." Significantly, the United States, at the time it voted in support of the resolution in 1967, also interpreted the resolution as requiring a full Israeli withdrawal and formally communicated this position to foreign governments, including Jordan, from whom Israel conquered the West Bank. See Donald Neff, "The Differing Interpretations of Resolution 242," *Middle East International* 404 (September 13, 1991). See also Noam Chomsky's introduction to this volume.

23. In addition to Edward Said's *The End of the Peace Process*, see his *The Politics of Dispossession* (London, 1994) and *Peace and Its Discontents* (New York, 1996). For additional analysis from a similar perspective see Noam Chomsky, *Fateful Triangle: The United States, Israel and the Palestinians*, updated edition (Boston, 1999), pp. 533–65; Norman G. Finkelstein, "Whither the 'Peace Process,'" *New Left Review* 218 (July-August 1996); Finkelstein, "Securing Occupation: The Real Meaning of the Wye River Memorandum," *New Left Review* 232 (November-December 1998); Graham Usher, *Palestine in Crisis* (London, 1995).

24. In this context Israel and the PLO have irreconcilably conflicting interpretations of the sole instrument identified in Oslo as the basis for a permanent settlement, Resolution 242 (Resolution 338 basically reaffirms it). Since formally accepting 242 in 1988, the PLO has insisted that its withdrawal clause applies to the 1967 occupied territories in full. Israel contests this and has previously argued both that it already fulfilled its obligations under 242 in April 1982, when it completed its withdrawal from the Sinai Peninsula (which constitutes 90 percent of the territories occupied in 1967), and that the PLO as a nonstate entity cannot be considered a party to the resolution's implementation. In the context of Oslo, the true intent and proper interpretation of 242 is an irrelevant exercise, because the agreement makes no attempt to define the resolution and contains no provision for an independent and binding arbitration mechanism. See, however, note 22 above.

25. The letters are reproduced in JMCC, Occasional Document Series No. 7 (Jerusalem, 1996), pp. 259–61.

26. In this regard, see also Glenn Robinson's article in this volume.

27. The centrality of achieving statehood for the contemporary Palestinian national movement is discussed in Yezid Sayigh, *Armed Struggle and the Search for State: The Palestinian National Movement, 1949–1993* (Washington, DC, and Oxford, 1997). See particularly sections III and IV.

28. See further Finkelstein, "Securing Occupation."

29. The phenomenon of apartheid is often misconstrued as a system defined by pernicious racist legislation such as existed in South Africa and/or strict racial segregation as was practiced in the American South. According to the relevant UN convention, which defines apartheid as a crime against humanity, the defining characteristic of the phenomenon is (as the meaning of the term implies) the separate administration of persons within a single territorial unit on the basis of race or ethnicity. Explicitly racist laws that confirm such policies and the institutionalized forms of discrimination that result from such administrative separation are thus *consequences* of apartheid. Israel's consistent claims since 1967 that it subjects the Palestinian civilian and Jewish settler populations in the territories to separate legal regimes, and issues them with distinct identity cards, vehicle license plates, and so on for purely "administrative" reasons, therefore provide formal confirmation

of its practice of apartheid. One could also note that whereas South African apartheid legislated the inferiority of the majority, the Israeli version promulgates the superiority of the minority and does so in more subtle ways. In this context, the establishment of the PA as a territorially restricted ethnic authority with limited jurisdiction derived from Israeli control (which surrounds it on all sides) is virtually indistinguishable from the South African homelands policy, and the Israeli policy of "separation" on which it is based would seem to constitute the institutionalization of apartheid.

30. Figures provided in *Report on Israeli Settlement in the Occupied Territories* (of the Foundation for Middle East Peace, www.fmep.org) and Rassem Khamaisi, "Settling the Land: A Pattern of Domination," *Palestine-Israel Journal of Politics, Economics, and Culture* VII:3&4 (2000).

31. PASSIA, *Diary*, p. 257, citing *Law Annual Report* 1999. One dunam = 0.1 hectare or 0.25 acre.

32. *Ibid.*, pp. 257–58, citing *Law Annual Report* and Peace Now.

33. See for example the map (produced by Jan de Jong) in Geoffrey Aronson (ed.), "Settlement Monitor," *Journal of Palestine Studies* XXIX:1 (Autumn 1999). For more on these "bypass" roads see Jeff Halper, "The 94 Percent Solution: A Matrix of Control," *Middle East Report* 30:3 (Fall 2000).

34. The World Bank Group, "Poverty in the West Bank and Gaza," *Palestine-Israel Journal of Politics, Economics, and Culture* VII:3&4 (2000). See also Sara Roy's article in this volume.

35. See further Akram Hanieh, *The Camp David Papers* (Ramallah, 2000), also in *Journal of Palestine Studies*, Vol. 30, No. 2 (Winter 2001); Edward Said's article in this volume (and particularly the maps of Jan de Jong); Jan de Jong, *Palestinian Planning Imperatives in Jerusalem, with a Case Study on Anata* (Jerusalem, 2000).

36. In this respect it is important to recall that the Palestine Mandate "provisionally recognized" the independence of Palestine, precisely in order to camouflage the inherently colonial character of the arrangement.

37. See "West Bank Final Status Map Presented by Israel—May 2000" by Jan de Jong, in Geoffrey Aronson (ed.), "Settlement Monitor," *Journal of Palestine Studies* Vol. 30, No. 1 (Autumn 2000). According to De Jong, furthermore, the Clinton plan would give Palestinians only approximately 85 percent of the West Bank, whereas Israel's response reduced this area to 80 percent. The relevant maps can be consulted at www.fmep.org.

38. Unlike the United National Leadership of the Uprising (UNLU) of the previous intifada, which consisted of Fatah, the PFLP, DFLP, PCP, and (initially) Islamic Jihad, the NIF also includes all PLO factions (including the alphabet soup of fronts sponsored by Damascus and Baghdad) and all Islamist factions. The only exceptions are the openly schismatic groups, namely the Fatah-Revolutionary Council of Sabri al-Banna (Abu Nidal), the Fatah-Provisional Command of Sa'id Maragha (Abu Musa), and the Palestine Communist Party-Provisional Command (Arabi Awad). The Islamic Liberation Party (Hizb al-Tahrir), which still retains a number of adherents in the West Bank but is as a rule politically aloof, has exempted itself.

39. In the aftermath of their expulsion from the site in October 2000, settlers stated quite openly that they never seriously believed Joseph is buried in his alleged tomb, and that they put forward the claim primarily to force an Israeli state increasingly beholden to Jewish fundamentalist forces to retain control of a site in the center of an Arab town.

40. The autonomous, activist wing of Fatah has generally come to be known as the *tanzim* ("organization"). Formally, however, Fatah in its entirety is known as *harakat fath* ("the Fatah movement") or *tanzim fath* ("the Fatah organization"), and membership in Fatah and the *tanzim* are thus one and the same (Fatah cadres often refer to fellow members as *ibn tanzim*, "son of the organization"). Furthermore, while Fatah retains a number of formal and clandestine militias, none are known as the *tanzim*, in the sense of a separate, distinct apparatus within Fatah. This notwithstanding, the name appears to have stuck. For more on this wing of the movement see Graham Usher, "Fatah's Tanzim: Origins and Politics," *Middle East Report* 30:4 (Winter 2000).

41. To illustrate the point, the PA blamed "criminals" and "collaborators" for the assassination. The following day, the Anti-Corruption Unit (*wihdat mukafahat al-fasad*) of the Al-Aqsa Martyrs' Brigade (*kata'ib shuhada al-aqsa*), a new militia spawned by the activist wing of Fatah, pointedly took responsibility for the killing.

42. For a description of the various forms of Israel's "closure" policy, which has been in effect since 1993, see Sara Roy's article in this volume. During the current uprising, Israel has also deployed "comprehensive closure," in which Gaza international airport, the airspace above the Palestinian territories, and coastal waters are ordered closed, VIP permits issued to senior Palestinian officials that normally exempt them from closures are revoked, and tanks occupy main junctions within areas under full Palestinian control to intensify their geographical fragmentation. In March 2001 the Sharon-Peres government erected ninety-one new roadblocks in the West Bank, dividing it into sixty-four distinct enclaves, each of which can be opened or closed at will. The much smaller Gaza Strip was divided into at least four such regions. Such roadblocks, consisting of trenches dug through asphalt roads, earthen barricades, and concrete barriers, typically presided over by tanks and armored vehicles and accompanied by massive uprooting of trees and vegetation, often turned the areas concerned into a moonscape.

43. For full details consult Elam, "'Peace' with Violence"; Cordesman, *Peace and War*, pp. 83–89.

44. For a comprehensive account of the political transformation of the PLO from its early origins to the eve of Oslo see Sayigh, *Armed Struggle and the Search for State*.

45. Graham Usher, "Gaza Agonistes," *Middle East Report* 31:1 (Spring 2001).

46. Although the rise and increasing effectiveness and influence of Hamas during the early 1990s was a main factor behind both Israel's and the PLO's decision to conclude the Oslo agreement, it would be an exaggeration to assert that the Islamist movement was capable of overtaking the PLO at that time.

4. DECLINE AND DISFIGUREMENT: THE PALESTINIAN ECONOMY AFTER OSLO

SARA ROY

Introduction and Overview

Tragedy, wrote Jean Anouilh, is "restful" precisely because "hope, that foul, deceitful thing, has no part in it."[1] The Al-Aqsa Intifada has introduced a new and perhaps unprecedented phase into the long and bitter conflict between Israelis and Palestinians. This phase is characterized by great violence and brutality, massive destruction, extremism, and regression.

The current phase of the conflict is often seen as a tragic departure from the period of "peace" and development that preceded it. The common belief purveyed in the Western media is that Palestinians foolishly rejected magnanimous Israeli concessions made at the Camp David Summit in July 2000 and opted instead for violence, hoping thereby to gain more. The majority of Israelis, convinced that Palestinians are unwilling to live peaceably, responded by installing a right-wing government that promised a military solution to the Palestinian "problem." The resulting crisis appears to have no end.

The current crisis, far from representing a break with the recent past, is a logical and inevitable extension of it. The Al-Aqsa Intifada did not emerge in a vacuum but emanated from a context of continued occupation and dispossession that characterized the entire Oslo peace process and its impact on Palestinians. Nowhere is this more visible than in the weakening of the Palestinian economy and the resulting impoverishment of the Palestinian people. While it is beyond the scope of this chapter to detail the vicissitudes of the Oslo process in all their dimensions, an examination of the economic sector under Oslo will reveal one critical component motivating the current uprising.

The peace process not only failed to ameliorate, let alone end, Palestinian economic decline or the terms upon which it is based; it accelerated that process by introducing into the Palestinian economy new dynamics that further attenuated an already diminished socioeconomic base.[2] Arguably, there never has been a period since the imposition of Israeli control in 1967 when the Palestinian economy has been so vulnerable. When measured against the advances made by other states in the region, the Palestinian economy is weaker now than in 1967.[3]

The economic losses to Palestinians during the post-Oslo period have been devastating. The average unemployment rate, for example, increased over ninefold between 1992 and 1996, rising from 3 percent to 28 percent, one of the highest unemployment rates among nearly 200 countries and political

Left: Preparing to walk down a road heavily guarded by the Israel Defense Forces in Khan Yunis, Gaza

entities, according to the World Bank. Real Gross National Product (GNP) declined 18.4 percent between the end of 1992 and the end of 1996. During the same period, real per capita GNP fell a dramatic 37 percent, with a concomitant increase in poverty rates.[4] Poverty, especially among children, is now visible in a manner not seen for at least twenty-five years.

Rather than becoming more modern, internally integrated, and complex, the Palestinian economy is becoming more atavistic, disarticulated, and fragmented. Indeed, since the initiation of the Oslo process, the Palestinian economy has moved toward a structure that is increasingly characterized by small production units using local inputs to produce for the domestic market, with more and more people divorced from the means of production and deskilled. The economic patterns taking shape in the West Bank and Gaza Strip are strikingly similar to and, in certain respects, more harmful than those that characterized Palestinian economic activity during direct Israeli military occupation.

Palestinian economic contraction, which appears all the more startling in a globalizing world economy, not only constrains growth but limits its impact. Economic gains, when they do occur, are reversed easily and swiftly, suggesting in turn that economic growth, let alone development, is the exception and not the rule today. Poverty, not prosperity, characterizes the local landscape. People and the communities in which they live have become more vulnerable and weaker.

The reasons for Palestinian economic regression are many and interrelated but turn on one primary axis: closure. Israel's closure policy, which restricts and at times bans the movement of labor and goods from the occupied West Bank and Gaza Strip to Israel, to each other, and to external markets, represents the single most deleterious factor shaping the nature of Palestinian economic activity and Palestinian life in general. Closure was first imposed in March 1993, prior to the signing of the first Oslo accord in September of that year, and has never once been lifted. Throughout the Oslo process, closure has been used to divide, isolate, and punish Palestinian communities. With the Al-Aqsa Intifada, closure has found its most extreme expression, encirclement and siege, fragmenting and disconnecting Palestinian communities in a manner that has seriously damaged individual and collective well-being. Yet, closure remains largely unknown and unrecognized in the West.

Closure has long been an economic fact of life in the West Bank and Gaza, a permanent system that has introduced a host of new and intractable problems into an already weakened and structurally distorted economy, further attenuating the possibility of economic growth and reform. These problems include: high and fluctuating unemployment, permanent unemployment for a growing segment of the labor force, the declining mobility of labor, diminishing trade, weakening agricultural and industrial sectors and declines in domestic production, reduced investment in needed export-oriented industries, low levels of infrastructural development, rising levels of poverty and child labor, and increasing demand for relief and social assistance. Closure has also resulted in the geographic isolation of the West Bank and Gaza Strip, a reality without precedent since 1967, and the spatial separation of their populations. This bifurcation not only has immense implications for the reconstruction of the

Palestinian economy but also for the implementation of a viable and sustainable political solution to the Israel/Palestine conflict.

The Palestinian Authority (PA) has played an important albeit secondary role in shaping the current economic environment. Despite some achievements in establishing a reasonably efficient and competitive banking system and a functional tax system, the PA has failed to establish a regulatory and institutional environment that would attract high levels of foreign investment. The latter is critically needed for the growth of the private sector, which is a prerequisite for economic development.

Moreover, some of the policies instituted by the Palestinian government demonstrate an outright hostility toward economic reform and modern institution building. These policies, which are characterized by secretiveness and a lack of transparency, include the establishment of monopolies (and price fixing) over a range of essential commodities, collusion with influential private-sector interests rather than promotion of free competition, mismanagement of the public sector, and increasing corruption within the bureaucracy.[5] Furthermore, the PA's disrespect for its own people, as seen in its consistent disregard for human rights and the rule of law, and its authoritarianism and repression, have had a pernicious effect on the economy and society alike.

While the PA has contributed to the adverse economic situation in the West Bank and Gaza, it is the government of Israel that remains the primary determinant of Palestinian economic life, and it is Israeli policy that will be the focus of this discussion.[6] The historical construction of the Palestinian economy has remained fundamentally unchallenged in the post-Oslo period. Despite certain policies of territorial (and functional) separation imposed by the Israeli government since the signing of the first Oslo Agreement in 1993, Palestinian economic dependence on and integration with Israel remains marked.

Israel's continued domination of the Palestinian economy is not accidental. The continuation of pre-existing power relations between Israel and the Palestinians, and the structures that underlie them, is a characteristic feature of the Oslo agreements. These agreements were designed not to alter the structures of occupation but to maintain them, albeit in new, somewhat less direct forms. In this way, the Oslo agreements, like the policies that preceded them, preclude needed economic restructuring. Therefore, it is not the specific policies of any given Israeli government per se that obstruct "peace," as many observers have maintained; it is the agreements themselves.

Oslo and the Economic Protocol: Defining the Parameters of the Palestinian Economy

The policy parameters of the interim period (1994–2000) were established fundamentally by four agreements between the State of Israel and the Palestine Liberation Organization: the Declaration of Principles (DOP/Oslo I) in September 1993, the Protocol on Economic Relations (Paris Agreement) in April 1994, the Agreement on the Gaza Strip and Jericho Areas (Cairo Agreement) in May 1994, and the Israel-Palestinian Interim Agreement on the West Bank and Gaza Strip (Oslo II) in September 1995. Collectively, these documents define a legal framework for Palestinian economic activity, especially economic relations with Israel. Certain features of this framework are worth noting.

Perhaps the most significant feature of the Oslo process is the abandonment of international law in favor of bilateral negotiations between two parties of grossly unequal power. Despite the appearance of symmetry between Israel and the PLO, it is Israel that possesses almost total power while the PLO/PA possesses almost none. As such, the various Oslo agreements overwhelmingly reflect Israeli interests and concerns. Israel has the power, unchallenged by any official actor, to force unilaterally its own terms on the implementation process even if they violate the agreements themselves. Furthermore, under the terms of the DOP, Israeli military law, including many restrictions on economic activity, remains in force during the transitional phase, effectively placing the West Bank and Gaza Strip under the continued authority of the occupation regime, which retains all of its powers and prerogatives.[7]

A key feature of Oslo II, which detailed the extension of limited self-rule to the West Bank, was the division of the West Bank into three areas (A, B, C), each under varying degrees of Palestinian and/or Israeli control. By March 2000, area A, under full Palestinian control, had grown to only 17.2 percent of the West Bank.[8] Since Israel retains security control over area B and full control over area C, in practical terms, Israel actually controls almost 83 percent of the West Bank.

While the absolute area under full or partial Palestinian control has increased (and is expected to increase further as part of a permanent settlement), these areas are noncontiguous and constitute, in effect, isolated enclaves separated by areas under the complete jurisdiction of Israel. Hence, even if Palestinians are given authority over larger enclaves, and thus more of the West Bank, the enclaves will remain fragmented and disconnected. This also applies to the much smaller Gaza Strip, which effectively is divided into three enclaves. Palestinians have no control over borders, internal or external to the West Bank. That control remains with Israel, and Palestine's only borders are with Israel. Indeed, according to Amnesty International, by December 1999, the Oslo agreements had created 227 separate West Bank enclaves under the full or partial control of the PA. Approximately 88 percent of these areas are less than two square kilometers in size. Critically, *all* Palestinians in the West Bank live within six kilometers of Area C lands.[9]

Hence, the division of the West Bank into different areas, itself inconceivable in other national contexts, has given Israel a new mechanism with which to control the Palestinian people. Not only is the population demographically separated, it is difficult to imagine how a viable economy could be created in over 227 tiny enclaves that are severed from one another, let alone from Palestine's logical trading partners in surrounding countries.

The Protocol on Economic Relations—the Oslo accord that defined economic relations between Israel and the Palestinian territories—called for the introduction of certain new economic powers for

Palestinians and for the elimination of some longstanding restrictions. Yet decision-making authority over the most critical aspects of the Palestinian economy was maintained wholly by Israel, formally legalizing Palestinian economic dependence on Israel and Israeli control of the Palestinian economy, arguably for the first time. For example, under the terms of the agreements, key resources (including the critical factors of production) such as land, water, labor, and capital remain subject to Israeli jurisdiction for the entirety of the occupied territories. By mid-2000, Israel retained direct control over more than 20 percent of the Gaza Strip in addition to its 59 percent share of the West Bank. In these areas, Israel also has legal authority over zoning, building, land registration, and all other resources.

In that portion of the West Bank under both Palestinian and Israeli authority (Area B), the PA has partial administrative control while Israel has complete authority over the disposition of land, water, etc.[10] It is only in Area A that Palestinians exercise total control over their resource base. However, most of the land "returned" to the Palestinians "is the least desirable and least productive, from an economic point of view."[11] The bulk of Palestinian agricultural land, a key component of the local economy, is located in Area C and is therefore outside the PA's legal and economic domain.[12]

Between 1994 and 2000, the Israeli government confiscated approximately 35,000 acres of Arab land in the West Bank, much of it agricultural and worth more than $1 billion, for the construction of bypass roads and settlement expansion. Ironically, Yasir Arafat agreed to this confiscation as part of the Oslo II Interim Agreement. Similarly, in 1999, after the Barak government was installed, Israeli authorities confiscated some 10,000 acres of Arab land in the West Bank and Gaza Strip for Israeli settler use.[13] Indeed, between September 1993, when the Declaration of Principles was signed, and April 2000, the number of settlers in the West Bank grew by 85 percent, from 100,000 to 185,000 people, and the number of settlements increased by thirty.[14] In addition, 250 miles of settler bypass roads had been built on expropriated lands. These roads run like a grid throughout the West Bank, encircling and truncating Palestinian enclaves.

Critically, the Israeli authorities have also retained control over all borders, which means control over the movement of labor and goods, the closure notwithstanding.[15] The Economic Protocol states: "both sides will attempt to maintain the normality of movement of labor between them, subject to each side's right to determine from time to time the extent and conditions of the labor movement into its area."[16] This clause, which is meaningless to the PA since no Israeli seeks employment in the Arab sector, gives Israel the legal right to restrict the entry of Palestinian labor according to its own criteria and methods.[17] Furthermore, no Palestinian laborer or product can exit the West Bank or Gaza without an Israeli permit. Both workers and goods also require a permit from the PA, which only adds another layer of bureaucracy to an already cumbersome process, since no movement is possible without Israeli authorization. Thus, even though closure was imposed before the implementation of the Oslo agreements, the agreements, in effect, legalized and institutionalized closure as a policy measure.

Because of the small size of the Palestinian economy, trade is a critical component of development. However, given Israeli control of borders as established in the Economic Protocol, Palestinian trade continues to be wholly mediated through Israel. The protocol calls for a quasi-customs union between Israel, the West Bank, and Gaza. A customs union permits free trade or open borders between participating economies and imposes joint and identical import restrictions (for example, tariffs) on trade with other countries. In the case of Israel and the occupied territories, the quasi–customs union arrangement (something between a customs union and a free-trade area), which reflects Palestine's continued extreme dependence on the Israeli market, has been characterized by certain modifications and restrictions.

The Economic Protocol allows Palestinian trade with the Arab world. However, imported goods are subject to a range of restrictions, including quotas agreed to by both sides for more than sixty tariff items. These items must meet Israeli quality standards for imports. According to the World Bank, these standards are considered to be "above what would be desirable given Palestinians' income levels. Even in the midst of border closures (when Israel's closing of the border led to meat shortages in the Gaza Strip), meat could not be imported from Egypt because of quality standards restrictions."[19] Furthermore, only certain goods could be imported from Jordan and Egypt, in quantities agreed to by both sides, while the quantities of others would be approved according to demonstrated Palestinian need.[19]

Another modification written into the Economic Protocol calls for the imposition of quotas on Palestinian exports, notably agricultural exports. Although Israel theoretically opened its borders to Arab agricultural products, this opening is a restricted one, a measure meant to protect Israeli farmers. For specified Palestinian exports, Israel's borders were to be opened gradually over a five-year period, with annual quotas imposed.[20] These agricultural exports—poultry, eggs, potatoes, cucumbers, and tomatoes—are most competitive with Israeli products and constitute approximately 60 percent of Gaza's agricultural production. In addition, one Israeli export to the Palestinian economy, melons, was included.

The Economic Protocol also gives Palestinians the legal right "to export their agricultural produce to external markets without restrictions."[21] Yet these markets are largely inaccessible given Israel's almost total marketing monopoly over key agricultural exports. Access is further weakened by Palestinian reliance on Israeli marketing mechanisms and inexperience with international marketing.

Given the noncompetitive nature of Palestinian industrial products and the expansion of Israeli subcontracting ventures at the time of the Economic Protocol's formulation, fewer restrictions were imposed on industrial trade between Israel and the territories. Yet industrial subcontracting and the trade to which it gives rise create limited employment for Palestinians, transfer low levels of technology, depend on labor-intensive production methods, and generate low value-added.

As a result, Palestinian industry post-Oslo remains as weak and dependent as it was pre-Oslo.[22] The agreements have secured for Israel an uncontested Palestinian market—a source of low-technology, low-cost goods for Israel and a repository for high-priced manufactured goods from Israel. Closure has made the Palestinian subcontractor even more dependent on his Israeli manufacturer. Even so, the marketing uncertainties created by closure have compelled Israeli suppliers to transfer production to neighboring countries like Jordan and Egypt, where such uncertainties do not exist and where labor costs are cheaper.

The Economic Protocol's structural terms of reference describe what could be called a "best case" scenario for the interim period. Yet even under this more optimistic scenario, whose positive effects largely have been vitiated by the restrictions of closure policy, the West Bank and Gaza would remain a captive market for the Israeli economy in both labor and goods. This is because the "customs union" articulated by the Economic Protocol was accompanied by certain critical restrictions on the Palestinian economy.

First, the PA cannot establish or pursue independent trade relations with third countries since Israel, with certain specified exceptions, determines trade policies (tariffs, quotas, and standards). This means that the PA is legally prevented from seeking new markets for its exports and for new sources of cheap imports.[23] Indeed, Palestinians cannot import goods from countries that do not have trade links with Israel, which includes the majority of Muslim countries.[24] (The PA's ability to establish trade links with other countries is crucial. Not only would such links reduce Israel's share of Palestinian trade but it would promote expanded domestic production and employment, thereby reducing the dependence of Palestinian labor on the Israeli market.)

Second, the PA has no guarantees of uninterrupted access to those markets it can enter either for its exported finished products or for imported raw materials for production. Furthermore, Israel's ability to impose closure frequently impedes and even prohibits Palestinian access to these markets.

Third, the PA has no strategic decision-making power in other areas of economic policy (for example, fiscal and monetary).[25] Thus, the "customs union" established between Israel and the Palestinian economy "continued to reflect Israeli policy and was not a coordinated trade policy as is the case with many other customs unions in the world."[26] Stated differently, as a result of the Oslo agreements the Palestinian economy lost its significant share in the Israeli labor market, upon which it was extremely dependent, and it effectively forfeited free access to international markets.

The terms prescribed by the Economic Protocol do not significantly alter existing structures or decrease Palestinian dependence on Israel. On the contrary, these terms deepen Palestinian-Israeli ties by keeping the West Bank and Gaza Strip economically linked to Israel while weakening their economic links to each other as well as to the rest of the world. For example, the Economic Protocol provides for the transfer by Israel of value-added taxes (VAT) and customs revenues to the PA. Although these transfers are very important because they account for a majority share of the PA budget—in 1996 they equaled 65 percent of the PA's tax revenues and 14 percent of GDP—they also reveal ties of economic dependence that place the PA in a weak and vulnerable position vis-à-vis the Israeli government.

Overall, the Economic Protocol and other Oslo agreements serve to "split up the West Bank and Gaza into a number of largely separate economic units with little economic interrelationship among them, breaking up an already small domestic market into even smaller ones."[27] Indeed, the lack of a geographic basis for the PA and the absence of defined borders with Israel, Egypt, and Jordan lie at the core of the problems facing the Palestinian economy. This absence is not accidental but a reflection of official Israeli preferences (of both the Labor and Likud parties) and Israel's power to enforce them. Indeed, according to the arrangements prescribed in the Oslo agreements, the Palestinians cannot separate from Israel at all. The core of the problem was and is Israeli occupation and Israel's continued domination of Palestinian life and resources.

Closure Policy

Between 1967 and 1987, Palestinians and Israelis had open access to each other's towns. During this time Palestinians, under the general exit permit, had considerable freedom of movement in Israel, the West Bank, and Gaza. The borders were open for people and goods, forming the basis of Moshe Dayan's functional integration policies. Dayan, who had a significant role in determining occupation policy in the years immediately after the 1967 conquest, believed that integrating the territories into Israel was the best way to hold on to them. During the first intifada, which began in December 1987, Israelis avoided Palestinian areas but Palestinians continued to have access to Israel, although the number of workers began to decline. Gazan workers wishing to enter Israel during this time were required to obtain a magnetic card from the Israeli authorities.

During the Gulf War, however, Israeli policy toward the Palestinians underwent a fundamental shift. In January 1991 Israel canceled the general exit permit for Gazans and West Bankers. Initially this move was regarded as a temporary measure, given the heightened political tensions and the imposition of curfews. However, even after tensions subsided and the curfew was lifted, all Palestinian workers were still required to obtain a permit to work in Israel. Similarly, Israeli employers began to face harsher sanctions for failing to register their Arab employees. Hence, after January 1991 Palestinians became more costly to employ, which led to a sharp decline in Palestinian workers in Israel.[28]

Although the revocation of the general exit permit constituted the real start of the closure policy, it was not until March 1993 that closure was first imposed as a permanent and administrative measure affecting all sectors of society and demographically bifurcating the Gaza Strip and West Bank. The March 1993 closure was a response to heightened levels of violence by Palestinians against Israelis inside Israel. Since then, closure has become an institutionalized system and has never been removed, although its intensity is subject to change.

The Israeli government officially justifies closure as a security measure despite the fact that the Israeli security establishment itself has stated that closure is of limited value against extremist attacks. Closure remains in place for at least two reasons: it serves an important psychological function for the Israeli public, and it is used as a political weapon that forces Palestinian officials into accepting short-term economic improvements over long-term territorial and political solutions.[29] It also serves as a form of collective punishment against the Palestinian people.

Closure affects the movement of labor, people, and goods. It has cut off the Gaza Strip and, to a lesser degree, the West Bank from Israel, and it has severed most movement between the West Bank and Gaza. (Closure has also restricted Palestinian access to foreign markets.) By 1998 virtually all physical, demographic, and commercial interaction between Gaza and the West Bank had ceased. Stories abound of how Palestinians living in the West Bank, for example, have been unable for years to obtain the requisite permits to visit family and friends living in the Gaza Strip.[30]

Furthermore, by restricting Palestinian access to Jerusalem, Israel's closure policy has physically separated the northern and southern regions of the West Bank, whose primary road connections pass through Jerusalem. Since East Jerusalem is the commercial heart of the West Bank, closure has devastated Jerusalem's Arab economy as well. The psychological impact has also been dramatic. The physical division of the West Bank has become so pronounced that families living in the northern region do not want their children to marry spouses from the southern region because they fear they will not be able to see them (even though the distance between the north and south West Bank is no more than forty miles).[31] A young worker in Gaza said: "I used to dream about having my own country. Now I dream about getting out of the Gaza Strip. All I want is to be able to work."[32]

Closure has three forms: general, total, and internal.[33] General closure describes the restrictions imposed on the movement of labor, goods, and the factors of production between the areas described above. Typically it is accompanied by long delays at border crossings and prolonged searches. According to the UN, general closure is enforced by "fixed checkpoints at key border crossings to control mobility and a comprehensive system of differentiated permits to control movement of laborers, business people, medical personnel and patients, students, religious worshipers and other categories of people."[34] These border checkpoints have slowed the mobility of people and goods and significantly increased transaction, production, and operation costs.

Total closure, the complete prohibition on any movement, is typically imposed in anticipation of or after an extremist attack in Israel.[35] The duration or frequency of total closures can never be predicted, adding greater risk to an already uncertain situation. During total closures, even Palestinians holding work permits to enter Israel are denied access, as are duly registered cars and trucks owned by Palestinians. Only Israeli-owned and -operated vehicles can cross borders.

Internal closure, which refers to restrictions on movement between Palestinian localities within the West Bank itself (as well as in Gaza), was made possible by the geographical cantonization of the West Bank legalized in the Oslo II Agreement. Since these urban enclaves are not contiguous, movement in and out of these towns or to nearby villages is, depending upon circumstance, partially or totally restricted, effectively separating one Palestinian community from another.

Between March 1993 and March 1996, any Palestinian wishing to enter Israel or Jerusalem (and by extension, the West Bank and Gaza) alone or with their cars and trucks had to obtain a permit from the Israeli authorities. It is through the permit system, in large part, that the closure policy is enforced. Since March 1996, it has been very difficult to obtain passes, especially for West Bank-Gaza travel. Between March 1996 and June 1997, for example, only 500 non-VIP passes were issued (out of a population of over 2.5 million).[36] The VIP passes are restricted to Palestinian government officials who can move more freely between areas but are also subject to restrictions in movement, especially during periods of total closure.

In 1998, only married men and women over the age of 23 could obtain permits.[37] In fact, by early 1998, less than 4 percent of Palestinians living in the West Bank and Gaza Strip had permission to enter Jerusalem.[38] Clearly, closure policies have led to the creation of groups or classes of people who increasingly are categorized by their ability to exercise freedom of movement, now a privilege, not a right.

Furthermore, these policies have institutionalized a very specific structural configuration that increasingly is characterized by the isolation of the Gaza Strip from the West Bank and Israel, and by the integration of the West Bank, or critical areas and resources of the West Bank, into Israel. This integration is economic (by mid-2000 there were more than three times as many West Bankers working in Israel as Gazans, a dramatic reversal of historical patterns) and physical (the expansion and construction of settlements and settlement infrastructure in anticipation of Israeli annexation). The physical, bureaucratic, and economic structure that has emerged in the Gaza Strip and West Bank since Oslo insures that when a Palestinian state is established it will be weak, internally fractured, and incapable of unified action.

The Economic Impact of Closure Policy[39]

In the years between 1993 and 1996, the Israeli government imposed 342 days of *total* closure in the Gaza Strip and 291 days in the West Bank.[40] Thus, for almost one-third of each year between 1993 and 1996, Palestinians were prohibited from any physical or economic movement outside the West Bank and Gaza, and on the remaining days were subject to closure in a less extreme form. In 1996 alone, closures in the Gaza Strip increased by 35 percent and in the West Bank by 57 percent over the year before.[41]

Closure's damaging impact has had many expressions. In 1996, for example, losses resulting from closure equaled 39.6 percent of Gaza's GNP and 18.2 percent of the West Bank's GNP.[42] Furthermore, the World Bank estimated the "annual costs of closure and permit policies at about 11–18 percent of GNI [gross national income] in the West Bank and 31–40 percent in the Gaza Strip for the period 1994–96."[43]

The most stunning and immediate effect of closure policy was the fluctuating unemployment rate and declining income level among Palestinian workers in Israel. Between 1992 and 1996, the unemployment rate among Gazans and West Bankers increased almost tenfold. The highest levels occurred during total closures, when all labor movement was frozen. After the total closure of March-April 1996, for example, 66 percent of the Palestinian labor force was either unemployed or severely underemployed.

As Israel eased the closure, unemployment levels decreased but still remained high, standing at 10–20 percent in the West Bank and 18–30 percent in the Gaza Strip between 1997 and mid-2000. The costs from closure to an already weakened economy have been prohibitive, amounting to hundreds of millions of dollars.

Closure's impact is also seen in declining Palestinian trade levels (where imports vastly exceed exports), and the changing character of domestic production, toward more traditional activities and lower production levels. In trade as in labor, Israeli policy remains defining. Closure policies have dramatically obstructed trade and have vitiated the longer-term, positive effects of any trading arrangement. Old trading patterns have been preserved, for example, Israel's dominance as a trading partner, the one-way trade structure (which denies Palestinian producers free access to Israeli markets while their Israeli counterparts have unlimited access to Palestinian markets), and have constrained access to international markets, including Egypt and Jordan, Palestine's natural trading partners. But new patterns also have been introduced, such as the separation of the Gaza Strip and West Bank markets, historically important economic outlets, and the receding of the Israeli market as a repository for Palestinian exports. If such patterns continue, Palestinian economic activity will turn increasingly toward a more insulated and circumscribed base.

These negative trends have resulted in the steady impoverishment of the population since 1993. The number of poor living below the poverty line (defined as a household with two adults and four children with a yearly consumption of less than $2.10 per day), was around 21 percent of the total population in mid-2000, with 25 percent of all Palestinian children living in poverty. Palestinian economic distress finds its most powerful expressions in rising child labor rates, particularly among children 12–16 years of age, and in changing consumption patterns, in which the consumption of food overwhelmingly dominates other expenditures, such as education and health. There should be no doubt that as long as closure is maintained as policy, Israeli control over Palestinians and their livelihood is assured.[44]

Closure as Separation[45]

The idea of separating from the Palestinians is an old one, dating back to the earliest days of the Yishuv in the British Mandate. Closure is, in effect, the method by which Israel has implemented the policy of separation (retaining an economic linkage in the form of cheap labor and captive export markets). Separation was revived by, and underlines the substance and implementation of, the Oslo agreements. According to Meron Benvenisti, the former deputy mayor of Jerusalem and an Israeli analyst and historian,

> The separation…is not only a strategy designed "to remove Gaza from Tel Aviv." It is in fact a complex master plan, which is founded on a dual separation between Palestine in its British Mandate boundaries from the neigh-

boring states; and second, an internal separation between Jewish and Arab demographic blocs within the country. The concrete control (known as "security") of all the international borders, which Israel is succeeding in retaining at the land crossings, the Gaza airport and. . .seaport, enables it to implement the internal separation…

Control of the external wrapper is essential for the Oslo strategy, because if the Palestinians control even one border crossing—and gain the ability to maintain direct relations with the outside world—the internal lines of separation will become full-fledged international borders, and Israel will lose its control over the passage of people and goods. Puncturing the external system will necessitate the establishment of a vast array of physical obstacles, crossing points and customs barriers between the enclaves of the "internal separation," and will expose the absurdity of the tortuous and noncontiguous borders of the ethnic cantons on which all the ideas of the permanent settlement are based.[46]

During his successful election campaign in 1999, Ehud Barak ran on a platform of "Peace Through Separation: We Are Here; They Are There." Barak ordered his government to prepare a "separation plan along the seam,"[47] the political and ethnic boundary line between Israel and the PA. Barak's vision of separation was to be achieved through the construction of checkpoints, walls, fences, trenches, bridges, canals, and tunnels. At present there are sixteen Israeli checkpoints around Bethlehem alone and a wall separating the city from Jerusalem, in what Benvenisti calls "an absurd border crossing at a nonexistent border."[48] There is also an electrified fence around the Gaza Strip. Since the Al-Aqsa uprising began, hundreds of checkpoints and barricades—earthen and concrete—have been erected at the entrances of Palestinian villages and towns throughout the West Bank and Gaza, isolating many of them.

In its more benign form, separation would impose boundaries on a separate Palestinian entity. In its more extreme form, known as unilateral separation, first articulated by Benjamin Netanyahu and later drafted by Barak's government (should a Palestinian state be declared without Israeli coordination), the West Bank and Gaza would be hermetically sealed off from each other and from Israel with a complex system of roads, tunnels, and army roadblocks that would become international border crossings, costing close to $1 billion.

Soon after the induction of Ariel Sharon's government in March 2001, the new prime minister ordered the sealing of Palestinian localities throughout the West Bank and Gaza Strip through the digging of trenches, the destruction of roads, and the erection of physical barriers. For example, the Israeli army dug trenches two meters deep and dozens of meters in length to close off Ramallah to approximately 65,000 people living in twenty-five surrounding villages. Since these trenches cannot be physically crossed, people are not only cut off from work but from hospitals, health clinics, and schools. In the process of trench digging, furthermore, not only were roads themselves damaged (and in some cases destroyed) but so too were water, electricity, and telephone networks.[49]

Unilateral separation as defined by Barak and, now, Sharon would also deny Palestinians work in Israel, sever economic relations and delink the infrastructure upon which such relations are based—telecommunications, electricity, and water, now deeply entwined between the two populations. Also included in Barak's plan was an exitless twenty-eight-mile elevated highway from Gaza to the West Bank that Palestinians could use without touching Israeli soil. This highway would cost approximately $250 million to construct and would be lined with watchtowers.[50]

One version of this elevated highway—"safe passage"—was enacted on October 25, 1999, between Gaza and Hebron. Held up as an important achievement of the peace process, the safe-passage corridor, which is for Palestinians only, is a hermetically sealed route separated completely from Israeli traffic and under the full control of Israel. "Safe passage" represents a substantial loss to Palestinians and their economy when compared with the freer and more open borders to which they had access prior to 1993. Two months after the safe passageway had been opened, however, more than 5,000 Palestinians who had applied for permits to use it had been denied permission by the Israeli authorities.[51] And those who are granted a permit are vulnerable to arrest by Israel security forces at any time.

This scenario of partition and separation, which harks back to nineteenth-century imperialism and twentieth-century cold war, may seem absurd and Orwellian but it remains the subject of serious discussion by Israeli and American officials.[52] Yet as Edward Said correctly points out, "Neither Palestinians nor Israelis can be made distant from the other. In the area between Ramallah in the north and Bethlehem in the south [alone], 800,000 Israelis and Palestinians live on top of each other, and cannot be separated. That is the truth."[53] Any attempt to separate them, therefore, will have to be forcibly imposed and will fail.

Conclusion: The Al-Aqsa Intifada

The second Palestinian uprising, which began in September 2000, arose in response to Israel's continued attempt to fragment and weaken the Palestinian community through dispossession, denial, and closure. The Al-Aqsa Intifada perhaps marks a watershed in Palestinian-Israeli relations in that both sides, convinced that the other is unwilling to compromise and live in peace, have assumed absolutist positions. For Palestinians absolutism means resisting Israeli occupation through violence and other means until the occupation withdraws. For the state of Israel, with its overwhelming power, absolutism means extinguishing Palestinian violence through extreme methods until Palestinians concede to Israeli terms. These methods include: continued settlement expansion, accelerated home demolitions, the shelling of Palestinian localities, the razing of Palestinian property and destruction of Palestinian lands (often agricultural), the physical blockade of Palestinian communities, and the widened and intensified use of total closures. It is the last two of these policies that have proved the most damaging.

Given the weakened state of the Palestinian economy before the current uprising, it is not surprising that economic conditions have deteriorated further and faster since the Al-Aqsa Intifada began. For the first time in the history of Israel's occupation, Palestinians face a humanitarian crisis, which began to emerge within just weeks of the uprising's start.[54] By January 2001, close to 1 million people, or 32 percent of the population, were living below the poverty level.[55] This represented an increase of 350,000 people over the 650,000 living in poverty prior to the uprising, or a 50 percent increase in the number of impoverished in just four months.[56] By April 2001, just three months later, the number of people living below the poverty line doubled from 1 million to over 2 million, or 64.2 percent—almost two-thirds—of Palestinians, according to the Palestinian Central Bureau of Statistics (PCBS). Poverty is greatest in the Gaza Strip, where 81.4 percent of the population is now impoverished compared with 55.7 percent in the West Bank.[57]

This rapid increase in poverty is due primarily to the loss of employment in Israel and in the domestic economy, itself a result of the widespread and prolonged imposition of total closure. During the 123 days between October 1, 2000, and January 31, 2001, economic borders were closed ninety-three days, or 75.6 percent of the time. Internal closures were in effect 100 percent of the time in the West Bank and 89 percent in the Gaza Strip.[58]

Between October 2000 and March 2001, 250,000 Palestinians lost their jobs, according to the United Nations Relief and Works Agency (UNRWA).[59] Not only has the crucial job market in Israel been lost but the domestic market has also contracted, in part because of Israel's destruction of Palestinian agricultural land. Between October 2000 and April 2001, 181,000 trees were uprooted from Palestinian land and 3.7 million square meters of Palestinian cultivated lands were destroyed.[60] As a result, approximately 40,000 agricultural workers have stopped working on their farms. By obstructing the importation of raw materials and construction materials, closure has wreaked havoc on Palestinian trade, industry, and commerce, depriving more than 100,000 Palestinians of employment in the West Bank and Gaza.[61] By April 2001, the overall unemployment rate was 38–40 percent (compared with 11 percent in the first nine months of 2000), and it was as high as 60 percent in Gaza.[62]

The dramatic declines in employment represent an income loss of $3.6 million per day and a 47 percent decrease in per capita income.[63] The gross domestic product has fallen by half, and the economy has lost at least $1.15 billion.[64] In early April the Palestinian Finance Ministry maintained that the total losses to the Palestinian economy (including the commercial, industrial, agricultural, and tourism sectors) between late September 2000 and March 20, 2001, equaled $3.87 billion.[65] According to the PCBS, 49.2 percent of households have lost more than half their income during the intifada and 11 percent have lost all of it.[66]

Given the vast declines in personal income resulting from the loss of work, the majority of assistance given Palestinians has been in the form of food. In February 2001, the UN World Food Program began distributing monthly flour rations to 250,000 Gazans, the first time this agency has implemented large-scale food distribution in the Palestinian territories.[67] At the same time, UNRWA distributed food parcels consisting of flour, rice, lentils, sugar, whole milk, and cooking oil to 120,000 families in Gaza (or 64 percent of the refugee population) and to 46,000 families in the West Bank.[68] The International Committee of the Red Cross (ICRC) also implemented a "Closure Relief Program," in which relief packages were distributed to 35,000 people in sixty West Bank villages that have been isolated by the closure.[69] Yet, although 48.1 percent of households surveyed by the PCBS received some aid since the uprising began, 88 percent indicated that it was less than $100 in value.[70]

The Palestinian people now face not only the continued contraction and disfigurement of their economy, but a humanitarian crisis that is altogether unprecedented. Hunger is now a fact of life for the majority of people, as is the despair and rage that attend it. This appalling situation does not and will not affect Palestinians alone.

Economic recovery cannot occur in the absence of aspiration and hope. As Anouilh pointed out, the absence of hope is one condition of tragedy. Closure is not only a structural phenomenon, it is a psychological one as well. At a minimum, it is vital that closure be removed, and with it all barriers, human and otherwise. If this occurs, the violence will end. If it does not, the violence will spread, perhaps threatening the entire region.

This chapter, in large part, is reprinted from Sara Roy, "Postscript," The Gaza Strip: The Political Economy of De-Development, *Second Edition (Washington, DC, 2001), pp. 333–94. Reprinted with permission of the publisher. Parts were originally published in 1998 in Sara Roy,* The Palestinian Economy and the Oslo Process: Decline and Fragmentation, *Emirates Occasional Paper Number 24, Emirates Center for Strategic Studies and Research, Abu Dhabi, United Arab Emirates.*

Notes

1. Cited in Anne Marie Oliver, *The Fate of Literalism in Hamas, The Israeli-Palestinian Conflict, and Beyond,* Paper presented at the Center for Middle Eastern Studies, Harvard University, Cambridge, MA, April 2001. Original source: Jean Anouilh, *Antigone* (Paris, 1946, 1957).

2. Sara Roy, "De-Development Revisited: Palestinian Economy and Society Since Oslo," *Journal of Palestine Studies*, Vol. 28, No. 3 (Spring 1999), p. 64.

3. George T. Abed, "Beyond Oslo: A Viable Future for the Palestinian Economy," in *The Economics of Middle East Peace: A Reassessment*, ed. by Sara Roy [Research in Middle East Economics, Volume 3] (Greenwich, CT, 1999), pp. 29–58.

4. UNSCO, *Economic and Social Conditions in the West Bank and Gaza Strip, Quarterly Report.* Prepared by Salem Ajluni, et al. (Gaza: United Nations Office of the Special Coordinator in the Occupied Territories, April 1, 1997), pp. i & 6.

5. Abed, "Beyond Oslo." See also Ghassan Abu Sitta, "The Failure of the Palestinian Authority," *Middle East International*, July 3, 1998, pp. 16–17.

6. For a detailed discussion of the Palestinian Authority and its policies, see Sara Roy, "The Crisis Within: The Struggle for Palestinian Society," *Critique: Journal for Critical Studies of the Middle East*, No. 17 (Fall 2000), pp. 5–30.

7. See Joel Singer, "The Declaration of Principles on Interim Self-Government Arrangements: Some Legal Aspects," *Justice*, No. 1 (February 1994), pp. 4–13.

8. Geoffrey Aronson, *Recapitulating the Redeployments: The Israel-PLO Interim Agreements*, Information Brief, No. 32 (Washington, DC: Center for Policy Analysis on Palestine, April 27, 2000). See also Rex Brynen, "Recent Political Developments," in *Development Under Adversity: The Palestinian Economy in Transition*, ed. by Ishac Diwan and Radwan A. Shaban (Washington, 1999), pp. 33–44.

9. Ibid. The Amnesty International Report is titled *Israel and the Occupied Territories: The Demolition and Dispossession of Palestinian Homes.*

10. See Palestine Economic Policy Research Institute (MAS), *MAS Economic Monitor: Monitoring the Palestinian Economy*, Palestine Economic Forum Home Page, June 1997, August 19, 1997.

11. Atif Kuburi, *Economic Decline and Dependency in the West Bank and Gaza Strip*, Information Brief No. 36 (Washington: Center for Policy Analysis on Palestine, July 5, 2000).

12. Abdul Jawad Saleh and Hisham Awartani, *Palestinian Agriculture: Where To?* (Nablus, West Bank: Center for Palestine Research and Studies, 1997).

13. The Palestinian Society for the Protection of Human Rights and the Environment (LAW), *LAW Director Meets Chris Patten, European Commissioner for External Relations*, April 6, 2000, on website: www.lawsociety.org.

14. Aronson, *Recapitulating the Redeployments.*

15. Sara Roy, "The Palestinian Economy After Oslo," *Current History* (January 1998), p. 20.

16. *Protocol on Economic Relations Between the Government of the State of Israel and the PLO Representing the Palestinian People*, Paris, April 29, 1994, Article VII, p. 1.

17. Other analysts offer a very different interpretation of this clause. For example, see Arie Arnon, Israel Luski, Avia Spivak, and Jimmy Weinblatt, *The Palestinian Economy: Between Imposed Integration and Voluntary Separation* (Leiden, 1997), p. 83: "the free movement of labor between Israel and the Palestinian Authority, agreed upon in the Protocol, was an important achievement for the Palestinian side." For a more positive interpretation of the Israeli-Palestinian economic agreement, see Ephraim Kleiman, "The Economic Provisions of the Agreement Between Israel and the PLO," *Israel Law Review*, Vol. 28, Nos. 2–3 (Spring-Summer 1994), pp. 347–73; the International Monetary Fund, "West Bank and Gaza Strip Adopts Outward-Oriented Economic Strategy," *IMF Survey* (January 22, 1996), pp. 25–28; and "The Paris Protocol: To Implement or Not to Implement?" *Palestine Economic Pulse*, Vol. II, No. 5 (September-October 1997), pp. 2–3.

18. The World Bank and the Palestine Economic Policy Research Institute (MAS), *Development Under Adversity? The Palestinian Economy in Transition*, Jerusalem, October 30, 1997, Chapter 6, p. 5 (pre-publication draft version).

19. *Protocol*, Article III.

20. *Protocol*, Article VIII.

21. Ibid.

22. Fadle Naqib, *Prospects for Sustained Development of the Palestinian Economy: Strategies and Policies for Reconstruction and Development* (Geneva: UNCTAD, November 1995), pp. 179–80.

23. Arnon, et al., *The Palestinian Economy*, p. 236.

24. Nur Calika, "The Trade System," in The International Monetary Fund (IMF), *The Economy of the West Bank and Gaza Strip: Recent Experience, Prospects, and Challenges to Private Sector Development* (Washington, DC: Middle Eastern Department, IMF, May 1998), pp. 51–54 and fn. 5.

25. Arnon, et al., *The Palestinian Economy*, p. 236.

26. Ibid, p. 110. See also Palestine Economic Policy Research Institute (MAS), *Palestinian-Israeli Trade Relations: Free Trade Area or Customs Union?, MAS Policy Notes*, Issue No. 1, August 1996; idem, *Palestinian-Israeli Trade Relations: Trade Policy Options for the West Bank and Gaza Strip*; Osama A. Hamed and Radwan Abu Shaban, "One-Sided Customs and Monetary Union: The Case of the West Bank and Gaza Strip Under Israeli Occupation," in *The Economics of Middle East Peace: Views From the Region*, ed. by Stanley Fischer, Dani Rodrik, and Elias Tuma (Cambridge, MA: MIT Press, 1993), pp. 117–48;

Karim Nashashibi and Oussama Kanan, "Which Trade Arrangements for the West Bank and Gaza?" *Finance and Development*, Vol. 31, No. 3 (September 1994), pp. 10–13; Judy Maltz, "Ending 27 Years of One-Sided Trade: Implications of the Israeli-Palestinian Economic Accord," Palestine Economic Forum, www.palecon.org/peacedir/peacemedia94/pm1.html, August 20, 1997; and Ruba Husary, "The Opportunities Offered to the Palestinian Economy by the New Trade Regime," Palestine Economic Forum, www.palecon.org/peacedir/peacemedia94/pm1.html, August 20, 1997.

27. Sara Roy, "U.S. Economic Aid to the West Bank and Gaza Strip: The Politics of Peace," *Middle East Policy*, Vol. 4, No. 4 (October 1996), p. 61; original source: Foreign Investment Advisory Service, *The West Bank and Gaza: Creating a Framework for Foreign Direct Investment* (Washington: International Finance Corporation and the World Bank, June 1995), p. 3.

28. Amira Hass, West Bank correspondent, *Ha'aretz*, Lecture, Center for Middle Eastern Studies, Harvard University, May 1999.

29. Sara Roy, "Economic Deterioration in the Gaza Strip," *Middle East Report* (July-September 1996), p. 39. The use of closure as a political weapon was clearly seen in August 1997, when, after two suicide bombings in Jerusalem, the Israeli government withheld tax clearances from the PA, making the transfer of these monies contingent on certain political conditions.

30. See Gideon Levy, "Family Pictures," *Ha'aretz*, July 14, 2000.

31. Amira Hass, Lecture, Harvard University, May 1999.

32. Interview, Gaza, May 2000. See further Amira Hass, *Drinking the Sea at Gaza: Days and Nights in a Land Under Siege* (New York, 1999).

33. See UNSCO (April 1, 1997), pp. 41–42 for taxonomy of closure; and IMF, *The Economy of the West Bank and Gaza Strip: Recent Experiences, Prospects, and Challenges to Private Sector Development* (Washington: International Monetary Fund, May 1998), pp. 25–27.

34. Ibid, p. 44.

35. Human Rights Watch, *Israel's Closure of the West Bank and Gaza Strip* (Washington, July 1996), p. 3.

36. U.S. Department of State, *Gaza's Economy: Neither the Worst of Times nor the Best of Times*, Unclassified Cable, Tel Aviv 09841, June 1997.

37. The Palestinian Society for the Protection of Human Rights and the Environment (LAW), *The Consequences of the Israeli Siege on the West Bank and Gaza*, Jerusalem, August 7, 1997. See Government of Israel, "Economic Relations Between Israel and the Palestinian Authority (Revised May 25, 1998)," in *The Prime Minister's Report*, Vol. 2, No. 18, June 4, 1998. E-mail: pmr@pmo.gov.il.

38. Salim Tamari, Lecture, Middle East Studies Association meeting, San Francisco, November 23, 1997.

39. Some of this material first appeared in Roy, "The Crisis Within," pp. 19–22, and parts of it are reprinted here with permission.

40. Palestine Economic Policy Research Institute (MAS), *MAS Economic Monitor: Monitoring the Palestinian Economy, Palestine Economic Forum Home Page/June 1997*, August 19, 1997.

41. Ibid. In 1998 and 1999, Israel imposed twenty-one and thirteen days, respectively, of total closure. See Palestinian Center for Human Rights, *Annual Report* (Gaza City: PCHR, 1999).

42. *Development Under Adversity?* (1997), Executive Summary, p. 8. For a detailed description of the economic impact of the August-September 1997 total closure, see the United Nations Office of the Special Coordinator in the Occupied Territories and The World Bank, *Closure on the West Bank and Gaza, August-September 1997 Fact Sheet,*

www.arts.mcgill.ca/mepp/UNSCO/closure080997.html, March 10, 1998. See also Israel Foreign Ministry, Information Division, Measures Enacted to Ease Closure, Jerusalem, September 17, 1997, www.israel-mfa.gov.il; and the Palestinian Center for Human Rights (PCHR), *Submission of the Palestinian Center for Human Rights to the United Nations Human Rights Committee*, July 1998, email: pchr@trendline.co.il.

43. Patricia Alonso-Gamo, Max Alier, Thomas Baunsgaard, and Ulric Erickson von Allmen, *West Bank and Gaza Strip: Economic Developments in the First Five Years Since Oslo* (Washington: International Monetary Fund, 1999), p. 13.

44. See Lee Hockstader, "Dependence Shapes Emerging State: Reality of Israeli Control Tempers Dreams of Autonomy," *Washington Post*, September 8, 2000.

45. Taken and reprinted from Sara Roy, *The Palestinian-Israeli Crisis: An Analysis*, paper presented at a symposium, The United States in the Middle East: Politics, Religion & Violence, Center for International Studies, University of Delaware, February 21, 2000. To be published by the University of Delaware Press (2001).

46. Meron Benvenisti, "The Illusion of Soft Borders," *Ha'aretz*, October 14, 1999.

47. Aluf Benn, "Trenches, Obstacles to Be Built Between Israel, PA," *Ha'aretz*, June 21, 2000.

48. Benvenisti, "The Illusion of Soft Borders."

49. Amira Hass and Amos Harel, "IDF Digs Trench to Keep 65,000 Villagers Out of Ramallah," *Ha'aretz,* March 8, 2001; The Palestinian Society for the Protection of Human Rights and the Environment (LAW), "Israeli Authorities Tighten Siege on Palestinian Territories," March 12, 2001, www.lawsociety.org; and Health, Development, Information, and Policy Institute (HDIP), "Israeli Siege Intensifies, Strangling Palestinian Health and Education Services," March 12, 2001, www.upmrc.org.

50. Suzanne Goldenberg, "Israeli Plan to Build Fences, Not Bridges," *The Guardian*, October 23, 2000; and Aluf Benn, "No 'Irreversible Steps' Included in Barak's Unilateral Separation Plan," *Ha'aretz*, January 15, 2001. See also *idem*, "Sharon Reiterates His Separation Plan," *Ha'aretz*, January 16, 2001.

51. Roy, "Postscript," p. 375.

52. See Aluf Benn, January 15, 2001; and "Has Oslo Run Its Course? A Washington Think Tank Offers a Strategy to President-Elect George Bush," *Ha'aretz*, January 17, 2001. For a discussion of separation and its failure in other international contexts, see Oren Yiftachel, "The Mirage of Oslo," *Tikkun*, January/February 2001.

53. Edward Said, "What Can Separation Mean?" *Al-Ahram Weekly*, November 13, 1999.

54. Peter Morris, Caroline Abla, and Jack Myer, *Humanitarian Assessment for West Bank and Gaza*, Report Submitted to the USAID/West Bank/Gaza Mission, December 19, 2000. Internal Document.

55. United Nations, *The Impact on the Palestinian Economy of Confrontations, Mobility Restrictions and Border Closures, 1 October 2000-31 January 2001, Summary* (Gaza Strip: Office of the United Nations Special Coordinator in the Occupied Territories [UNSCO], February 2001); and The World Bank, *Poverty in the West Bank and Gaza (Summary)*, West Bank and Gaza Office, February 5, 2001.

56. Ibid.

57. Palestinian Central Bureau of Statistics (PCBS), *Impact of the Israeli Measures on the Economic Conditions of Palestinian Households*, Press Conference on the Survey Results, Ramallah, Palestine, April 2001; and "Two-Thirds of Palestinians Live Below Poverty Line," *Ha'aretz*, April 25, 2001.

58. UNSCO (February 2001).

59. The Palestinian Initiative for the Promotion of Global Dialogue and Democracy (MIFTAH), *Special Report: Intifada Update, September 28th, 2000 until April 7th, 2001*, Ramallah, West Bank; *Ha'aretz* (April 25, 2001); "Closure Drove Two Million Palestinians Into Poverty-UN," *Jordan Times*, March 11, 2001; and UNSCO (February 2001).

60. Ibid.

61. "PA Supplies Minister Outlines Economic Hardships Due to Israeli Measures," *Al Quds*, Jerusalem, January 22, 2001 (via FBIS).

62. PCBS, *Impact of the Israeli Measures; Jordan Times* (March 11, 2001); and *Ha'aretz* (April 25, 2001).

63. MIFTAH, *Special Report*.

64. "Palestinians—Shaky Solidarity," *The Economist*, February 17, 2001; and UNSCO (February 2001).

65. *Al Hayat al-Jadidah*, Internet edition in Arabic, April 9, 2001.

66. PCBS, *Impact of the Israeli Measures*; and *Ha'aretz* (April 25, 2001).

67. "UN Agency Begins Food Distribution in Gaza Strip," *Reuters*, February 27, 2001.

68. United Nations, *UN Relief and Works Agency Launches New Emergency Appeal, as Situation in West Bank and Gaza Continues to Deteriorate*, Department of Public Information, Press Release, February 22, 2001, New York.

69. International Committee of the Red Cross (ICRC), *Israel and the Occupied/Autonomous Territories: The ICRC Starts Its "Closure Relief Programme,"* Press Release, February 26, 2001.

70. PCBS, *Impact of the Israeli Measures*.

5. THE PEACE OF THE POWERFUL
GLENN E. ROBINSON

The specific causes of the dissolution of the Oslo peace process into violence during fall 2000 are well known to close observers of Palestine, and are discussed in detail elsewhere in this volume. Those causes can be seen at different levels: the broad failure of Oslo to end Israel's military occupation of the West Bank and Gaza after seven years of negotiations; the more specific failure of the Camp David summit in July 2000 to lay out a just and viable vision of peace; and the "spark" of Ariel Sharon's arrogant visit to the Haram al-Sharif/Temple Mount in Jerusalem on September 28, 2000. Israel's excessive use of force in responding to pent-up Palestinian frustration only deepened the cycle of violence.

While the reasons for Palestinian discontent were not difficult to understand, they tended to elude most American media accounts of the conflict. These stories largely portrayed the violence as "Arafat's war" (to use Thomas Friedman's provocative phrase), a deliberate war launched by the Palestinians against Israeli peacemakers. In this way of thinking, when decision time came for the Palestinians at Camp David—the historic opportunity to accept a generous Israeli offer and put an end to the conflict—Yasir Arafat balked, still more comfortable playing the role of guerrilla leader than statesman. Arafat then returned home and ignited the war that would happily prevent him from ever having to make the hard choice for peace.

Besides showing a breathtaking ignorance of history and Palestinian politics, this line of argument contains within it what I call the "microwave" theory of political violence. That is, Arafat could simply push a button and immediately create a rush of frenzied energy, and then push another button to immediately stop it. The notion of Palestinians-as-automatons would rightly be dismissed as ludicrous, perhaps even racist, if applied to nearly any other people in the world. It is an equally absurd path to comprehending the tragic turn of events in Palestine.

The media were not alone in their ignorance. The Clinton Administration's "peace team" had numerous warnings of trouble ahead throughout 2000 but chose to ignore them. For example, the path-breaking Israeli-Palestinian parliamentarian Azmi Bishara warned in June 2000 (as he had repeatedly) that "the maximum Israel is prepared to compromise won't reach the minimum expectations of the Palestinians. I do not think it is either war or peace, but there is a confrontation coming."[1] Some American analysts were explicit in predicting a coming wave of violence as a result of the Oslo process.[2] Even Arafat begged the Americans not to go forward with the Camp David summit because the parties were not yet ready to strike a final deal. If the summit failed, he argued, instability would almost certainly follow. His pleas fell on the deaf ears of an American team that was overly anxious to cut a final peace deal in the last days of Clinton's presidency.[3]

Conflictual personalities, bad policies, uninspiring visions, and failures of political summitry are insufficient to explain fully the violence and instability wrought by Oslo in both Palestine and Israel. Rather, this turmoil should be understood in deeper, structural terms—that of a hegemonic peace. In this chapter, I will argue for the necessarily hegemonic nature of the peace process and its consequences, and then show how hegemonic peace is linked to the structure of regime power in Palestine.

The Hegemonic Peace

The term "hegemonic peace" should not be taken as a normative judgment, but rather as an analytical statement. What are the expected consequences of a peace process between two polities of vastly unequal power? A hegemonic peace is defined as a peace between two significantly unequal powers that nevertheless retain the autonomy to accept or reject the terms of settlement. It is not a peace between relative equals, nor is it a "peace" completely imposed on an utterly vanquished enemy. Unlike these last two types of peace, a hegemonic peace tends to be destabilizing to both the hegemon (in this case Israel) and to the weaker party (Palestine). The Israeli-Palestinian peace process is clearly hegemonic in nature, accurately reflecting the broad imbalance of power between Israel and Palestine.

While the notion of a "just peace" is held dear by so many, peace treaties invariably reflect power, not justice. The Israeli-Palestinian negotiations and agreements since 1993 were no different. On every major issue, Israel's power held sway over Palestine's justice. To begin with, all of the key issues were left for last—at Israel's insistence. Only at Camp David, for the first time, were the central issues of Jerusalem and refugees—among others—discussed. On each core issue, Israel held the power on the ground to decide what to implement. No refugee could return without Israel allowing him to do so; no settlement could be dismantled without Israel's say-so; no land could be returned to the Palestinians without Israeli consent. While Palestinians may have wanted these things to happen, only Israel could make them happen. The peace process should be understood more as an internal Israeli debate about how much to concede of all that it controlled, rather than as negotiations between Israel and Palestine. Most of that internal Israeli debate centered on how much of the 22 percent of Palestine not captured in 1948 should be returned to the Palestinians. Israeli hawks wanted to maintain permanent Israeli control over all the Palestinian lands, while Israeli doves were willing to cede virtually all of the West Bank and Gaza.

There was no comparable Palestinian leverage on Israel. There were no illegal Palestinian settlements in Israel; there were no Israeli refugees pining to return to Gaza; there were no Palestinian troops occupying Israeli lands. The only leverage Palestinians had over Israel was the autonomy to say "no" to Israeli proposals. This autonomy was not inconsequential, because saying "no" hampered

Israeli normalization with the Arab world, and it could bring on serious instability—as the violence of 2000–2001 demonstrates. Still, in the final analysis, it was Israel that controlled what would happen—or not happen—on the ground.

A hegemonic peace tends to be far more unstable than one based either on a reasonable balance of power or on complete domination. A balance-of-power peace tends to be stable because both sides know that the other side can inflict significant and unacceptable levels of damage if the peace breaks down. The cold war and the concept of MAD—Mutually Assured Destruction—between the US and the USSR demonstrated nicely the stability of a balance-of-power peace, however "cold" it may have been. Serbia sued for peace in Bosnia only after Muslim and Croat forces (with significant aid from the United States) started winning battles in western Bosnia, thereby demonstrating that the playing field had leveled. Conversely, the US occupation of Japan and parts of Germany following the Second World War demonstrates the stability of total domination, where the dominant power is relatively free to remake the institutions and politics of the defeated adversary. Indeed, at times the domination of many of these polities by another has been so total that they have become mere footnotes in history: consider the former countries of Normandy and Nubia, the Papal States and the Confederacy.

Hegemonic peace, by contrast, is quite unstable for both parties. Following the First World War, the allies were powerful enough vis-à-vis Germany to extract a one-sided and vengeful peace at Versailles, but not so powerful to remake Germany in their own image. The predictable result: instability on both sides, and another war. Israel imposed a one-sided formal peace treaty on Lebanon following its 1982 invasion, resulting in instability and violence, and ultimately the collapse of the hegemonic peace. India has been able to dominate, but not transform, Kashmir.

There is a compelling logic for why a hegemonic peace produces instability for both polities. For the weaker party, explaining instability is rather obvious. There will necessarily be a great deal of opposition to the government for signing a peace that so obviously compromises national rights in the eyes of the population. Political opposition at the social level strengthens, while the "capitulating" government feels compelled to crack down on dissent. Polarization occurs that, in simple terms, pits the state against its own society.

Ironically, a hegemonic peace is often destabilizing for the powerful party as well. Objectively, such a peace is usually viewed by outsiders as disproportionately benefiting the more powerful party. Internally, however, dissent against the government focuses on the perceived lack of necessity to make any significant concessions at all. By definition, the powerful party is not compelled by the weaker party to concede anything. Thus, the greater the level of "uncompelled" concessions by the hegemon, the more intense internal opposition will be. The opposition in the hegemonic power uses a discourse created in wartime to assert that any meaningful concessions are not only unwarranted given the circumstances of power and (their own constructed) morality, but are a sign of weakness and betrayal by the government.

Indeed, the hegemonic dynamic strongly characterized the Oslo peace process in Palestine. While moments of exhilaration occurred, such as during the fall 1995 Israeli withdrawal from some major urban areas in the West Bank, for the most part the peace process failed to deliver Palestinian national rights. Through the years, as the failure of the PLO to deliver in its negotiations with Israel became more apparent to more Palestinians, dissent increased. In turn, the PA had to use various types of repression to ensure that the opposition was contained within manageable limits. The violence during the fall of 2000 strengthened Palestinian unity temporarily, but it was only a matter of time before the internal contradictions in Palestine once again came to the surface. The polarization, repression, violence, and instability born of a hegemonic peace will likely continue into the future.

Israel also continued to suffer from instability brought on by a hegemonic peace process. While Palestinian oppositional discourse rejected as unjust the terms of the peace, the oppositional discourse in Israel, speaking the language of power, rejected as unnecessary any significant concessions at all to a much weaker—and much hated—party. As with Palestine, this pattern had been apparent in Israel since the first Oslo accord was signed in 1993. The large opposition in Israel consistently berated Yitzhak Rabin, Shimon Peres, and Ehud Barak for their "selling out" of Zionism when there was no significant external pressure on Israel compelling it to make concessions. Even the rejectionist Netanyahu government was harshly criticized by the opposition in Israel when it signed (but never fully implemented) the Hebron and Wye River accords.

While the assassination of Rabin in 1995 was the most obvious example of the instability born of a hegemonic peace, the sharply vitriolic turn of Israeli public discourse since Oslo is perhaps a better indicator of the impact of this kind of peace on the Israeli body politic. Public vilification of Labor Party leaders as Nazis and killers of Jews became commonplace among the Israeli opposition after Oslo. Twice since Oslo, an incumbent Labor government was voted out of office for pursuing "unwarranted concessions" to the Palestinians, both times by significant majorities among Israeli Jews. Sharon's electoral victory over Barak in February 2001 was particularly lopsided. Hegemonic peace with Palestine brought turmoil to Israel in a way that its peace treaties with Egypt and Jordan never did.

Compare Israel's three peace treaties with Arab countries. While Israel was clearly more militarily powerful than Egypt, still their peace treaty of 1979 was between two strong states that had shown they could cause considerable damage to each other. There was a rough parity. That peace, however "cold," has stood the test of time. Few in Israel question its wisdom. Broadly speaking, a similar statement can be made for how Israel's public has greeted the Jordan-Israel peace treaty: there is no significant force in Israel that has denounced Israel's government for making that peace deal, because there was no significant concession Israel was compelled to make (its popular reception in Jordan, on the other hand, has been quite hostile).

It is only with the Palestinians that peace has proven so destabilizing to Israel. Given Israel's domestic political cleavages, there is no reason to assume that any final-status peace deal will change this. In fact, if the post-Oslo years of assassination, recrimination, and vitriolic public discourse are prologue to Israel's future, then the "kulturkampf"—an intense and often nasty polarization of Israel's domestic politics—predicted by one of Israel's more astute scholars will likely be at hand.[4]

The "Tunisians"

The hegemonic nature of the Oslo peace process likewise had a significant impact on the structure of regime power in Palestine. The most significant internal Palestinian political cleavage since Oslo was not between Hamas and the PLO, but between the "insiders" and the "outsiders." The Palestinians from the West Bank and Gaza (the insiders) openly referred to the 100,000 or so Palestinians who returned to Palestine after Oslo as "outsiders." More precisely, since the PLO headquarters returned to Palestine from Tunisia, the PLO returnees were known as the "Tunisians." The great irony of the Oslo accord is that it brought to power in Palestine an outside political elite that did not lead the revolution—the 1987–93 intifada—but rather promised to end it. The 1993 Declaration of Principles specified that a strong Palestinian police force would cooperate with Israeli and US security and intelligence units in crushing the intifada.

The "Tunisians"—the returnees or outsiders—dominate the PA bureaucracy in Palestine and were largely responsible for establishing authoritarian rule in Palestine. Starting at the very top with Yasir Arafat, the Tunisians held most of the key positions of power in the PA. While Arafat had the stature and history to largely protect himself from personal criticism, the same could not be said of any other "outsider." Outsider domination was particularly strong in the police and security apparatuses. Indeed, of the fifteen or so police and security services in Palestine (the exact number is unknown since most are illegal under the terms of Oslo), all but two were dominated by outsiders loyal to Arafat.

For some observers, there is nothing surprising in the creation of another Arab dictatorship. Why should Palestine and the PA be any different from so many other countries in the Arab world? Such arguments, generally focusing on an essentialist, anti-democratic understanding of Arab-Islamic political culture, miss the point of the political—not cultural—origins of PA authoritarianism. In fact, Palestinian leadership in the occupied territories before the Oslo agreement had many of the attributes, or precursors, of democratic rule: it had a dynamic and pluralistic civil society that acted as a proto-state under military occupation; it had a well-educated and professional middle class; and it had, through the PLO, a long-held ideological commitment to democratic rule in a liberated Palestine.

In order to understand the authoritarian nature of the PA one needs to examine the internal logic of power consolidation by the PA in the West Bank and Gaza Strip in the post-Oslo period. The Oslo accords brought to power in Palestine an exiled PLO elite that had many familial and emotional ties to the Palestinian population in the West Bank and Gaza, but with whom it had little practical political experience. Personalized authoritarianism was the tool that the PA—at base, an organization of the "Tunisians"—used to consolidate its position of power over a society and an "inside" counter-elite that it did not fully trust or control.

The Evolution of Palestinian Civil Society

Since the late 1970s Palestinian civil society has been perhaps the most active and vibrant in the Arab world. Ironically, Palestinian civil society in the West Bank and Gaza owed a great deal of its growth to the unintended consequences of Israeli policy decisions. First, following the 1967 war, in which Israel captured the West Bank and Gaza Strip (along with the Golan Heights and Sinai Peninsula) from its Arab neighbors, Israel opened its labor markets to Palestinians from the occupied territories. Employing Palestinian labor (in the agricultural and construction sectors primarily) served both communities. For Israel, the plentiful supply of cheap labor helped fuel an economic boom; for Palestinians, even the discriminatory wage rates provided an income well above what could be made at home. Within a few short years, 40 percent of the total Palestinian labor force was employed in Israel. The Gaza Strip became completely dependent on jobs over the Green Line in Israel to sustain its population.

Opening Israel's labor market to the lower rungs of Palestinian society had profound social and political consequences. The most immediate and important consequence was to disrupt and eventually destroy the traditional patron-client networks that linked the urban-based Palestinian landed elite to rural communities and, to a lesser degree, refugee camps. It also exposed working-class Palestinians in a direct way to the everyday humiliations of being a conquered people. In short, to borrow a phrase, Israel's labor policies had the unintended consequence of making peasants into Palestinians. These Palestinians provided fertile grounds for recruitment into the mobilization efforts that began in the late 1970s by an emergent civil society.

The second Israeli policy that proved consequential in the development of Palestinian civil society was the decision to allow Palestinians to open universities in the West Bank and Gaza Strip. The first to open, in 1972, was Birzeit University, a transformed teacher's college. It was followed in the subsequent fourteen years by universities in Bethlehem, Hebron, Nablus (al-Najah), Jerusalem, and Gaza (Islamic University), and was joined further by numerous community colleges. Prior to 1972, only the sons of the local elite could afford to acquire a university education either in the Arab world or abroad; by the fall of 1987, nearly 20,000 Palestinians were enrolled in Palestinian universities and colleges in the West Bank and Gaza.

The opening of Palestinian universities created a large local educated elite distinct from traditional Palestinian landowners. This new elite based its position on educational achievement and broadly reflected the society from which it emerged: 70 percent of Palestinian university students came from refugee camps, villages, and small towns. It was this new elite—educated, non-landed, and less urban—that built the institutions of civil society in the 1980s and subtly mobilized disaffected Palestinians against both the Israeli military occupation and the old Palestinian landowning elite; it was this new elite that sustained the Palestinian uprising, or intifada, of 1987–93; and it was to marginalize this elite—primarily made up of "inside" PLO cadres—that Arafat's PA resorted to authoritarian politics.

The eclipse of the Palestinian landowning elite was helped along directly by a third Israeli policy, that of land confiscation. Begun under Labor Party rule, land confiscation accelerated dramatically when the conservative Likud party came to power in Israel in 1977. Land confiscations took many forms, from direct and "legal" expropriation to (more commonly) the use of land for "security" reasons. Most Jewish settlements built in the occupied territories (and they are specifically for use by Jews, not Israelis per se) are built on lands taken for "security" purposes or declared state lands by Israel. By 1993 and the signing of the Oslo accords, two-thirds of the West Bank and half of the Gaza Strip had been confiscated from or otherwise made off-limits to Palestinians.

The biggest political loser in the land confiscations was the Palestinian landowning elite, who sometimes lost land directly and in any case showed that it could no longer control or influence the fate of Palestinian lands. Unable to control the land—a key source of power and patronage—the landowning elite was further marginalized. As a result, Israel lost a key element of social control in the West Bank and Gaza, as this elite historically had acted as the intermediary between the Israeli state and Palestinian society.

Thus, the origins of Palestinian civil society were largely a byproduct of the rise of a new elite through Palestinian universities, the eclipse of the old elite (which, like landowning elites everywhere, was anathema to institutional politics and social transformation) through land confiscation, and the transformation, through Israel's labor policies, of a Palestinian population open to new forms of social organization and mobilization. These three elements combined to make possible the building of new social institutions upon which to base organized economic, social, and (ultimately) political activity. Indeed, during the late 1970s and early 1980s, each of the four major factions of the PLO created its own labor unions, women's committees, agricultural and medical relief committees, student groups, and community assistance programs.

Throughout the 1980s, and especially during the Palestinian uprising, the individuals and institutions active in civil society formed what can only be called a proto-state, organizing its members and providing an (incomplete) network of social services. Authority in this nascent state structure had three defining characteristics. First, it devolved into lower strata of society, both reflecting the changing social structure of Palestinian society and making Israeli attempts to capture or disrupt this authority more difficult. Devolved authority reflected the grassroots nature of the politics of the new elite. Second, authority was practiced institutionally, as opposed to residing in individual personalities. Institutional politics and authority distinguished the new elite from the political practice and authority of the old landowning families, who relied on personal ties to govern. Third, authority was pluralistic, and even democratic, in its decision-making. Given the grassroots nature of authority in the new structure, the new elite had little choice but to incorporate multiple voices into the making and implementing of decisions.

Given this pluralistic past and the validation (on paper, at any rate) of democratic institutions in the Oslo accords, why did the PA turn authoritarian?

The Politics of Antithesis

The creation of an authoritarian, personalized political system in Palestine can only be understood in the context of the consolidation of power by a new regime within the parameters of the Oslo process. The central political task of the new Palestinian Authority, in keeping with the usual practice of the weaker regime in a hegemonic peace, was to undermine the power and position of the PLO elite on the ground in the West Bank and Gaza, which had built the institutions of civil society and had led the intifada. In order to accomplish this task and therefore to consolidate its own new-found position of power, the PA had to create a "politics of antithesis," that is, a politics that undermined the very foundations of the authority of the new intifada elite by completely changing the rules of the political game.

Whether this particular means of consolidating power was done consciously or reflexively is not important; that it was done—and done rather successfully—is clear. It was also not surprising, as any new regime seeks to solidify the bases of its own power. The intifada-based structure of authority posed the greatest potential challenge to the new regime and thus was systematically attacked. It was done in three general areas, corresponding to the three salient characteristics of the new "inside" elite.

First, the PA replaced the devolved grassroots authority of the intifada elite with centralized decision-making. The intifada leadership had embedded its authority in the grassroots of society both because they themselves came from more modest social roots than the old landowning elite and because it made Israeli control much more difficult. All revolutions seek to disperse authority in order to survive; states seek to centralize it in order to function. The same is true of the PA, which tried to recapture authority at the center.

The second policy of antithesis was to attack the institutional basis of the authority of the intifada elite through the personalization of politics. It is crucial to remember that the institutions of civil society built in the 1970s and 1980s primarily by PLO cadres in the West Bank and Gaza were more than just altruistic measures to alleviate suffering. These institutions represented the actual manifestations of the political ideology of the new elite. For this elite, politics was all about organizational and associational ties, not about creating cults of personality. Thus, the extreme anti-institutional policies of the PA must be understood in a systematic way, and not just as some cultural legacy. By attacking the institutions of civil society and institutional politics in general, the PA undermined the political center of the intifada elite, making effective challenges to the new order far more difficult.

Finally, the intifada elite both espoused and practiced relatively pluralistic politics, not altogether different from the "outside" PLO. Although the system was not a paragon of democracy, many different streams of political thought and practice were tolerated and even encouraged. The kind of authoritarianism developed in Palestine after Oslo had no real precursor in modern Palestinian politics. However, when the "outside" PLO came "inside," the political logic changed. Because the intifada elite espoused and practiced pluralism and democracy, the PA justified and practiced authoritarianism.

One final point needs to be made about the "politics of antithesis." While it is convenient short-hand, the "inside-outside" PLO dichotomy is not a completely accurate conceptual tool to explain political instability and authoritarianism in Palestine. While "outsiders" were clearly the single most important part of the PA—up to and including Yasir Arafat himself—outsiders alone did not make up the entirety of the PA. Indeed, the PA built its rule, in part, with the help of strategic groups within Palestinian society. The core issue is about the consolidation of power by a new regime over a society with an existing structure of everyday authority. The geographic origins of the new regime alone are not necessarily important; the political logic of its consolidation of power is, as is the context within which it occurs.

PA Authoritarianism

PA authoritarianism was bolstered at the most basic level by the multiplicity of police and security organizations employing in excess of 40,000 personnel for a total population of 3 million (one of the highest such ratios in the world). There was no formal hierarchy or reporting system connecting these forces. Rather, they each reported directly to Arafat personally, lessening the possibility of a "coup coalition" being formed. The mission of at least one security force was to report back to Arafat on the activities of the other security forces. The disturbing results of the activities of these forces have been well documented by numerous human rights groups, both foreign and Palestinian. Sadly, the PA adopted a number of "techniques" learned originally from their Israeli occupiers.

More significant in the long term than the sad but common tale of violations of human rights was the manner in which the PA attacked institutional life in the West Bank and Gaza, and the way in which power and politics became personalized. The anti-institutional nature of the PA was seen in its behavior toward both governmental and nongovernmental organizations (NGOs).

NGOs, the backbone of Palestinian civil society and the institutional expression of the new elite, were hit particularly hard by the PA. In spite of the fact that NGOs proved crucial in providing key services to a Palestinian population under siege during the intifada, the PA implemented a two-pronged attack on their very existence. The more crude prong was the PA's policy of intimidation and harassment against NGO personnel. Leaders were arrested, detained, and/or pointedly questioned by multiple security and police forces about the activities of their NGO or their personal politics. This last point is important, because many of the very best NGOs were affiliated with PLO factions that opposed or were ambivalent toward the Oslo agreements. NGO personnel were asked to fill out PA questionnaires that, among other things, asked about their politics, the politics of family members, and whether they or anyone in their family had spent time in prison. NGO leaders viewed this as simply a means of intimidation.

A second, more effective means for undermining Palestinian NGOs was to control their resources. Many such NGOs were dependent, in part, on aid from international donors, both private and public. The PA consistently lobbied foreign donors to funnel all monies directly to the PA, which in turn would distribute them as it saw fit. While the PA did not end direct external contributions to Palestinian NGOs, it was able to put a significant dent in them. Again, those NGOs affiliated with opposition political factions were particularly hard hit, even though they were typically the most professional and effective of all the Palestinian NGOs.

While generally adopting indirect methods to attack NGO finances, the PA also utilized more direct approaches. It sought to take on direct control of the leadership of the NGOs, their budgets, and even their existence. In a handful of cases, the PA closed down NGOs or fired their directors. The single most important episode, however, was the promulgation of a draft law regulating the relationship between NGOs and the PA. The draft law, if adopted, would have eliminated Palestinian NGOs as an autonomous element of civil society and made them, in effect, semi-governmental agencies. The draft law, formulated without any consultation with the NGOs, was based on Egypt's Law 32, the most repressive law regulating NGOs in the Arab world. The NGOs, with critical assistance from international donors, were able to defeat this particular law. The one that was ultimately promulgated, in 1999, was better, but it still gave ultimate oversight responsibility for NGOs to the Ministry of the Interior—the ministry synonymous with internal repression in much of the Arab world.

The PA's disregard for institutional politics and procedures extended to its own legislative and judicial branches as well. Under the terms of Oslo, the elected Palestinian Legislative Council was to be the decision-making body in the Palestinian areas under self-rule. In spite of opposition boycotts and questionable election engineering, an eighty-eight-member Council was seated in closely watched elections in January 1996. Even though Fatah candidates won a decisive majority of seats—fifty—the PA (more precisely, the Executive Authority of the PA) consistently ignored the wishes of its parliament. Resolutions, laws, and hearings were routinely ignored by the PA. The Council's impotence prompted the leading vote-getter in the 1996 elections, Haydar Abd al-Shafi, to resign in protest.

The judicial branch of government likewise found itself in an untenable position. The PA often simply ignored judicial decisions when it found them disagreeable. This was particularly true of decisions ordering security forces to release prisoners being held illegally. Noncompliant judges were illegally removed when they prove too nettlesome. The Chief Justice in the West Bank, Khalil Silwani, was pressured into resigning in early 1996. His replacement, Amin Abd al-Salam, was chosen because he was thought to be more compliant. When Abd al-Salam proved just as stubborn when applying the law to PA activities, he too was fired. In order to bypass the court system altogether (and to impress the United States and Israel with its seriousness of purpose in cracking down on "terrorists"), the PA established security courts, and even created a parallel Attorney General specifically for the security courts. These courts were condemned by all impartial observers as legal frauds and worse; they often included midnight trials, no or inadequate defense counsel, and harsh sentences with no right of appeal.

The PA's policy of personalizing power was seen most clearly in the construction of a cult of personality around

Arafat himself. Arafat's picture could be found everywhere in Palestine, from posters plastered on walls and buildings to banners fluttering from telephone lines. His likeness even greets visitors at Palestinian "border crossings."

Personalized politics breeds corruption because power is vested in key individuals instead of in the offices themselves. It is not surprising, therefore, that corruption has been rampant in Palestine. One prominent case of corruption showed clearly that personal ties, especially to Arafat, mattered more than official position. The Minister of Agriculture, Abd al-Jawad Salah—one of the most popular and independent Palestinian politicians—publicly charged that high-ranking officials in his own ministry were producing false Palestinian licenses for Israeli citrus so that it could be marketed in Jordan under the terms of the Jordanian-Palestinian trade regime. Salah had ordered them to stop and had twice reported the scam and all of its participants to the PA Attorney General, yet the scam continued unabated. The reason for inaction was that Salah's deputy, Azzam Tibila, protected those involved. Tibila, unlike his boss, was an Arafat appointee and strong Arafat loyalist and thus had more real power than the Minister of Agriculture himself. Salah resigned in disgust.

The single most important example of systematic—yet perfectly legal—corruption was the establishment of economic monopolies over the importation of key basic commodities. The recipients of these monopoly rights invariably were companies owned by families of important PA officials, further erasing the line between public and private goods. Select PA officials made economic fortunes as a direct result of their political standing.

Given the close relationship between corruption and political power in Palestine, no significant reform was undertaken. When a 1997 Palestinian Inspector General's report found that nearly half of the PA's budget for the year before had been wasted through fraud and mismanagement and went on to identify those ministers most implicated in this corruption, no action was taken. Indeed, instead of demanding the resignations of those ministers, Arafat merely enlarged the size of his cabinet to allow more individuals access to patronage funds.

The Return of the Intifada Elite?

The most significant development to come out of the failure at Camp David and the subsequent Al-Aqsa Intifada was the discrediting of the "Tunisians," who had driven the Oslo train on the Palestinian side. Their *raison d'être* was to deliver Palestinian rights through the Oslo peace process, and at this they were seen to have failed miserably. Conversely, the Al-Aqsa Intifada was led not by the Tunisians but by the inside PLO (primarily Fatah) cadres who had cut their political teeth a decade earlier in the first intifada.

Interestingly, the official Palestinian police and security forces played only a small role in the early weeks of the Al-Aqsa Intifada. The people doing most of the shooting on the Palestinian side instead came from the *tanzim*, a rag-tag militia made up of veterans of the first intifada. The *tanzim* had no rigid hierarchy and was not a disciplined—or even very effective—military force. However, given the insider credentials of most of its members, it had a popular legitimacy on the Palestinian street unrivaled by the repressive and generally hated other security forces, or *mukhabarat*. The *tanzim* was one of only two of the plethora of armed forces in Palestine that was dominated by insiders. The other one—and the only official one—was Jibril Rajoub's Preventive Security Force in the West Bank.

The voice of the *tanzim* was the secretary general of Fatah in the West Bank, Marwan al-Barghouti. Barghouti was a young (41 at the time of the Al-Aqsa Intifada), popular, and charismatic figure among Palestinians, as much at home in Palestine's Legislative Council, where he was an elected parliamentarian, as he was in confrontations with Israel. A veteran of the first intifada, Barghouti spent years in Israeli jails—institutions that have "graduated" many of Palestine's best and brightest. Barghouti had been expelled from Palestine by Israel for his leadership in the first intifada.

Barghouti had a strong personal bond of loyalty to Arafat, which is why he was able to push the envelope on criticism of the PA. He was an outspoken voice for democracy in Palestine and against the corruption of the PA. Most of the very large Fatah movement also remained loyal to Arafat, in part because of the privileged position it had been afforded in Palestine. Fatah cadres represented the most important "insider" pillar of PA rule. However, this loyalty did not translate into automatic support on every issue, and it certainly did not mean total control. There were too many factions and cleavages within Fatah to treat it as though it were a single entity that spoke with a unified voice.

Power in Palestine today is more complex than the microwave theory allows. The regime has clear social bases of support even beyond the "Tunisians" and the Fatah movement, including the old landowning notable families from Palestine's past, and those Palestinians that benefit from the PA's large patronage machine. The PA does not rule by repression alone; far from it. What the failure of Camp David and the subsequent violence may have done, however, is to cause a fundamental shift in the ruling coalition in Palestine.

With the exception of Arafat himself, members of the Oslo elite—the outsiders—were conspicuous by their political absence following the failure at Camp David. Many virtually disappeared from the Palestinian public scene in the territories, including Mahmoud Abbas, the presumptive successor to Arafat, Ahmad Qurei, the Speaker of the Legislative Council, and Nabil Shaath, a cabinet minister and the PA's unofficial representative to Western donors and businessmen. Arafat faced a dilemma in the aftermath of Camp David: either maintain his ruling coalition as is, even with the need for greater repression, or shift the dominant coalition away from the "Tunisians" and toward the intifada elite. Each strategy carried its own set of risks for Arafat. The Tunisians were more dependent on his personal pleasure and therefore more politically reliable, and they were more likely to strike a deal with Israel. The deal they would strike, however, given its hegemonic nature, might precipitate a Palestinian civil war. The intifada elite would bring a great deal more popular legitimacy to PA rule but would be much harder for Arafat to control. Unfortunately for Palestinians, the logic of hegemonic peace suggests that Arafat must ultimately return to the ruling coalition he patched together after Oslo, and re-marginalize Barghouti and the rest of the intifada elite.

The intifada elite would be less willing than the "Tunisians" to agree to a deal with Israel that does not meet basic Palestinian rights. Moreover, as the *tanzim* activity in the Al-Aqsa Intifada suggests, they are also more willing to engage Israel in political violence to attain those rights than were the architects of Oslo. On the other hand, given their more democratic bent and grassroots popularity, the intifada elite is much better suited to make any agreement that is reached with Israel stick. In short, this type of coalitional transition would, in the long run, create a more stable Palestine better able to live at peace with Israel. While the logic of hegemonic peace mitigates against this scenario being realized, one cannot dismiss the possibility. As Barrington Moore noted long ago, sometimes violence is the necessary—if unfortunate—midwife to a better political future.[5]

Parts of this essay appeared in Current History, *January 1998,* Current History, *January 2001, and "News and Analysis," Center for Policy Analysis on Palestine, September 12, 2000.*

Notes

1. *San Jose Mercury News*, June 28, 2000.

2. See, for example, Glenn E. Robinson, "Palestine After Arafat," *The Washington Quarterly* 23:4 (Autumn 2000). Online version can be found at www.twq.com.

3. Akram Hanieh, "The Road to the Summit," *The Camp David Papers*, Al-Ayyam newspaper, August 2000. Online version can be found at www.al-ayyam.com. See also Hanieh, "The Camp David Papers," *Journal of Palestine Studies*, Vol. 30, No. 2 (Winter 2001).

4. Ilan Peleg, "Conclusion," *The Middle East Peace Process* (SUNY, 1998).

5. *The Social Origins of Dictatorship and Democracy* (Beacon, 1966).

6. THE AGONY OF BEIT JALA

On the outskirts of Bethlehem, a few miles south of Jerusalem, lies the predominantly Christian Palestinian town of Beit Jala. Since the new intifada erupted, Beit Jala has become a focal point of the conflict, often coming under rocket, tank and heavy machine-gun fire from the Israel Defense Forces. The IDF says its attacks are a response to Palestinian small-arms fire from Beit Jala aimed at the nearby Jewish settlement of Gilo. Nevertheless, numerous human rights organizations have condemned the IDF for its disproportionate response and for indiscriminate fire against a heavily populated civilian area.

The following is a letter from Nidal Barham, an English teacher at Beit Jala's Talitha Kumi Lutheran School, to friends in Germany, written on December 26, 2000. Barham lives about three miles from Beit Jala, in the town of Beit Sahour, which has also come under heavy IDF attack.

Dear Birgit, Roland and Marlene,   Dec. 26th, 2000

How pleased I was to talk to you yesterday. I hope the situation will be better in summer and you will be able to visit us. I'm looking forward to seeing you again.

When you asked about us last night, I told you that things were all right. I didn't want to spoil the happy moments while talking to you and expressing my warmest Christmas greetings. I'm truly sorry for not sending you a card this year. It's the first time in more than thirty years that I haven't sent cards to relatives and friends abroad on this occasion. Fear, sorrow and grief have been over-whelming the last three months. It has been a very gloomy Christmas, and I'm quite sure that very few people thought about Christmas cards.

Last night I promised you, dear Roland, that you would find a long, detailed letter near your fax machine when you got back to work because all of you wanted to hear about the situation here. Thanks a lot for your true concern. I think that talking merely about my family will help you get a good impression of the horrible life we have been living.

First of all, we thank God day and night that we live in the center of the town, because houses two kilometers from our house have been shelled, destroyed or burnt. These houses are adjacent to an Israeli camp of soldiers, which has been attacked by a few Palestinian fighters a few times. Owners of these houses have moved and they are staying with relatives in safe places—if there are any. When helicopters are used, even churches and mosques are not safe. Four of these families are our cousins, whose mother, 80 years old, had to leave her house as well. My aunt is longing for her room, where, according to her, she feels peace and finds comfort while surrounded by her children, grandchildren and familiar belongings. Worst of all is the uprooting, without any notice, of all trees between her house and the camp. Everything is allowed to Israelis under the claim of security. My aunt used to tell us stories about those trees: where she and her late husband brought each plant from, when each one was planted and how she used to carry buckets of water on her head for long distances to water them. "I grew each tree and looked after it as I did my own children," she used to say. No one has dared to tell her what has happened to her trees. They are still waiting for the right time.

My husband, brothers, and brothers-in-law are unemployed now. The majority of Beit Sahourians earn a living working in tourism, trade, construction in the Bethlehem area or Israel, and, recently, in the casino [in Jericho]. All these fields of work have been greatly affected by the political situation. I don't have figures or statistics; all I can say is that the busiest place in Beit Sahour now is the Orthodox Club, where most of the unemployed gather to play cards or chess or to have a cup of coffee. By chance, my father is responsible for the canteen there for this year. Since work has flourished, one of my brothers is helping him.

The last two years, people started to feel that life was probably getting less difficult and work would be better. As a result, many young men started building their own houses or renting a new flat, got married, bought cars, got loans from banks and started small projects. Now, these people are in big trouble. They have no income to afford all these commitments. They can hardly afford medical care or school fees for their children. One of these young men is my brother. He sells goods to merchants in Bethlehem, Hebron and Ramallah and gets a commission. His work was good enough to encourage him to build a house for his family instead of paying rent for a very small flat. "I lived in cells for nine years and want to have more room around me," he says (he was in prison under the Israeli occupation for political reasons). He made commitments to pay the builder a monthly sum of money for eight years. The Palestinian towns and cities are under siege most of the time. Therefore, traveling between them is not allowed. Sometimes my brother risks his life using unusual, unsafe routes to deliver some goods, and very often he is not paid.

Some women haven't lost their jobs yet, which is supposed to be a blessing for the family. Switching roles, the man at home and the woman working outside, adds more pressure on some families, since this situation is too much to bear for some men. Taking into consideration the feeling of insecurity and frustration, most people are continuously under stress. "I don't like school very much, but I prefer staying here rather than going home," a 12-year-old girl told me. When I asked her the reason she told me that her parents, brothers, and sister either watch news on TV or shout at each other. "All of them are nervous. I'm not used to this kind of life. I can't take it anymore," she complained. "You are right. It's not easy or nice to live like that," I said, "but, after all, they are normal human beings living in an abnormal situation. Don't blame them. If they don't feel free to let their anger out at home, where should they do that? Remember that they love you and that they've never been like that," I added. I'm not sure whether I helped this student or added to her burden. A few days later she told me that she started to understand her family more. "I love them and forgive them too," she said. I think we need more than one social worker at school if this situation will go on.

Nadia [Barham's daughter] works in Jerusalem, as you know. When the intifada started on the 29th of September, many injured Palestinians were sent to hospitals. The operating rooms are next to Nadia's office. Unable to work while wounded people and their relatives were outside the door, she left her office. She saw horrible scenes. Some had lost an eye or both, others an arm or a leg. Some were bleeding, others fainted. Mothers were screaming and lamenting. Men were searching for their relatives. Bodies came in and out. When my daughter came home, she said nothing. We were watching TV and following what had happened in Jerusalem that day. Nadia's tears were falling heavily while watching. Her father and I felt that the day had been very heavy for her, so we tried to turn the TV off, but she refused. After almost an hour she agreed and then she started telling us about the unforgettable scenes she witnessed in the hospital. Nadia was sick the following days and refused to eat. We took her to the doctor. "Tension," he said, after a series of blood tests and X-rays. She lost six kilos and hasn't regained them.

Nadia goes to Jerusalem six days a week. So far, she has a permit, so she takes the usual way. She has to pass a checkpoint, which is usually a hot place for confrontation between young Palestinian men and Israeli soldiers. Nadia has a mobile, and to make sure she passes that place safely, we keep calling her until she reaches Jerusalem, and on the way back also. She is tired, bored, and frustrated. She expected a better life and more amusement when she graduated. She took a one-week vacation, visiting her sister in Jordan. I hope the border will not be closed again, because she may lose her job if she doesn't come back on time.

Bassam [Nadia's son] is in high school this year. He's going to sit for the government exams (Tawjihi) by the end of this scholastic year. This is a decisive year for all Tawjihi students. Bassam can't concentrate on his studies. He wants to listen to people talking about the situation and discussing politics. He has become news-addicted like the rest of us. Almost every night we hear the sounds of explosions. He just can't isolate himself and be separated from what's happening in order to get good results. "What for?" he sometimes wonders, like many teenagers, who have started to feel that there is no hope to ensure a good life, whatever they do.

Bassam had a very painful experience last month. The father of one of his friends was killed when he left his home to give first aid to some wounded people whose houses had been shelled. Bassam screamed with enormous sorrow and hit his fist against the wall when he heard the news. He left the house early the next morning. His friends gathered and went to be with Daniel, the martyr's son. I saw my son become a mature, responsible man that day. He did things I had never thought he could do. He went to the hospital to fetch the body, which was half-burnt and torn to pieces. He also carried the coffin with other young men. When the funeral was over, he refused to come home with me. He felt that he had to be with his friend Daniel. I didn't want to leave Beit Jala and leave my son behind me, since I thought more shelling would take place there after the funeral. He refused to listen to me and made himself scarce. When I reached Beit Sahour it was being shelled.

Do you see, dear friends? We live in horror. Life is unbearable during this difficult time. Please pray for us, pray for peace. We do need it now.

Yours,

Nidal Barham

The following essays were written in January and February 2001 for this book by Barham's English students at Talitha Kumi school in Beit Jala. The students, aged 14–16, were asked to describe what their lives have been like since the uprising began.

SAMAR HAZBOUN

As I was watching the beautiful stars from my window, like I do every night, I heard the gunshots. At first I thought it was going to stop after an hour or two, just like every night. Later the gunshots got stronger and louder. I decided not to listen to it or bother myself with my negative thoughts because I get tired of this ritual shelling. So I lay myself into bed to forget all about what was going on in this cruel world.

I tried closing my eyes, but the feeling of fear was much too strong. I looked at my sister and asked her whether she was afraid. She looked at me for a while and then closed her eyes as if she couldn't hear anything. She must have been trying to deafen herself too so as to get some peace. For some reason I felt nervous and restless. It was 11:30 exactly, and this weird feeling came over me. I started crying for an unknown reason. I don't remember falling asleep.

At 6 o'clock in the morning I woke up as usual and got dressed. When I was having breakfast, my Dad was listening to the news on the radio. They announced that a German doctor [Harry Fischer] from Beit Jala was shot and had passed away. My thoughts started racing. Eventually, I realized that it was my best friend's dad who was dead. Tears wet my cheeks. I told my mother that I wanted to call Raphaella, but my mom refused and told me that it would be better if I waited.

I was upset. I was confused and didn't listen to my mom. Raphaella's mom answered the phone. She sounded very sad. When she knew I was on the phone, she gave it to Raphaella. I tried to sound as normal as possible and said, "Hi." She replied, "Hi, Sam." I have never asked her "How are you?" but this time I did. "We are still alive, but my Dad passed away." All words suddenly became meaningless, and not knowing what to say, I whispered, "Coming right away."

Raphaella's father was savagely executed. Killing a father of three children is a crime. A hero doctor was killed by Israeli rockets, which smashed his body and tore it into pieces. Why? Is this the reward of a good job? Is this the price doctors pay when duty calls? He left home to help injured neighbors. What was done is evil. But who cares? They are Israelis. They see themselves as almost holy and claim that they are victims. To them Palestinians are nothing more than garbage they must get rid of. When will people all over the world know the reality of these hypocritical, cruel Israelis?

RAPHAELLA FISCHER

[Raphaella is the daughter of Dr. Harry Fischer, the German doctor who was killed by Israeli shelling in Beit Jala in November while he was trying to tend to wounded civilians.]

Dear Diary,

I haven't talked to you for a long time. It's not because I didn't have time but because words can't express how I feel deep inside. Those pictures in my head, which will never leave my sight, can't be described.

Oh dear, what can I say? Looking back at the day when my father was taken away, I remember feeling that my soul was leaving to another zone. For some reason I couldn't understand, I felt like the whole world was going to end, so I screamed and felt I was going to die. In reality, a part of me is now missing and I'm cracked up with misery.

This painful grieving feeling struck me while I was at my Dad's funeral. I tried so hard to hide it, but my tears gave me away. Something in my chest began to squeeze my heart and lungs. I couldn't breathe anymore. My head started spinning. I thought I was going to die again. No, I wouldn't allow this to happen. I had to keep undismayed.

I couldn't hide the mournfulness or the rage that was building up, longing to burst out. At the funeral, one feeling was clear: I hate nobody, but someone must be blamed. Who is responsible for the victims in this bloodshed? Why must there be tears in children's eyes? Look at their faces, see the fear ruling their lonely souls. Who can tell me how to live in peace, when fear controls our hearts? How many more have to die? How many souls have to be dispatched for a lie that has become the truth? People only see what they want, they only listen to what they long to hear, and they manipulate words to reach their aims, while others are being destroyed and stepped on. Why? Shall we always pay the price? We are captured in spiders' webs, trying to escape. Who can help?

ELIAS ISSA HALABI

Agreements to make peace with devils? What kind of peace would it be? Why us? What do mothers' tears mean to those killers? Is it fair? Are human rights just for Americans and Israelis? Can't anybody help? Why should Palestinians drink from the cup of death? Should I lose faith? Or should I continue dreaming of this thing called "peace"?

No one knew it would be like this. It started suddenly, with stones. More stones with more injuries. The killers started to use guns, then tanks and warplanes. It's a real war, but the main problem is that it's one-sided. Babies, children, and old people are dying every day. It's a bloody mess. Life was easy before: school, parties, picnics, youth meetings—we were having fun. But not anymore. It's like a great dream has ended as a nightmare. Our houses, schools, even churches are not safe.

I remember after returning from school one day, around 4, I heard the helicopters approaching. They started shooting bullets everywhere. My parents were at work. My brother, my sisters, and I were at home. My grandfather and my aunt came to our house because their house was not safe. Some bullets had broken the windows and doors. Thirty minutes later my parents came home, after many difficulties. God had protected them.

We ran to the first floor to hide. Hours passed and we were still hiding. We could do nothing but pray. The helicopters left after midnight. We tried to sleep but couldn't because the tanks started shooting. More fear—you could touch it and hear it. Suddenly we heard a sound like bombing. The Israeli soldiers sent us a present: three rockets and more than 100 bullets in the balcony. After an hour we went to see the damage and when the soldiers saw us, they started shooting at us, so we ran away. That same night they killed my friend's father [Dr. Fischer] while he was trying to help someone who had been injured from the rockets. They killed a father of three in such a brutal way. It really was like a day from a horror film.

Israeli soldiers and Jewish settlers attack houses, land, people, schools, even ambulances. They are killing and injuring more and more every day. But no matter how many they kill and injure, we will continue fighting until we reach our goals and take our rights, because God is with us, and when God is with us, no one can be against us.

MARY RIZK ALLAH

It was early winter, when people are supposed to start preparing for Christmas. I was sitting in my warm bedroom writing cards to send to friends and relatives. I played some Christmas songs to help me cheer up.

Sounds of explosions broke the silence of the night, and they were much louder than the songs. Everyone in the house jumped up and shouted, "Get on the floor!" I was shocked and couldn't move. Someone pushed me and I found myself lying down like the others. The sound of Christmas carols was mixed with the sounds of the Israeli machine guns, which started firing in all directions, regardless of the consequences.

I closed my eyes and started praying. With the sound of each bullet or missile, I thought it was going to strike me or one of my family. Every time, I thanked God that it hadn't, but at the same time prayed that nobody else in our neighborhood would be hurt. To my surprise, I lost feeling in my body. I felt that I had no legs, no arms, no face. Was it because of the cold floor? Was it because I had been wounded somewhere? I tried to figure it out, and finally realized that it was because of fear—only fear.

A few hours later silence dropped heavily upon the area. We tried to rest in our beds again. My body was as heavy as a stone, so my sister and brother helped me drag myself to the bed. Our eyes refused to close. As the sun rose we were still gazing at each other, unable to say a word.

How horrible this experience was. I hope we will never live through this situation again. May the Lord protect my friends, family, and all children.

SAWSAN GHNEIM

I will never forget Wednesday, November 15, 2000. Late at night, I was studying for an Arabic exam. My parents and sisters were sleeping. My brother was visiting one of his friends. I heard the sounds of bombing. It was in an area not too far from Beit Jala. Gradually, the bombing came closer and closer. I could hear it a couple of kilometers from our house. Fear seized my heart. I woke up my parents and my sisters. The firing kept getting closer and closer. We felt great panic. I started crying and so did my sisters. My mother was thinking of a safe corner. Suddenly, bullets began breaking the windows of our neighbors' houses.

My father shouted, "Come on, quickly!" In a hurry, we opened the door of the house and went out. We couldn't see the stairs because of the dust. My old grandmother was still downstairs. At that time my brother and his friend showed up. As we were were sneaking out of the house, the Israeli soldiers rained us with bullets. It seemed they thought we were Palestinian fighters. Until now I can't understand how none of us were killed or wounded. It was a miracle. The only safe place, we thought, would be my uncle's house, so we headed for it. On the way, we met him coming in his car to pick us up. But we couldn't sleep at his house; we were waiting for the shelling to stop.

When morning came, the war settled down and we went back home. But it wasn't our home anymore; it was the home of missiles, rockets, bullets and scattered bombs. Nothing in the house was in normal condition: blankets were holed, clothes and curtains were burned, windows and beds were destroyed, bullets were inside the refrigerator, and the washing machine was broken. It was unlivable. The mayor expressed his sorrow and is paying for our stay in Bethlehem Hotel till we find another house to rent.

KLARA SHIHADEH

It's a silent night. The pale moon is shining on our sad town; the stars are twinkling brightly in the clear sky. The sound of bells joining the evening prayer are rising up high to heaven, and we are sitting in the dining room, having supper.

Suddenly, a red shade covers the moon. The light is extinguished and all the house is shaking. The sound of shooting, the impact of rockets and the explosions of bombs followed by the screams of people, the crackling of flames and the sirens of ambulances break into the silence of the night.

We are completely scared, our whole bodies are trembling and our hearts are crying.

My parents are searching for a place to hide. After perplexing for a while, they decide to take refuge in our basement. We rush out into the red dust and smoke, passing through the shooting. The cold wind blows into our hot faces. Suddenly, a red bullet passes near my sister's back. It could have killed her, but God's angels are surrounding us. Terrified and stricken, we get to the small old door and my father decides on a corner, hoping that his heart has led him to the right decision. With pain in our hearts and tears in our eyes we sit on the cold floor, huddling under an old blanket.

My mother is hugging my sister, praising God for protecting her child. Peering around anxiously into the darkness, I can see the shadows of old furniture, clothes and provisions. These shadows cause strange, curious feelings deep in my heart. A small, soft hand is touching my arm. Looking through a small window, pointing to a beautiful star that appears brightly in the sky, my little brother says, "Klara, look at that star, it's our grandmother. She has heard the shooting, she's very worried about us. She has asked Jesus to change her into a star, so that she will be able to see us. And now, seeing us all safe, she is twinkling happily in the sky. She knows that God is protecting us."

None of us are able to destroy his happiness and consolation by telling him the truth. These words have moved great feelings in my heart. My brother has touched me so much that I start hugging him kindly, kissing his small, round face and giving him love that is springing from a fountain inside my heart. In fact, he seems to be very relaxed. He is still observing that star with big eyes, believing it is his grandmother. I'm also watching that star, wondering what death is like and imagining how horrible and painful it would be if my sister were killed. I really thank God with all my heart for protecting her.

Knowing that our lives are in danger makes me experience strange and terrible feelings. I feel myself at the edge of life, wondering if I'll see the sunrise once more, if I'll sleep in my bed again, if I'll live until peace is achieved. With each shot and rocket impact, with each explosion and siren, I start thinking of all my relatives, friends, classmates and teachers, hoping that none of them are harmed and asking God to protect them all. Sad, frightened and patient, we go through a night of doubt and sorrow, waiting until the morning breaks to see what has happened to our small town.

Slowly the sun rises, shining on destroyed houses, injured people and crying children. Trying to give them new hope and helping them to forget their tragedy by beginning a new day may lead to a better future.

CHRISTINA ABUSLEIMEH

The situation has been very difficult and life has been miserable in our city due to the political changes in the area and because of the siege that has been imposed upon us. So far, I go to school five days a week, as usual. The main street to our school is closed now because it is located in C zone (the land under Israeli occupation). The school building itself is in A zone (under the Palestinian Authority). Therefore, a new gate was opened from the other side of the school compound to enable students to reach it. Taking into consideration the difficult situation the students are going through, the school administration canceled the first-term exams. Despite this cancellation, we still have to study and do homework. The problem is that a lot of students don't live in their houses anymore. Because they are staying in relatives' houses, they don't have any kind of stability and can't concentrate on studying. Very often the city is shelled in the afternoon; consequently, the electricity is out almost every night. A lot of students don't get enough sleep at night and have to go to school in the morning. Almost every night, my family spends many hours in a safe place in the house, and we go to bed for a couple of hours in the morning. It's very exhausting.

My father leaves home almost every night, whether he is on duty in the hospital or not. Since the hospital where he works is in emergency most nights and he is one of the main surgeons, he can't stay at home whenever a city, town or [refugee] camp is attacked in the Bethlehem area. We are always worried about him. The hospital as well as the ambulances have been attacked several times.

In other words, we are living a nightmare. We are trying to live this abnormal situation as normally as possible. How long we can stand this life is anyone's guess. Please, pray for us.

RANEEN AL-ARJA

Since the second intifada started, many tragedies have struck Palestinian towns, camps and cities. Beit Jala has had its share as well.

One day last October started normally, but at about 11 o'clock, four Palestinian bullets were shot and, as usual, never reached the settlement nearby. The response came back immediately: a heavy rain of bullets and rockets. Unfortunately, my mother and many other relatives were attending a funeral. People were in the street when the Israeli army started shelling. People started screaming and running away. They were afraid to death when they saw that some had been injured. My grandparents' house was the nearest, so a lot of people took shelter there. Two cars were bombed and started burning, one of my cousins was shot in the shoulder, and a little boy was shot in the head.

My mother phoned and asked us to call the ambulance and the fire engine. We could feel panic in her voice, which vanished before we could ask her why. Two hours later, she came home. She could hardly breathe, her face was pale, and her body was shaking. While crying, she told us about all that had happened.

It took us a few days to recover from this shock and to live our life normally. The second horrible experience didn't give us a break. The house of my uncle was severely attacked twice in the same week. The house, 600 meters away from ours, is very near the tunnel that leads to a safe road [bypass road] between Jerusalem and the settlements around Hebron. When Israeli soldiers at the checkpoint started shooting, we realized that they were attacking my uncle's house. We phoned to make sure they were all right. We heard his three little girls screaming and crying on the phone. He said that the house was shaking and they would try to leave if possible, but they couldn't. We were terrified. How painful it was to feel that our relatives were in danger and we were unable to do anything but pray for them.

More than 800 bullets hit their house. All the furniture was damaged. My uncle's daughters and wife couldn't live there anymore. They left the country. Even now his daughters have nightmares and cry while sleeping. The first thing they ask us on the phone is, "Are they still shooting?"

JAVIER KHAROUFA

November 12 was one of the worst Sundays for the people of Beit Jala. If you ask anyone about that day, you will hear lots of stories about the same event—not because people make things up but because the same event affected everyone in a different way.

A lot of people were at church to attend the Sunday service and to offer condolences to the relatives of two people who had passed away. After attending the funeral of both, my parents and uncles went to church. My brother, sister, and I, along with my cousins, stayed at home. After breakfast, some started playing in the garden, others started doing homework. My sister and I sat on the balcony. From the tune of the church bells, we knew that the funeral had started.

While carrying the dead bodies to the cemetery, people started to hear the sound of bombing. Suddenly, Israeli soldiers started shooting bullets and rockets at the town. All of us ran quickly to the ground floor. My little brother and my cousins started shouting and trembling. I realized that I had to pretend I wasn't afraid, in the hope that I would be able to reduce their fear and calm them down. It seemed that ages passed before my cousin came running into the house while bullets were passing by him. My little cousin and brother were comforted when they saw him. A few minutes later, my mother came in. She had used a safe road and climbed a wall. She had to hide in one of the houses in our neighborhood. My mother was crying when she told us her story, but at the same time she was smiling because we were safe.

We waited till we felt it was safe to leave the house. In a few minutes we were standing on one of the safe streets. There, we saw lots of parents waiting for a chance to reach their homes. Mothers were crying and fathers were waiting anxiously and trying to figure out what to do and how to reach their children. When the attack was over, we went home. On our way we saw a lot of destruction. Some houses were burned, but thank God very few people were injured. Fortunately, no one died.

LINDA BADER

The tourism industry here is one of the best in the world. Because Palestine is the Holy Land of three religions, our country attracts tourists from all over the world.

The year 2000 was expected to be one of the best seasons in years. But once the intifada against the Israeli occupation started, news of bloodshed spread quickly and travelers began to cancel their plans. Only a few groups have come to the Holy Land since September 2000; consequently, hotels are empty, tourist buses are not operating, restaurants are closed, and gift shops have laid off their employees. My dad, a travel agent, is out of work, and tour guides have no work either. The situation has also affected businesses related to tourism, like those that sell olive wood, mother-of-pearl, and other souvenir products.

The beginning of this century is not better at all. I hope the political situation will be solved and Palestinians will have their free country. Then the tourists will start coming again.

PATRICIA AL-TEET

The first time Beit Jala was shelled, people were surprised and wondered what had happened. Children, of course, took more time to realize what was going on, and I'm sure they will take much more time to recover from the stress and confusion. It seems that no matter how hard parents try to secure and improve their children's lives, unexpected circumstances destroy their efforts.

Beit Jalians, like parents all over the world, try their best to educate their children, often taking on extra work to pay for school. Nowadays, some kids miss school because they didn't get enough sleep at home or because they are hiding in a corner of their house or staying in the house of a relative. Those who sleep for a few hours and are able to go to school can't study at home because they have to take refuge before the shelling starts. School administrations and teachers are trying their best to take these circumstances into consideration, but school should involve some reading, writing, and evaluation.

Each couple plans to have their own house if their parents can't build them one. Building a house is both a dream and a necessity because we don't have any kind of social insurance; people plan at least to not pay rent when they are unable to work. A lot of children help their parents prepare material for the builders in order to save money. Children really live the construction of each stone in their rooms. How much they dream of the rest they will feel when the house is finished, and how horrible to see those dreams vanish without any kind of mercy.

Children come first in priorities in parents' lives even if these children are married. It is very hard to see your children deprived of a good education or become homeless, but it is even harder when it comes to daily bread and health care. The number of unemployed is increasing and the economic situation is deteriorating. It is unbearable when parents can't afford the minimum standard of living; what is even worse is that now Israel is threatening to blockade the Palestinian areas and prevent us from getting water, electricity, or fuel. In other words, children are the first victims of all this. No wonder they don't laugh from their hearts anymore. They've lost their childhoods, and their crime is that they are Palestinian.

7. THE PALESTINIANS OF ISRAEL
AN INTERVIEW WITH AZMI BISHARA

When the intifada broke out in late September 2000, the Palestinian citizens of Israel expressed their solidarity by observing a general strike and engaging in demonstrations in their towns and villages. These protests were met, according to Human Rights Watch, "with repeated excessive use of lethal force against unarmed Palestinian demonstrators who posed no imminent danger of death or serious injury to security forces or to others."[1] Israeli security forces killed thirteen Palestinians and injured hundreds more, some seriously.

The October clashes occurred after several years of organizing, in which the Arab citizens of the Jewish state have increasingly asserted their national rights as Palestinians and their equal rights as citizens of Israel, protesting everything from land confiscations to unequal distribution of state resources. At the forefront of this movement is Dr. Azmi Bishara, a Palestinian Member of the Knesset representing the National Democratic Alliance (Tajammu). The following interview with Bishara was conducted in Arabic in Jerusalem on January 29, 2001, by Mouin Rabbani.

***

Let's start with the living conditions of the Palestinians inside Israel. It's known that unlike Palestinians in the occupied territories, they have citizenship, the right to vote, and many of the rights that are available to the other citizens of Israel, so it would seem that they are living in a full democracy. But your whole platform is based on what you term systematic discrimination, and even the practice of apartheid, against Palestinian citizens of the state. So perhaps you could give a brief overview and elaborate on this issue.

In order to properly understand the structure of discrimination against the Arabs in Israel you have to understand the historical processes that produced and sustain it, because there is no real distinction between the relevant structural issues and historical processes. In other words, it is not simply a matter of a group of citizens who are being discriminated against. Rather, they are an indigenous population, who constitute what is left of the Palestinian people in this country, and who during the early years of the state, when they were under direct military rule between 1948 and 1966, were treated by it as a fifth column, a group that constitutes an actual or potential threat to state security. After this initial period, they were treated as a group that had to be integrated and have its national identity eliminated within the framework of the Israeli state. When all is said and done, this is the state of the Jews and not their state; therefore, the discrimination that is practiced against them is structural, institutionalized. Israel is in a state of permanent denial vis-à-vis Palestinian identity and Palestinian history.

Left: Jerusalem's Old City seen from the Mount of Olives

The Palestinian citizens of Israel are discriminated against both in the negative sense, because they are not Jewish, and also in the positive sense, because they are Arabs: they remind Israel of the original conflict and of the question of Palestine. These are two different kinds of discrimination that researchers generally neither understand nor appreciate. For example, there are many foreign workers in this country who are discriminated against because they are not Jewish. But this is different from the discrimination we are confronted with. We are subject to two distinct types of discrimination; the first concerns disparities in the allocation of state budgets and those kinds of things, while the second concerns the denial of our identity and the contradictions that exist between the state and our identity and memory, our presence within it, our membership in the Palestinian people and connection with the wider Arab world.

If you don't understand the particularities of these two distinct factors, you can have only a partial understanding of why people took to the streets in October of 2000. You wouldn't understand the act of solidarity with the Palestinian people in the occupied territories and the Arab world that the demonstrations expressed, or why the state shot at unarmed Arab citizens and killed them.

Could you elaborate a little further on what you term the two distinct forms of discrimination, for example in budget allocations?

It's everything. In fact, you have to examine where there isn't discrimination, not where there is. Because, I mean, it's hardly a state secret. The first and most important initiatives undertaken by the state concern issues relating to the denial of the collective identity of the Arabs in Israel. Issues like land. The state had an ideological problem accepting the relationship between the Arabs and their land. The state was founded on the denial of this relationship and the perception that this relationship poses a threat to the state. So you saw expropriations, on a massive and continuing scale. More and more and more, and not always because the state had a specific need for the expropriated lands. Sometimes—usually—it did. But its need for the land is not the whole story and doesn't adequately explain the process. There was also an ideology involved. That is why, after the state was established and after Arabs became citizens, 85 percent of their lands were expropriated. Six laws were adopted for the specific purpose of expropriating Arab lands. The word "Arab" did not appear in a single one of these laws. It didn't have to, because the only land owned by private individuals was Arab land, which is precisely what was expropriated.

Of course, there is also budgetary discrimination by the state. The state spends only half the amount on the education of an Arab as it does on that of a Jew. But such figures reveal only part of the story. They do not explain to which school the Arab child goes, who is responsible for his curriculum, what its content is, and so on. There is discrimination in everything.

A term that perhaps best exemplifies the meaning of discrimination is "unrecognized villages." The very term is irrational, and one that in the context of a modern state does not make sense. These are villages—some established before 1948 and some after—that exist in Israel's midst and are treated like unrecognized states. When the state drafts development plans, it simply ignores these unrecognized villages. When planning new roads, for example, or the extension of services like water and electricity, no effort is made to connect these villages to the expanding infrastructure. And after the plans are made, and it is suddenly discovered that the size, location, or existence of this village contradicts the implementation of the development plan, it is not the plan that is amended but the village that is considered to be in its way. One group of people that exists here is simply ignored, while others are brought here from Poland, Russia, and elsewhere and have communities planned and built for them.

The contradiction between the Jewish state and its Arab citizens can also be seen in public administration and government corporations, in the types of jobs Arabs have, or more accurately don't have. We undertook a number of initiatives to challenge this situation, based on the legislative model used by African-Americans in the United States—affirmative action—and we recently scored some achievements. The legislative proposals I introduced have been termed a constitutional revolution, because there are now specific laws that mention Arabs by name and call for their improved representation in these sectors. This is, however, only a contribution: to expose and challenge reality, enhance the civil rights consciousness of the Arab population, and give us legal tools to combat discrimination. The laws in and of themselves are not going to solve the problem, of course. We've simply given people legal instruments with which to fight discrimination.

Was previous discrimination based on formal legislation, institutionalized practice, or a combination of both?

Practice. The Israeli establishment is intelligent enough not to adopt laws that specifically prohibit Arabs from assuming certain jobs on the basis of their identity. But in practice, they never appointed an Arab to those jobs. Israel is not going to state that its budget for 2001 will discriminate against the Arabs. But in practice, there are so-called "priority areas," and the Arab regions are the state's last priority.

In the past decade, virtually every Israeli political party has included statements in their electoral campaigns publicly recognizing that discrimination exists, and that they would equalize budgets once in office. Fifteen years ago this would never have happened; none of them would even recognize the existence of discrimination. Today they do, but then nothing happens and the issue is forgotten, until there is a new election or an uprising in which people get killed and wounded and so on, and then the same promises are made once again.

You've elaborated on the discrimination that is practiced by Israel against its Palestinian citizens. At the same time, we are talking about a community whose members are citizens of the state, who have the right to vote and form political parties, and who form approximately a fifth of the electorate. Given this reality, why has it taken almost half a century for this community to begin successfully confronting insti-

tutionalized discrimination through passage of parliamentary legislation of the type you just described? Was the community prevented or inhibited from exercising its formal political rights, or just very slow in mobilizing its clout and resources?

Until the late 1970s, Israel did not permit the establishment of Arab political parties, on security pretexts of course. (In the early 1960s the Al-Ard [Land] Movement, an Arab nationalist party, was declared illegal by the authorities.) At the same time, during the period of direct military rule the Zionist parties—Labor, for example—established lists of Arab parliamentary candidates, not because they supported the establishment of an Arab political party or any such thing, but because Arabs were forbidden from joining the Zionist parties. So Labor would sponsor lists of Arab candidates affiliated with it and sharing common interests. The lists were composed of mukhtars, tribal and clan leaders and other traditional leaders, who would get those they controlled to vote for Labor. These people, who served as electoral agents for the Zionist parties, were a social class rather than a political phenomenon, a traditional leadership that maintains its position by mediating between the state and society. The existence of this class is in my view the most important indicator of the existence of an occupation, which always includes the presence of collaborators.

Traditional leaders who entered the Knesset would actually vote with the Labor Party for the extension of military rule over Israel's Arabs. When such resolutions extending the military government would come before the Knesset, the Likud would vote against but the traditional [Arab] leaders would vote for it, with the Labor Party. A change began in the late 1970s, when the Progressive Movement registered as a legal political party, and thereafter the Progressive List for Peace—a joint Arab-Jewish party—registered as well.

How do you explain this change, in which the Israeli authorities began to permit the establishment of Arab political parties as legal organizations?

I would explain it in terms of the increasing power of the Israeli state—internally in its relationship with its Arab citizens, regionally in terms of its military power, and also in terms of the increasing strength of its democratic institutions, which allowed for greater political freedoms at the margins. After Land Day on March 30, 1976 [in which six Arabs were killed and hundreds wounded by security forces during large demonstrations], the state came to the conclusion that it was preferable to deal with us by relaxing its controls somewhat, lest the accumulating pressure be released in a different way. Of course, initially they believed the Arab parties would be traditionalist and moderate, but we exploited the margin of maneuver available to us and are less beholden to the establishment. That is why they are now accusing us of violating the law in the Israeli Supreme Court.

It seems that almost every Arab member of the Knesset has been placed under investigation for "incitement."

Yes, there are a lot of investigations under way, although none have been formally charged. But these are individual cases, relating to a position taken here or there by this or that person. What I am talking about are the attempts to ban political parties in their entirety, like the Tajammu Party. The Supreme Court stated that we are treading a thin red line between legality and illegality. Recently, for example, the former head of the General Security Service [Shabak, or Shin Bet], Ami Ayalon, gave a lengthy press interview in which he threatened to have us declared illegal. He stated that our existence contradicts the Jewish character of the state and that the Attorney General should therefore consider placing us beyond the limits of the law. So there are investigations launched against individuals, as well as efforts to declare entire parties outside the law.

In any event, during the past years the margins for legal political activity have been expanded, and this has led to the emergence of new parties that look at the same issues from a different perspective. Take, for example, the issue of equality. Traditionally, the Arab parties have defined it as the absence of discrimination. We no longer approach the issue of equality as something that exists when something else is removed, but rather seek to define it positively. That is to say, equality means a state of all its citizens, because you can't have equality in the context of a Jewish state. This is for two reasons. The first is because Israel as the state of the Jewish people gives rights to people who are not citizens of the state at the expense of people who are, and second because it excludes Arabs who are citizens of Israel. So you have two contradictions here.

And this is a matter of law and legislation?

Yes, this is a matter of law. Israel is constitutionally the state of the Jews, which means it is the state of many people who are not citizens of it, and at the same time not the state of many people who are its citizens. The state recognizes Israeli citizenship, but it does not recognize the concept of Israeli nationality. This is because it insists on its Jewish identity. I was once asked why I am against the concept of "Israelization" [the common term for acceptance of and integration into the Zionist framework of the state]. My answer was that I'm against the Israelization process which marginalizes Arab national and cultural identity that existed before the emergence of the state of Israel; but the problem is also with the state itself, which recognizes no such thing as Israeli nationality.

Which brings me to my second point. Israel is not only the state of the Jews, providing rights to people who are not citizens and excluding people who are. It is also a Jewish state. This means that in Israel there is no distinction between nationality and religion—there is no separation between church and state. If you don't distinguish between national and religious identity you can't possibly distinguish between church and state. In fact, there is no way to join this nationality. The Arabs in Israel don't want to join it. They are part of a nation, which is the Arab nation, which came into formation prior to the establishment of Israel. Our situation is not like that of the Jews, nor like that of some of the Africans, who were taken to the Americas. In our case the national idea began to develop in the nineteenth century. Nationalism arrived in this region at approximately the same time that Zionist thought began to develop in Europe. So in our case the Zionists came into contact with a people who were already in the process of national formation. And Zionism approached the concept of integration as a Jewish issue. Israel is a melting pot for Jews, not a melting pot for its citizens. So the only way to join is by [religious] conversion. There is no other way. Because we are not talking about the American nation, where citizenship is your ticket to join. Or even the French, where—though less than in the United States—citizenship is still a way to join. What we are saying is that in this structure you can't speak about equality.

At the same time, you are a member of the Israeli Knesset. Your command of the Hebrew language is equal to that of any Israeli Jewish intellectual. When you say that equality is impossible in the context of a Jewish state, you are speaking as someone who legislates not only for greater equality for your own, Arab community, but also on issues that are internal to Israeli Jewish society, and on which you have the right to vote. So on what basis are you saying that not only is there no equality, but that there can be no equality? I'm trying here to clarify the inherent contradictions between Zionism and democracy. That is, this is not like apartheid South Africa: Arabs are not told, with the force of law, "Go to your ghetto, stay out of sight, we don't want to hear your voice."

No, there is no need to. If the Arabs in Israel were to become a majority then you might have such a South African situation. But here you don't have to. Arabs are a minority.[2]

So they are tolerated on account of their demographic insignificance?

Yes, I think so. Of course. But they're not really that tolerated. There are clear limits to the toleration of this minority, which are also the limits of Israeli democracy. The popular upheaval [*habba sha'biyya*] of October 2000 showed limits of another kind. An act of solidarity between the different sectors of the Palestinian people, an expression of political rage, was met with bullets. The limits of Israeli democracy are best exposed when it is confronted with the national question, as opposed to demands for this or that particular right.

Anyway, as far as the contradictions are concerned, these go deeper than the question of who has the right to vote and sit in Parliament. The apparatus of the state as a whole—Parliament, the executive branch, the army, the security establishment, the judicial branch, the prison authority—have until now always been a part of the Zionist movement. There is of course a level of toleration for outsiders, but when push comes to shove these are all fully mobilized against the Arab population. The most important indicator of the recent popular upheaval is that, all of a sudden, the mask came off. It became apparent that we are a tolerated population, provided the situation permits. The popular upheaval of last October is not the only instance. On Land Day in 1976 the same thing happened.

There is another issue of central importance. This is the role of military service as a criterion for obtaining regular rights from the state, or am I misinterpreting the reality?

No, you are not misinterpreting it. This state, which is very strongly based on what I would call

Jewish virtues, also has a strong tradition of republican (not liberal), secular virtues. During the period of the Yishuv [the pre-state Jewish community in Palestine] as well as during the initial stages of the Israeli state, these republican, secular virtues were dominant. Among its leading symbols were the army and of course patriotism, but the dominant one was that of the "pioneer," a combination of the physical labor involved in agriculture and the military activity involved in settlement. In other cases they would use imagery derived from the Old Testament and so on, in the process deleting 2,000 years of Jewish diaspora existence. The embodiment of this ideology was David Ben-Gurion, who referred to this as the new moral Jewish imperative. It involved what was termed "the negation of the diaspora," all the way to the period of King David. The real Jewish history—the whole Talmudic period—suddenly vanished, and the Old Testament became the basis. The entire richness of Jewish history was thrown into the dustbin without a second thought. The entire period between the Israel of the Old Testament and the modern state of Israel was redefined as a historical vacuum. This was the dominant thinking during the period of the Yishuv.

There is a direct affinity between secular Zionism and the Old Testament. But the Jewish religion is not the Old Testament. The Jewish religion is the Talmud. It is a religion that was developed in the diaspora. The Old Testament is a popular myth of origin and a folklore, not religion. The Orthodox religion is the Talmud, the codex, religious laws, interpretations, what we in Arabic would call *fiqh* [the "science" of religious jurisprudence] and the *sunna* [the religious traditions], and there are of course the different sorts and patterns of popular religion affected by the other prevailing traditions in the different diasporas and so on.

At the same time, Orthodox Jewry, which was anti-Zionist, maintained the traditions of the diaspora, and neither Zionism nor the negation of the diaspora made much of an entry into this community. It maintained its emphasis on Jewish virtues, which are different from republican Zionism. It remained this way until 1967, when there was a process of amalgamation between the two. The two legitimacies in Israel joined: Jewishness and Zionism, Jewishness and settlement, Jewishness and military prowess. Two different virtues, both considered equally valid and legitimate. Orthodox Judaism moved toward Zionism, and Zionism moved toward Orthodox Judaism.

This must have made the situation increasingly complex for the Arab community.

It certainly did. Much more complex. What you had after 1967 was an overlap between the concept of Eretz Yisrael ("the [biblical] Land of Israel") and Medinat Yisrael ("the [Zionist] State of Israel"). That year there began an overlap in consciousness, between the traditional Jewish consciousness and the contemporary Zionist one. This is very important. Because based on these two new "tickets" to legitimacy, you don't necessarily have to serve in the army, you can also perform your national service in a yeshiva.

So your entry ticket is either through the army or the yeshiva, neither option of which is open to the Arab community.

Either through the army or the yeshiva, or actually just by being Jewish. Even if you desert. More recently, however, within the secular Jewish camp there have arisen new processes of differentiation, which focus more on the individual and his rights—the idea that rights are not derived from membership in a group but from being an individual citizen. This is something that we could find a way to coalesce with.

These appear to be based on more traditionally democratic concepts.

More on democratic concepts that emphasize rights as deriving not from your membership in a group but from your being a citizen of an entity. These are producing a new dynamic, which we could cooperate with. But as a matter of principle, in a very ideological sense, we are incapable of serving in the army. It is not just an army of occupation, but an army that was established on the principle of the negation of our presence in this land. To wear that uniform is an act of perversion, of deformation.

You mean for an Arab to wear that uniform?

You can't wear it without violating a thousand moral barriers, and a thousand identity barriers. And this relates not only to the occupation of the West Bank and Gaza Strip. It is historical. The only possible democratic response is to say that, in principle, in a liberal democratic state, rights and responsibilities should be separate. You cannot make equality of rights conditional on equality of responsibilities.

Does such conditionality exist in Israel?

Yes, of course, in numerous spheres, involving numerous individual as well as collective rights.

For example?

Eligibility for housing loans, for example. But most importantly in matters of employment. For numerous types of jobs you are asked if you have served in the military. And on this basis numerous companies do not employ Arabs. They may employ Arabs as cleaners or as security guards, which apparently doesn't pose a risk. But to work as an engineer inside the premises, no. It's interesting. Many academics and engineers are therefore unable to find work and leave the country. Especially those engaged in fields like electronics, mechanical engineering, chemical engineering.

Would you say that the state has adopted a policy of "transfer" toward the Arab citizens? I don't mean this in the sense of actively deporting them, but in encouraging them to leave through various means.

There was. But now it is difficult, because people are more aware of their rights. I am certain that we live in a state that is hyperconscious of demographic issues, a state that obsessively counts, each day, how many Arabs and how many Jews live in it. In a very obsessive way. This is very important. You are constantly made aware that you are considered a demographic threat, a demographic bomb. The state is constantly counting: how can the state stem Jewish emigration from the Galilee and settle more Jews there, and so on. They are constantly counting and compiling statistics.

Of course, there is also a perpetual campaign to encourage Jews to settle in Israel, while Arab immigration is actively discouraged. This is very important. Here you see the essence of the state. Take the example of an Arab citizen of Israel who marries a person from the West Bank or Gaza Strip. In any other country, a foreign spouse is automatically provided with a residency permit and is eventually eligible for citizenship. Even in Switzerland, which is considered the most difficult European country in this respect, the spouse is entitled to live there and eventually receives a residency permit and citizenship. In Israel it takes years and years just to obtain residency status for the spouse. It creates extreme difficulty, because without a residency permit you are not entitled to health and medical insurance. It makes it excruciatingly clear that this state does not want more Arabs, only more Jews. No other explanation is possible. And don't forget, this is a state whose entire campaign against the Soviet Union during the 1970s was based on the Soviet refusal to permit family reunification, to permit spouses to immigrate to Israel in order to join their wives or husbands here.

We have thousands of such cases like this: men who marry women from Jordan, the West Bank or Gaza Strip. These women come here and have to remain illegally in order to be with their husbands, which means they can't travel or go anyplace, can't get proper medical treatment. I personally deal with hundreds of such cases: people who have been here five, six, seven years as a result of marriage, have already had several children, and still don't have residency permits.

Could you tell us when your political party was established, on what platform, and why? Were you previously a member of a different party?

A long time ago, until 1980, I was a member of the Communist Party. I left it before perestroika. Our party [the National Democratic Alliance] is an attempt to transform thought into a political platform over a longer period of time, when the establishment of new political platforms has throughout the world become difficult on account of the disintegration of ideologies, globalization, and so on. In our specific situation, we are faced with multiple disintegrations: Arab nationalism, Oslo, the Palestinian national movement, the global left. We emerged as a result of three experiences: that of the left, that of the Arab national movement, and that of the Palestinian national movement. Plus a lot of liberal democratic ideas. We tried to turn this into a political party. It has been a very difficult process, especially because we are not professional politicians. Most of us are from an academic background. Some of us were previously active in other parties, the main result of which was disappointment. Our success was a surprise. What we succeeded in doing was in establishing a democratic framework for the expression of Arab and Palestinian nationalism on the basis of a secular platform.

In any event, we acted to give expression to this platform in an Israeli context, which complicated matters further. Our role is to affirm the relationship between democracy and citizenship, between equality and citizenship; to affirm our national identity as a necessity for our ability to function in a modern society, without being an impediment to democracy.

This project is expressed on two levels. The first concerns the idea of a state of all its citizens and the development of our program of equality in the context of the struggle with Zionism. And the second is affirming our national identity as part of the modernization of Arab society and against concepts of tribalism, sectarianism, and other such alternatives.

When was the party established?

It was established in 1995, although we first began to organize immediately after the Gulf War. After Oslo, we had the impression that the Arabs within Israel were approaching a state of disintegration. There was no basis for preserving our national identity. There was a visible movement toward the Labor Party, during the period of Yitzhak Rabin and Shimon Peres [1992-96]. It was a period of genuine danger to the Arab national identity in Israel. Not because Israel was becoming more democratic, but because the sources of Arab identity were becoming increasingly weak. First the Arab national movement, the pan-Arab movement, disintegrated. Then the Palestinian national movement collapsed, or rather changed significantly. The Palestinian National Authority was established, a project very limited in scope. We saw a process of disintegration developing: if you cease to be an Arab Palestinian you are not going to become a Jew, a Swiss, or a Dane, you will become a Muslim or a Christian. The disintegration of our identity would lead to its replacement with partial, sectarian identities set against one another, and this is in fact what began to transpire, almost immediately. The events in Nazareth, for example [in which the Islamist movement was pitted against the municipality over the former's insistence on building a mosque next to the Church of the Nativity]. If anything, we felt we came too late.

You decided to contest the Knesset elections.

We decided to contest the elections after a long internal debate. A section of the movement had rejected even voting in previous Knesset elections. We came to the conclusion that it was not possible *not* to contest the elections, for the following reasons: the first is that the existence of Arabs in Israel, whether they enter the Knesset or not, is an existence filled with contradictions. If you are a lawyer, or whatever. If you carry an Israeli passport and enter Jordan on an Israeli passport, or the PA territories on an Israeli passport. There are contradictions involved here regardless of the choices you make. Refusing to enter the Knesset does not avoid them. They remain as part of your life.

The second issue is that refusing to enter the Knesset for national reasons will separate the national movement and national identity from the challenges of daily life confronting society. We came to the conclusion that the national movement had become isolated and politically sectarian and ceased to be relevant because it was unable to perceive the desire of the average Arab citizen for equality.

In 1999 you entered the prime ministerial elections as well. What is the background to this?

There were many factors involved. First, we wanted to expose the contradictions I have been discussing—between the Jewish state and its Arab citizens. It was obvious from the moment I pursued my candidacy that there was no way an Arab could become prime minister of Israel.

There were attempts to bar your candidacy.

Legislation was introduced by a Member of the Knesset, Michael Kleiner, but it didn't pass. Although it was obvious that an Arab can't become prime minister of Israel, we used the candidacy to establish a national and political identity distinct from the Labor Party. It was a precious opportunity to discuss Barak and the Likud and present a third alternative. There were of course also many Jews who weren't enamored of either candidate.

You mean to get away from the complex of being a reserve army of voters for the Labor Party?

Exactly. There was also a third issue. We gave the young generation options, a choice. And don't forget, a lot of people in the world, in Europe and the United States, didn't even know there are Arabs in Israel. Because my candidacy received a lot of international press coverage, we became part of the map. All of a sudden a lot of people discovered there are Arab citizens in Israel, and it gave us opportunities to present our case and our issues. This was very important.

We turn now to the popular upheaval by the Arab community in Israel in October 2000. There are several interpretations. The first sees it as a reaction to the discrimination or apartheid practiced against the Arab community in Israel. Another perspective sees it as an act of solidarity with the Palestinians in the West Bank and Gaza Strip. Isn't there a contradiction between these interpretations?

No, I think they complement each other. I don't think either interpretation is sufficient. There is no doubt there was a genuine display of solidarity, which was the result of what people saw in the media, the images that were projected into every home. Another factor is that the Barak government violated every promise it made to the Arab citizens of Israel. And then of course there was the factor of discrimination, and there had of course been demonstrations against land confiscation in the not too distant past [in the town of Umm al-Fahm]. But the overt, advertised, and clear reason for the demonstrations was political: solidarity with the Palestinian people [in the territories] in their battle against Barak's effort to impose his conditions on them. At Camp David the US-Israeli alliance sought to impose an unjust peace upon the Palestinians. It's beyond doubt that this was an act of political solidarity, and that is why these events, more than any conference or publication, confirmed the national identity of the Arabs in Israel. Within days it reversed years of deterioration in this national identity. It confirmed that we are an integral component of the Palestinian people and part of the Arab nation, which is preserving its identity. And maybe the most important aspect of this popular upheaval is that it was not motivated by demands concerning the concrete daily needs of the community. It represented a higher level of consciousness and direct entry into the political arena in order to demand justice.

So then the question is why now? There's been no lack of issues, whether specific to the Arab community in Israel or relevant to the Israeli-Palestinian or Arab-Israeli conflicts, that could have precipitated such an upheaval.

It happened now because there was a situation of expectations and none of them were met.

Expectations arising from Oslo?

No. Resulting from the election of the Barak government. On two levels—the level of peace and the level of equality. Barak failed on both counts, and the situation in fact got worse. It was not only the [September 29, 2000] Al-Aqsa massacre, but also the events in the West Bank and Gaza Strip during the next several days, which were televised into every home. Additionally, Hezbollah and Israel's withdrawal from Lebanon had raised people's morale. All these issues came together.

Concerning the specific events, could you give a description of what exactly happened? I think at one point there was an attack on your house.[3]

There was an attack on my house. On September 30 we called a general strike. That day, three were shot dead. The next day eight more were killed. And more the next day. We saw that every time there was a general strike more people were getting killed, so we stopped the strike. What took place was a very strong popular upheaval characterized by civil disobedience. Popular demonstrations, closure of streets, general strikes, and so on.

The Northern Command of the Israeli Police—and specifically its chief officer, commander Alik Ron—has for several years openly held the view that the Arabs need to be taught a lesson, and without doing so the problem of radicalization won't be solved. I'm talking about a police officer who gives press conferences to express such views, names us by name, and so on.

It was obvious that they had something in store for us, and had been preparing for quite some time. Their actions during October 2000 amounted to a military occupation of the Arab villages in Israel. It was not an issue of discrimination, but rather one in which all the masks came off.

In my view their actions exposed the nature of the Barak government more than anything else did. Not so much because they did or did not give orders to open fire, but because we repeatedly warned them, and specifically Minister of Public Security Shlomo Ben-Ami, that there was a disaster waiting to happen. I myself wrote Ben-Ami more than ten times, concerning incidents of excessive use of force. Cases in Jaffa where people would be beaten to a pulp, and then falsely charged. A demonstration at the Hebrew University, where Arab students were beaten up in front of my eyes, and subsequently those who were attacked, rather than their attackers, were arrested and charged. Even now, after the upheaval, this is still going on. I, a member of the Knesset, for example, was shot. A member of the security forces aims at a member of Parliament who is defending a home in Lydda, shoots at him, he is wounded, and the incident is not even investigated!

Therefore, this is not a question of offering apologies or expressing regret, neither of which can be accepted. They— Ben-Ami and Barak—are personally responsible for the killing of thirteen people. They did not need to die. During the exact same period, Jewish mobs attacked Arab towns and villages, and also my own home, in actions reminiscent of Europe during the 1930s. Not a single demonstrator was arrested or charged. Neither for mob attacks against Arab civilians, nor for attempting to burn down the home of a member of the Knesset. Imagine what would have happened if 300 Arabs had attacked the home of a Jewish member of the Knesset and tried to burn it down!

I think this is one important difference between the events of October 2000 and Land Day in 1976, namely the participation of mobs now as opposed to 1976, where the repression was conducted only by the security forces.

Yes, non-uniformed thugs and marginal elements of Jewish society played a prominent part in October 2000. They didn't just attack Arabs, but also places like Jewish-owned restaurants that employ Arabs. Jewish-owned property that was inhabited by Arab tenants was burned down. There were numerous physical attacks against Arabs; a lot were severely beaten. Many such incidents, involving severe violence, took place in the Hatikva neighborhood of Tel Aviv, Tiberias, Ramat Gan, and many other places. In East Jerusalem settlers went on the rampage several times. There were attempted pogroms against the Arab population: beatings, burnings of homes. Natzeret Illit [the Jewish settlement established above Nazareth, which Arabs refuse to call Upper Nazareth because it is not part of the city] was the most important such act. Not a single Jew was wounded. Not only was not a single Jew wounded, but three policemen were wounded by Jewish demonstrators. On our side hundreds were wounded, many severely, including those who lost an eye, required intensive care, sustained broken bones, and so on—in addition, of course, to the thirteen Arabs who were killed.

This was during the tenure of the Peace Now government, when the "peace movement" held the reins of power. And that is why I say that it was during this period that all the masks came off. The right was in opposition, so there was nobody on our side. The movement that is supposed to defend our rights was the one that was killing us. If the right had been in power the peace movement would have been demonstrating with us against it. But it was doing the killing, so the entire Israeli society was mobilized. From the army to the media, shapers of public opinion. It was unbelievable. They were blaming us not for taking to the streets, but for doing so while they were in power. It was full of rage and fury. Their line was, "You are embarrassing us, you're threatening our interests. How dare you do this to us?" Their egocentrism is beyond description.

By the way, this is something you don't find among the right wing. The right at least sees things as they are. But the left was not unlike Barak's conduct in the occupied territories, as if to say, "If you demonstrate even against me, it's obvious Israel doesn't have partners." So there was an important element of paternalism in the government's actions. This was what distinguished the reactions of people like Amos Oz and A.B. Yehoshua. They attacked us without mercy or reservation, and were nowhere to be seen during the entire upheaval. Not an ounce of solidarity. This is not something we are going to forget. When push came to shove these intellectuals who consider themselves the conscience of Israeli society sided with the killers against the killed. Full stop. And we're talking about aggression against citizens of the state. Of course, some of them came afterward, solely to express their condolences. But even in the houses of mourning they saw fit to start blaming us. No such thing as a political statement blaming the police for their use of deadly force, blaming Alik Ron and calling for his dismissal, or anything of the sort.

And this they would have done if Benjamin Netanyahu had been in power?

Of course they would have. And this makes them hypocrites of the worst sort. They therefore created an inseparable moral gap between us. Between the liberal Jewish Israeli elite, on the one hand, and the liberal, progressive, democratic Arabs. Not only do we reject their paternalism; we reject them emotionally as well as morally. Don't forget, we were left entirely alone, and in fact attacked, when we were most in need of their solidarity, when it really counted. I was receiving numerous death threats on a daily basis, and my house was attacked. Not one Zionist writer, intellectual, or member of the Knesset has condemned any of this. Silence, deafening silence. I felt like a Jewish intellectual in Europe during the 1930s, whose neighbors all of a sudden can't recognize him anymore. Unbelievable. Of course the anti-Zionist Jews, many of whom are my personal friends, behaved quite differently and honorably so. But apart from them, nobody. The Speaker of the Knesset, whose primary responsibility is to defend this body and its members, who gets paid to do so, never condemned these attacks. Unbelievable.

Regarding the attacks of the Jewish mobs, do you think these were genuine attacks, in the sense of elements of Jewish Israeli society inciting the mob and launching these attacks, or were they encouraged and/or directed by the state and security forces?

No. They were genuine. But they were also encouraged by the security forces and protected by them. Most important, the actions of the mobs were legitimized by the actions of the police, who were shooting at us and killing us. This combination of actions made our lives very cheap indeed. Once the police began acting in this way and killing people, anything became acceptable; the limits were removed.

I think in Nazareth the police played an important role in assisting the mobs.

Yes. The police entered the city with the mob and began shooting at people who were defending their homes, killing two of them and wounding many others.

I would like to return now to your platform of transforming Israel into a state of all its citizens. To put it simply, you seek to convert Israel from a Jewish state into a state like any other democratic one, for example the United States or Spain.

This platform is really a compass, according to which we map our path. It is not a political program, in the sense of something I propose as legislation in the Knesset to be voted on, to change the character of the state. The Zionist project is over 100 years old, and it's going to be around for a while. This is a long struggle.

Our platform leads us to examine the sensitive junctures in this setup, like the demolitions of Arab homes and the legal and legislative issues surrounding such matters. If the state claims to treat its citizens equally, we want to see that claim carried out. Our platform gives us instructions, strategic objectives, and possibilities to divide our agenda into smaller questions that are relevant to our overall goal. And it gives us the opportunity to propose a whole series of issues and questions that have not been discussed before. At the same time, it has transformed the struggle for equality from a discussion about toleration into a discussion about rights. Equality is my right; I refuse to be simply tolerated. Secondly, we conduct our struggle for equality while preserving our national identity. So to get back to your question: no, Israel is not going to be transformed from a Jewish state to a state of all its citizens.

It seems your struggle is similar, say, to demanding the introduction of capitalism in the Soviet Union, because at the end of the day you are proposing a platform that stands in direct contradiction to the essential character of what is an ideological state.

Exactly. I think that the state will become a state for all its citizens only if it ceases to be a Jewish state. And this can only happen if it first becomes a binational state. The phase we are in now is the struggle to create a binational state, or rather to popularize the concept of a binational state, in which we preserve our national identity. At the same time, we are demanding equality for the nationalities within the state. To neutralize the role of the state in issues of religion, for example. We now have a state in which there are two groups, a Jewish majority and an Arab minority. The only way this will become a state for all its citizens is if, first, these two groups are no longer defined as a majority versus a minority but as two equal groups with equal identities treated on an equal basis. And this can only happen within a binational framework.

The principle of binationalism will not lead to the immediate failure of the concept of separation between Israel and the occupied territories, at least not during this generation. But we will have opened the road in this respect.

There is a criticism of your platform which states that the real, and also the achievable, agenda for Palestinians today is the struggle for equality within Israel and the struggle for independence in the occupied territories. And what you are doing, by proposing binationalism and a state for all its citizens, is in effect moving the goalposts to unachievable terrain, and thereby undercutting struggles that have a reasonable prospect of success.

We are not proposing binationalism. We are practicing it. We're not that childish and immature. To the contrary, our position is that if a Palestinian state is created in the West Bank and Gaza Strip this would be a big achievement for the Palestinian people. And we don't just make statements in this respect, we struggle on behalf of the establishment of such a state. And we struggle to ensure that no deal is achieved that provides the Palestinian people with less than this.

But we also look at the longer term. We raise the question as to what such a state will achieve with respect to the situation within Israel. We talk about equality while realizing fully that equality for Arabs within the framework of a Jewish state is an impossibility. Therefore, within the state of Israel, the question about the contradiction between the concept of equality and the reality of a Jewish state needs to remain on the agenda. These tensions and this question will remain precisely because we continue to propose the concept of a state for all its citizens.

The proposal of a state for all its citizens is made on the basis of two identities. One is the identity of a majority and the other is the identity of a minority. This is not binationalism. Binationalism is where you have an equal status accorded to national identities, as in Belgium, for example. This will happen if the road is opened to it in the future. We don't see a contradiction at present. To the contrary, we have initiated our struggle and we actively participate in the struggle of the Palestinian people to establish an independent state in the territories occupied in 1967. But if the principle of separation fails—and perhaps it will be Ariel Sharon who causes it to fail—then another and entirely different discussion becomes possible and necessary.

Many of your proposals concern issues of identity and cultural autonomy and the right to preserve these in a larger political entity. On this basis I ask the following question: While granting that Israel is a colonial-settler state, do Jews in Israel in your view have the right—whether out of principle or in practice—to retain an ethnic majority in order to ensure their own culture? Do they have the right to preserve for themselves what you are demanding for yourself?

When you are speaking of groups and collective entities you don't speak in the language of rights. Do the Jews have rights? Every individual Jew has rights, but the Jews as a group do not have rights. They are a group with an imposed identity. They are not practicing it as a right. You have the state, and the state apparatus that is constructing its own version of the Jewish identity and imposing it on both Jews and history. Out of many and quite different Jewish histories it is constructing a single Jewish history, a national history. It is creating a new identity—that of a uniform, continuous, and unchanging Jewish identity that is said to have existed throughout history—and imposing it on Jewish society.

 Having said that, there is an identity that has developed among Jews in the state, and there is a rich Hebrew culture. I see it with my own eyes, and it is of course a very legitimate identity and culture.

A particularly Israeli Jewish one?

Hebrew culture. Around language, around experience, around the Israeli experience. There is a new culture that was constructed and developed here. Whatever I may think of it, it is there. There is now a collective group, it has an identity, and I would say it even has a national identity now, which is a

Hebrew national identity. But it is not recognized by Zionism or the Israeli state. The biggest contradiction here is that they do not recognize the product of their own work! Zionism succeeded in creating a national group that Zionism does not recognize. Instead, it insists on a traditional religious collective group called the Jewish community. The only thing Zionism has succeeded in creating is the Hebrew nationality in Palestine; it was created from literally nothing and the consistency of the political project that bred it demands admiration. From nothing, and now it has institutions, a state apparatus, rules of the game, democracy for the Jews, a high standard of living, a language, and a culture—a very rich culture, with internal differentiations, and so on. Yet Zionism refuses to recognize any of this and continues to insist that the Jews in New York and Moscow and South Africa and Ethiopia are a single collective, unified on the basis of religion. So the biggest contradiction in the future, in my view, is their refusal to recognize the nationality that they have constructed (every nationality is constructed; there is no nationality that has not been constructed) and their insistence on this primordial, larger, and unconstructed thing, which is religious affiliation.

On this same point—what you are demanding when you talk about cultural autonomy and rights of groups, whether of a minority or otherwise—isn't there a contradiction between collective and individual rights?

No. There is a long tradition of philosophical discussion about these subjects, and liberal democratic thought has developed in these respects. Liberal democratic thought used to reject the concept of groups and grant rights only to the individual. And then you had republican democratic thought, in which the individual is not recognized but derives his rights from affiliation with or commitment to a certain collectivity of origins (ethnicity) or of patriotism (republican virtues) among others. Now in the contemporary phase of modernity this is all in flux and new possibilities are arising. It is possible to strike a balance between collective and individual rights, as long as we see that collective rights are derived from individual rights and not the other way around. It is the right of the individual to have a national identity and belong to a national group, and not the other way around.

Historically, of course, it was the other way around. Historically, people were individualized within a collective group; the individual emerged from the group and not the group from the individual. The society, the community, came first, and then the individual. Although historically false, I need to start with the individual, and I presume that society is a network of voluntary contracts between individuals. I have to suppose this in order to have a liberal democratic approach to society. Now, you can balance between individual and collective rights. On some issues—murder, for example—there is no cultural autonomy. A murder is a murder. No collective group will have the right to give it a ritual or cultural interpretation and say that it is a legitimate act. There have to be shared and common values accepted by and equally applicable to everyone, like personal freedom, human dignity. But on issues of language and culture, for example, you provide autonomy.

I have one last question. Previously, you said that disappointment with the Barak government was an important background factor in explaining the October 2000 upheaval. More broadly, how did Oslo affect Palestinian society within Israel? At the beginning, there was a lot of talk of "now we are no longer seen as a fifth column," "Arabs in Israel will form a bridge between Israel and the Arab world," and so on.

There are a lot of conflicting and contradictory perspectives on this question. Many people, for example, sought to justify their Israelization by stating that the PLO had betrayed us and left us with no choice but to become good Israelis, and so on. This is in my view no more than a justification offered by people who never wanted the PLO to begin with. These are people who wanted to advance the process of Israelization all along. Oslo removed a burden from their shoulders. It became possible for them to write about the process of Israelization, and they were able to soothe their bad conscience by claiming that they had been abandoned by the PLO rather than abandoning their attachment to their national identity. The advocates of Israelization began stating, "Look, now there is peace. Weren't you always demanding that the Labor Party make peace with the PLO? Well, it just has, so why don't we all join it? Why don't we join the army as well?" Contesting this is one of the reasons our party exists, and in fact it speeded up the process of establishing it. We had to contest this trend at the ballot box, because we felt the momentum toward the Zionist parties was gathering pace.

At the same time, the PLO, in the context of its engagement with the peace process, ceased to make any demands regarding the rights of the Arabs in Israel. Its demands began to be made of the Arabs rather than on their behalf. They wanted us to become a reserve army for the Israeli peace movement. Paradoxically, the Palestinian national movement began to have more in common with the Arabs collaborating with mainstream Zionist parties than with us. These forces weren't an irritant to it or to the peace process, and they were seen not as forces that would debate the PLO or engage in solidarity with the Palestinian people or get involved in specific causes, but as forces that would support those within Israeli society who were prepared to negotiate with the PLO.

We of course rejected this. We rejected the idea of being a bridge, because we didn't want people walking all over us, which is, after all, the main function of a bridge. A bridge is an object, not a subject. Imagine, people living within the frontiers of the state, who have a very rich experience, and you ask them to lie down so you can walk on their backs! Here a contradiction was created with my own demands and my own identity. We are a part of the national struggle of the Palestinian people that is no less important than any of its other components. Preserving the national identity and lands of a million Palestinians within Israel is no different from what is going on in the Gaza Strip or the West Bank. We are part of the Palestinian national struggle, but the fact that it takes also the form of solidarity with the just cause of the Palestinians under occupation and the Palestinian refugees does not mean that we just obey anybody who asks us to put it aside and support any solution even if it is unjust, or give up our national identity and disintegrate our society in order not to alienate the Labor

Party, for example. So in the beginning this created a certain level of tension between the Palestinian National Authority and the young democratic national movement that we established within the Green Line, but experience made them not only respect our will, but also listen to what we have to say.

Notes

1. Human Rights Watch, *Investigation into the Unlawful Use of Force in the West Bank, Gaza Strip, and Northern Israel*, Vol. 12, No. 3(E), October 2000.

2. There are about 900,000 Palestinian citizens of Israel, 19 percent of the total population. "History of the Arabs in Israel," Adalah: The Legal Center for Arab Minority Rights in Israel (www.adalah.org).

3. In November 2000, Prime Minister Ehud Barak announced the formation of an official Commission of Inquiry, under the chairmanship of Supreme Court Justice Theodor Or, to investigate the October events. The Or Commission began hearing testimony in mid-February, soon after the election of Ariel Sharon, and is still in session as this book goes to press. So far, police involved in the clashes have contradicted initial Israeli government claims that live ammunition was not used against the demonstrators. In addition, police have testified that Northern District Commander Alik Ron gave instructions by remote telecommunication to officers on the ground during the events, ordering them to fire live ammunition at specific demonstrators, in conditions where the officers' lives were not in danger (Israeli officials have never claimed that any of the demonstrators used firearms). Dr. Stephen Males, an expert in riot control who accompanied an Amnesty International investigation into the October events, said, "My view was that the police failed in their policing role—they used weaponry and tactics more suitable for an armed conflict than for crowd control." One of the policemen testified that when he was off-duty he joined a mob of Jewish rioters who stoned Bishara's house in Nazareth.

8. GAZA: A REPORT FROM THE FRONT

ALISON WEIR

February 2001

I don't want to be overly dramatic, but I was sort of shot at yesterday.

I say "sort of" because I don't think the Israeli soldiers in their tower were trying to hit me, or the people with me. If that had been their purpose I have no doubt that they would have. There is massive evidence here that their aim is quite good. I think they were simply asserting their power. And I think they were trying to intimidate me, as a foreigner, into leaving the area.

There were no "clashes." There was no stone-throwing. Everything was quiet. I was being shown around Khan Yunis, a bullet-riddled refugee camp in southern Gaza filled with ragged, barefoot kids and angry, resigned, perplexed parents. "Why are they doing this to us?" people kept saying to me. "Why they do this Palestine people? They say we guns. Where guns? Why America help Israel? Why America not help Palestinians?"

Houses were riddled—and I mean riddled—with bullets. There were two-foot-wide holes in roofs where mortars had come through. People showed me around their homes. For the most part they had moved into areas away from the outside, where, they hoped, they would be safe—huddled on mattresses on the floor. They showed me around one house right at the periphery of the camp. It had lovely, bullet-riddled archways inside, the remains of a tiled kitchen. When the children saw I was curious about the bullets, they gathered them for me by handfuls—smashed, distorted pieces of metal that tear through walls and people. I'll try to bring some back. I wonder if Israel will let me bring my souvenirs of their country.

They opened a door a few inches for me—they were afraid to do more, they know what happens if you do—and I could see a guard tower a few hundred meters away. Even I was afraid—usually so easily brave, armed with my middle-class American feeling of invulnerability. I've read too many reports of injuries in just such situations, seen too many pictures of people with bandages over eyes that have been shot out. Earlier in the day I saw a picture of four boys probably about 7–12 sitting on chairs in a waiting room somewhere, looking at the camera with no expression on their faces, and each with a large piece of gauze where one of their eyes should be. They were the lucky kids—these were only rubber bullets, and they hadn't gone into the brain. Did I say no expression? Perhaps the expression is beyond describing…of being old far beyond their small bodies.

So when I looked out at the guard tower where soldiers with sniper scopes and binoculars were no doubt watching us, I too was nervous.

Left: A young boy ducks to avoid potential Israeli gunfire in Rafah, Gaza

We continued to wander around the camp—groups of smiling children coming up, saying *salaam*, hello, giggling. The streets were Gaza sand. The ocean is probably only half a mile away, but these children never get to swim in it. There are soldiers in between. Instead they play in the dirt.

I needed batteries for my camera, so we went to a tiny store. The owner gave us small glasses of strong coffee, and would take no money for the batteries.

Intense, frustrated, he pointed out what his life had become. He showed the inevitable bullet holes in his store, the larger hole where a missile had entered a store room, destroying what looked like fifty five-gallon jugs of oil. He showed me his house next door—full of bullet holes, and told me about his children, who luckily had remained uninjured, if trauma and subjugation don't count as injuries. He told me that all he wanted was peace, to live his life. Again, he asked why Israel was doing this, why America was doing this.

What could I answer? All I could try to do was explain that Americans don't know that this is going on—that their newspapers and television don't tell them. And so Americans think it is a complicated issue, and that it doesn't involve them.

Amazingly, I don't find people hostile toward me, as an American, even though they so clearly know America's role in their suffering. By the way, "suffering" is a word they use often in trying to tell me what their lives are like. They always smile at me, shake my hand. When they hear I am from America, they virtually always say, "Welcome."

We wandered over to another house, on the other side of town. I saw a family home no longer livable—bullet holes everywhere, large hole in the roof—another once-lovely home, and probably loved home, with an interior garden and children's toys, and bullets scattered on the floor.

It was when we went outside of this home that the gunshots occurred. We were behind a wall, so it didn't feel scary. Of course, feelings lie—I had seen numerous holes through such walls. They showed us another way out. At the time, I didn't take the gunshots personally. Once again, as a middle-class American, I didn't think anyone was firing near me on purpose—I thought it was just an accident, a coincidence. But as I've thought about it further, I think I was wrong. Why then? There? In that particular part of town?

And this would fit the pattern I've heard about lately. A few days ago when the UN team investigating human rights violations was here in Gaza they were shot at. The Canadian ambassador was shot at. A young American documentary filmmaker I met this morning had been in Khan Yunis a few days ago, and had been shot at. He showed me footage of the Israelis shooting at him: He is letting the camera roll as he walks on a dirt road following five or six small boys. None are throwing rocks. It is quiet. There is a tank at the end of the road—this is nothing unusual. They continue walking. Suddenly there are gunshots, the camera tilts. No one is injured. But the army has made its point. Except it didn't work. He went back today.

I asked him if he had a time frame for making his documentary. He said until he ran out of money or got shot, whichever came first. It wasn't much of a joke.

Have you heard about the American stringer for AP who was shot a few months ago?—a young woman, her name is in another notebook (I'm at an Internet cafe in Gaza City with the slowest computers on earth)—but I think she was about 26. Mark, a 30-year-old freelance English photographer I've just met, knew her, and told me about it. The Israelis shot her in the pelvis, destroying her spleen and uterus. They say it was an accident. She says they knew quite clearly that she was a journalist. Israel is apparently investigating how this could have happened. Was this reported in the press? Will we hear the results of the investigation? Wouldn't you think this would have been headlines? Shouldn't it have been? If she had been shot by Palestinians don't you think it would have been?

Another man today told me about working with a Fox film crew, when suddenly they were shot at by the Israelis. They barely managed to escape, and they filmed it all. But Fox never aired it. He told me the problem with the US coverage wasn't the crews, it was management back in the States. I believe him.

Some people in the refugee camp told me about a new gas bomb the Israelis shot at them last weekend. They said it had black smoke, and a "good" smell. At least forty people are still hospitalized from it—I'm going to pin the number down tomorrow. Apparently there are people in several hospitals, so the true number could be considerably higher.

From the refugee camp we went to Al Amal Hospital. I saw a 22-year-old man in the ICU. He was moaning and had IVs in both arms. He said it felt like knives in his intestines. Sometimes he had trouble breathing. His mother and aunt were hovering over him. His little sister was sitting next to him. I went to another ward and saw six more. I met a father who was obviously distraught—two of his sons were in the hospital. I saw two men have seizures while I was there.

They all said the same thing. They had just been going about their lives when suddenly "bombs" came into their houses. Some had been outside, and had gone in to rescue people because they thought the house was on fire. But they said there was no flame, just black smoke, and a good smell. In most cases nothing happened immediately, but after ten to fifteen minutes they collapsed. Some became unconscious. Israel is, as usual, denying that there was anything unusual about this gas. As usual, they are lying.

Apparently, this also explains a lot of the bias in the US press. The reporters in Jerusalem and Tel Aviv get their numbers and "facts" from military spokesmen. Information from Israeli sources is printed; information from Palestinian sources isn't.

You see, an Israeli is one of us. A relative, a friend's relative, a colleague's relative. We hear distorted versions of what is going on from these friends and colleagues, and we think they know what they're talking about. And that they're not biased. Because they sound so reasonable and confident and knowledgeable. They say just enough about what is wrong about Israel, about the "two sides," to seem neutral. This is BS.

The problem is when you know the truth, it is far too much to describe, far too cruel…far too diametrically opposite what we used to think and what everyone still thinks to express. It is hard not to sound fanatic, over-wrought, biased. The lie is too big, the repression too complete, the Palestinians' lives too horrible to write about reasonably. I find it difficult to write anything—rare for me—because there is so so so much. You have to retrieve and redefine the very words out of the newspeak that Israel has created of "closures" and "bypass roads" and "security."

So I think maybe I should try to take on just one topic at a time—and for now, this new gas. Today I was going to visit the Ministry of Health for more information, and then back to the Khan Yunis hospitals with Mark to take photos. But he didn't show up at the scheduled time. Probably something just came up. But over here you always worry. Tomorrow I'll go.

There is so much to try to describe. Who will ever believe all this? Israel couldn't possibly be this cruel, this arrogant. Who will believe it? They must have a good reason. There are two sides here, of course…just the way there was in South Africa's apartheid period.

I also visited two tiny encampments of women and children living in tents on the dirt. They were people who used to have homes in Khan Yunis, but the Israelis decided to make a road through them— for "security"? to divide the people? to terrorize them? just because they wanted to? who ever knows? an absolute conqueror doesn't have to explain—so they bulldozed their homes and their date palms and orange groves.

The people are living in the dirt. They show me a bent-up aluminum wash pan that they retrieved from where their homes had been—everything else, they said, was "under the land." Again, they asked me why America was helping Israel do this to them. Why did Bill Clinton do this? Would George Bush still do this? They're on a first-name basis with our presidents. And we don't even know about them. One old, newly poor woman knew all the international news—she had been given a radio and listens to BBC, French broadcasts, German broadcasts, etc. She hears the Israeli statements. The US government positions. She's living in rags in the dirt now. Four months ago she and her husband had two homes—they had just built another one for their son, who had been married just two months when his new home was bulldozed.

The Palestinians have been pleading for an international team for months to come over to protect them from the Israelis—but the US keeps blocking this. Why? How could this be even imagined to threaten Israel's "security"? But you'll be happy to know that the international community isn't ignoring them—it contributed the fly-covered, floor-less tents that the people are living in. Meanwhile, how much aid did we give to Israel today? Eight million was it? Sixteen million? And tomorrow we'll give it to them again, and the next day, and the next day, and the next day…

They gave me tea, as we sat surrounded by dirt, and told me to tell America to stop doing this to them. I'll try. Maybe you could try too.

9. PALESTINE'S TELL-TALE HEART
OMAR BARGHOUTI

Introduction

More than a century and a half ago Edgar Allan Poe wrote "The Tell-Tale Heart," in which a young man decides to kill a kind old man who "never wronged" him, simply because "he had the eye of a vulture." Whenever he looked at the eye, his "blood ran cold," as it "chilled the very marrow" in his bones. But in order to kill the old man, he had to shine a ray of light on his "pale blue eye," alone in the otherwise complete darkness, so as not to see anything else "of the man's face or person." When he was about to commit the murder, he heard "a low, dull, quick sound"; it was the "beating of the [terrified] old man's heart." It only increased his fury, "as the beating of a drum stimulates the soldier into courage."

After suffocating the old man, he dismembered his corpse and carefully concealed the parts under the floor planks. The old man's last shriek before dying, however, alarmed the neighbors, who called the police. Upon their arrival, the young man received them with confidence, even inviting them to search the old man's room, bringing chairs for them, and "in the wild audacity of [his] perfect triumph, [he] placed [his] own seat upon the very spot beneath which reposed the corpse of the victim." He began to hear a ringing sound, which grew in intensity despite all his attempts to speak louder to cover it up. It grew louder by the minute, until he felt that he "must scream or die." "Anything was better than this agony," he thought, until he finally screamed, "I admit the deed!—tear up the planks!… It is the beating of his hideous heart!"[1]

The second Palestinian intifada is to Israel the tell-tale heart of the old Palestine, which has obstinately refused to rest in peace, even half a century after it was dismembered, entombed and shrouded in forgetfulness. The *Nakba*—catastrophe—of 1948, in which more than 750,000 Palestinians were driven off their native land, has come to dominate the political discourse. In response, Israelis from across the political spectrum, stirring up a deep-rooted "victimology," as Rabbi Mayer Schiller calls it,[2] cry "existential threat!"

Israeli researcher Meron Benvenisti puts the blame for this "unwelcome" remembrance on the Israeli establishment's effort to garner an increasingly elusive internal cohesion: "the Zionist establishment has found a new *raison d'être*: To encourage the pampered warriors of the 'final battle [of 1948]' and to lubricate the axis of the 'threat to Israel's existence.' The temptation to erase an entire half-century is so strong that even the government itself has succumbed to it and is reinforcing a sense of deja-vu."[3]

Left: A rock thrower hit in the head by an Israeli rubber bullet gets carried to safety in Ramallah

One Ariel Sharon supporter, a recent immigrant to Israel from the former Soviet Union, was perhaps more representative of Israeli public discourse when she said, "The country is on the verge of annihilation! We need someone to save the country, someone who will say publicly that Oslo is a suicidal process. We have to stop giving territory to the Palestinians, because the more we give, the more appetite they have. Look at the map! Israel is surrounded by a sea of wild, cruel and hungry Arabs."[4]

An examination of the hard facts of the intifada—the grossly disproportionate suffering of the Palestinians—cannot corroborate this wildly exaggerated "threat." On the contrary, it indicates that Israeli officials and intellectuals are crying wolf. From this viewpoint, evoking apocalyptic fear, often by warning of a second Holocaust, expresses an addiction to media manipulation and the inversion of truth in a desperate attempt to cover up the slow massacre, to evade the moral responsibility involved, and to beg for sympathy from an increasingly skeptical world.

Agreeing that such calls are terribly exaggerated, more sophisticated Zionist intellectuals view the purported "existential threat" in sharply different terms. Yossi Beilin, Ehud Barak's Justice Minister, expressed a common theme in Zionist ideology when he asserted that "the long conflict with our Arab neighbors was not part of the plan of the founders of Zionism," who strove "to live a normal, peaceful life in this country." Slipping into perpetual conflict will therefore "bring a fatal winter to the Zionist dream," whereby "those who are young and flexible enough will leave the country, and Jews who live in developed countries will not consider joining us."[5] Singing the same tune, *New York Times* columnist Thomas Friedman reminds us that although Israel is a "powerful, powerful country—a nuclear-armed Sparta" that is not about to collapse as a result of Palestinian intifadas, its soft underbelly lies within, "from a sense that the country was trapped forever in a grinding conflict," which could eventually "prompt Israel's best and brightest to leave."[6]

Addressing the crucial need for normality, Henry Kissinger, who advocates a Palestinian "formal renunciation of all future claims," writes, "Israel regards peace as a culmination of the struggle for a homeland and defines it as a normality that ends claims and determines a permanent legal status."[7] This "normality" is essentially defined as the perpetuation of the Zionist project, embodied in the existence of Israel as the Jewish state. And since the intifada, with its various dimensions discussed below, radically disturbs or threatens the prospects for achieving such a goal, it is by definition viewed by Zionists as an existential threat.

This fear for the existence of the state is not simply a transitory demonstration of collective paranoia; nor is it just an extreme case of populist fear-mongering. In fact, its consistent articulation in the official as well as the intellectual discourse indicates something much more deep-rooted. It is my contention that Israel's "existential fear," when interpreted as a concern for the continuity, legality and moral foundations of Israel qua Jewish state, is quite genuine, though morally deplorable. It emanates from several compelling facts exposed by the Al-Aqsa Intifada, whose heartbeat has resurrected the initial crime committed by the Zionists in 1948 against the indigenous Arab-Palestinian people. As the Israeli writer Benjamin Beit-Hallahmi says, "Israelis seem to be haunted by…the curse of the original sin against the native Arabs. How can Israel be discussed without recalling the dispossession and exclusion of non-Jews? This is the most basic fact about Israel, and no understanding of Israeli reality is possible without it. The original sin haunts and torments Israelis: it marks everything and taints everybody. Its memory poisons the blood and marks every moment of existence."[8]

I will focus on three aspects of the current intifada that touch on this perceived existential crisis:

1) the brutality used by Israel in its attempt to suppress the Palestinian revolt, revealing a dehumanization reminiscent of that which permeated the "original sin";

2) the brief yet full participation of the marginalized Palestinian citizens of Israel in the intifada, shattering the illusion of coexistence with colonialism and beginning the process of relinking them with their Palestinian co-nationals in the West Bank, in Gaza, and in the diaspora;

3) the prominent rebirth of the Palestinian and Arab near-consensus on the Right of Return for the *Nakba* refugees and their descendants, which has inspired a long-dormant debate on the moral foundations of the Jewish state.

Dehumanization

International human rights organizations, the United Nations, and people of conscience throughout the world have been unanimous in condemning Israel's excessive use of force. Amnesty International went as far as declaring that "there is a pattern of gross human rights violations that may well amount to war crimes."[9] I shall concentrate here on the moral dimension of this issue, by examining the dehumanization involved in treating one particularly vulnerable and innocent sector of Palestinian victims: children.

Few issues evoke as wide a consensus of denunciation as the intentional injury of a child. The overwhelming evidence, carefully gathered by human rights workers and journalists alike, proves beyond doubt Israel's deliberate shooting of Palestinian children during this intifada. The language of dehumanization has seen fit to brand these children as "enemies," "beasts," "tormenting attackers" and "terrorists." Even some Israeli army officials have been appalled at the intentional killings. *Ha'aretz* quoted a senior officer saying, "Nobody can convince me we didn't needlessly kill dozens of children."[10] Some of the most revealing instances will help substantiate this claim.

Even before the current intifada, in Hebron in 1996, an Israeli settler fatally pistol-whipped 11-year-old Hilmi Shusha. The Israeli judge first acquitted the murderer, saying the child "died on his own as a result of 'emotional pressure.'" After numerous appeals and under pressure from the Supreme Court, which termed the act "light killing," the judge reconsidered and, as the new intifada was raging, sentenced the killer to six months' community service and a fine of a few thousand dollars. The boy's father accused the court of issuing a "license to kill."[11] Gideon Levy of *Ha'aretz* described the fine as the "end-of-the-season clearance price" on children's lives, and referred as well to the findings of the Israeli human rights organization B'tselem, which documented dozens of similar cases in which perpetrators were either acquitted or received a slap on the wrist.[12]

Several human rights organizations, including the Boston-based Physicians for Human Rights, have documented a pattern in which Israeli sharpshooters have targeted the eyes or knees of Palestinian children with "clear intention to harm." Tel Aviv University professor Tanya Reinhart writes, "A common practice is shooting a rubber-coated metal bullet straight in the eye—a little game of well-trained soldiers, which requires maximum precision."[13] The snipers could see only those eyes, the "vulture eyes," without the face, the person, the human child behind the eyes, and they "took them out" with "professionalism."

What is revolting to Palestinians in the above events is not just the extreme cruelty but also the painful memories they stir up. A Jewish veteran of the 1948 Zionist conquest of Palestine was quoted in the Israeli paper *Davar* describing an exceptionally disturbing aspect of the 1948 massacre in the Palestinian village of Dawayma by Israel's 89th Commando Battalion during the Negev Offensive, saying, "To kill the children [the Jewish soldiers] fractured their heads with sticks. There was not one house without corpses."[14] The chief British investigator of another 1948 massacre, at Deir Yassin, where some 250 Palestinian civilians were slaughtered by the Irgun and Stern terror organizations, documented that "many infants were also butchered." The killing of 12-year-old Muhammad al-Durra on September 30, 2000, captured by a French video crew and transmitted all over the world, and the slow death of a 10-year-old girl from Nablus of a burst appendix due to the siege,[15] must be seen in this context, as conforming to a rule, rather than being sad exceptions.

Outside the children's world, Israel's ethical record was hardly less astounding: Extrajudicial executions (now "legalized" by Israel's Attorney General[16]), shooting unarmed, handcuffed detainees,[17] preventing ambulances for hours from saving the lives of the wounded,[18] killing innocent passers-by because of "battle fatigue," taking "photographs of themselves with their [badly battered Palestinian] victims, holding their heads by the hair like hunting trophies,"[19] were all acts in this ghastly repertoire of death. One scene was described in a letter to *Ha'aretz* from a former Israeli army officer, who said, "I was shocked to see [Israeli army] soldiers dragging a bleeding young Palestinian in the streets of Hebron. The shocking image showed our soldiers as sadists who rejoice over the killing of a young man, and drag his body to our settlers to rejoice, dance, exchange candy and congratulations and kick the not-yet-dead body."[20] (Immediately after the Deir Yassin massacre in 1948, Irgun leader Menachem Begin sent a note to the attackers saying, "Accept congratulations on this splendid act of conquest. Tell the soldiers you have made history in Israel."[21]) The conscientious ex-officer said, "It reminds me of cheetahs and hyenas, which kill and drag their prey. The problem is these animals kill to survive. Our soldiers kill to maintain the occupation, an apartheid system."

Unfortunately, such utterances of moral outrage by Israelis have been rare in this intifada. Only a small minority have publicly protested the immorality of the killings. Most representatives of the "left" were chiefly concerned about the adverse effect on the Israeli image abroad, as polls have shown. Their support of Barak's internationally condemned policy as "restrained," "geared toward peace," "politically necessary," and a "measured response to Palestinian violence" exposes their true moral decadence, another aspect of which will be revealed in the discussion of their views on the Right of Return. In November 2000 Barak showed the extent of his concern for Palestinian life, saying, "If we thought that instead of 200 dead [Palestinians] there, that 2,000 dead would end this whole issue…then we would use more force."[22]

For Palestinians too young to remember 1948, the Israeli practices and underlying ideological convictions have been a crash course in history, politics and ethics. For those Palestinians old enough to remember, it is as if the Israelis have been giving a repeat performance after a thunderous wave of "encore!" by a cheering Israeli public (those who have not cheered have, with a few commendable exceptions, stood by in apathetic silence). The long-forgotten initial colonization finally took center stage, inspiring an entirely different discourse.

Palestinians in Israel: Self-Emancipation Versus "Normalcy"

With sharp insight, Frantz Fanon notes:

> Colonialism is not simply content to impose its rule upon the present and the future of a dominated country. Colonialism is not satisfied merely with holding a people in its grip and emptying the native's brain of all form and content. By a kind of perverted logic, it turns to the past of the oppressed people, and distorts, disfigures and destroys it.[23]

Though the "C" word has hardly ever been mentioned in the context of Israeli rule within the pre-1967 borders, the intifada gave to the long-oppressed Palestinian minority an opportunity for catharsis, for the emancipation of their fettered collective memory, even as it drew greater attention to their more tangible fetters. For fifty-two years the Palestinians in Israel could not express the fact that they too were under settler-colonial rule, albeit an earlier phase, with all its classical traits, including humiliation, dispossession, economic enslavement, political marginalization, denial of their historical narrative, even of a glimpse of hope for a life free of racism. They were not allowed to re-attach their severed history or to mend their fragmented identity so as to be whole again.

The intifada gave utterance to long-suppressed frustrations and aspirations, allowing them to pour out in a torrent of transformative energy. Surprised by this uprising from within, the vast majority of Israelis reacted in disbelief, even shock, which was to be expected after the long denial of their "other Palestinian problem," as the *New York Times* called it, and their naïve presumption that Palestinians in Israel had accepted an eternally subordinate role in the Jewish state. The Israeli media reflected a pervasive sense of disappointment, if not betrayal, at the "inexplicable" actions of the "Israeli-Arabs," who ignored all their "privileges" and went out in force to express their fervent support for Palestinians in the territories. Some went as far as accusing them of "fifth column" politics. Military "precautions" were taken near Arab towns after a security report at the highest echelons termed the Israeli Palestinians "hostile populations"[24] and a menace to "Jewish security." Israeli President Moshe Katsav, in a no-doubt unconscious acknowledgment of the fact that most Israeli Jews view Israeli Palestinians as an alien population, expressed his gratitude that the "riots have brought Israelis closer," forgetting that one-fifth of his constituents were on the receiving end of the live bullets, the hate propaganda and the blame.[25]

The protests by Arab citizens were harshly suppressed by live ammunition, with "an intention to kill or injure," as Amnesty International's reports disclosed. Polls show that most Israelis accepted the official government line that it was acting in self-defense, in "retaliation" for "violence initiated by the Arabs," even though the demonstrators were unarmed. This idiosyncratic Israeli concept of "retaliation" reflects what I term snapshot vision: one that freezes reality in time and space, decontextualizes it, and presents it as the truth. If X enslaves Y for years and, at one point, unexpectedly, Y rebels, X cannot logically claim that Y started the violence. It is precisely the violence inherent in X's domination that accumulates in Y's consciousness, eventually provoking him/her to rebel. As Paulo Freire puts it, "Never in history has violence been initiated by the oppressed. How could they be the initiators, if they themselves are the result of violence? How could they be the sponsors of something whose objective inauguration called forth their existence as oppressed?"[26]

Gideon Levy was one of the few Israeli Jews to recognize the Israeli Palestinians' changing identity. He wrote in *Ha'aretz*, "The Arab society in Israel is undergoing an upheaval, and its representatives in Israel's parliament are undergoing a parallel upheaval. Instead of a submissive, groveling society, which on Independence Day hoists two Israel flags and not just one, as the late writer and activist Emil Habibi remarked with such pungent sarcasm, a proud, militant society is now emerging."[27] Another serious attempt to understand this transformation was presented in a research report conducted by a nonconformist group of twenty-six academics, both Jews and Arabs, and presented to Ehud Barak after the uprising began. Seeking to remedy the grave disintegration in the relationship between the state and its Palestinian citizens, it called on the government to adopt far-reaching and comprehensive measures to redress the injustice done to the latter. It says:

> The State of Israel, its institutions and its values well express the national interests and cultural feelings of the Jewish majority. Accordingly, Israel's civil boundaries are in fact identical with the boundaries of Jewish nationalism, and the rights granted to Jewish citizens of Israel are greater in number and more significant than those granted to the Arab citizens of Israel. The state is built around the heart of Jewish historical memory, which emphasizes the heritage of the exile, the Holocaust and the recovery, while its basic values and its institutions sanctify the world of concepts related to this memory only.[28]

Acknowledging the Palestinian "ethnic-national" identity of the Arab citizens of Israel, the report calls for recognizing and apologizing for the *Nakba* and suggests that only an official recognition of this crucial "episode" may set the foundation for future reconciliation and true coexistence. The reason for this connection, the report says, is that after the 1948 war, "the Arab citizens found themselves subjects of a state which was forced on them, which does not represent their political vision, and which in fact is built on their destruction."

Recently, and to the same effect, a group of prominent Israeli artists organized an exhibit in Tel Aviv during which a manifesto was distributed, espousing some relatively radical views on the conflict. Their statement said:

> If the state of Israel aspires to perceive itself as a democracy, it should abandon, once and for all, any legal and ideological foundation of religious, ethnic and demographic discrimination.... The State of Israel should strive to become the State of all its citizens. We call for annulment of all laws that make Israel an apartheid state, including the Jewish Law of Return in its present form. The phrase "a State of all its citizens" is a primal cornerstone in the establishment of a democracy. This is not analogous in any way to a call to dismantle the Jewish State, as is so often argued in the current political discourse in Israel. Between "everything" and "nothing" stretches a wide zone of potential reforms, within which reconsideration and a revision of the meaning of the "Jewishness" of the State should ensue.[29]

But there is nothing more discriminatory, exclusive and oppressive to the indigenous Palestinians than the very Jewishness of the state. As long as Israel is defined as essentially and exclusively Jewish in its national character, its original inhabitants, whether Muslim or Christian, will be precluded from asserting their national identity. Furthermore, no degree of exclusivity or hegemony of Jewish identity can ever be morally binding on the native Palestinians, as it would essentially entail their acquiescence in the outcome of the first phase of Zionist colonization of their homeland. Unethical acts do not become less so with passage of time. In fact, with the intifada and the revival of calls for the right of return for all Palestinian refugees, the initial ethnic cleansing in 1948 rushed to the forefront of the collective memory of the Palestinians in Israel, as everywhere else. The cause of the refugees, after all, has always been the very heart and soul of the question of Palestine.

The Right of Return

On the issue of ethnic purity and chauvinism, Israeli politicians and intellectuals, even those self-proclaimed as "the left," have made the far-right parties of Europe sound as humane as Mother Teresa. The crucial difference, however, is that in the case of Israel, the immorality is aggravated by the fact that, unlike the foreign immigrants to Europe, the "other" is in fact the original inhabitant of the land. The most recent equivalent of the Palestinian refugee crisis has been the plight of the Kosovars, expelled from their towns and villages by Serbia and later returned after a brief war waged by NATO against their tormentors. Discussing the similarities with his customary insight, Gideon Levy writes:

Out of sight, out of heart: the pictures from Kosovo are transmitted to the Israelis from afar. Only the memory of the Holocaust brings those pictures closer, for those who do remember. But Kosovo was indeed here, for those who do not remember, and Kosovo may very well occur here, for those who are not concerned.... Between December 1947 and September 1949, about 600,000 to 760,000 Arab-Palestinians fled or were expelled from their homes, turning overnight into refugees. Their world was ravished over them, and they haven't yet recovered.[30]

The clearest indication of the moral collapse of almost all shades of the official Israeli left was when they revealed their position on the Palestinian right of return. On the far right stands Knesset Member Rehavam Ze'evi of the Moledet party, who advocates "transfer" of the Arabs who are still in "Eretz Yisrael" as a condition for peace with them; it is safe to assume his thoughts on return. In what amounts to a virtual consensus among Israelis, Ehud Barak declared in an interview with the BBC that "insisting on the right of return [to Israel] is putting a question mark on the very *raison d'être* of Israel."[31] Self-proclaimed peaceniks, including such influential figures as A.B. Yehoshua and Amos Oz, who both endorsed Barak as the "candidate of the peace camp,"[32] echoed Barak's categorical position in large advertisements placed in several newspapers, saying, "We shall never be able to agree to the return of the refugees to within the borders of Israel, for the meaning of such a return would be the elimination of the State of Israel." Barak's relatively liberal foreign minister, Shlomo Ben-Ami, acknowledged some justice in the Palestinian demand for this right but quickly offered the Palestinian leadership a sobering choice between two options: "justice or peace."[33] From Ben-Ami's point of view, the two are mutually exclusive in the context of the Arab-Israeli conflict. Yossi Sarid of the "leftist" Meretz party termed it "suicidal."

Uri Avnery, a veteran peace activist, severely criticized the Yehoshua-Oz position, and he ridiculed the suggestion of the pioneering Israeli historian Benny Morris to allow only a "trickle" of refugees to return, which is blatantly inconsistent with his "important role in exposing the expulsion of 1948." Avnery recognizes this right as the "core of the Palestinian national ethos," yet he censures Barak for bringing it up, "kicking the sleeping lion in the ribs" by insisting prematurely on "end of the conflict" language at Camp David. Proposing an "annual quota of 50,000 for ten years," and keeping in mind Israel's absorption of 50,000 Jewish immigrants a year, Avnery's proposal is meant to preserve the "Jewish character" of the state and does not jeopardize "the demographic picture."[34] A more sophisticated attempt was presented by Danny Rabinowitz, who suggested "dropping the definite article 'the' " before the phrase "right of return" in order to sway that right from the "maximalist" interpretation that is demanded by international law.[35] University of Maryland scholar Jerome Segal suggested controlling the "rate of returning refugees" so as to maintain "the character of Israel as a Jewish State." In language reminiscent of passé racialist ideology, Segal also proposed making a distinction between older and younger refugees, the former being "less threatening," mainly because they are "well past childbearing age."[36]

In response to those who have called the right of return impractical, Salman Abu Sitta has demonstrated that, in addition to being required by international law, return is quite feasible and could be carried out without causing major disruption to the livelihood of Israeli Jews (see his essay in this volume). Curing the injustice done to the Palestinian refugees, nevertheless, necessitates delving into the taboo issue of the "Jewish character" of Israel.

Conquest of the "Desert": A Selective Vision

Far from achieving normalcy, Israel remains the sole colonial state on the planet. Zionists have developed a special ability to filter out this and other facts that contradict their imagined version of reality; this, coupled with selective amnesia, is part of their attempt to deal with Israel as if it has always been a normal state.

This self-inflicted visual and memory impairment is challenged by nothing as much as by the very presence of the telltale cactuses all over the country. Before the *Nakba*, those resilient thorny trees were used by Palestinian farmers to embellish their lands and to form the natural borders of a homestead, a land plot or even a village. They were thus immediately targeted for uprooting, as some of the few remaining witnesses to a culture that once thrived, to a land that was opulent and nourishing, and to the uprooting, massacres and expulsions that characterized the establishment of Israel. In their relentless destruction of Palestinian farmlands, today's settlers and soldiers carry on in the tradition of their predecessors' first crusade. But the story of the cactuses goes back even further.

When the first Jewish settlers set foot in Palestine, they must have been astounded by the sight of what the seventeenth-century English poet, George Sandys, called "a land that flowed with milk and honey…adorned with beautiful mountains and luxurious vallies."[37] But they must have also noticed the curious cactuses, which in their European minds could grow only in the desert. So they shut out of their consciousness everything but those cactuses and dubbed the place a desert, a barren land yearning for civilized white hands to till it and make it bloom. Those who accidentally happened to be living there for centuries were not just dehumanized, as colonists always do to natives; they filtered them out of their vision and minds entirely. The land was proclaimed to be "without a people."

Goyimrein Land: A Self-Fulfilling Prophecy

The early Zionists eventually admitted the reality that Palestinian Arabs inhabited Palestine. Consequently, they started planning how to deal with them, so as to reduce their threat to the project of settling European Jews in their land. Since the Zionists had no use for the natives, and in fact wanted their lands for the "conquest of labor," natives had to be removed. To justify this purge, the standard dehumanization tools of European colonialism came in handy. In 1925, in a letter to Senator O.O. Grusenberg, Vladimir Jabotinsky, founder of the Revisionist school of Zionism, wrote that the establishment of a Jewish majority in Palestine would "have to be achieved *against the will* of the country's Arab majority."[38] That would not have constituted a moral burden for Jabotinsky, since he "had utter contempt for the Arabs," considering them "decidedly inferior to Europeans and unworthy of a place in the Holy Land."[39] One of Jabotinsky's American followers, William Ziff, described the Palestinian Arabs as a "sickly and degenerate race" that was "low on the scale of human development."[40]

David Ben-Gurion also made it clear that unless they are "convinced" to leave, "we will expel the Arabs and take their places."[41] Israeli author Simha Flapan says, "That Ben-Gurion's ultimate aim was to evacuate as much of the Arab population as possible from the Jewish state can hardly be doubted."[42] Naturally, the Palestinians were not convinced that they should leave; hence Ben-Gurion's Plan Dalet, and many others like it, had to be implemented, resulting in thirty-four documented massacres, 531 depopulated Arab villages and towns, and a flood of more than 750,000 refugees.[43] Thus the Zionists came close to realizing the prophecy of a *goyimrein* (gentile-free) land. A former director of the Israeli army archives said, "In almost every Arab village occupied by us during the War of Independence, acts were committed which are defined as war crimes, such as murders, massacres, and rapes."[44] Further confirming the above facts of Israel's creation, Israeli new historian Ilan Pappe wrote on Israel's responsibility for creating the Palestinian refugee problem, "The Jewish military advantage was trans-lated into an act of mass expulsion of more than half of the Palestinian population. The Israeli forces, apart from rare exceptions, expelled the Palestinians from every village and town they occupied. In some cases, this expulsion was accompanied by massacres [of civilians].… Expulsion also was accom-panied by rape, looting, and confiscation [of Palestinian land and property]."[45] By the end of 1948, the majority of the Palestinian people had become refugees. Palestine became Israel, the Jewish state.

Even a humanist as nonviolent as Gandhi could understand why the Palestinians resisted the Zionist onslaught in their homeland. As far back as 1938, he wrote:

> My sympathy [for the Jews] does not blind me to the requirements of justice. The cry for the national home for the Jews does not make much appeal to me. The sanction for it is sought in the Bible and the tenacity with which the Jews have hankered after return to Palestine.… Palestine belongs to the Arabs in the same sense that England belongs to the English or France to the French. It is wrong and in-human to impose the Jews on the Arabs. What is going on in Palestine today cannot be justified by any moral code of conduct. The mandates have no sanction but that of the last war. Surely it would be a crime against humanity to reduce the proud Arabs so that Palestine can be restored to the Jews partly or wholly as their national home.[46]

From another perspective, the very idea of Jewish nationalism, or Zionism, was initially "opposed by practically every rabbi in Europe" as a "vile heresy." Prominent Jewish figures also opposed this idea. Edward Montagu, a Jewish Cabinet minister serving in the British government during World War I, called Zionism a "mischievous political creed" and strongly resented the attempt to establish a Jewish state in Palestine, "driving out the present inhabitants."[47] The first president of Hebrew University in Jerusalem, Rabbi Judah Magnes, said, "A Jewish home in Palestine built up on bayonets and oppression [is] not worth having."[48]

Decolonization: Renaming, Reclaiming Palestine

As in every other case of colonialism, the only logical, legal and moral reparation for the native population is embodied in the imperative of decolonization. But if all we can see of the Jewish presence in Palestine is its negation of our own moral right to the land, then we will possess only half the truth. The other half is that we must view the Jews in Palestine qua humans, above and beyond everything else. Otherwise, only revenge can settle the score. Palestinians have a moral obligation to make a distinction between "annulling the wrong," as Hegel calls it, and revenge. The former aims to negate that which makes the colonist so, not to eliminate the human behind the colonist, for being so. Revenge, however, primarily focuses on venting long-suppressed anger, frustration and humiliation, which leads to immoral acts, as witnessed in abundant cases of national or ethnic strife. It therefore "falls into an infinite progression and descends from one generation to another ad *infinitum*," as Hegel says. To "annul the wrong," we ought to conceptualize a demand for justice "no longer contingent on might" but on universal principles of ethics, which uphold the utmost value of humanity above everything else.[49]

We must always be vigilant to the fine line between reversing colonial oppression and undeservedly oppressing the former oppressors. Crossing this line, failing the test, would doom the Palestinians to the abhorrent future of becoming themselves what they have always detested and struggled against: oppressors.

Two particular models of decolonization are commonly discussed: Algeria and South Africa. The former is a paradigm for the classical case of expelling the colonists, while the latter is a new experiment, specifically designed to accommodate the particularities of the South African colonial experience. In that case, apartheid was abolished, while the white inhabitants survived it after agreeing to dismantle it and become equal citizens under the new democratic constitution. In the case of Palestine, this represents an important example, especially because of the many similarities between Zionism and apartheid, and in particular because there is no mother country for the Jews to go back to. Expelling the colonists is not a moral option in the case of Palestine.

There are diverse solutions to the conflict that could satisfy the test of moral duty, international law and universal human rights. Clearly, a Jewish state is the perpetuation of colonialism, inequality, and dispossession. An alternative that has been put forth by Jewish intellectuals—many decades ago by philosopher Martin Buber and Rabbi Judah Magnes—and most recently by such Palestinian intellectuals as Azmi Bishara and Edward Said, is the binational state in historic Palestine. This is based on the principle of "self-determination for both peoples,"[50] as Said has put it. The underlying assumption is that there are two nations, one composed of Israeli Jews and one of Arab Palestinians, which must have the same rights. To equally encompass both, such a state would have to be democratic—as Bishara has proposed, "a state of all its citizens." Realizing the Palestinian right of return is assumed in this case as a necessary first measure to undo the injustice, the original sin.

However, binationalism makes two problematic assumptions: that Jews are a nation, and that such a nation has a right to exist as such in Palestine. But since arguing against these points is well beyond the scope of this essay, I shall propose what I consider a preferable solution: a secular democratic state, to be constructed through the process of decolonization, whereby a transnational identity evolves, an actual "fusion of horizons," as the philosopher Hans-Georg Gadamer calls it, uniting the Jews of Palestine and the Palestinians and therefore not allowing for the exclusion or hegemony of either group. It goes without saying that such a new identity must reconcile the contextual requirements of the region, as well as the universal rights of all its citizens.

Menachem Begin once said: "My friend, take care. When you recognize the concept of 'Palestine,' you demolish your right to live in Ein Hahoresh. If this is Palestine and not the Land of Israel, then you are conquerors and not tillers of the land. You are invaders. If this is Palestine, then it belongs to a people who lived here before you came."[51]

This *was* Palestine, and there is no reason why it should not be renamed Palestine. Granted, it would entail a comprehensive process of decolonization and transformation, and that is never easy. However, Israelis ought to recognize this challenge to their colonial existence not as an existential threat to *them* but rather as an auspicious and magnanimous invitation to dismantle the colonial character of the state, to allow the Jews in Palestine finally to enjoy normalcy, as equal citizens of a secular democratic state—a truly promising land, rather than a false Promised Land. Only then will the past be properly eulogized and dignified in memory, and the tell-tale heart given a proper burial.

Notes

1. Edgar Allan Poe, "The Tell-Tale Heart," in *Works of the Late Edgar Allan Poe* (1850), www.pambytes.com/poe/stories/heart.html.

2. Rabbi Mayer Schiller, quoted in "Issues of the American Council for Judaism," Summer 1998, cited in "The Origin of the Palestine-Israel Conflict," www.cactus48.com.

3. Meron Benvenisti, "The Final Battle in a Cyclical War," *Ha'aretz*, November 30, 2000.

4. Lee Hockstader, *Washington Post*, January 16, 2001.

5. Yossi Beilin, "Moving Forward After Oslo," *Ha'aretz*, November 7, 2001.

6. Thomas Friedman, "A Mideast Policy for Mr. Bush," *New York Times*, January 19, 2001.

7. Henry Kissinger, "The Peace Paradox," *Washington Post*, December 4, 2000.

8. Benjamin Beit-Hallahmi, *Original Sins: Reflections on the History of Zionism and Israel* (1993); cited in "The Origin of the Palestine-Israel Conflict," www.cactus48.com.

9. Reuters, "Amnesty Slams Israel for Role in Mideast Violence," November 1, 2000.

10. *Ha'aretz*, December 12, 2000.

11. Reuters, January 22, 2001; Phil Reeves, "Fury as Court Frees Settler," *The Independent*, January 22, 2001.

12. Gideon Levy, *Ha'aretz*, January 28, 2001.

13. Tanya Reinhart, "Don't Say You Didn't Know," Indymedia (www.indymedia.org), November 6, 2000.

14. *Davar*, September 6, 1979, quoted in Michael Palumbo, *The Palestinian Catastrophe* (London, Boston, 1987), p. xii.

15. Gideon Levy, *Ha'aretz*, January 7, 2001.

16. *Ha'aretz*, February 1, 2001.

17. *Ha'aretz*, January 8, 2001.

18. Report of Mary Robinson, the UN High Commissioner for Human Rights, November 2000.

19. Lee Hockstader, *Washington Post* and *San Francisco Chronicle*, September 19, 2000.

20. "Letters," *Ha'aretz*, January 17, 2001.

21. Jabotinsky Archives, quoted in Palumbo, p. 55.

22. Keith Richburg, *Washington Post*, November 17, 2000.

23. Frantz Fanon, *The Wretched of the Earth* (London, 1965), p. 170.

24. Mazal Mualem, *Ha'aretz*, November 1, 2000.

25. *Ha'aretz*, October 5, 2000.

26. Paulo Freire, *Pedagogy of the Oppressed* (New York, 1972), p. 41.

27. Gideon Levy, *Ha'aretz*, November 12, 2000.

28. *Ha'aretz*, November 27 and December 6, 2000.

29. Israeli artists manifesto, Beit Ha'Am. Curators: Tamar Getter, Aim Deuelleluski, Roee Rosen.

30. Gideon Levy, *Ha'aretz*, April 4, 1999, translated by Omar Barghouti.

31. BBC, www.bbc.co.uk, January 5, 2001.

32. A.B. Yehoshua and Amos Oz, "Support Barak Conditionally," *Ha'aretz*, December 19, 2000.

33. Barbara Demick, *Philadelphia Inquirer*, January 16, 2001.

34. Uri Avnery, "The Right of Return," www.indymedia.org.

35. Danny Rabinowitz, *Ha'aretz*, January 4, 2001.

36. Jerome Segal, *Ha'aretz*, February 1, 2001.

37. Quoted in Edward Said, *The Question of Palestine* (New York, 1979), p. 11.

38. Vladimir Jabotinsky, quoted in Palumbo, p. 12.

39. Ibid, p.13.

40. William Ziff, quoted in Palumbo, p. 13.

41. David Ben-Gurion, quoted in Palumbo, p. 32.

42. Simha Flapan, *The Birth of Israel: Myths and Realities* (New York, 1987), p. 90.

43. Salman Abu Sitta, *Palestinian Right of Return: Sacred, Legal and Possible* (London, 1999), pp. 11, 15, 26.

44. Norman G. Finkelstein, *Image and Reality of the Israel-Palestine Conflict* (New York, 1995), p. 110.

45. Ilan Pappe, "Israeli Historians Ask: What Really Happened Fifty Years Ago?" *The Link*, January-March 1998.

46. Gandhi, essay on Jews, 1938, www.cactus48.com.

47. Palumbo, pp. 5, 9.

48. Rabbi Judah Magnes, *Like All the Nations*, ed. by Brinner & Rischin, www.cactus48.com.

49. G.W.F. Hegel, *Philosophy of Right*, tr. by T.M. Knox (Oxford, 1967), p. 73.

50. Edward Said, "The One-State Solution," *New York Times Magazine*, January 10, 1999.

51. *Yediot Ahronot*, October 17, 1969, cited in Arie Bober, ed., *The Other Israel* (New York, 1972), p. 77.

10. FLOUTING CONVENTION: THE OSLO AGREEMENTS
ALLEGRA PACHECO

It's clear that the ones who initialed this agreement have not lived under occupation. You postponed the settlement issue and Jerusalem without even getting guarantees that Israel would not continue to create facts on the ground that would preempt and prejudge the final outcome. And what about human rights? There's a constituency at home, a people in captivity, whose rights must be protected and whose suffering must be alleviated. What about all our red lines? Territorial jurisdiction and integrity are negated in substance and the transfer of authority is purely functional.... At least you should have done something about Jerusalem, settlements and human rights. Strategic issues are fine, but we know the Israelis and we know that they will exploit their power as occupier to the hilt and by the time you get around to permanent status, Israel would have permanently altered realities on the ground.

—Hanan Ashrawi, quoting her initial comments to Abu Mazen upon seeing the Declaration of Principles (1993)[1]

The Middle East peace process officially began with the Madrid Conference in 1991. The Madrid talks were multilateral and were held under the auspices of the former Soviet Union and the United States, with the European Community participating. Representatives of the State of Israel and Palestinian civilians from the occupied territories held bilateral negotiations in Madrid aimed at resolving the Palestinian-Israeli conflict. These talks stalled over several issues, including Israel's refusal to cease settlement expansion. In 1993, the Israeli government and the Palestine Liberation Organization initiated a secret alternative-negotiating track in Oslo, Norway. These secret talks succeeded in producing a Declaration of Principles (DOP), which was signed by Israel and the PLO on the White House lawn in September 1993.

The DOP terminated the public Madrid talks and set in motion a series of agreements known in common parlance as the Oslo Agreements: the 1994 Gaza-Jericho Agreement (Oslo I), the 1995 Interim Agreement on the West Bank and the Gaza Strip (Oslo II, or Taba agreement), the January 1997 Hebron Protocol, the October 1998 Wye River Memorandum, and the September 1999 Sharm el Sheik Memorandum.

Oslo II was by far the broadest and most concrete agreement concluded between the PLO and Israel. This agreement facilitated the withdrawal of the Israeli army from six West Bank Palestinian cities (2 percent of the territories), implemented the election of the Palestinian Authority and the Palestinian Legislative Council, and partitioned control of the occupied territories between the Israeli military and Palestinian Authority. Oslo II also established detailed and complex security, economic, legal, and political arrangements and coordination offices between the Palestinian Authority and the Israelis, creating a "new Oslo order" in the territories. Despite the Israeli military withdrawals under Oslo II, the agreement

Left: An Israeli flag marks the home of Ariel Sharon in the Muslim Quarter, East Jerusalem

was never implemented in full. The Hebron Protocol in 1997 and the opening of the safe-passage route from Gaza to the West Bank in 1999 were the only significant steps implemented afterwards.

The Fourth Geneva Convention: The Law of Military Occupation

There are many international conventions that protect persons from human rights abuses, including the Convention for Civil and Political Rights, the Convention Against Torture, the Convention on the Prevention and Punishment of Genocide, etc. However, there is a specific body of international humanitarian law aimed at protecting civilians under military occupation that incorporates many of these human rights. The law is codified in the Fourth Geneva Convention Relative to the Protection of Civilian Persons in Time of War (hereafter "the Convention").

Completed in 1949 by a special committee under the auspices of the International Committee of the Red Cross (ICRC), the Convention was designed to protect the civilian population of occupied areas and prevent the occupier from permanently changing the status of the territories. The Convention's restrictions on the occupying army and its dominant humanitarian focus reflected a global aspiration to prevent a recurrence of the atrocities of World War II:

> At the end of the Second World War, unprecedented as it was in extent, the time had obviously come to revise the Geneva Conventions once more and extend them in the light of experience.... The discussions were dominated throughout by a common horror of the evils caused by the recent World War and a determination to lessen the sufferings of war victims.[2]

Since its inception, the Convention has become the internationally accepted guideline for armies to follow in their treatment of civilians for all occupations and is considered reflective of customary principles of international law. The Convention's official commentary, published in 1958 and edited by Jean S. Pictet, provides the legislative history and intent behind its sections and is intended to serve "all who…are called upon to assume responsibility in applying the Geneva Conventions, and to all, military and civilians, for whose benefit the Conventions were drawn up."[3]

In a military occupation, civilians are for all practical purposes stateless and remain vulnerable to the mercy of the occupier to protect them. The Convention provides a body of rules to protect them. Accordingly, the Convention contains over 100 provisions prohibiting human rights violations like torture, illegal detention, house demolition, deportation, and humiliation and degradation of the civilian population.

Another major goal of the Convention is to facilitate an uncomplicated withdrawal of the occupying power at the end of hostilities and avert all claims by the military occupier to the occupied territory and its resources. The Convention proscribes the military occupier from taking any action that makes its temporary presence permanent. Policies by the occupier such as mass confiscations of civilian property or settlement of the occupier's own civilians in the territories are therefore absolutely prohibited.

Likewise, any "peace" agreement that purports to transfer or legitimize sovereign claims by the occupier or restricts or cancels the rights of the occupied population to its territory is absolutely prohibited.

Respect for the Geneva Convention is therefore a critical political issue for Palestinian negotiators and other interested parties. It strengthens and legitimizes Palestinian demands for a complete Israeli withdrawal from the territories, undermines Israeli claims to sovereignty over annexed Jerusalem or the other territories, and holds Israeli officials accountable and responsible for protecting Palestinian human rights.

The Applicability of the Convention in the Occupied Territories

In June 1967, the Israeli military occupied the West Bank, Gaza Strip, East Jerusalem, and the Golan Heights. The Israeli government annexed East Jerusalem and the Golan Heights and applied Israeli civil law to these areas.[4] The West Bank and Gaza Strip were not annexed but remained under Israeli military occupation.

Initially, the Israeli military applied the Geneva Convention.[5] However, when it became clear to the Israeli government that applying the Convention would drastically limit its control and would accord the Palestinian civilians greater freedom than the army preferred, the government developed a complicated legal argument to justify rejecting the applicability of the Convention. This legal theory was developed in 1971 by Israel's Attorney General Meir Shamgar, formerly the Military Advocate General for the Israeli army. He later became the president of the Israeli Supreme Court. In presenting his theory, Shamgar admitted that "the divergence of approaches…did not turn on theoretical legal problems but much more on their political repercussions."[6]

Shamgar and others contended that if Israel recognized the applicability of the Convention, then it would effectively be recognizing the prior sovereign rights of Jordan and Egypt over these areas, a legal status that did not suit Israeli political interests. Without a prior sovereign, there could not be an occupation. Instead, under the Israeli perspective, these areas were simply administered—a legal status for which the Geneva Convention didn't apply. This legal lacuna would be filled by the vaguely worded and antiquated Hague Regulations from 1907 and Israeli military orders that would in good faith protect the interests of the Palestinian civilian population.

Later, the Israeli Supreme Court added another argument against the applicability of the Convention, holding that even though Israel had signed and ratified it, the country was not bound by the Convention because Israel had not passed the requisite legislation to incorporate it into Israeli law. This position clashed with the recognized legal doctrine that countries are bound to a treaty once it's been signed and ratified. Mindful that its position conflicted greatly with the entire international legal establishment, the Court affirmed that it would abide de facto by the humanitarian provisions of the Convention.

The International Community's Position

Israel remains alone in its legal position. Indeed, the entire international community holds that the West Bank, Gaza, and East Jerusalem are under occupation and therefore that Israel is bound to abide by the Convention's rules and restrictions.[7] Hundreds of UN General Assembly resolutions and committee decisions reaffirm the applicability of the Convention in the territories. Even the United States has recognized the applicability of the Convention in the territories. Every major human rights organization, including the ICRC (the original drafters of the Convention and responsible for its implementation), Amnesty International, the International Commission of Jurists, and the Israeli human rights group B'tselem, considers the Convention binding.

The international position is consistent with the intent of the drafters of the Convention. The rights of civilians under occupation are embedded and not subject to debate. The official commentary to the Convention makes clear that the question of the political status of the occupied territory cannot be used to undermine the rights of civilians and their internationally accorded legal protections:

> The words in question [Article 1 "in all circumstances"] also mean that the application of the Convention does not depend on the character of the conflict. Whether a war is "just" or "unjust," whether it is a war of aggression or of resistance to aggression, whether the intention is merely to occupy territory or to annex it, in no way affects the treatment protected persons should receive. [8]

The Israeli Supreme Court's position on the Convention's non-applicability is just as problematic. Indeed, many human rights and legal scholars hold that after fifty years, the Geneva Convention has become part of customary international law, making it universally applicable even without ratification.[9] Some legal scholars, including Israeli scholars, add that Israel does not need to ratify the Convention to be bound by it. This is because the Convention deals with a situation inherently outside domestic law and an area outside of Israel—where of course its internal law wouldn't apply. The Court's application of the "humanitarian provisions" is quite disingenuous since the Convention is a humanitarian document in full. Indeed, the Court has never listed which humanitarian provisions apply, making such a position wholly arbitrary and unenforceable, as subsequent Israeli court decisions (many by Meir Shamgar himself) demonstrate.

Israeli Human Rights Violations of the Convention During Its Occupation

Since 1967, the Israeli military has consistently violated nearly every provision of the Fourth Geneva Convention. Human rights organizations worldwide, from Amnesty International to Israel's own B'tselem, as well as the United States government, have issued hundreds of statements and reports criticizing Israel's violations. Among the lists are: torture of over 50,000 Palestinians; over 1,500 Palestinians deported; annexation of East Jerusalem; construction of over 150 Jewish settlements; illegal transfer of over 400,000 Israeli civilians into the occupied territories; repeated collective punishment, including the ongoing closure since 1993, which has limited freedom of movement for 99 percent of the Palestinian population; demolition of over 8,000 homes and villages in East Jerusalem and the West Bank and Gaza; pillage of Palestinian natural resources, including water, quarries, and trees; and the illegal appropriation of over 70 percent of the occupied territories. Most if not all of these violations continued unabated during the Oslo peace process.

The Convention's Applicability After the Oslo Agreements

Under the Convention, its rules and protections remain applicable even after hostilities end and a cease-fire is implemented. The Convention's general application remains in effect until the military occupier fully withdraws and ceases to control the lives of the civilians.

> Article 6:
> In the case of occupied territory, the application of the present Convention shall cease one year after the general close of military operations; *however, the Occupying Power shall be bound, for the duration of the occupation, to the extent that such Power exercises the functions of government in such territory, by the provisions of the*
> *following Articles of the present Convention: 1 to 12, 27 General, 29 to 34, 47, 49, 51, 52, 53, 59, 61–77, 143* [emphasis added].[10]

The Convention is replete with catchall phrases like "applies in all circumstances" or "in any case or in any manner whatsoever" to emphasize the continued applicability of the Convention in occupied territories, despite peace agreements and other arrangements that do not end the occupation completely.

> Article 1:
> Protected persons may in no circumstances renounce in part or in entirety the rights secured to them by the present Convention, and by the special agreements referred to in the foregoing Article, if such there be.

These statements are inserted to guarantee protection for the civilian population until protection is no longer needed—until the foreign army has completely withdrawn and a final political settlement is implemented. Thus, as long as the Israeli military is present in the occupied territories and controls the lives of the Palestinian civilian population, the Convention remains in effect, despite any agreement or arrangement reached.

During the Oslo period the Convention's general application remained in effect because the Israeli military remained an active occupying force and maintained ultimate control of most aspects of Palestinian lives. Dozens of military bases stocked with tanks, armored personnel carriers, and various other weapons, along with dozens of military checkpoints throughout the territories, operated round-the-clock. Israeli soldiers and special units deployed throughout the territories remained in active combat duty, killing over 750 Palestinians.

The army also continued to employ thousands of Israeli soldiers and officers to manage the bureaucracy of the occupation as the "Civil Administration"—the headquarters of the Israeli occupation—

remained open for business. Military detention centers and courts in the territories also functioned continuously throughout the Oslo period and prosecuted thousands of Palestinian civilians suspected of offenses against the military occupation. This reality seriously undermines the Israeli claim that it was ever simply "administering" the territories or that the Oslo Agreements had terminated the occupation and the relevancy of the Convention.

The heavy use of military force during this second intifada—tanks, US-manufactured helicopter gunships, thousands of soldiers, snipers, assassination teams, and the military's total control of Palestinian movement, trade, and access, including sieges and curfews throughout the territories— makes the applicability of the Convention even more compelling today.[11]

Critical Legal Miscalculations Under the Oslo Agreements[12]

One of the greatest flaws of the Oslo agreements was that they did not commit Israel to abide by the Convention and cease its human rights violations. At most, the agreements contain two broadly worded, ambiguous clauses, vulnerable to multiple and self-serving interpretations that the Israeli side, as the controlling power, exploited for its interests:

Article XIX: Human Rights and the Rule of Law
Israel and the Council [Palestinian] shall exercise their powers and responsibilities pursuant to this Agreement with due regard to internationally accepted norms and principles of human rights and the rule of law.

Had the Palestinian negotiators received a written commitment from the Israeli side to abide by the Convention and to refrain from specific human rights violations, the legal dispute regarding the applicability of the Convention could have been resolved and the Convention would have had a greater basis for enforcement. However, the above clause simply maintained the status quo of the legal debate and enabled Israel to continue to argue that it was not bound by the Convention and that its settlement construction, house demolitions, and land confiscations do not violate human rights.

As support for their contention that Israel made a commitment in Oslo to stop settlement building and land confiscations, Palestinians point to provisions in the Oslo Agreements that commit both sides to maintaining the status quo of the territories during the interim period:

Article XXXI:
6. Nothing in this Agreement shall prejudice or preempt the outcome of the negotiations on the permanent status to be conducted pursuant to the DOP…
7. Neither side shall initiate or take any step that will change the status of the West Bank and the Gaza Strip pending the outcome of the permanent status negotiations.
8. The two Parties view the West Bank and the Gaza Strip as a single territorial unit, the integrity and status of which will be preserved during the interim period.

Like the human rights clauses, these sections are vaguely worded and leave interpretation open to debate. The actions that constitute "changing the status" of the territories or undermining the status of the territories as a "single territorial unit" are left to the imagination. The Supreme Court of Israel ruled time and again that these clauses were not meant to stop Israeli abuses. The ambiguity of these clauses permitted Israel to argue that its settlement expansion or road-building were not violating the agreements but actually consistent with the agreements. Such was Israel's position from the start, as quoted by *Ha'aretz*:

> The agreements between Israel and the Palestinians since 1993 do not include any prohibition of construction or expansion of settlements.... The only limitation undertaken in the agreements is that neither side will act to change the status quo of the West Bank and Gaza before the discussions of the final status. Upon reaching those discussions...Israel's position, as stated by its leaders, is that most of the settlers should remain where they are.[13]

Thus, during the seven years of the Oslo process, Israel doubled its Jewish settlement population in the West Bank and Gaza to almost 200,000. In East Jerusalem it grew to 170,000. More than 18,330 new housing units were constructed, according to the Israeli Bureau of Statistics, and thousands of dunams of Palestinian land were confiscated to expand the settlements.

The first Palestinian negotiating team in the pre-Oslo peace talks in Madrid in 1992–93 clearly understood the importance of the Convention as a guideline for negotiations. They also sensed the political implications of obtaining explicit commitments from Israel to refrain from human rights violations and recognize the applicability of the Convention.

Having endured years under the Israeli occupation, the Madrid negotiators correctly anticipated that without a commitment by Israel to halt the violations, Israel would entrench its sovereign interests during the interim period, making complete withdrawal nearly impossible. Ironically, the Israelis chose these Palestinian negotiators, refusing to recognize them as an independent team and insisting that they be attached to the Jordanian delegation, preferring them since they were from the occupied territories and ostensibly not part of the PLO. These "local" Palestinians made the human rights issue one of their major points during the negotiations, which ultimately contributed to the failure of the talks. As Hanan Ashrawi later described it:

> Our daily Human Rights Status Reports continued, as did the Israeli refusal to receive them in written form, so we resorted to reading them at the beginning of each meeting as well as at the beginning of each press briefing.... [W]e insisted that we deal only with categories and issues on the basis of the Fourth Geneva Convention.... [W]e kept up a continuous flow of memoranda to the Israeli and American sides on issues such as settlements and land confiscations, deportation, torture and maltreatment of prisoners, administrative punitive measures, the de jure applicability of the Fourth Geneva Convention and the Hague Regulations, different forms of punishment, summary executions, and the activities of the undercover units (death squads), as well as concrete proposals and plans for implementation. They went unheeded.... The hands-off policy of the United States and its automatically pro-Israeli stance fueled the flames of Palestinian exasperation and contributed directly, though incrementally, to the back-channel talks between the PLO and the Israeli government.[14]

The US Middle East peace team, headed by Dennis Ross, played a critical role in pressuring these pre-Oslo Palestinian negotiators to back off from the human rights issues and the applicability of the Convention. In the summer of 1993, the United States even proposed a draft Declaration of Principles to the Madrid team that omitted any commitment by Israel to abide by the Geneva Convention and cease its settlement expansion and land confiscations in the territories and Jerusalem. On July 1, 1993, Faisal Husseini, the head of the Madrid Palestinian negotiating team, responded to Secretary of State Warren Christopher, arguing that the draft was totally unacceptable because, aside from the omissions, it opened up for negotiation Israeli sovereignty claims to the territories and Jerusalem, in total contravention to the Convention and international principles:

> By stating that any party has the right to claim territorial sovereignty in the permanent status negotiations, the draft contradicts the terms of reference in UN Security Council Resolution 242, including the principles of territory for peace, that of the non-admissibility of acquiring territory by war, and putting an end to the occupation. The draft omits these and other long-standing US policy principles, such as the legitimate political rights of the Palestinian people, the applicability of the Fourth Geneva Convention and Israeli withdrawal.... As for Jerusalem, the US has, in the letter of assurances to us, stated that it does not recognize Israel's annexation of East Jerusalem.... The draft invites us to agree to much less than that and to wait until the permanent status negotiations before raising the question of Jerusalem. You will understand that this is totally unacceptable to us, all the more so in view of Israeli acts on the ground which are predetermining both the interim arrangements and the final status, and the repeated declarations by Israeli leaders concerning Jerusalem which run contrary to long-standing US policy.[15]

Unable to persuade the Palestinian negotiators to concede their rights, the Israeli and US negotiators rediscovered the PLO in 1993. Many of the PLO representatives had lived in exile and were less familiar with the occupation and with the political connection between the human rights violations, the Geneva Convention, and Israel's territorial expansion plans. They also did not have a qualified legal team with them to advise them on the terms. Within two months of the Madrid team's rejection of the US draft DOP, the PLO stunned the world and announced that it had secretly and independently agreed in Oslo to a Declaration of Principles with the Israeli government. In this declaration, the PLO team agreed to give away what the Madrid team had valiantly struggled not to concede throughout the two years of the Madrid talks. It agreed to make negotiable Israeli sovereignty claims to the territories, natural resources and settlements; to postpone negotiations on Jerusalem until final status; to waive any obligation to explicitly stop settlement building, expansion, and other human rights violations; and to waive any obligation to abide by the Convention. The DOP was the first step in the Oslo peace process.

The following is a summary of some of the significant legal miscalculations made by the Palestinian Oslo negotiators that paved the way for Israel's continued settlement expansion and solidification of its control over the territories and East Jerusalem. The effect of Israel's unmitigated expansion and entrenchment of its control led Palestinians ultimately to reject the entire Oslo process and embark on the new intifada against both the Israeli occupation and the Palestinian negotiators.

1. Agreeing to continued Israeli control in East Jerusalem

After the war in 1967, the Israeli government annexed 6.5 square kilometers of East Jerusalem and 64.5 square kilometers of the occupied territories into the Israeli Jerusalem municipality. This area is referred to as annexed East Jerusalem. The annexation, which violates the Geneva Convention, has never been recognized by most nations, including the United States and the countries of Europe, and the area is still considered occupied territory by the world community.

Article 47 of the Convention states, "Protected persons who are in occupied territory shall not be deprived, in any case or in any manner whatsoever, of the benefits of the present Convention by…any annexation by the latter [Occupying Power] of the whole or part of the occupied territory." And the commentary clearly points out that "occupation as a result of war, while representing actual possession to all appearances, cannot imply any right whatsoever to dispose of territory…an Occupying Power continues to be bound to apply the Convention as a whole even when, in disregard of the rules of international law, it claims during a conflict to have annexed all or part of an occupied territory."[16] Many Israeli scholars hold the view that "the most basic tenet of the law of belligerent occupation is that occupation as such does not transfer title to the territory."[17]

Instead of adhering to the Convention's prohibition, the Palestinian negotiators agreed to open up for negotiation the annexation of East Jerusalem and to postpone this discussion until final status. Postponing the issue of Jerusalem to final status effectively kept East Jerusalem under full Israeli control. As a result, during the Oslo period, the Jewish settler population rose from 22,000 to 170,000 in annexed East Jerusalem,[18] while the Israelis issued 322 new house demolition orders against Palestinians. More than ninety-two Palestinian houses were demolished in East Jerusalem during this period.[19]

When final-status talks began in 2000, the Palestinian negotiators did not adhere to the recognized international and legal position delegitimizing any Israeli sovereign claim to Jerusalem. Instead, they engaged the Israelis in the debate as to which areas of annexed Jerusalem would remain in Israeli hands. So caught up were the negotiators in the imbroglio over Jerusalem that Palestinian claims were reduced to dividing one square mile of the Old City into tiny areas of varying sovereignties. When talks finally broke down and the new intifada began, the Palestinian negotiators had set a terrible precedent for the future status of East Jerusalem and for illegal annexations elsewhere.

2. Making 60 percent of the West Bank negotiable

Under the Convention, a military occupation is temporary and at its termination the occupier must withdraw completely from the territory. The occupier does not acquire any sovereignty rights to the land or resources as a result of its occupation.[20] Not one inch of occupied territory should be open to negotiation. And yet, the very essence of the Oslo agreements affirms that Israel's claims to land in the West Bank are valid and thus open to negotiation. Conceding to such a claim undermines the Convention itself and the rights of the civilians, who are the landowners and users of the territory and its natural resources.

According to the Convention, Israel's extensive confiscation of Palestinian property to build Jewish settlements and roads does not confer sovereignty. In fact, it amounts to a grave breach of the Convention, which is considered a war crime.

> Article 147:
> Grave breaches…shall be those involving…extensive destruction and appropriation of property, not justified by military necessity and carried out unlawfully and wantonly.

In addition, the Convention obligates every contracting party to arrest and prosecute any person who committed, or ordered to be committed, a grave breach.

> Article 146:
> …Each High Contracting Party shall be under the obligation to search for persons alleged to have committed, or to have ordered to be committed, such grave breaches, and shall bring such persons, regardless of their nationality, before its own courts.

Contrary to the letter and spirit of the Convention, the Oslo agreement opened up for negotiation more than 60 percent of the West Bank and Gaza. This area constituted over 4,000 square kilometers, much of it agricultural, which the Israeli military destroyed and turned into settlements, bypass roads, and Israeli-owned, maquiladora-style industrial zones.

Under Olso, the West Bank was partitioned into three separate categories for negotiations. Area A: complete transfer of security and civilian matters to the Palestinian Authority (approximately 17.2 percent by 2001). Area B: Israeli control over security, Palestinian control over civilian matters (approximately 23.8 percent by 2001). Area C: approximately 59 percent, under Israeli military and civilian control, to be negotiated.[21]

Instead of focusing the Oslo Agreement on full Israeli withdrawal from Area C, financial compensation for the billions of dollars of property loss and the indictment of those officials responsible for such unjustified appropriation and destruction, the Palestinian negotiators turned their backs on the victims of Israel's plunder. They engaged Israel's contention that its massive presence and investment in Area C legitimizes its claims to sovereignty.

Equally problematic was the Palestinian concession not to challenge Israel's property rights in Areas A and B obtained through these very same war crimes.

> Oslo II—Annex III:
> Article 22(3):
> The Palestinian side shall respect the legal rights of Israelis (including corporations owned by Israelis) related to lands located in the areas under the territorial jurisdiction of the Council.

> Article 16(3):
> The Palestinian side shall respect the legal rights of Israelis (including corporations owned by Israelis) related to Government and Absentee land located in the areas under the territorial jurisdiction of the Council.…

There is no parallel commitment by the Israeli government to respect the property and legal rights of Palestinians in Area C. As a result of this disproportionate Palestinian concession, during the Oslo years the Israeli government appropriated tens of thousands of dunams of land for nonmilitary use and added to its list of war crimes. The agreements did not provide any mechanism to stop this. The tragedy of all this was made clear in the latter days of the Clinton presidency, when Israeli negotiators were depicted as having made historic concessions in the name of peace in their agreement to return West Bank land to the Palestinians. This land was never theirs to return.

3. Legitimizing illegal Jewish settlements

The Arab Studies Society, headed by one of the Madrid negotiators, Faisal Husseini, described one of the main purposes of entering into the Madrid negotiations:

> When Palestinians decided to attend the Peace Conference in Madrid under special severe conditions, they were having the hope to save whatever they could from the remaining land of Palestine, stopping the settlements' invasion over Palestinian land in the West Bank (including East Jerusalem) and Gaza Strip. Their step aimed to stop settlements from cutting the ties and links among the Palestinian land, stopping all procedures that aim to change the reality of the Occupied Territories....[22]

When the Palestinian negotiators agreed in Oslo II to leave Area C in Israeli hands, they lost control of the majority of West Bank land and thus the possibility of stopping settlement expansion. Like the worst predictions of the Palestinian Madrid negotiators, Israel used this Oslo interim period to create facts on the ground to expand settlements and take other actions to predetermine the outcome of the final-status negotiations.

Jewish settlements are built on land confiscated from Palestinian private landowners or villages. Despite the fact that they are located in the territories within Palestinian areas, Jewish settlers are subject to Israeli law, rights, and privileges, creating an apartheid-like legal and rights structure. For example, if a Palestinian is arrested in the area where a settler resides, the Palestinian is adjudicated by Israeli military orders and courts, while the settler benefits from Israeli civilian courts.

Article 49 of the Convention prohibits the establishment of settlements in the occupied territories: "The Occupying Power shall not...transfer parts of its own civilian population into the territory it occupies." The Commentary explains that this prohibition was designed to prevent a recurrence of policies carried out in Europe by the Nazis during World War II. "It is intended to prevent a practice adopted during the Second World War by certain Powers, which transferred portions of their own population to occupied territories for political and racial reasons or in order, as they claimed, to colonize those territories."[23]

Neither the DOP nor the Oslo II agreement contains any provisions prohibiting or restricting the establishment or expansion of Jewish communities in the West Bank. The question of settlements was postponed until final status. In presenting the Oslo II agreement to the Knesset, Prime Minister Yitzhak Rabin stated, "I wish to remind you, we made a commitment…to the Knesset not to uproot any settlement in the framework of the Interim Agreement, nor to freeze construction and natural growth."[24]

By postponing settlements until final status, the Palestinians opened the way to Israeli sovereign claims to the West Bank land where the settlements were located. Indeed, when final-status talks began, annexing settlement blocs into Israel was the top Israeli demand, and Palestinian negotiators, according to press reports, were pressured into agreeing to this illegal annexation. Any agreement signing away these blocs undermines the Convention's strict prohibition against settlements. The new intifada prevented the negotiators from signing such an agreement.

4. Agreeing to construction of bypass roads

As part of the Oslo II negotiations, the Israeli government proposed that it pave several roads to facilitate the IDF's redeployment. According to numerous reports—which have never been refuted by PA officials—the Palestinian Authority agreed without conducting a thorough investigation of the maps of the road plan. The plan actually involved full-scale construction of a 400-kilometer alternative highway system for settlers, parts of which the Israeli government had prepared years before.[25] Until the Oslo process, the Israeli government never had the pretext of Palestinian consent to confiscate the huge amounts of Palestinian land needed to pave these roads. The PLO signature to Oslo II gave the Israelis just what they needed.[26]

In the fall of 1995, when the bulldozers began to appear in every region of the territories, tearing up agricultural land, the Palestinian Authority made faint-hearted protests. Abu Ala, chief Palestinian Oslo negotiator, convened a press conference on October 26 and announced that Oslo II did not at all relate to the bypass roads. "I always said that these roads are part of settlement acts and therefore I oppose them now and forever." However, when asked by reporters if the PA had submitted an official complaint to the Israelis, Abu Ala refused to answer.[27]

By November, Israeli newspapers reported that Jamil Tarifi, head of the Palestinian civil affairs committee for the PA, had agreed on behalf of the PA to reconsider its objections to the bypass roads. The PA was persuaded by the Israeli position that suspending road construction would delay Israeli redeployment from the cities and the entrance of the PA into those cities.[28] Three weeks later, Israel began uprooting and leveling approximately 5,000 dunams of one of the best Palestinian grape vineyards in the West Bank, destroying a centuries-old industry in the Halhoul area. In a panic, Palestinian residents called Tarifi, who was at the airport, and pleaded with him to make the PA intervene. Tarifi is reported to have told them, "I have no time; I am traveling abroad."[29]

The PA's capitulation to the bypass-road confiscations also facilitated Israel's contention that these roads were essential to the peace process. Responding to a letter about the confiscations, Itamar Rabinovich, then Israel's ambassador to the United States, wrote: "let me just say that it appears…that the 'confiscation' of the land…seems to be part of the redeployment of Israeli forces in the West Bank in implementation of Palestinian self-rule.… In other words, this would be part of the effort to finally bring about peace between Israel and the Palestinians."

When some Palestinian landowners petitioned the Israeli occupation authorities and courts against the widescale land confiscations, the government argued that the PA had consented to the roads through the Oslo agreements and that this effectively barred private landowners from contesting the confiscations. Attempts to obtain official cooperation from the PA in the High Court petitions were in vain. This severely undermined the legal struggle, as lawyers representing the Palestinian landowners stood alone in their claims. Indeed, during one Supreme Court hearing, when lawyers argued that the roads were designed to establish Palestinian cantons, Justice Michel Cheshin responded angrily, "Are you making a speech in the market square? This is how you argue in the court? This is not serious!"[30]

The extensive destruction of thousands of acres of Palestinian land for no public or military purpose, but rather to serve the illegal Jewish settler population, was clearly a violation of the Convention and fell under its war-crime definition in Article 147. After the network was completed in 1999, it became another Israeli claim to sovereignty.

Again, the PA failed to make use of its rights under the Convention and failed to prevent this grave breach of the Convention. The PA did not actively stop the roads or support the legal and grassroots resistance to them. Once the roads were paved, the PA did not demand control over them, compensation for the extensive destruction, or criminal indictments against those who carried it out. By fall 2000, it accepted the roads as a fait accompli and focused its negotiations on other areas.[31]

The bypass roads formed "moats" strategically placed around most Palestinian populated and agricultural areas, cutting off nearly all semblance of Palestinian territorial contiguity. These roads facilitated the Israeli siege of Palestinian cities, towns, and villages during the new intifada, which caused over $2 billion in damages to the fledgling Palestinian economy. The siege also resulted in massive food shortages and the threat of starvation, leading the UN World Food Program to distribute food to families in Gaza.

5. Legitimizing Jewish settlements in Hebron

Despite the illegality of Jewish settlements under the Geneva Convention, the PA agreed in the 1997 Hebron Protocol to allow the Jewish settlements in that city to remain.[32] Moreover, instead of demanding its full sovereign rights, the Palestinians gave the Israeli military direct sovereignty over one-fifth of the city. It also allowed the Israelis to retain overall security jurisdiction for the areas surrounding Hebron and to retain authority to detain, arrest, interrogate, try, and imprison all Hebron residents. The Hebron Protocol divided the city into two parts. H-1 would be under PA rule, and H-2—with a population of 400 Jewish settlers and 40,000 Palestinian civilians—would be under Israeli control. The Hebron Protocol effectively left these 40,000 Palestinians under Israeli military occupation:

Section 2(b):
Israel will retain all powers and responsibilities for internal security and public order in Area H-2. In addition, Israel will continue to carry the responsibility for overall security of Israelis.

Section 10(b):
In Area H-2, the civil powers and responsibilities will be transferred to the Palestinian side, except for those relating to Israelis and their property, which shall continue to be exercised by the Israeli Military Government.

The H-2 section became the prototype for Israeli apartheid, as Jewish settlers were subject to Israeli civilian laws with all the according rights and privileges of Israeli citizens. The 40,000 Palestinians residing there were separated and controlled under Israeli military rule, with a few civil responsibilities like education and health delegated to the PA. Not only did the PA agree to the presence of settlers and the army's control over 40,000 Palestinians and property, but it also committed its own police in Hebron to protect the illegal settlers: "The purpose of the above mentioned checkpoints will be to enable the Palestinian Police…to prevent entry of armed persons and demonstrators or other people threatening security and public order, into the above-mentioned area [H-2] (3b)."

As a result of continued Israeli military rule in H-2, settlement construction continued. During the new intifada, the Israeli army placed all 40,000 Palestinian residents under curfew for weeks, while the 400 Jewish settlers roamed free and armed. The army also used these settlements during the intifada as bases to shoot at and bomb Palestinian neighborhoods of H-2.

6. Legitimizing prohibition on freedom of movement

The Universal Declaration of Human Rights guarantees the right of each person to freely enter and exit his country. Article 27 of the Convention requires the occupying power in all circumstances to respect the manners and customs of the protected persons, which include free movement. Palestinians in the territories are denied this right under the Israeli closure policy. Solidified during the Oslo period, closure prohibits free movement of Palestinian goods and persons in and out of the occupied territories. The Israeli military enforces closure through bureaucratic requirements of permits and magnetic ID cards and through dozens of military checkpoint crossings dispersed throughout the territories.

Closure functions only one way: it seals the occupied territories for Palestinians only; all 400,000 Jewish settlers in the West Bank, Gaza and East Jerusalem maintain total freedom of movement with political, social, and economic privileges and advantages. By the end of the 1990s, most Palestinians had endured seven years of closure and the resultant deterioration of their economic conditions. Such a setting opened the floodgates for mass support of the violent uprising against the Oslo peace process.[33]

Throughout the Oslo years, the Labor-led governments used closure as a pretext to convince uninformed supporters of peace that "separation" would be the first step in the implementation of the two-state solution. Prime Minister Ehud Barak's campaign slogan in the summer of 1999 reflected this approach: "Peace Through Separation: Us Here, Them Over There." And yet, this slogan, billboarded around cosmopolitan cities like Tel Aviv, was closer to America's Jim Crow ideology or South Africa's apartheid than to a call for Palestinian statehood.

Closure was also justified to protect Israeli security interests. After a bombing or military attack and during every major Jewish holiday, the Israeli military closed the checkpoint crossings. In one fell swoop, 3 million Palestinians were denied freedom of movement.

The Geneva Convention prohibits collective measures and punishment:

Article 33:

No protected person may be punished for an offense he or she has not personally committed. Collective penalties and likewise all measures of intimidation or of terrorism are prohibited.... Reprisals against protected persons and their property are prohibited.

Closure solidified Israel's economic and military control over Palestinians and facilitated the Israeli military's siege of Palestinian villages and towns during the 2000 uprising. All Palestinians were required to obtain permits from the Israeli security authorities to move in and out of the territories. The planning and construction of Jewish settler bypass roads and settlements throughout the territories were fundamental in successfully implementing the separate but unequal character of Israeli occupation, and in laying the groundwork for the segregation or apartheid emerging out of the Oslo Agreements.

Under Oslo II, the PA never once required the Israeli government to dismantle the closure policy and its total control of movement of 3 million Palestinians. Indeed, the Oslo Agreements were replete with convoluted arrangements to accommodate the Israeli closure policy. Instead of demanding the lifting of closure, the PA agreed to facilitate the bureaucracy by acting as go-between for Palestinian permit applications. Any request for a permit to leave the area or travel between Gaza and the West Bank or to enter Jerusalem now went first through the PA, which then transferred the application for Israeli approval. At border crossings, an Israeli clerk sat behind a one-way mirrored window located behind a Palestinian clerk, who would pass the Palestinian passport behind him for Israeli approval before allowing the traveler to proceed. The Israeli clerk was kept hidden to provide an aura of independence, but in reality there was none. Not only did the Israeli officials have total discretion to refuse exit or entry, but also they maintained jurisdiction to arrest any Palestinian traveler and take him from the border crossing to prison inside Israel.

The safe-passage route—the traverse between Gaza and southern West Bank—was another example of the PA's concession of fundamental movement rights under the Convention. Undermining the right to free movement, the PA agreed to another complicated system of rules and restrictions for Palestinian travel between Gaza and the West Bank. Any travel had to be approved by the Israeli authorities, who could at entry point arrest any Palestinian they chose. In addition, Israeli holidays and schedules determined hours of operation.

One reason that the Palestinian negotiators did not link talks with ending the closure is that senior PA officials were exempted from closure and permit requirements. They obtained special VIP permits that allowed free movement through checkpoints. Their free movement enabled the PA to maintain very profitable monopolies over the distribution and sale of supplies, resources, and industries in Palestinian areas. For the rest of the Palestinian population, however, closure caused a marked decline in the standard of living and devastated the Palestinian economy. Seven years of closure and restrictions on Palestinian freedom of movement during Oslo resulted in a threefold increase in unemployment, a lower standard of living, and a 21 percent decline in Palestinian gross domestic product.[34] In February of 2001, months after the superclosure or siege that the Israeli army imposed on Palestinian areas, the World Food Program reported that Palestinians had become among the poorest people in the world.

7. Legitimizing pillage of Palestinian water resources

As an occupier, the Israeli government has no sovereign claims to the water resources in the territories. And yet, since 1967 Israel has plundered and pillaged over 80 percent of those resources.[35] Israel's water company, Mekoroth, has drilled thirty-two wells in the occupied territories. These wells not only serve the Jewish settlements; they have become "the principal reservoir of drinking water for Tel Aviv, Jerusalem and Beer Sheva and the most important long-term source in the [national] water system."[36]

Article 33 of the Convention states succinctly, "Pillage is prohibited." Pillage is defined in the American Heritage Dictionary as: "To rob of goods by violent seizure; plunder 2. To take as spoils."

The Convention permits the occupying power to requisition foodstuffs and supplies for its army and personnel, but even that small right is restricted. The food and supplies can be requisitioned only after Palestinian civilian needs are accounted for, and only after the occupying power has paid for the supplies.

> Article 55:
> The Occupying Power may not requisition foodstuffs, articles…available in the occupied territory, except for use by the occupation forces and administration personnel, and then only if the requirements of the civilian population have been taken into account…. the Occupying Power shall make arrangements to ensure that fair value is paid for any requisitioned goods.

Israeli control of most of the Palestinian water supply is used as leverage to control the population. This Israeli use and control over water to pursue its own interests, including discriminatory pricing policies, directly contravenes the letter and spirit of the Convention. Indeed, in February 2001 Palestinians reported that the Israelis closed off the water supply to the cities of Bethlehem and Hebron, denying water to over 300,000 Palestinian civilians. Despite the fact that every Jewish settlement in the Hebron and Bethlehem district continued to receive a continuous flow of water, and that this was the rainy season, the Israeli government contended that some wells had run dry. In an area suffering from several years of drought, control of water has become a crucial issue for the Palestinian community.

Under the Oslo Agreements, the Israeli government recognized a vague, undefined Palestinian water right in the West Bank, yet this right and ownership of water became a negotiable issue for final-status talks.

> Annex III:
> Article 40:
> 1. Israel recognizes the Palestinian water rights in the West Bank. These will be negotiated in the permanent status negotiations and settled in the Permanent Status Agreement relating to the various water resources.
> 5. The issue of ownership of water…in the West Bank will be addressed in the permanent status negotiations.

Under the Convention, since the occupier has no right to the water or other natural resources of the occupied territories, the occupier is prohibited from using those resources to serve its own civilians and from transferring them outside the territories. The fact that Israeli citizens need the water does not give them the right to claim it. Under international law, the Jewish settlers have never had any legitimate basis to continue residing in the occupied territories, nor to demand a share of Palestinian water.

Not only did the Palestinian negotiators agree to engage Israel in its claims to water, but the negotiators agreed to the continued and unfettered pumping of Palestinian water wells for use by illegal Gazan Jewish settlements and Israeli military bases. The Palestinians, on the other hand, were required to pay the Israelis for any water obtained from the Israeli water company.

> Annex III—Schedule 11
> 2. …the existing water systems supplying water to the Settlements and the Military installation Area, and the water systems and resources inside them shall continue to be operated and managed by Mekoroth Water Co. [Israeli Water company]…
> 4. …the [Palestinian] council shall enable the supply of water to the Gush Katif settlement area and Kfar Dorom settlement by Mekoroth.
> 5. The Council shall pay Mekoroth for the cost of water supplied from Israel and for the real expenses incurred in supplying water to the Council.

In a "normal" withdrawal from occupation, the occupying power would set up a joint committee to discuss arrangements for paying the new Authority in the territories for a constant water supply. Under the Oslo agreements, the Palestinians granted the redeploying Israeli power rights to the natural resources of territories it theoretically no longer occupied.

8. Legitimizing Israel's continued imprisonment of Palestinians

According to the Convention, when the occupier withdraws, it is required to "hand over" all prisoners from the territories to the authorities of the liberated territory.

> Article 77:
> Protected persons who have been accused of offences or convicted by the courts in occupied territory, shall be handed over at the close of occupation, with the relevant records, to the authorities of the liberated territory.

The Commentary says, "This provision is of prime importance; the absence of such a rule would have allowed an Occupying Power with not too many scruples to take detained persons with it in its retreat and thus to circumvent the prohibition on deportation in Article 49 and 76."[37]

When the Israelis withdrew from Palestinian cities in 1995, instead of releasing all Palestinians held in military prisons it transferred many of them to prisons inside Israel. Throughout the Oslo process, the Israelis arrested, tried and/or convicted an additional 13,000 Palestinians. Aside from not releasing the prisoners, their deportation caused enormous hardships. It obstructed family visits, since the closure policy restricted entry of Palestinians to Israel.

The Oslo Agreements did not provide for the release of all Palestinian prisoners, nor did it prohibit Israel from deporting prisoners to Israeli prisons or making new arrests. It only offered a series of staged releases of an unspecified number of prisoners at unspecified dates. The releases were listed as "confidence-building" measures, making them nonbinding and dependent on the new relations and trust between the two parties. The absence of any guarantee by Israel to cease imprisoning Palestinians allowed the Israelis to exclude from these conditions all prisoners arrested after 1993, later changed to September 1995 (the date of Oslo II).

One of the most damaging and aberrant terms of Oslo II is the Palestinian agreement to divide prisoners into categories according to the offense committed.

> Annex VII 2(c):
> The following categories of detainees and/or prisoners will be included in the above-mentioned releases:
>   c. detainees and/or prisoners charged with or imprisoned for security offenses not involving fatality or serious injury.

This clause, which later developed into the "Jewish blood on their hands" condition, was used by the Israelis to justify not releasing hundreds of Palestinian prisoners. Because there was no concrete time frame and commitment to release all the prisoners, Palestinians were forced to negotiate each individual release within this Israeli framework. Those convicted of a minor offense like throwing rocks became worthier of release than a resistance fighter who engaged in military activities. Most prisoners were humiliated by this situation; some felt completely abandoned by the PA, especially those whose own military commanders, who were now senior officials in the Authority, agreed to these conditions. These frustrations led to several prisoners' strikes and mass solidarity actions in the streets and contributed to the erosion of popular support for the Oslo Agreements.

Instead of negotiating a complete release and the cessation of Israeli arrest and imprisonment of Palestinians, the Agreement allowed the Israelis to use the political prisoners as bargaining chips to force further concessions from the Palestinian negotiators. By September 2000, over 1,000 prisoners remained incarcerated in Israeli prisons. Six months later, during the new intifada, this number had doubled.

Agreements Like Oslo Are Null Under the Convention

The drafters of the Convention clearly envisioned an Oslo situation and prohibited it:
Article 7:
No special agreement shall adversely affect the situation of protected persons...nor restrict the rights which it confers upon them.

Article 47:
Protected persons who are in occupied territory shall not be deprived, in any case or in any manner whatsoever, of the benefits of the present Convention by...any agreement concluded between the authorities of the occupied territories and the Occupied Power.

The harsh experience of the Vichy regime after the Nazi conquest of France provided all-too-familiar reasons for the Convention's drafters to prevent the recurrence of such a situation. The drafters sought clearly and unequivocally to prevent instances whereby the occupying power would prop up a questionable government that would then ostensibly be authorized to make agreements with the occupying power at the expense of the rights of the occupied civilians.

Agreements concluded with the authorities of the occupied territory represent a more subtle means by which the Occupying Power may try to free itself from the obligations incumbent on it under occupation law; the possibility of concluding such agreements is therefore strictly limited by Article 7, paragraph 1, and the ``general rule expressed there is reaffirmed by the present provision [Article 47].[38]

Concerned primarily with protecting the rights of civilians under occupation, the Geneva Convention contains a built-in protection to guard against a situation such as Oslo, in which those rights are signed away. The principle is clear: the rights of Palestinian civilians under the Geneva Convention are protected. No authority, not even the Palestinian Authority, has the right to concede them. Conceding sovereignty over land, water, settlements, roads, and prisoners is a violation of the Convention. Any agreement or sections of an agreement that attempt to do this are therefore illegitimate and should be rendered unenforceable.

Independent Attempts to Enforce the Geneva Convention

In the midst of the Oslo process, Palestinian human rights groups became increasingly alarmed at Israel's continued settlement expansion and land confiscation for roads and settlements, which was protected and legitimized by the agreements. The Palestinian Authority took no significant action during the entire negotiation process to link negotiations to the cessation of these and other human rights violations.

Frustrated, Arab and Palestinian human rights groups took their cause to the international community and embarked on a campaign to enforce the Fourth Geneva Convention in the territories. While this campaign began more than thirty years after the Israeli occupation and during a peace process supervised by the US government, this seemed to be the only viable approach to pressure the Israeli government to cease its violations.

The campaign centered on Article 1 of the Convention, which confers responsibility on every party to the Convention to ensure its enforcement: "The High Contracting Parties undertake to respect and to ensure respect for the present Convention in all circumstances."

As the first article of the entire Convention, the drafters intended to emphasize that without each party's active enforcement of the Convention, the entire document would be ineffectual. According to the Commentary:

> The use…of the words "and to ensure respect for" was, however, deliberate: they were intended to emphasize the responsibility of the Contracting Parties…. It follows, therefore, that in the event of a Power failing to fulfill its obligations, the other Contracting Parties (neutral, allied or enemy) may, and should, endeavor to bring it back to an attitude of respect for the Convention. The proper working of the system of protection provided by the Convention demands in fact that the Contracting Parties should not be content merely to apply its provisions themselves, but should do everything in their power to ensure that the humanitarian principles underlying the Conventions are applied universally…. It is clear that Article 1 is no mere empty form of words, but has been deliberately invested with imperative force. It must be taken in its literal meaning.[39]

The campaign's momentum grew as Israeli Prime Minister Benjamin Netanyahu became increasingly unpopular worldwide. At a certain point the PLO and, ironically, the Palestinian Authority joined in. On February 8, 1999, the UN General Assembly voted almost unanimously (resolution ES-10/6) to call for the convening of a meeting of the parties to consider enforcement measures of the Convention in the occupied territories.

The resolution was important on a larger level for international humanitarian law. It was the first time that contracting parties to the Fourth Geneva Convention met to discuss its enforcement. The meeting would have historical precedence not only for the Palestinian civilians in the occupied territories, but for the direction of international humanitarian law and the future success of the Convention in protecting civilians under future occupations. Nabil Shaath, a senior Palestinian Oslo negotiator and a minister in the Palestinian Authority, affirmed:

> If this convention can be successfully applied in one very specific case in which there is international consensus about Palestine, then international humanitarian law will be able to provide protection, not only to the Palestinians, but to the rest of humanity wherever they suffer from the encroachment of war and occupation.[40]

Despite the meeting's importance for strengthening international law, protecting the Palestinian civilians and curbing Israeli human rights violations, the US government vehemently opposed convening it and echoed Israel's contention that it would interfere with the peace process. Along with Israel, the US government lobbied vigorously and put enormous pressure on the member countries and the Palestinian Authority to halt the convening of the Convention. The pressure had no justification, since the Israeli government refused to commit in any political agreement with the Palestinians to stop its violations of the Convention in the territories. As UN Secretary General Kofi Annan wrote in a prepared statement for the preparatory meeting on June 14, 1999: "Pending a political settlement, the most effective way to ensure the safety and protection of the civilian population of the occupied territories would be the full application of the provisions of the Convention."[41]

The pressure mounted and more countries joined the Israeli and US efforts to stop the meeting. With few allies in its camp, the PA representatives, led by Shaath, finally conceded to the pressure. Ehud Barak had just defeated Netanyahu in the Israeli elections, and the United States and Israel argued that convening such a meeting would undermine hopes of reviving peacemaking without confrontation. An unnamed Palestinian official stated, "The Palestinian Authority's decision to adjourn indefinitely the UN conference after convening Thursday is meant as a good will gesture to Israel's new government."[42]

In its opening statement to the meeting, the Palestinian delegation urged the participants to defer the rest of the conference. The meeting was then adjourned indefinitely. The Israeli government made no commitment to abide by the Convention or to stop its human rights violations. A year later the intifada exploded and Barak was listed by Israel's Peace Now as the biggest settlement builder since 1992.

Following the deferment, Amnesty International issued a scathing statement describing the decision as an "abdication of responsibility."

> Amnesty International is appalled by a 10 minute meeting of High Contracting Parties to the Geneva Conventions, convened today in Geneva, which failed to consider enforcement measures to ensure that Israel respect its obligations under the Fourth Geneva Convention.... It is a supreme irony that, on the 50th anniversary of the Geneva Conventions, a conference that was set up to bring back to the limelight the plight of the protected population of the Occupied Territories lasts only 10 minutes. Today marks a scandalously missed opportunity to reaffirm international humanitarian law.[43]

The Palestinian leadership again missed a perfect opportunity to enforce the Convention and bring an end to most of the human rights violations its constituents were suffering from under the guise of the Oslo process: settlement building, land confiscations, transfer of prisoners, bypass-road building, and solidification of Israel's confiscation of Jerusalem. The international community's abandonment of the Palestinian position severely weakened the force of the Convention and hopes for an advance in international humanitarian law enforcement.

One can speculate how the political situation may have developed had the meeting convened, followed by world community action to enforce the Convention. In October 2000, following the outbreak of the intifada, the Arab League requested that the Swiss government, which is entrusted with the Geneva Conventions, convene the signatories. As of the writing of this article in March 2001, no meeting has been set.

Conclusion

The Fourth Geneva Convention was designed to protect the rights of civilians under occupation and to prevent the occupying power from permanently changing the status of the occupied territory and its civilians. The thirty-four-year-old military occupation has done just the opposite: thousands of human rights violations have been committed, along with seemingly irreversible changes in the landscape and population of the area. Had the Israeli government abided by the letter and spirit of the Geneva Convention and not transferred almost half a million Israelis into the territories, perhaps it could have successfully withdrawn from the territories and the parties could have succeeded in establishing a viable and independent Palestinian state.

Many Palestinians and peace activists worldwide were lulled into thinking that the Oslo agreements would end the Israeli occupation and create such an independent state. In reality, the agreements created an atmosphere for Israel to make permanent its military and settler presence throughout the territories and to prevent Palestinian territorial contiguity. With the influx of 400,000 Israeli Jewish settlers into the territories, and the linking of their economy and most of their natural resources, including water, to Israel, withdrawal and separation at this stage do not seem possible. As the former head of Israel's domestic intelligence service, Ami Ayalon, remarked recently, separating the territories from Israel today would be like separating Siamese twins—causing irreparable damage to both societies.[44]

One may contend that it is the benefit of hindsight that makes these arguments so compelling. And yet the rights of the Palestinians under the Geneva Convention were unambiguous, present and known to the Palestinian negotiators at every step. Had the Palestinian Authority asserted its inalienable rights under the Convention as the basis for negotiations, we may have had a very different situation today.

The Palestinian Authority's total disregard for the very international law that protected its people's rights was irresponsible and a contributing factor to the continued suffering of 3 million Palestinians remaining under Israeli occupation. The PA's willingness to concede Palestinian rights enshrined in the Fourth Geneva Convention lacked legitimacy and rendered those concessionary parts in the Oslo Agreements unenforceable. Since the Convention remains applicable in the territories, it can never be too late for the Palestinian leadership to reassert its rights under the Convention. Indeed, the Oslo II agreement makes explicit that signing the Agreement does not prevent either party from reasserting its rights and claims.

> Article XXXI:
> 6. …Neither Party shall be deemed, by virtue of having entered into this Agreement, to have renounced or waived any of its existing rights, claims or positions.

Those who argue that the Palestinian Authority had the right to disregard the Convention in a bilateral agreement are mistaken. The Convention clearly prohibits any agreement that abrogates the rights of civilians under occupation. Moreover, with the expiration of its elected term at the end of

May 1999, the PA thereafter did not have a legitimate, democratically elected mandate to conduct such agreements. The fact that in May 1999 both the PA and the Palestinian Legislative Council unilaterally extended their terms of office instead of holding elections reflects their own admission that they did not have the support or the will of the people behind them.

One of the successes of the new intifada has been to bring to a screeching halt the Oslo process and Palestinian concessions and compromises on international humanitarian law. With Oslo in abeyance and the chances for a viable independent Palestinian state remote, now may be the time to consider alternative solutions, like the democratic secular state model, which actually implements international law and guarantees full equality, dignity, and freedom for both Palestinians and Israelis. No matter what political course is taken, the Oslo experience makes clear that there will be no chance for a genuine settlement of the conflict unless the process is consistent with the Geneva Conventions, international law, and Palestinian rights.

I would like to thank Susan Akram for her comments and Mimi Asnes for her invaluable research assistance. Although this article covers legal issues, it is not a standard law review article. For an in-depth legal discussion see B'tselem, *Settlement in the Occupied Territories as a Violation of Human Rights: Legal and Conceptual Aspects*, March 1997, researched and written by Yuval Ginbar, www.btselem.org; Emma Playfair, ed., *International Law and the Administration of Occupied Territories* (Oxford, 1992); Allegra Pacheco, "Occupying an Uprising: The Geneva Law and Israeli Administrative Detention Policy During the First Year of the Palestinian General Uprising," *Columbia Human Rights Law Review*, Vol. 21, No. 2, Spring 1990.

Notes

1. Hanan Ashrawi, *This Side of Peace* (New York, 1995), p. 260.

2. Jean S. Pictet, ed., *ICRC Commentary to the IV Geneva Convention*, 1958, pp. 6, 8.

3. Pictet, *Commentary*, p. 2.

4. The annexation of East Jerusalem and the Golan Heights has never been recognized by the United Nations or the United States. This article will not discuss the disposition of the Golan Heights, which was formerly under Syrian sovereignty and not part of the Oslo agreements.

5. Anis Qassem, "Legal Systems and Developments in Palestine," 1980 *Palestine Yearbook of International Law*, pp. 19, 30. Initially, the Israeli government recognized the applicability of the Convention to the West Bank and Gaza Strip, and the Israeli military instructed the military courts to adhere to it. This order was revoked five months later, but general staff regulations and opinions of the General Advocate headquarters continued to order soldiers to act in accordance with the provisions of the Convention.

6. M. Shamgar, "Legal Concepts and Problems of the Israeli Military Government—The Initial Stage," in Shamgar, ed., *Military Government in the Territories Administered by Israel 1967–1980* (Jerusalem, 1982), pp. 13, 14.

7. Pacheco, "Occupying an Uprising," pp. 519, 530–31.

8. Pictet, *Commentary*, p. 16.

9. See, for example, the final document of UN International Meeting on the Convening of the Conference on Measures to Enforce the Fourth Geneva Convention in the Occupied Palestinian Territory, including Jerusalem, June 15, 1999. "Participants stressed the universal character of the Geneva Conventions and the fact that their provisions have been accepted as norms of international customary law." UN Press Release, GA/PAL/809, June 15, 1999.

10. These provisions refer to the sections of the Convention unrelated to the immediate exigencies of war, like mobile hospitals and evacuation from danger zones. This list includes sections of the Convention that prohibit settlements, deportations, unfair trials, torture, confiscations, and restrictions on movement.

11. For more information on US weapons used in the intifada, see the National Lawyers Guild's report, *The Al Aqsa Intifada and Israel's Apartheid: The U.S. Military and Economic Role in the Violation of Palestinian Human Rights*, (www.nlg.org).

12. This section will not address the miscalculations in the Oslo agreements of the rights of 1948 Palestinian refugees, since it requires an extensive discussion of additional bodies of law not covered by this article. See Salman Abu Sitta's article in this book.

13. Aluf Benn, "PLO's Anti-Israel Diplomacy Gets Boost From Intifada," *Ha'aretz English Internet*, February 13, 2001.

14. Ashrawi, *This Side of Peace*, pp. 198–99.

15. Mahdi F. Abdul Hadi, PASSIA, *Documents on Palestine*, Vol. II, December 1997, p. 137.

16. Pictet, *Commentary*, pp. 275–76.

17. Y. Dinstein, "The International Law of Belligerent Occupation and Human Rights," *Israeli Yearbook of Human Rights 8* (1978), p. 105.

18. Saleh Abdel-Jawwad, "Against History," *Al-Ahram Weekly*, March 15–21, 2001.

19. "Severe Hardship and Existential Problems of Palestinians in Jerusalem as a Result of Israeli Policies," Orient House Department of International Relations, October 1998.

20. According to Oppenheim, in "The Legal Relations Between an Occupying Power and the Inhabitants," *Law Quarterly Review* (1917), p. 364, "there is not an atom of sovereignty in the authority of the occupant." Quotation cited in A. Pellet, "The Destruction of Troy Will Not Take Place," in Playfair, *International Law and the Administration of the Occupied Territories* (Oxford, 1992) p. 174.

21. These areas contain the most important groundwater reserves for the Palestinian population.

22. "Statistical Study About Land Confiscation—Settlements Since the Declaration of Principles Up to March 1, 1995," Arab Studies Society, Land Research Committee, Jerusalem.

23. Pictet, *Commentary*, p. 283.

24. October 5, 1995, as quoted in the Statement by the Jewish Communities in Judea, Samaria and Gaza, Jerusalem, January 21, 1997. See PASSIA, *Documents on Palestine*, Vol. II, December 1997, p. 327.

25. For example, Hebron bypass road no. 35 was part of the "Gaza-Amman" road planned in 1991 by the Israelis even though then no peace agreements had been signed between the Israelis and either the Jordanians or the Palestinians. "High Court Hears Petition Against Paving of Hebron Bypass Road; Gov't Representative: No House Will Be Demolished," *Ha'aretz*, November 1, 1995.

26. The Israeli land confiscations and overall plan to use the roads and settlements to divide the West Bank into isolated cantons were publicized by human rights organizations as early as 1995. These warnings went largely unheeded by the PA and the international community. See, for example, "Legal Organizations Demand Cancellation of Confiscation of 71,000 Dunams in the West Bank," *Ha'aretz*, September 19, 1995; "Statistical Study About Land Confiscation–Settlements Since the Declaration of Principles Up to March 1, 1995," Arab Studies Society, Land Research Committee, Jerusalem; "Since June 1993, the Israeli government confiscated 128,788 dunams of Palestinian land," Land and Water, Property Violations Report, April-June 1995. As Jan de Jong pointed out in "Palestine After Oslo II: Preparing the Final Map" (*News From Within*, December 1996, pp. 3–8), "The primary means of unleashing the settlements' urban potential is the construction of the bypass roads. Much of what is displayed on the map will be completed by the end of the year, not coincidentally on the eve of the next Israeli elections. This construction will improve the settlers' road network and allow transport to key destinations in the West Bank without having to pass through Palestinian areas. With strictly limited entry and exit points largely restricted to areas under Israeli authority, it will render the transfer of intermediate areas to Palestinian authority as mainly a nominal affair, without consequences for the Jewish settlements. Israelis will continue to have large tracts of land throughout the West Bank."

27. "Abu Ala Harshly Attacks the Paving of the Bypass Roads," *Ha'aretz*, October 27, 1995.

28. "The Palestinian Authority Will Reconsider Its Objection to the Paving of the Bypass Roads," *Ha'aretz*, November 1, 1995.

29. Press release, Hebron Solidarity Committee, November 23, 1995.

30. "High Court Rejects Petitions Against the Paving of Nablus and Jenin Bypass Roads," *Ha'aretz*, September 8, 1995.

31. Had it done its legal homework, the PA would have realized that most of the orders for the military to use Palestinian land were for five-year periods. Even if the PA did not want to assert Palestinian rights under the Convention, they could have demanded that the military orders not be extended. See Pacheco, "Dazed in the Circles of Justice: Legal Challenges to the Bypass Roads Land Confiscations," *News From Within*, Vol. 12, No. 3, March 1996, p. 19.

32. This despite the fact that even Israeli human rights groups were calling for total IDF withdrawal from Hebron and the dismantling of Jewish settlements there. See: B'tselem: The Israeli Information Center for Human Rights in the Occupied Territories, "Summary of Report of Human Rights in Hebron," September 1995: "B'tselem urges the government of Israel to dismantle the settlement in the city of Hebron and remove Israeli security forces from the city. The absurd reality of Hebron, where a minority of 450 settlers dictate the lives of 120,000 Palestinians, and the illegality of the settlement of Hebron under international humanitarian law require these actions.... Any political solution which preserves Jewish settlement in the city and Israeli control over it, wholly or partially, will inevitably lead to additional violations of the human rights of the Palestinian residents of Hebron."

33. Interview with Marwan Barghouti, West Bank secretary general of Fatah, Media Monitors Network, January 16, 2001: "First of all, I believe that Al-Aqsa Intifada has expressed a new Palestinian state of mind refusing to live under the current circumstances or going back to the pre-September 28 status quo. Therefore, I see no point in proceeding with negotiations in the same framework that they were conducted during the past seven years, which led to nothing but more US support for Israel"; see also Robert Fisk, "Peace Is Dead, We Will No Longer Be Victims—Hanan Ashrawi," *Independent*, November 8, 2000.

34. Center for Economic and Social Rights press release, "Great Expectations—Bitter Realities: Human Rights Abuses and Economic Decline Under the Oslo Process," March 29, 2000.

35. PASSIA, *2001 Diary*, p. 252.

36. Israeli State Comptroller Report, February 1993, as quoted in "Special Report: The Socio-economic Impact of Settlements on Land, Water and the Palestinian Economy," Foundation for Middle East Peace, July-August 1998.

37. Pictet, *Commentary*, p. 366.

38. Pictet, *Commentary*, p. 274.

39. Pictet, *Commentary*, pp. 16–17.

40. Sherine Bahaa, "Righting Wrongs in Geneva," *Al-Ahram Weekly*, June 17–23, 1999.

41. "UN Meeting to Discuss Conference on Measures to Enforce Fourth Geneva Convention in Occupied Palestine Opens in Cairo," UN Press Release, PAL/C/2, June 14, 1999, p. 3.

42. Reuters, July 13, 1999.

43. "Fourth Geneva Convention Meeting: An Abdication of Responsibility," Amnesty International Online, July 15, 1999.

44. *Ma'ariv*, December 5, 2000.

11. A COMPARATIVE STUDY OF INTIFADA 1987 AND INTIFADA 2000

GHASSAN ANDONI

Ever since the beginning of the Middle Eastern conflict, Palestinians have fought to achieve their legitimate national and civil rights. With the colonial and expansionist character of the Israeli occupation, resistance has continued on many different fronts, using a variety of methods. Toward the end of the 1980s, as a result of the gradual shift of resistance into the occupied territories, Palestinians introduced the intifada as a new style of rebellion. The intifada combined the character of a civil rights movement with that of a national struggle for independence. Peaceful mass protest, limited violence such as stone-throwing, and limited, localized armed struggle coincided. The balance between the three methods has been subject to the test of efficiency and has varied according to the level of Israeli oppression. Comparing the first intifada (1987–93) with the current one in terms of context, methods, participation, impact, and goals can help us understand the complexity of the conflict and the various peacemaking efforts.

The End of Illusions

Until the 1980s, the liberation struggle was hampered by myths that were directly responsible for prolonging the life of the occupation. The first, which was widespread among Palestinians living inside the occupied territories, was the belief that if they remained steadfast, salvation would come from outside. The 1982 Israeli invasion of Lebanon, after which the PLO lost its last stronghold adjacent to occupied Palestine, stimulated intensive debate about the effectiveness of the modern Palestinian revolution as a diaspora movement. It forced Palestinians in the occupied territories to reclaim responsibility for national independence. Thus, even before the 1987 intifada the focal point of the conflict had moved into the occupied territories. The main issue on the Palestinian national agenda became challenging the sustainability of the Israeli occupation, with the eventual goal of ending it.

The second myth, which was widespread among Israelis, was the very sustainability of that occupation. The practice of introducing minor modifications to the system, which started with the creation in 1979 of the so-called Civil Administration after the Camp David accords between Israel and Egypt, was intended to prolong occupation indefinitely while at the same time avoiding the difficult problem of how to determine final status. The only two available options—annexation or Palestinian independence—were from the Israeli standpoint extremely problematic. The first was hindered by the complicated demography of the place: annexation—aside from the worldwide protest and diplomatic

Left: A mural of a young boy killed at a clash site in Shati refugee camp, Gaza

problems it would have provoked—would have brought about rough demographic parity between Jews and Palestinians in Israel, thus threatening the Jewish character of the state. Like the first option, the second flew in the face of Zionist ideology. It also would have forced a reversal of all the procedures implemented on the ground since the occupation began in 1967, not least among them the Jewish settlements.

The most immediate accomplishment of the 1987 intifada was that it seriously challenged the sustainability of occupation. In doing so, it forced a search for an alternative. All the issues brought about by the occupation were part of the agenda of massive resistance: settlements, the role of the military, civil and human rights, Jerusalem, recognition, and more. The only issue that was not at the forefront of the 1987 intifada was the longstanding problem of the refugees.

The Oslo process was an important manifestation of the recognition by both Israel and the PLO of two things: that occupation—at least as it was being enforced at the time—was not sustainable and needed to be replaced, and that it was necessary to move not only the conflict but also the Palestinian leadership into the occupied territories. The two sides had different and very contradictory understandings of the Oslo process. Israel, while accepting the need to replace the occupation with something else, was primarily interested in creating a system that addressed its demographic problem. Its goal was to quell the rebellion while maintaining overall control of the territories, and at the same time ensuring maximum separation of the Jewish and Palestinian populations. Israel also thought that by moving the conflict into the territories it would be easier to normalize relations with the Arab world and at the same time create a partner—the Palestinian Authority—that would help execute its security demands. The PLO envisioned the Oslo process differently, seeing it as the gradual replacement of occupation with national independence. The PLO also thought that moving into the occupied territories was a better way to continue the national struggle than the problematic diaspora revolution. A collision between the two different agendas was inevitable.

The major illusion of Oslo was that it was a peacemaking process. The two sectors who most believed in this illusion were mainstream Palestinians and the Israeli peace movement. The interim arrangements, dressed up in the meretricious garb of diplomacy, blinded both to the reality of continued occupation; one major failure of Oslo was that it did not address the critical question of Israeli settlements. When the illusions were finally stripped away with the Camp David talks in the summer of 2000, the Palestinians were faced with the unbearable misery of their life and lack of a future—especially the younger generation, the most sensitive compass in any nation.

Most Israeli politicians were convinced that by the end of the process, Palestinians would have to relinquish most of their national, religious, and human rights because of Israel's ability to dictate terms, especially with coordinated pressure from the United States. Therefore, and throughout the Oslo period, successive Israeli governments shared the same political bottom line: a united Jerusalem would be the eternal capital of Israel, the Jordan Valley would be forever controlled by Israel as a security asset, most of the Jewish settlements would stay and remain under Israeli sovereignty, and Israel would accept no moral, political, or historical responsibility for the Palestinian refugees. The Israeli public was indoctrinated with these guidelines on a daily basis; as a result, most were convinced that all are legitimate Israeli rights. The 2000 intifada brought an end to those illusions and set the region on a course toward reality without masks.

The Shifting Geography of Occupation

In 1987 Israel controlled every aspect of Palestinian life; there was no authority but the occupation authority. As a result, intifada activities were neither confined nor localized. Protests and clashes occurred in every neighborhood and street. The 1987 intifada was a genuine mass movement; most of the Palestinian population was directly involved in the resistance in one way or another. Methods ranged from peaceful protests and civil disobedience to limited violence. The conditions on the ground were almost identical in cities, villages, and refugee camps. Both locally and internationally, it was clear that the confrontation was between an oppressed people and a foreign occupier.

The Oslo interim arrangements created a different environment for Intifada 2000. The fact that the Palestinian Authority had sovereignty in some areas (aside from control over entrance and exit, of course) and shared sovereignty in others complicated the context in which the uprising took place. Confrontations were confined mostly to the borders between Palestinian-controlled areas and Israeli-controlled areas. This situation should have made it easier for the Israel Defense Forces to control and confine the conflict. Instead, because the government wanted to punish Palestinians for not accepting the dictates of Camp David, it decided to adopt an iron fist policy and use excessive firepower. As a result, the casualty tolls have been horrendous.

The existence of a Palestinian Authority and of areas that are defined as sovereign have allowed the Israelis to portray the conflict as a state of war, as if there were parity between the two sides. This situation gave Israel the excuse to mobilize its full military arsenal against Palestinians, which was unthinkable during even the most violent periods of the 1987 intifada. Under these conditions, Israel was using its power not to regain control but for punishment and political dictation. On the other hand, Palestinians had no short-term demands; rather, they were defending their legitimate rights. The intifada was envisioned as a necessary component of the negotiating process, without which Israel's dictation of the final-status terms would be inevitable. Therefore, Intifada 2000 cannot be concluded with interim arrangements. No one should have been surprised that the conflict would become painful once sensitive issues like Jerusalem and the rights of refugees were raised.

Several factors hindered mass involvement in the new intifada. Once armed groups became involved, the majority of the population stayed away from direct confrontation. Also, the Oslo agreements had led to the installment of the Palestinian Authority as a corrupt, one-party leadership; this lack of democracy cast a malaise over Palestinian society and politics. The public mistrusted the PA—was it a guarantor of Israeli security, as Oslo had stipulated, or was it the leader of the intifada?

From Grassroots to Hierarchy…and Back?

The 1987 intifada was at first highly decentralized, composed of local initiatives and led by local activists. In addition to the confrontations with Israeli soldiers, there was a gradual move toward civil disobedience in most regions of the West Bank and Gaza: Popular committees challenged Israel's Civil Administration; an underground school system was established after the Israelis closed the schools; Israeli products were boycotted; people threw out their military identity cards; and there was a tax rebellion, most famously in Beit Sahour. Because the resistance had wide popular participation and was diverse in methodology, it managed to confuse the Israeli army and had great potential for sustainability. But by the end of 1989, the PLO leadership had begun to centralize the uprising. As a result, the level of popular participation decreased tremendously, local leaders were marginalized, and semi-militant groups such as the Black Panthers, the Red Eagles, and the Qassam Brigades of Hamas became the main players. (Of course, ruthless Israeli repression—including killings, torture, and prolonged detention—was crucial in subduing the uprising; Beit Sahour was besieged for forty-five days, for example.) The intifada was already fading by 1990; the Gulf War diminished morale further. Finally, with the 1991 Madrid conference and the secret Oslo talks that followed, Palestinians lost the chance to combine negotiations with active resistance.

Intifada 2000, on the other hand, started explosively, with many confrontations and high casualties, quickly escalated into militant clashes that occasionally involved the Palestinian police force (although more often unofficial armed groups), and then normalized into less intense clashes with frequent military operations from both sides. This sequence took place even as negotiations sputtered on. By late spring 2001, the intifada stood at a crossroads. It looked like it would be concluded with a political agreement or it would evolve into a less violent but more effective uprising, with wider participation.

The ability of Palestinians to mobilize their power and the power of their potential allies in a more effective way could become the crucial factor in deciding the course of events. Mobilizing masses in a peaceful way against the symbols of occupation, such as checkpoints, military camps, and settlements, could nullify the only other option Israel has: unilateral separation. The concept of separation is based on the assumption that such symbols of control are sustainable. In addition, mobilizing refugees in a massive "return home" march from inside the West Bank and Gaza, and from the diaspora as well, would force that issue onto the Israeli agenda, however much it is now resisted. In other words, Intifada 2000 still has the potential to reverse the sequence of Intifada 1987. Signs for such a transformation began to develop after several months. The massive, peaceful demonstration against the blockade of the Ramallah-Birzeit road in March of 2001 forced a reversal of the Israeli plans to cut Ramallah off from the surrounding villages. This and other large peaceful demonstrations were indicators of a gradual change in the character of the intifada. Also encouraging was the participation of small Israeli peace groups, which finally began to make the transition from protest to resistance; this may herald the development of a genuine Israeli peace camp. The main challenge for this peaceful resistance is whether it can survive alongside continuing military operations from both sides. A dramatic move by Prime Minister Ariel Sharon against the Palestinian Authority might indicate to the Palestinian public that massive nonviolent resistance is the best way to counter Sharon's strategy.

Intifada 1987 took place without the complications created by having the Palestinian Authority. The earlier uprising never had to meet the challenges posed by shared authority, internal borders, negotiations, and security partnership between the PA and Israel. In the early weeks of Intifada 2000, the clashes between the Palestinian police and the IDF brought to an end the efforts to create a "security partnership." This change is of enormous significance: within the Oslo context, security partnership was the only way for Israel to sustain its control over Palestinians. Now that the illusion of having a security partner was ended, Israelis began to see the Palestinian Authority as either an enemy to fight against or an enemy to make peace with. (The intifada was not the first crisis between the PA and Israel; the severe clashes during the 1996 "tunnel crisis"—when Israel began construction under Jerusalem's Haram al-Sharif, leading to riots and gun battles in which dozens were killed—were an indication of what confrontations between the two could look like.) Thus Israel began to think more in terms of geographic separation. On the other hand, the Palestinian people perceived security partnership as their nightmare. There was almost a consensus among them that it must be ended. Therefore, Intifada 2000 was not a confined conflict, like the tunnel crisis, that could end with parties resuming efforts from the status quo ante. The collapse of security cooperation limited the future options to either geographic separation (removal of the settlements and establishment of firm borders between Israel and Palestine) or demographic separation (keeping the settlements and other areas under Israeli control while enforcing separation of relatively autonomous, highly populated Palestinian areas from the rest of Palestine), with the latter imposed through military force.

As for the negotiating process, Intifada 2000 managed to challenge the long-lived Israeli illusion that security obedience must come first. The infamous and one-sided Israeli stand that "we do not negotiate under fire" (the assumption that Israel can continue hostilities against Palestinians in the framework of negotiations, while Palestinians are not allowed the same policy) was undermined. The gradual modification of this stand—Israel did finally re-enter full political negotiations while under fire—is a significant change that could set the basic lines of future relations. After the election of Sharon, the main area of conflict was around precisely this issue. The primary reason for his election, in fact, was the Israeli public's lack of tolerance for negotiations in the context of open conflict. Again,

Palestinians can force a carefully formulated strategy in this regard by transforming the intifada into a massive, less violent resistance.

Therefore, even though the existence of the PA logistically complicated and severely confined intifada activities, the uprising dramatically corrected the relations between Israel and the PA to the benefit of the latter.

Youth and the Intifada

The involvement of young Palestinians in resistance to the Israeli occupation is not a new phenomenon, of course. At least since the first intifada, there has been a tradition of passing the conflict from one generation to another. It is transmitted to younger generations both experientially, through living it, and theoretically, through formal and informal education. Since Palestinians are subject to oppression and atrocities on a daily basis, it is impossible to create a different, specially designed environment to raise kids away from the conflict. While Israeli children in Tel Aviv, for example, can enjoy their childhood away from the day-to-day conflict, Palestinian kids cannot.

Looking at the introductory periods of both intifadas, we can see striking similarities in terms of the involvement of youth. Prior to Intifada 1987, the symptoms of generational defeat were evident. The Arab summit in Jordan earlier that year had totally ignored the Palestinian question, and Palestinians inside the occupied territories were in total despair and mostly pacified. Suddenly, a new generation stepped in with an unprecedented level of determination, renewed hope, and self-confidence, and they reoriented the entire community toward resistance.

By the time of Intifada 2000, Palestinians had lost interest in the peace process, having given up hope that they would get anything substantial out of it. The malfunctioning of the PA, on the one hand, and the continuity of the Israeli occupation, on the other, had forced Palestinians into a passive mode. Resisting occupation procedures and correcting the wrongdoings of the PA were almost unthinkable. Again, and as suddenly as in 1987, a new generation stepped in, renewed hope, and moved the whole community toward active resistance.

While in both cases the younger generation, mainly teenagers, played a key role in the active resistance, Intifada 2000 recorded a much higher level of casualties among them. Two factors are responsible for the high death toll among teenagers: one is that the points of conflict were confined to specific areas, which made demonstrators a more exposed target for Israeli soldiers and snipers. The other has to do with the Israeli army. It is evident that the army's iron fist policy is responsible for the high casualty tolls among both Palestinian demonstrators and bystanders. Because many of the clash sites are located at the borders of sovereignty zones, or in some cases inside crowded Palestinian cities, villages, and refugee camps, there has been a high percentage of casualties among noninvolved residents. Most of the children killed have been bystanders or residents of neighborhoods adjacent to clashpoints.

The Role of the Media

Both in 1987 and in 2000 the media played a significant role and had a serious impact on the course of events. The 1987 intifada was reported primarily by the Israeli and non-Arab international media, whereas one of the major factors influencing Intifada 2000 is the ubiquity of Arab satellite and local Palestinian TV stations. This additional coverage provided more fuel to the intifada and mobilized Arab masses on a scale never witnessed during the previous uprising. The uncensored flow of media, especially satellite television, into the living rooms of citizens throughout the Arab world presented a major challenge to Arab governments. While there are clear limitations on what the Arab governments can and are willing to do, pressure from the masses did force a higher degree of support. While the gap between what the masses want and what their governments can deliver is still huge, at least these leaders find it much more difficult to act as mediators or as nonaligned.

At the early stage of both rebellions, a significant image transmitted through major TV networks resulted in widescale sympathy for Palestinians. In the first intifada, it was of Israeli soldiers using huge stones to crush the bones of two young Palestinians after they were arrested. This scene was transmitted by CNN. The critical image in the second intifada, captured by a French video team, was the killing of the boy Muhammad al-Durra while he was seeking refuge with his father during a clash at the Netzarim junction in Gaza. In both intifadas, the early images were challenged by a flow of reports and photos conveying a far more negative view of Palestinians. Both started with images of oppressed Palestinians resisting occupation and developed into images of either meaningless violence or both parties being equally responsible.

Intifada 2000 was confused further in the media by the existence of the Palestinian Authority, with its sovereign areas and security forces. Because of the higher incidence of armed resistance in the current uprising, journalists wavered between reporting an uprising against occupation and reporting a state of war. Parents were accused of sending children to the battlefield and therefore of being responsible for their death. Reporting of particular incidents, in isolation from any broader context, confused the audience and created the false image of a series of miniwars, each one having a clear beginning and end, with blame neatly attributable to one side or the other. The roots of the conflict were considered irrelevant.

Unlike coverage of the 1987 intifada, Israeli media coverage of the new uprising was like that of a state-dominated industry. Listening to an army spokesman, watching TV reports, or reading Israeli newspapers was pretty much the same experience, with a few notable exceptions. The successful recruitment of Israeli media in the effort to defeat the intifada weakened their reliability and severely limited their Palestinian audience. The daily carnage on TV screens fueled the conflict, stimulating the desire for revenge. Children in particular were victims of these images, which will no doubt influence their future behavior and attitudes. No wonder that each generational crisis is more intense and violent than the previous one.

The Internet war is another interesting new development. In 1987 it was of course not available; in 2000 both sides used the Internet extensively as both a media and an advocacy and organizing tool. Thousands of activists with a computer and an Internet connection waged a media war in both directions. The massive flow of images, reports, and personal stories added considerably to the coverage of the crisis. While mass media were immersed in technical reporting, with the Israeli press sympathetic to the IDF and local Palestinian and Arab press sympathetic to the Palestinians, the Internet provided a diversity of information and images that covered all aspects of the conflict, allowing people—at least those with access to a computer—to evaluate more critically the top-down reporting. However, the influence of the Internet is still marginal as compared with the mass media.

Addressing the Outside World

The message to the Arab world of the 1987 intifada, which initially aroused widespread sympathy, was interrupted by the Gulf War. The uprising's achievements ended with the first bullet fired at the Iraq-Kuwait border in 1990. In addition, the poor and highly controlled coverage of the intifada through official state-owned media limited the influence of the uprising among the Arab masses.

Before the 2000 intifada, international efforts to solve the Palestinian-Israeli conflict were peaking, so the demand was not for more international involvement but to change the nature of that involvement. If the frustration prior to 1987 was lack of interest and involvement by outside parties, the anger in 2000 was at the effort of the United States and Israel to force an unjust solution on the Palestinians. Contrary to 1987, this frustration was directly addressed to the Arab masses; the result was widespread demonstrations that forced an Arab summit to convene. That summit backed the Palestinian struggle, promised considerable financial support for the intifada, and, more important, stressed the fact that Palestinians are the key to stability in the Middle East. While the commitments made at the summit might not be totally fulfilled, the intifada managed to force a process of gradual reform on the official Arab world. These achievements in the early weeks of the intifada encouraged both the PA and ordinary Palestinians to continue and intensify the uprising.

The 2000 uprising, which started within the general framework of intensive international efforts to solve the conflict through negotiations, was perceived as harmful to those efforts. Thus the level of international sympathy for Palestinians failed to match the level of Israeli atrocities. The attempt to build an international grassroots coalition in support of Palestinian rights is a good step forward, but it cannot have a significant impact in the near future. In addition, Intifada 2000, at least in its initial stages, failed to address the Israeli public directly. Because that public was exposed to the uprising only through its own, relatively uncritical media, there was a tremendous amount of fear and a tribal rallying behind the leadership; this was true as well for the Palestinian side. Thus internal differences were replaced by a sense of unity on both sides.

The Israelis

Prior to the 1987 intifada, Israel had prepared to fight enemies from without. That intifada provided a clear example of how powerful and dangerous an enemy from within can be. This forced Israelis at all levels of society to deal seriously with the difficult question of whether to recognize a Palestinian state and to consider the feasibility of demographic separation.

Intifada 1987 was an eye-opening event for many Israelis. It deeply affected public and official policy on the Palestinian issue. Until that eruption, most failed to see Palestinians as a people with national and human rights. The overwhelmingly nonviolent character of the rebellion and the unprecedented level of Israeli oppression encouraged many Israelis to work against the occupation as an essential requirement to achieve peace, and the uprising helped the Israeli anti-occupation movement in its campaign against state policy. While the peace movement continued to be marginal in numbers, the intifada brought about major changes in the way Israel dealt with the Palestinian problem. Recognition of the PLO and the gradual acceptance of the idea of establishing a Palestinian state are clear examples of this change. On the other hand, that uprising was confronted with the militant attitudes of the right-wing camp in Israel and with the settlers at its front lines. Israeli society was genuinely divided.

In 1987 there was a clear separation between the question of Israel's occupation and any worries about the existence of Israel. Intifada 2000, however, was oriented not simply around the general demand of ending the occupation but around the specific insistence on Palestinian control of East Jerusalem and the right of return. Because these two demands have much less sympathy among Israelis—with many perceiving the call for right of return to be a threat to the "Jewish character" of the state—the anti-occupation camp failed to develop as a genuine peace camp. The split in Israeli society, which did not come close to addressing basic Palestinian demands, was merely technical: whether or not to continue with negotiations during the crisis, whether or not to dismantle small isolated settlements, whether or not to accept a few thousand token refugees. Therefore, Palestinians have been facing an Israeli society that is, at least vis-à-vis the Palestinian question, more united than ever. Also, the fact that there has been more armed resistance in this uprising has severely limited the chances even for the radical and extremely marginalized Israeli peace groups to participate in anti-occupation efforts.

Conclusion

For the Palestinians, in order to avoid concluding this intifada without tangible achievements, thus merely laying the groundwork for the next one, it is crucial to begin the process of reforming the intifada. The uprising must move from resistance to achievement. The only way to do this is to diversify the intifada's actions, bring the masses back to the battlefield and directly confront the structures of occupation and control, such as settlements, military bases, and checkpoints, through massive, nonviolent resistance.

It is becoming more evident that whenever the opportunity arises to end the conflict with a solution that addresses the needs of both sides, the Israeli public drifts quickly to the right. Therefore, Israeli governments are unable to fulfill the requirements of a just and lasting peace. While reasons for this drift are disputed, and in all cases Israelis have looked for a Palestinian act to explain it, the fact is incontestable. There will never be a fair solution as long as Israel refuses to agree to a complete withdrawal from the territories occupied in 1967—including East Jerusalem—refuses to recognize its moral and historical responsibility for the Palestinian refugee problem, and insists on an intolerable level of control over Palestinian lives. Palestinians, for their part, are not willing to adjust to Israeli demands that contradict their legitimate national and human rights. Since 1967, the region has been subject to a major conflict about every ten years. Intifada 2000 may have begun a period when it is not confined in either space or time.

12. NOTES FROM DHEISHEH
MUNA HAMZEH

Friday, September 29, 2000, started off as another ordinary day in Dheisheh.[1] I say ordinary, of course, in the sense that it was another day in our lives under Israel's apartheid rule, a rule which had become all the more oppressive and demeaning since the Palestinian leadership signed the Oslo Accord with Israel in September 1993. For one thing, the permanent Israeli military checkpoint at the northern entrance of Bethlehem was still there, caging us in, forcing us to keep out of Jerusalem and from using Jerusalem roads to get to our offices, hospitals, universities, or wherever it is that we worked, or had business to tend to.[2] Fortified Israeli settlements, strategically built on confiscated hilltops surrounding Bethlehem, were also there to remind us that Israel, and not the Palestinian Authority, is in control of the land.[3] Square gray and yellow blocks of concrete were still standing on various sidewalks throughout the district of Bethlehem to remind us that the maps signed between Israel and the Palestinian Authority at the Interim Agreement in 1995 (Oslo II) intended them to be placed there as a dividing line between neighborhoods under full Palestinian control and neighborhoods under full Israeli control, regardless of whether or not these neighborhoods were located within the same boundaries of a given town or village.[4]

Just the day before, we had watched, in utter dismay and disgust, Israeli Knesset Member Ariel Sharon on our TV screens as he marched into the grounds of al-Aqsa Mosque under the protection of what appeared to be hundreds of armed Israeli security forces. Our feelings on that day remain vivid in my mind. Without such heavy protection, would Sharon have dared set foot on the grounds of the holy site? Apart from sending a direct insult to every Muslim, every Arab, and every Palestinian, what was the purpose of the visit? To show the Palestinians who is in control of Muslim holy sites in Jerusalem? An uneasy mood prevailed in Dheisheh. This time around, the Israelis were going a bit too far in testing the tolerance of the Palestinians.

Shortly before noon on that fateful Friday, I went to Bethlehem to meet Mia. A Swedish photojournalist and a friend, Mia was working on an anthropological film in Artas, an ancient village situated in a fertile valley just down the hill behind Dheisheh. I had promised to translate, on camera, some of the interviews Mia wanted to conduct with some elderly women in Artas. After several hours of filming, we were exhausted and decided to take a cab to a restaurant in Bethlehem. A nourishing meal was just what we needed after hours of hard work. As the cab approached downtown Bethlehem, the driver told us that he couldn't go any further.

Left: Israel Defense Forces pack up for the day in Hebron.

"There are clashes at Rachel's Tomb," he informed us.[5]

Having been tucked away in the quaint calmness of Artas a good part of the afternoon, we had no idea what was going on around us. The cab driver quickly filled us in.

"Following the Friday noon prayer at al-Aqsa, Israeli police and soldiers opened fire at worshipers, killing six Palestinians and wounding 220," he explained as we listened in utter disbelief.

Instead of keeping its forces away from the mosque during such a volatile time, Israel was obviously thirsty for blood. Otherwise, why send in so many security forces to al-Aqsa at a time when Muslims were still reeling from Sharon's visit to the holy site?

The driver let us off a few blocks away from Rachel's Tomb. As we started walking in the direction of the clashes, we could smell the horrible odor of tear gas in the air. Dozens of young Palestinians were hurling stones at the heavily armed Israeli soldiers who were responding by firing live, rubber-coated metal bullets and tear gas into the crowds. Every few minutes, an ambulance whizzed by, carrying yet another injured Palestinian to the Hussein government hospital nearby. Using my cellular phone, I called a friend in Shati refugee camp in Gaza. "All hell seems to be breaking loose here in Bethlehem," I told him. "What is the situation like in Gaza?" My friend replied that Gaza was quiet, with no demonstrations anywhere. Bethlehem and Jerusalem were apparently the only areas where fierce confrontations were taking place.

The shooting persisted. Mia and I took refuge inside a restaurant and watched the clashes from a window. I remember standing there, watching the trigger-happy soldiers firing at Palestinian youths and wondering if these same soldiers would have the *chutzpah* to show their faces in the Palestinian territories if they were stripped of their guns. During the first intifada, young men from the camp would occasionally catch a soldier who had somehow gotten separated from his patrol and lost his way. Stories would circulate about how terrified the soldier was, and how thankful he was to the young men for turning him over, unharmed, to his companions. And now, standing a few feet in front of me, were young soldiers with helmets, bulletproof vests, and loaded weapons, firing at unarmed civilians and then running back for cover from the flying stones. This is the real image of Israel. The image it tries so hard to hide from the rest of the world.

After inhaling too much tear gas for our liking, and watching too many young men sustain injuries and get rushed to the hospital, Mia and I decided to call it a day. It was nearing dusk and Mia had to find a cab that would take her back to her house in Jerusalem. We said our goodbyes and I headed home to Dheisheh. My eyes and my cheeks were burning from the strong sensation of the tear gas, and I was beginning to feel pain in my chest. When I arrived at my house, I sat down to watch live coverage of the confrontations on one of the local, privately owned Bethlehem TV stations. Little did I, or anyone around me, know that this day, September 29, 2000, was not an ordinary day after all. Little did we know that it was the beginning of what would become known as the second intifada, the Intifada of al-Aqsa. And little did any of us know that Israel had an even more vicious force in store for us. A brutal repression that none of us, not even the best analysts amongst us, could have predicted.

Within the first six days of the intifada, Israel's army and police had killed sixty-one Palestinians and injured 2,657, many of them children under the age of 18, and many of them killed or wounded from shots fired to the upper part of the body.[6] By comparison, during the same period four Israelis—three soldiers and one settler—were killed, while thirty-five Israelis were wounded, most of them lightly.[7] Israel's excessive use of force was devastating. We spent every waking minute watching TV, trying to keep up with the names and faces of the falling victims. But each day, it was becoming harder and harder to keep up. There simply were too many victims, too many injuries and too many names and faces to retain in our exhausted memory. News reports would tell us that one victim had just graduated from university, and another victim was getting married in one week, and a third victim had just fathered his first child, and a fourth victim was an only child. And we sat there, absorbing all this, never knowing if the next victim was going to be someone we loved, or worked with, or went to college with, or lived next door to. We lived with this horrifying feeling at the rise of each new day, and went to sleep with it at the end of each long night.

And if this wasn't too much for people to bear, Israel, as usual, quickly clamped down a strict closure on the Palestinian territories, collectively punishing us and preventing thousands of people from reaching their workplaces. None of us were able to leave the immediate areas where we lived. While thousands of Israelis went about their lives, getting up and going to work each morning, and while thousands of Israeli soldiers and security forces were shooting human beings as easily as they would shoot decoys in target practice, we were being caged in like animals, unable to have even a fleeting sense that our lives were normal. Fearing for the safety of children, schools in the Palestinian territories were also temporarily closed. There was no escape, not even momentary, from the events unfolding before us.

In those early days of al-Aqsa Intifada, we sat in our homes in Dheisheh, thinking that we were safe from Israeli gunfire. Unlike the first intifada, when Israeli soldiers were right there in our midst, this intifada was different. This time we were, or so we thought, living within the safe boundaries of the Zone A area controlled by the Palestinian Authority. Those who wished to partake in the clashes had to go to Rachel's Tomb, where the Israeli soldiers were stationed. Those who didn't want to participate could remain in the safety of their homes. How foolish we were to think that being in Palestinian-controlled areas gave us any protection or kept us safe. For you can always count on the Israelis to think of new ways to brutalize the Palestinians. If, unlike the first intifada, Israel no longer had troops stationed in every corner of the West Bank and Gaza Strip, there was another way. The Israeli-made Merkava tanks and US-made AH-64D Apache Longbow helicopters were the answer. If Israel couldn't send in soldiers to the areas controlled by the Palestinian Authority, then it would simply bomb the hell out of our towns and villages. To reward Israel, the US Defense Department signed a letter of offer and acceptance with Israel in February 2001 to sell Israel an additional nine Apaches, which will be manufactured by Boeing in Mesa, Arizona.[8]

The helicopters would start flying overhead shortly after sunrise, and they would keep circling all day long. Then, after sunset, they would keep their lights turned off and start bombing residential neighborhoods in the towns of Beit Jala, Beit Sahour, the village Al-Khadir, and Aida refugee camp, all located inside the district of Bethlehem. The three privately owned TV stations in Bethlehem would broadcast live coverage of the bombings. We would sit and watch, waiting to see if someone we knew just had his house shelled, or was injured or killed. Then we would start calling to check on friends in the areas that had just been bombed. Other nights, we would go up on the roof, crouch down, and watch the bombings of Beit Jala in the same way that Americans watch the fireworks during the Fourth of July festivities. Except in Palestine, these fireworks were real bombs and missiles, falling on real homes, where real people lived.

It made no difference, of course, whether or not we were up on the roof, watching TV, eating a meal, or sleeping. None of us had shelters in our homes, so there really was no safe place for us to hide from the rocket or tank fire. This is why we went up on the rooftops to watch the bombings, live before our naked eyes. And all the time, we felt like players in a game of Russian roulette. Except in this Israeli-style game, we weren't in control of the game. Anyone's house could be a target, and any of us could be the next victim. It was the Israeli military, not we civilians, who were manning the controls.

Something funny happens to your mindset when the bombs are falling around you. First you experience an intense fear, the sort that makes you feel pain in your knees and in your stomach. Then, after a few nights, you simply stop being afraid. You stop being afraid because all the children around you—nearly 53 percent of the population in Dheisheh are children under the age of 16—are so terrorized that you, as an adult, stop feeling fear. Instead, you feel a sort of crippling helplessness, an outrage, and a fury that children around you may get killed and there is absolutely nothing you can do to prevent it. This is a much worse feeling than fear. It is a feeling that makes you realize that your university degree, your social status, your money, and everything else about you is completely worthless in the face of this insane use of sophisticated weaponry that brings with it death and destruction.

But the Palestinians, after all these years of a brutal occupation, have not lost their spirit, something the Israelis have never been able to understand about us. The Israelis may have the weapons to kill us, but we have the spirit to cling to life. One of the most heartwarming scenes I used to watch from my living-room window almost each day was this elderly refugee who lived up the hill from me. I never knew his name, but around noon each day, he would slowly make his way down the hill as he leaned heavily on his cane. He would walk down to the mosque to pray and then sit in the sun outside one of the many family-owned grocery shops in the camp. On more than one occasion, the helicopters would be circling low overhead as the old man was on his way. Suddenly, he would stop walking and raise his bent back, lift his cane, wave it angrily at the pilot and shout, "Damn you, you son of a prostitute! Damn you to hell, you bastard!" And then just as suddenly, he would continue walking, muttering something incomprehensible under his breath.

The first month of al-Aqsa Intifada was nearing its end when I received a call from Tom Segev. A noted Israeli author and journalist who writes for the leading Israeli newspaper *Ha'aretz*, Segev had read, on the Internet, the diary entries I had been writing about the daily impact of the intifada on our lives in Dheisheh refugee camp and wanted to interview me as part of a review he was writing for *Ha'aretz* about my diaries.[9]

The very first question Segev asked me was, "Why an intifada, Muna? Why did you Palestinians give us an intifada, when we [the Israelis] had given you the Oslo peace agreement?" This question, so typically Israeli, showed just how little the Israelis understand the Palestinians, what we think and what we are going through. At the end of the Camp David II talks in July 2000, even a child in the Palestinian territories could have told anyone who cared to ask that an explosion was on the way. In Dheisheh, friends would come over almost every evening to socialize, watch the news and discuss the latest political negotiations. Most were convinced that the Israelis and the Palestinian Authority, with the full backing of the US administration, had already reached an agreement at Camp David, to the very last detail, and that what remained was imposing the agreement on an overwhelmingly disheartened Palestinian population. Most believed that Israel planned to shed some Palestinian blood in order to force the Palestinians to accept the latest agreement. Nobody, however, predicted a full-scale intifada.

Indeed, the spontaneity with which unarmed Palestinian civilians took to the streets showed just how fed up we were with the overall deterioration of conditions since the signing of the Oslo accords. Nothing in the past seven years had given us hope or faith that we had entered an era of real peace with Israel. On the contrary, house demolitions, land confiscations, uprooting of trees, arrests, restrictions on our movements, economic control, and closures were still very much a part of Israel's policy toward the Palestinians. The Israeli public, living in total isolation from the Palestinian territories, was totally blind to these realities. Somehow, the Israelis expected the Palestinians to remain happy as Israel's underdog. We were expected to be the subservient blacks who would remain obedient to our white masters. If we couldn't obtain Israeli military permits allowing us entry into Jerusalem, the Israelis expected us to be content to sneak past the military checkpoints. "Come on," Segev told me during the phone interview. "You and I know that you [Palestinians] sneak into Jerusalem without permits all the time." It is precisely this that the Israelis seem unable to understand: that we will never be content to sneak into our own capital city—where we have every right to be—through a back door or back window. What we want, expect, demand, and are fighting for is to walk in, as free men and women, through the front door.

From the rooftop of my house in Dheisheh, the Israeli settlement of Gilo comes into full view—another ordinary day in Dheisheh. Perched like a fortress on a strategic hill a few miles away, Gilo is a clear signal to us that Israel controls the land.[10] Bethlehem is completely caged in by Israeli settlements, all built on Palestinian land that was confiscated in 1967. To the south of Dheisheh, the settlement of Efrat keeps growing by the day, swallowing the highest hilltops to the southwest of Bethlehem.[11] While Israeli politicians have been trying to convince the world that Israel wants to relinquish large parts of the West Bank to the Palestinians in future peace agreements, we have been watching Israeli military bulldozers steadily confiscate more and more Palestinian land, expanding existing settlements and building new ones. According to the Israeli group Peace Now, construction of homes for Israeli settlers in the West Bank and Gaza Strip was up by 50 percent since the 1993 Oslo accords, thousands of them under Ehud Barak's government.[12] The contradiction between what Israel says to the rest of the world and what it does on the ground in East Jerusalem, the West Bank, and the Gaza Strip is so stark that none of us believe it is in any way serious about peace.

Isolating major Palestinian towns and their respective villages from one another by surrounding them with heavily guarded settlements ensures the continuation of Israel's apartheid rule by segmenting the West Bank into islands of disjointed bantustans. Furthermore, as during al-Aqsa Intifada, the Israeli military can use the grounds of the settlements, all strategically located, to line up its high-tech, state-of-the-art tanks and bombard the hell out of residential neighborhoods.

Appearing more befitting in a large American metropolitan city, Gilo's apartment buildings collide with the beautiful landscape of Palestine, with its fig, peach, and almond orchards and terraced hills. While the settlers plant green forests around their settlement, using water resources that are denied to the Palestinians, the Israeli military and armed settlers go on a vicious attack against Palestinian agricultural land. As if not satisfied with killing hundreds and maiming thousands of Palestinians, the Israelis are also keen on killing our trees. Within the first three months of the intifada, 181,000 trees belonging to Palestinian farmers were forcibly uprooted.[13] Israeli soldiers and settlers who've been uprooting trees represent the same country that appeals for money from American Jews to plant trees in Israel. I have been to American Jewish homes in the United States where I have seen plaques on mantels, with a print of a tree in the center, thanking so and so for his donation to plant a tree in Israel. After all, how can Israel project itself to the world as not just the only democracy in the Middle East but also the nation that made the "desert" bloom? It does so by skillfully pleading for sympathy money on the one hand, while at the same time destroying the living proof that Palestinians have always planted their country with trees. The stories that grandmothers in Dheisheh, the survivors of the 1948 expulsion of the Palestinians, tell their grandkids describe a simple village life where hardworking farmers plowed their land, planting it with wheat, vegetables, herbs, and olive and fruit trees, so they could live a relatively self-sufficient life. Back in 1948, Israel tried to convince the world that it had established its state on a land without a people. What has changed in Israel's behavior since then? Does Israel really believe that by killing the Palestinians and destroying their agriculture, they will somehow disappear off the face of the earth?

I am still unable to get used to all the open space around me and to my ability to move about so freely. I guess I am not yet weaned from being in the West Bank. It is going to take months before I become adjusted. There are no Israeli soldiers here in Austin. There are no tanks, no helicopters, no shooting of innocent people, many of them children. There are no kids lying in hospital beds, brain-dead from Israeli bullet wounds.

No, it is peaceful here in Austin. It is peaceful and I am free. Free to get in a car and drive anywhere in all this open space around me. There is so much of it that I feel both confused and overwhelmed. My heart, my mind, and even my body had grown so accustomed to confinement, for so many years, that I am at a loss as to how to handle my sudden freedom. In my confusion, I keep expecting to see checkpoints pop out of nowhere. I look out for tanks on the sides of the roads, and I feel the irksome presence of trigger-happy soldiers, waiting to stop me. But no one does. I am in Austin, Texas, not the Palestinian territories. There are no tanks, no soldiers, and no checkpoints. No one asks for my identification papers. No one intercepts me as I move about. I have to keep reminding myself that I am free.

I sit on a stone bench somewhere on the campus of the University of Texas and I absorb the open space. I stare at the trees above my head. I look down at the green grass underneath my feet. I watch the birds hopping on the footpaths in search of a morsel of food. And then I start to cry. I want to stand up and shout. I want to scream. But I know I can't. I can't have an emotional outburst. And so I smoke another cigarette and cry some more. My mind travels across the Atlantic, across the Mediterranean, and into the Palestinian territories.

I think of my friends Hourieh and Muyasar and wonder how they're doing. I picture the face of children like Marianna, Sanabel, and Alaa, and wonder if the sound of the bombing still frightens them. Where are the helicopters bombing right now? Who is getting insulted at which checkpoint? Who was injured today? Who was the latest victim of deadly Israeli gunfire? Who is able to get to work? How are people managing to scrape together enough money to buy food? I flip through the February 14, 2001, issue of the *New York Times*. In an article describing Israel's latest assassination of a Palestinian security officer,[14] I read that a recent UN finding shows that the Palestinian economy has been losing $8.6 million a day as a result of the intifada and Israel's blockade. The finding states that 38 percent of the Palestinian work force is now unemployed, with some 32 percent of the people living in poverty, a 50 percent increase since the intifada began at the end of September 2000. What will it take for America and the world to wake up and demand an end to Israel's aggression and brutality? When will the world demand an end to Israel's occupation of the Palestinians?

I fall into a restless sleep at night and dream that an Israeli army unit is chasing after my friends and me. We are somewhere in Gaza and we try to run for our lives, but we are suddenly cornered and the soldiers start shooting at very close range. The screams and the immense amount of blood force me to wake up. I am sweating and gasping for air. The dreams just don't stop. I've been out of the Palestinian territories for three months and the dreams still haunt me. I know it is going to take a long time—a long time before I'm not jumpy when I hear a helicopter flying overhead. I hear the helicopters here in Austin, but they are up there to file weather reports for local TV stations. I am still not convinced that they will not bring death and destruction. It is going to take a long time before I don't panic at the sound of an ambulance siren. And a very long time before I stop dreaming that the bodies of my friends are being riddled with gunfire.

Notes

1. The largest of three Palestinian refugee camps in Bethlehem, Dheisheh is home to nearly 10,000 refugees who were forced to flee their homes in the 1948 war. Their villages, numbering about forty-two, were destroyed by Israel during and after the war.

2. Situated on the Jerusalem-Hebron Road at the northern entrance of Bethlehem, this checkpoint was erected in 1991 to control the movement of Palestinians between Bethlehem and Jerusalem. Palestinians aren't allowed to cross this checkpoint without first obtaining a time-restricted, Israeli-issued permit. These permits are given only to a few hundred area residents at a given time, even though the population of the district of Bethlehem is about 150,000. Israeli citizens, including settlers, can freely cross the checkpoint at any time of the day or night without the need to obtain permits. And while Israelis are allowed to cross the checkpoint in their own vehicles, Palestinians are rarely given vehicle permits that would allow them to drive to Jerusalem in their own cars.

3. The tri-cities Bethlehem, Beit Jala, and Beit Sahour have been left with little land to accommodate natural population growth with the construction of the new Israeli settlement of Har Homa on the illegally seized Palestinian land of Jabal Abu Ghneim. Because of immense protest, the Israeli Labor government decided to freeze construction in early 1996. But in February 1997, the Israeli ministerial committee on Jerusalem approved the settlement plan, and bulldozers began construction that March. Whereas Har Homa seals the northern boundary of the Bethlehem area, the Etzion bloc of settlements limits Bethlehem's southern expanse. From the west, Bethlehem is surrounded by Betar Ilit settlement as well as two bypass roads, and by Tekoa settlement and a third bypass road from the east. The construction of Har Homa and the fenced military bypass road will connect it with the neighboring Gilo settlement, thus depriving Bethlehem of the only land left for its future development. This bypass road will also shift the border of Jerusalem farther south, deeper into the Bethlehem area. It is worth mentioning that in 1967 Israel unilaterally expanded the borders of East Jerusalem to include about sixteen square kilometers of Bethlehem. Source: The Applied Research Institute of Jerusalem: www.arij.org.

4. Since the Oslo II Agreement, the West Bank has been divided into three zones: A, B, and C. Zone A is under full Palestinian control and is made up of the big towns only. Zone B is under Palestinian civil control and Israeli security control. Zone C is under full Israeli control and includes the majority of the West Bank.

5. Situated on the Jerusalem-Hebron Road near Bethlehem's northern entrance, this small building marks the traditional Tomb of Rachel, Jacob's wife. Although considered holy to Christians, Muslims, and Jews, the Israeli military authorities have made it off-limits to Palestinians and have turned the site into a fortified and permanent military point, used by Israeli soldiers and snipers to fire at Palestinian demonstrators.

6. LAW, the Palestinian Society for the Protection of Human Rights and the Environment: www.lawsociety.org.

7. Israel Defense Forces home page: www.idf.il/english/announcements/previous_2000.stm.

8. "Israel Orders Nine Apache Longbow Helicopters," Associated Press, February 20, 2001.

9. Tom Segev, "Where Are You Anne Frank?" *Ha'aretz*, November 3, 2000.

10. The settlement of Gilo was constructed in 1970 on Palestinian lands belonging to the towns of Beit Jala and Beit Safafa and confiscated after the 1967 war. The present population of Gilo exceeds 30,000. Gilo was greatly expanded in the southern and western direction, resulting in the confiscation of more Beit Jala land. Source: www.arij.org.

11. Built in 1979 by the Likud government on confiscated Palestinian land, the settlement of Efrat lies southwest of Bethlehem and houses 5,700. Source: www.arij.org.

12. "Jewish Settlements in Territories up by 50 pct. since 1993: Peace Now," Agence France-Presse, December 4, 2000.

13. Gaza Community Mental Health Program: www.gcmhp.net/File_files/Losses.html.

14. Deborah Sontag, "Israel Hunts Down and Kills a Top Arafat Security Officer."

PART II

THE MEDIA WAR

13. THE US MEDIA AND THE NEW INTIFADA
ALI ABUNIMAH AND HUSSEIN IBISH

Introduction

Three weeks into the intifada, Israeli immigration minister Yael Tamir publicly demanded the recall of her government's consul-general in New York, Shmuel Sisso, holding him responsible for "Israel's failure in the press war," which, according to Tamir, "we're losing in New York because we are hardly making any effort to get the message out."[1] Whether because he had done his job exceptionally well, or because there was no job to be done, a survey of the US media strongly suggests Sisso could be forgiven for feeling grossly ill-served by Tamir's assessment.

The purpose of this brief study is to survey coverage of the intifada and evaluate whether Palestinian realities and points of view were given a fair hearing in major American news outlets, and if there was any truth to Tamir's belief that Israel was losing a "press war" in the American media. We examine patterns in opinion sections of major newspapers and look at a number of troubling trends in reporting and commenting on the uprising, including the commonly ignored fact that events are taking place in occupied territory, the claim that Palestinians want their children to be killed in order to embarrass Israel, the underreporting of Palestinian victims of violence, myths of Israeli restraint, attributions of omnipotence or unique evil to Yasir Arafat, and allegations that the uprising is driven by a trans-historical "clash of civilizations." We also look at the treatment of several crucial issues forming the background to the intifada, including the idea that Israel's proposals at the Camp David summit in July 2000 were "generous," moral inconsistencies on refugee rights in the cases of Kosovo and Palestine, and widespread claims that Israeli rule in occupied East Jerusalem is justified because Jews supposedly care more about the city than Arabs do. We close with a section outlining commentary we found to be balanced and pro-Palestinian, both of which are disturbingly rare.

Patterns of Exclusion: the *New York Times* and the *Washington Post*

From the first days of the intifada, the *New York Times* and the *Washington Post*, as the two most influential newspapers in the United States, devoted more space on their opinion and editorial pages to the Palestinian-Israeli conflict than to any other international issue, and more than any single domestic issue, save perhaps for the contested US presidential election.

The high standards that both papers proclaim did not translate into equal opportunity for proponents of Palestinian and Israeli perspectives. Both papers set the standard for unfair and exclusionary

Pages 230–31: Israeli police stand guard in the Muslim Quarter, East Jerusalem
Left: Shati refugee camp, Gaza

coverage. We conducted a comprehensive review of all the editorial and opinion articles published by both newspapers from the start of the intifada on September 29, 2000, to the end of January 2001. We divided the articles into three categories: those that predominantly expressed clear and unambiguous support for Israel's positions, those that expressed criticism and sympathy for both Palestinian and Israeli positions in substantial measure, and those that predominantly expressed clear and unambiguous support for Palestinian views. The *Washington Post* printed twenty-seven Op-Eds on the subject, of which twenty were strongly pro-Israeli, two were substantially sensitive to Israeli and Palestinian concerns, while only five were strongly sympathetic to Palestinian viewpoints. Of the *Post*'s thirteen staff editorials, twelve were strongly pro-Israeli, while only one was somewhat neutral.

During the same period, twenty-five of the *New York Times*'s thirty-three Op-Eds on the conflict were pro-Israeli, two were equally sensitive to Israeli and Palestinian views, and six took positions mostly sympathetic to Palestinian views. Of the *Times*'s fifteen staff editorials, fourteen were strongly pro-Israeli, and we categorized one as neutral only because it focused on internal Israeli politics and did not mention the Palestinians. Taking together all the opinion articles in both newspapers in this period, 81 percent were pro-Israeli, 7 percent were neutral, and just 12 percent were pro-Palestinian. But the numbers do not tell the whole story. Both papers made considerable efforts to include a wide range of Israeli, Jewish American, and other authors supportive of mainstream Israeli positions. By contrast, there were only three articles by Palestinians.

The *Washington Post* printed pieces by Dore Gold, a former Israeli ambassador to the United Nations and supporter of Ariel Sharon, and David Ivry, Israel's ambassador to the United States. Articles by Israel's Justice Minister, Yossi Beilin, and Israeli politician Natan Sharansky even appeared on the *Post*'s Op-Ed page on the same day, perhaps representing what the editors consider to be a balanced debate.[2]

The pattern of inclusion and exclusion in the *New York Times* was strikingly similar to that of the *Washington Post*. Once again, pro-Zionist viewpoints were aired in all their diversity. For instance, Avraham Burg, the speaker of the Israeli Knesset, and Amos Oz, a novelist, both wrote as members of the Israeli peace camp affecting bitter disappointment at Palestinian treachery and intransigence.[3]

Of the six articles in the *New York Times* mostly sympathetic to Palestinian viewpoints, only two Palestinians were among the authors, Palestinian-American academic Rashid Khalidi, and Jordanian-Palestinian journalist Rami Khouri.[4] Three articles were actually written by prominent Israelis.[5] Unlike the *Post*, therefore, the *Times* did include some Israeli voices outside or on the margins of the Zionist mainstream, but coupled with the virtual exclusion of Palestinian voices, this only underlined the extent to which Palestinians are not permitted to speak on their own behalf but must be represented by others, if at all.

Ensuring that Israel always has a "home team" advantage are the stables of strongly pro-Israeli columnists that both newspapers keep. Perhaps matched in their virulence are George Will and Charles Krauthammer at the *Washington Post* and William Safire at the *New York Times*. The *Post*'s Jim Hoagland and the *Times*'s Anthony Lewis were somewhat more mainstream in their support for Israel. The *Times*'s "angry but super-empowered" columnist Thomas Friedman occupies a unique position among American journalists. His eleven columns inspired by the intifada demonstrated his signature arrogance as well as the tension between his acknowledgment of harsh realities facing Palestinians living under occupation and his inability to fit them into a template of ardent Zionism.

The *Washington Post* and the *New York Times* are widely regarded as representing the pinnacle of American journalism, and they supply many of the opinion pieces that reappear in countless newspapers across the continent. Their representation of the world influences the coverage choices made by newspaper editors and TV, radio, and Internet content providers across America and even internationally. Hence, their gross distortion and naked partisanship in the Palestinian-Israeli conflict do an enormous disservice not just to their own readers but to the American public at large, in whose name US foreign policy is conducted on the basis of a deliberately crafted public "consensus" in which both newspapers consciously play a defining role.

The Missing Occupation

It is taken for granted in much global media coverage of the Palestinian-Israeli conflict that East Jerusalem, the West Bank, and the Gaza Strip are under military occupation by Israel. The conventional term for these areas, "the occupied territories," is language derived directly from UN Security Council resolutions, especially 242 (1967), and reflects a longstanding international consensus. But this fact was consistently omitted from US media coverage of the uprising. With the context of occupation omitted, reporting on events involving an uprising against an occupying army can become highly misleading and confusing.

When on October 7 the UN Security Council voted 14-0, with the United States abstaining, to condemn Israel's use of excessive force against Palestinians and called on Israel as the "occupying power" to abide by the Fourth Geneva Convention, US media ignored or downplayed the story. According to Fairness & Accuracy in Reporting, "only three of the top thirty-six US papers in the Nexis database—the *New York Times*, *Los Angeles Times* and *Newsday*—devoted articles to the vote."[6]

The *Washington Post* suggested that the occupation had already ended several years before when it wrote that negotiations between Israelis and Palestinians had to continue because "the possibility of reverting to the pre-Oslo days of occupation and violence is almost unthinkable." *Post* columnist Charles Krauthammer delved a little deeper into this spurious argument, demanding to know what Palestinians could possibly have any reason to protest in the intifada: "Israeli occupation? It ended years ago; 99 percent of Palestinians live under the rule of Yasser Arafat."[7] This sophistry, which originates in Israeli government releases and talking points, suggests that the existence of a set of tiny enclaves scattered throughout the occupied territories (making up a grand total of 17.2 percent of the West Bank, for example) in which Palestinians are nominally responsible for security, means that the Israeli occupation has ended.

While National Public Radio (NPR) reports occasionally acknowledged that the West Bank and Gaza Strip are Israeli-occupied and at times did an effective job of conveying the realities of that occupation, other reports presented Israeli settlers, whose presence in the West Bank is maintained solely by the military occupation, and indigenous Palestinians as being on equal terms. Linda Gradstein reported on increased attacks by Israeli settlers on Palestinian civilians but made no mention of the occupation, and portrayed the violence essentially as strife between two communities who are equally at risk and equally frightened of each other. "Many on both sides who live there have guns," Gradstein pointed out, and "many also feel threatened and scared." Nor did the report mention that while many on both sides may have guns, Israeli settlers are given their guns by the Israeli army, roam around freely with them, and are rarely punished for killing or injuring Palestinians.[8] A Palestinian civilian, meanwhile, may be shot dead on sight for carrying a gun and, in the context of the intifada, for bending down to pick up a rock.

Settlements such as Gilo, in occupied East Jerusalem, were consistently referred to as "Jewish neighborhoods." In a typical example, John Kifner reported in the *New York Times* that "Beit Jala is a staging area for attacks on the Jewish neighborhood of Gilo at Jerusalem's southern tip." In a report for NPR Jennifer Ludden told listeners, "For many Israelis, the southern Jerusalem neighborhood of Gilo symbolizes the dangers the peace process has wrought." Ludden declines to identify Gilo as a settlement even though she acknowledges that "Gilo…is built on land Israel confiscated from Arabs in 1967."[9] By not acknowledging that Gilo and similar sites are settlements, reports obscure the fact that these "neighborhoods" are illegal and grave violations of the Geneva Convention and the human rights of the occupied population. They also obscure the nature of the relationship between the settlers (now "neighbors") and the people on whose land they sit.

Sacrifice Mythology

From the beginning of the intifada, pro-Israel commentators argued that Palestinians alone were to blame for the fact that they were being shot by Israeli occupation forces, and that this was the intention of the Palestinian leadership. "Arafat has encouraged his youth legions to write their refusal in blood that is mostly their own," wrote Jim Hoagland in the *Washington Post*. Some claimed that Arafat was gleeful about the deaths of as many Palestinians as possible. As the *Fort Lauderdale Sun-Sentinel* put it, "He has returned to a tactic from the past: rile up the masses, send them out to their deaths as 'martyrs,' then tearfully parade their bodies before the world." *Post* columnist Charles Krauthammer claimed that "some telegenic massacre to rally the world to his side would be Arafat's fondest wish."[10]

Even more brazen was a widespread outpouring of condemnation of Palestinian parents and the Palestinian leadership for deliberately promoting the killing of Palestinian children in order to embarrass Israel. The calumny of "child sacrifice" was, to a large extent, the brainchild of the Israeli columnist and broadcaster Dan Margalit. Writing in the leading Israeli daily, *Ha'aretz*, and in other forums, Margalit called for an Israeli public relations offensive that would shift the moral responsibility for the deaths of so many Palestinian youths and children away from the Israeli army that killed them and onto Palestinians, whether the leadership or the children's parents. Margalit suggested that in order to "reduce the gap between the cold logic on Israel's side and the bloody photograph giving Palestinians the edge…. A planned and creative PR campaign would attack Arafat from an unexpected direction— that he sacrifices children…. If all officials repeated this contention, some of those graphic photos would work against Arafat."[11]

Pro-Israel commentators in the United States dutifully began to churn out columns designed to absolve Israeli soldiers from responsibility for the scores of unarmed children killed during the suppression of the intifada. "You feel as if you are watching a modern form of ritual sacrifice," wrote the *Times*'s Friedman, describing the circumstances in which Israeli soldiers routinely resorted to deadly force against rock-throwing kids.[12]

Almost none of the reports from journalists on the ground, especially those that focus on the deaths of specific children, support this claim in any way. Jessica Montell of B'tselem, The Israeli Information Center for Human Rights in the Occupied Territories, which looked into the allegations, reported that the organization "has found no evidence of organized exploitation of children" during the intifada.[13]

This racist argument is based on a dehumanization of Palestinian parents and families and a suggestion that Palestinians love their children and value life less than other people. It mirrors the "blame-the-parents" strategy adopted by segregationists in the American South, who turned dogs and water hoses on children in Birmingham, Alabama, during the civil rights movement, and, ironically, by British forces in Palestine, who killed Jewish teenagers during pro-Zionist disturbances in the late 1940s. And the Israeli Foreign Ministry claims mirror almost verbatim those made by the South African government during the 1984–85 uprising against apartheid. The *Los Angeles Times* reported at the height of the township uprising, in which hundreds of black youths were gunned down by South African forces, that "senior police officers have complained recently that their efforts to deal with unrest are hampered by the rioters' tactics, including the use of women and children as 'human shields,' the absence of suspected leaders from the front lines of most protests and the increased attacks on police."[14]

What is astonishing is that the major American media allowed themselves to be a ready vehicle for such absurd claims, apparently without any sense of how cynical and transparent the arguments were and certainly without any sense of a need for balance. No editorial argued, for example, that Israeli soldiers, bred on a diet of Jewish chauvinism and anti-Arab racism, enjoyed shooting Palestinian children and that this accounted for the large numbers of dead kids. Had such an article been submitted, would it have had any chance of passing editorial muster? Could it have been printed in a major American paper? Almost certainly not. Nor, when several Israeli children were injured in a bomb attack on a settler bus in the occupied Gaza Strip, did any editorials comment that Israeli settlers were cynically and deliberately endangering their children by forcing them to live in armed camps on land confiscated from another people in the middle of occupied territory. However, the far more absurd and degraded claim that Palestinian parents actually want their children to be killed found ready space in the opinion sections of most major newspapers.

Reporting the Dead

While editorialists did their utmost to propagate the absurd notion that Palestinians under occupation were "besieging" Israel and, acting on orders from Arafat, deliberately throwing themselves and their children into the line of fire in order to embarrass Israel, reporters by and large did a far better job of presenting things as they were. The contradictions were so grave that it often seemed that editorial board members weren't reading their own reporters' stories on the conflict.

But there were some patterns that consistently detracted from the quality of the coverage. Reports about the deaths of Palestinians were typically vague, impersonal, or sometimes nonexistent, while deaths of Israelis were often prominent and humanized the victims by reporting details of their life and death. Because of the volume of the coverage, we will focus on only a few examples that we consider typical of common practices.

On October 4, barely a week into the intifada, at least seven Palestinians were killed by Israeli forces, bringing the total dead since the start of the intifada to over sixty. Coverage of this day's events was, to say the least, muted in major US papers. The front page of the *New York Times* on October 5 featured a lengthy article about Secretary of State Madeleine Albright's meeting with Yasir Arafat and Ehud Barak in Paris. It was only on page ten that an article appeared describing the violence, and only in the ninth paragraph did the *Times* report that,

> For the second time in five days, a small boy was killed at the crossroads near Netzarim, a Jewish settlement in the Gaza Strip, where Israeli troops again battled snipers and rioters with rockets and automatic weapons fire. The boy was identified as Muhammad Abu Assi, 9, who witnesses said had been seen throwing stones at the heavily fortified Israeli Army post there.[15]

On NPR Linda Gradstein reported that November 1 was "one of the fiercest days of fighting since the clashes began almost five weeks ago." The description she gave of the violence was that "six Israeli soldiers were injured and pinned down for several hours before the army was able to evacuate them. There was also heavy fighting in the Gaza Strip. Israeli troops shot dead three Palestinians, all teenagers." This report gave more emphasis to the six wounded soldiers than to three dead children. The next morning, November 2, referring to the previous day's events, Gradstein reported without any further elaboration that "three Israeli soldiers and seven Palestinians died in heavy fighting."[16]

Addameer, a Palestinian human rights organization that ran a daily news and information service in the first weeks of the intifada, documented six Palestinian deaths on November 1. Three of the deaths were of teenagers who may have been throwing stones at Israeli forces. Two more Palestinian civilians, not alleged to have been involved in any incidents, were killed by Israeli helicopter gunships conducting air raids on their villages.[17]

Only one Palestinian was killed on that day in what could be described as "heavy fighting," in a gun battle in the village of Al-Khadir near Bethlehem. Two of the Israeli soldiers were killed in this battle, and a third Israeli soldier in a separate battle at a military outpost near Jericho. Hence, "heavy fighting," like "clashes" and "crossfire," was a phrase that hid the grim reality of how most Palestinians were actually dying. That a description of a confrontation between a boy with a stone and a tank firing heavy machine guns, or civilians being killed in their homes by helicopters, as "heavy fighting" is highly misleading, not to say inaccurate, did not appear to cause concern.

While NPR skimped on details of Palestinian deaths when they did report on them, they often simply didn't report them at all. Eight Palestinians and a German doctor were killed by Israeli forces on November 15, amid heavy Israeli air attacks in several parts of the occupied territories. NPR's flagship morning and afternoon news programs did not carry any reports of the deaths. The following day the only brief acknowledgment came in the introduction to a report by Jennifer Ludden about what life is like for Israeli soldiers guarding a Jewish settlement in the occupied West Bank near Jerusalem.[18]

But while Palestinian deaths and funerals were of little interest to NPR, the same was not true of the far smaller number of Israeli deaths. NPR, like most other US media outlets, focused intensive attention on the October 12 killing of two Israeli soldiers in plain clothes who entered Ramallah, according to the Israelis, by mistake. Palestinians, enraged at the more than 100 deaths over the previous weeks, and reportedly acting on a rumor that the two men may have been undercover agents, seized the men from Palestinian Authority custody and killed them, dumping one of the bodies from a window. Images of this gruesome event, captured on film, played for supporters of Israel a galvanizing role similar to that played by the video of 12-year-old Muhammad al-Durra, who had been shot dead in his father's arms a week earlier, instantly becoming a symbol of Palestinian suffering and resistance under occupation.

While al-Durra's death was widely reported, and was almost a unique case of a Palestinian victim being humanized and given a name, many media outlets took seriously Israeli claims that the boy was caught in "crossfire," or reported faithfully Israeli claims that he had earlier been "throwing stones," as if that would justify shooting at him for forty-five minutes while he was lying on the ground pleading for his life. It was obvious to media the world over that the boy, his father (who survived), and the ambulance driver shot dead while trying to rescue them were all deliberately shot by Israeli snipers. Talal Abu Rahma, the photographer who filmed the murder, stated under oath, "I can confirm that the child was intentionally and in cold blood shot dead and his father injured by the Israeli army." As late as February 2001, the *Washington Post* was still reporting the death as an accident of crossfire.

When the two Israeli soldiers were killed in Ramallah, however, such journalistic inquisitiveness and skepticism all but disappeared. The *Chicago Sun-Times*, which had virtually ignored 100 Palestinian deaths over the previous two weeks, ran the photo of one of the alleged killers of the Israeli soldiers holding up his blood-covered hands. An October 13 banner headline screamed "Blood on His Hands." This illustrated a widespread sense of outrage that reporters expressed for the killing of the two soldiers that had been unavailable for dozens of Palestinian children shot down over previous weeks.

Linda Gradstein reported on one of the funerals of the two men, giving many details about the dead soldier, against a background of sobbing, wailing, and recitation of Kaddish (the Jewish prayer for the dead). The young, pained voice of the dead soldier's 8-year-old daughter, saying she never wanted him to go into the army, rang out. And we learned that in his civilian life the soldier had sold children's toys and candy.

While we agree that the killing was tragic and the funeral heart-rending, we do question the double standard at work in coverage. What is the effect of reporting on the funerals of Israeli victims of violence, when NPR and the others had not done any similar reports on dozens of Palestinian funerals? In a single report on the funeral of an 18-year-old Palestinian in Gaza a few days before, NPR's Jennifer Ludden did convey some of the sadness and loss that Palestinians were feeling, but nevertheless she portrayed mourners as violent and even death-seeking. Ludden stated that "even in grief, many of the victims' families support the continuation of the Palestinian uprising," and she closed the report saying that the young man's mother "says she's now preparing her youngest son to become a martyr."[19]

There is no reason to doubt the accuracy of Ludden's report, but it may have been equally true to say of those at the Israeli funeral that even in grief most Israelis continued to support the use of violence against Palestinians, or that Israeli mothers are preparing their sons to go into the occupied territories to maintain the illegal occupation, or that some Jewish mourners expressed anger at and hatred for Arabs.

Coverage of Israel's behavior in the occupied Palestinian territories reflects a widespread pattern whereby people with whom reporters can identify, who are seen as "Western" or "like us," are humanized. In the Middle East this includes only Jewish Israelis. The coverage of Arabs in this conflict, as with the Israeli occupation of south Lebanon, is typical of the treatment the Western media often accords non-Western, Third World peoples, whose humanity, interests, and personal stories are regularly given short, if any, shrift. This is a reflection of a deep-seated attitude that some people are the subjects of history, while others are its objects. The leading Israeli daily, *Ha'aretz*, noted this pattern in an October 3 story titled "Our Victims Are Stories, Theirs Are Mere Numbers."

Rules of Engagement

As the number of Palestinians killed by Israeli occupation forces relentlessly rose, Israel and its advocates in the US media held firmly to the notion of Israel's "purity of arms"—that deadly force is only used when unavoidable, and never against innocent civilians. "Israelis are doing much soul-searching about having to shoot and kill in self-defense," was a typical assertion. Israeli ambassador David Ivry wrote, "Israel has shown the greatest restraint possible," and "an Israeli soldier may respond only when shot at first or in a life-threatening situation."[20]

The theme of Israeli "restraint" and strict rules of engagement was widely repeated in the media. Only when the carnage became too difficult to justify or ignore did leading newspapers offer tentative criticism of Israel's actions, but such criticism was almost always advanced along with the notion that Israel was under deadly threat from the occupied Palestinians. Considerable efforts were made to rationalize or minimize Israel's use of deadly force. Confronting a rising Palestinian death toll, and little evidence that Israelis faced any similar threat to their own lives, the *New York Times* seized the occasion of Palestinian protesters sacking Joseph's Tomb (a shrine in the heart of the Palestinian town of Nablus that the Israelis had turned into a military outpost used to fire at Palestinians) to declare that "the Israeli anxieties that have led Mr. Barak to threaten to unleash full military force against Palestinian targets are readily understandable." Fully one and a half months into the intifada, the *Washington Post* again acknowledged that "Israel's measures against the rioters are sometimes excessive," but it labeled Israel's use of helicopter and missile attacks on Palestinian towns and cities as "largely symbolic reprisal attacks."[21]

Human rights organizations that examined Israel's claim of "restraint" and strict adherence to "rules of engagement" were unambiguous about what they discovered. In a November 3 statement after one of its medical teams traveled to the occupied territories to investigate the violence, Physicians for Human Rights (USA) said that "the Israel Defense Force (IDF) has used live ammunition and rubber bullets excessively and inappropriately to control demonstrators, and that based on the high number of documented injuries to the head and thighs, soldiers appear to be shooting to inflict harm, rather than solely in self-defense." A Human Rights Watch investigation of clashes in Israel, the West Bank, and the Gaza Strip came to similar conclusions, adding that Israeli security forces "made significantly little use of tear gas, even when evidence suggests that tear gas was more effective in dispersing protestors." A report by an Amnesty International delegation also found indiscriminate and excessive use of force by the Israeli occupation forces and noted that "the impunity for those who commit human rights violations and the lack of investigations into so many deaths at the hands of security forces has led to a breakdown in the rule of law which has grave consequences for the region."[22]

Reportage on the whole also contradicted the outlandish claims made on editorial pages, often of the same newspapers. A notable example was a lengthy investigative report in the *New York Times Magazine* by Michael Finkel, who responded directly to Israel's claims that its soldiers shot only when they were under threat. In a striking passage about the clashes at Karni Crossing in the Israeli-occupied Gaza Strip, Finkel recounts:

> I spent two weeks at Karni during daylight hours, and in my time there, the Israeli Army fired live ammunition almost every day. Sometimes only two or three shots, sometimes a dozen or more. On occasion the shots were fired when cars or buses needed to enter or exit the settlement, at other times I could ascertain no reason for the shooting. Not once did I see or hear a single shot from the Palestinian side. Never during the time I spent at Karni did an Israeli soldier appear to be in mortal danger. Nor was either an Israeli soldier or settler even slightly injured. In that two-week period, at least 11 Palestinians were killed during the day at Karni.[23]

Despite such reporting, the consistent testimony of human rights organizations, and the inexorably growing list of dead and injured months into the intifada, many commentators in the media continued to propagate the myth of Israeli "restraint" and orderly use of force only when required by legitimate self-defense.

Arafat the Almighty, Arafat the Demon

From the first moments of the intifada, US editorial writers were almost unanimous in claiming that the violence was instigated, orchestrated, and sustained by the Palestinian Authority and particularly Yasir Arafat, and they expressed their outrage at the "siege" the Palestinians were imposing on the hapless Israelis. The fact that almost all the victims of the violence were Palestinians shot down in their own towns and villages by occupation soldiers was not permitted to interfere with this consensus. The *Times*'s Friedman chastised Arafat for choosing to "provoke the Israelis into brutalizing the Palestinians again and again." Underlying these arguments is the notion that Israel is helpless and lacks any agency while Arafat and the Palestinians are all-powerful and force Israelis to do things they do not want to do. In the same paper Israeli commentator Meron Benvenisti mockingly quipped that those who espouse this view "cannot forgive [Palestinians] for forcing Israeli soldiers to kill Arab children."[24]

Arafat's omnipotence extends not only to his own people, who presumably respond to his orders like robots, but he is depicted as having the power to control events throughout the Middle East. Friedman, for instance, warned President Hosni Mubarak of Egypt that if Egypt did not warmly embrace Israel, it would leave "Egypt and other Arab regimes vulnerable to Yasir Arafat's inflaming their public opinion and bringing people into the streets, where they could start protesting all sorts of things besides Israel." In a "news analysis" tellingly entitled "Fork in Arafat's Road," Jane Perlez of the

Times posed the entire future of the Middle East as a "choice" that Arafat alone must make. No consideration was given to the fact that this "choice" was determined by the United States and Israel and presented in the form of "peace proposals" as a *fait accompli.*[25]

Commentators fond of reminding us that Israel is the "only democracy" in the Middle East, with a vigorous public debate on all issues, do not think it a great contradiction to propose that Arafat's control of events extends even to choosing Israeli leaders. As soon as early elections were called in Israel, NPR's Daniel Schorr was among the first of many to suggest that the onus to save the peace process, and with it Barak's political life, lay squarely on Arafat. In an editorial on the day of Ariel Sharon's election as Israeli prime minister, the *Chicago Tribune* accused Arafat of resorting to violence and "in doing so, he has accomplished the seemingly impossible: He has helped turn Israel, which last summer might have made unprecedented compromises for peace, into a nation pulling back from the final land-for-peace decisions that were at the heart of the 1993 Oslo peace accords." That the "unprecedented compromises" fell far short of ending Israeli control of Palestinian life and meeting the minimum requirements of international law was not considered by the editorialists. More chillingly, perhaps to shield Israel from future criticism for the possibly grim consequences of electing someone with Sharon's record, the *Tribune* held Arafat responsible in advance for Sharon's actions. "Arafat has placed his people at risk," wrote the *Tribune*, "that Sharon will engineer a more severe crackdown on Palestinian resistance."[26]

After Sharon's February 6 election victory, Friedman ingeniously shifted attention away from the fact that Israelis had just voted into office an infamous war criminal, arguing instead that "the press is asking exactly the wrong question about the Sharon election. They're asking, who is Ariel Sharon? The real question is, who is Yasir Arafat?" Thus not only do Israelis have no responsibility for whom they vote, it also doesn't matter who leads them, not because of objective aspects of the Israeli-Palestinian conflict, but because of the deficient, not to say evil, character of the Palestinian leader.[27]

Arafat was systematically demonized in major US newspapers. While Prime Minister Barak was routinely described as "brave," "generous," and a man who "has proven his commitment to peace," characterizations of Arafat, on the other hand, revealed a hostility rarely applied to other national leaders, let alone other Nobel Peace Prize winners. The "arch-terrorist," who had been redefined as a major statesman, was instantly restored to "arch-terrorist" status as soon as he was perceived as challenging Israel rather than cooperating with it.

The *Washington Post* excelled in the demonization rhetoric, especially in blaming Arafat for all Palestinian suffering. In perhaps the ultimate expansion of the rhetoric of demonization, the *Post* placed the blame for any and all Israeli victimization of Palestinians at the feet of Arafat: "Israeli Prime Minister Ehud Barak was said yesterday to be meeting with advisers to consider a plan to contain violence by essentially quarantining much of the Palestinian population. This would be a dreadful outcome, impoverishing further many Palestinians. Most of the world all the more would see the Palestinians as the victims, and they would be right. But their chief victimizer would be their leader, who refused to accept or speak up for the peace that could improve their lives." The ultimate effect of this argument is not just to demonize Arafat but to absolve Israel of any responsibility for its brutal and illegal actions.[28]

Clash of Civilizations

When all other pro-Israel explanations for the uprising failed, a number of commentators turned to the cliché of a "clash of civilizations." This notion, originated by Bernard Lewis and popularized by Samuel Huntington, sees the West as a coherent, distinct, and superior segment of humanity that is being increasingly challenged by inferior but highly dangerous "Islamic" and, to a lesser degree, "Confucian" civilizations. In the case of the intifada, Israel is represented as an outpost of the West surrounded by the rival civilization, as represented by the Palestinian protesters. This supremely reductive and overtly racist argument wipes clean any specific features of the intifada, the Palestinian-Israeli or even the Arab-Israeli conflicts, subsuming all of them under the rubric of a generalized struggle between "us and them." Palestinian experiences of dispossession, exile, and occupation are irrelevant in this model—since their behavior is conditioned only by cultural differences—as are international law and conventional concepts of morality. Its function is to make the reader identify fully with the Israelis, who are supposedly defending the survival of all of Western civilization, and yearn for the total defeat of the Palestinian enemy.

One would not be surprised, perhaps, to discover such an argument in the *New York Post*, a Murdoch-owned tabloid more extreme in its pro-Israel stance than any sizable Israeli paper. *Post* columnist Rod Dreher does not disappoint: "As the only outpost of the West in that irrational desert, we owe the Israelis our loyalty in what is likely to be a long and painful time of trial by fire." "The Israelis," Dreher continues, "whatever their failings, are fighting for us and for our civilization. Americans used to understand that. Arafat and his mobs are reminding us once again of what's truly at stake here. This isn't a clash of Palestinian mobs versus Israeli troops. This is a clash of civilizations. And it's far from over."[29]

Although one might have hoped that at least the country's leading newspapers would decline to embrace this loathsome discourse, the "clash of civilizations" argument was deemed "fit to print" in the *New York Times* and the *Washington Post*. Reuel Marc Gerecht, a former CIA official, set forth in the *New York Times* that both the Palestinian uprising and the bombing of the USS Cole are "above all else, violent expressions of the age-old confrontation between Islam and the West." Gerecht frames the entire conflict in terms of Muslim religious atavism: "Palestinian Arab nationalism is younger than its Israeli Jewish counterpart, but the Muslim reluctance to concede that 'Muslim lands' can ever legitimately be relinquished to infidels is age-old, imbedded into Islamic law and custom." This is typical of the way in which Islam is treated as a factor in the conflict by Western commentators: as a source of intolerance and fanaticism. In contrast, invocations of the role of Jewish traditions and beliefs in Zionist ideology and behavior are almost always cast as legitimizing factors that only underscore the justice of Jewish claims and the depth of genuine feeling they reflect. The high priest of the "clash of civilizations" interpretation of the uprising was certainly George Will of the *Washington Post*. His column "A Feast of Retreats" was among the first and certainly the most influential of its kind, arguing that "this is not a dispute between Israelis and Palestinians about land, it is a clash of civilizations and is not solvable by splitting differences."[30]

Israeli Generosity

The extremely pro-Israel reactions to the uprising by the vast majority of US media is based on the perception that at the Camp David summit, Israeli Prime Minister Ehud Barak presented Palestinians with a "generous" offer that was wantonly spurned by an intransigent Palestinian leadership, who then launched an irrational campaign of anti-Israeli violence. This perception reflects an uncritical acceptance of official Israeli spin, designed to make Israel's refusal to bring the occupation to a complete end seem forthcoming and Palestinian insistence on a fully sovereign, viable state seem unreasonable.

It should be noted that—unless they were privy to details they have yet to share with the public—none of the journalists had a good sense of what exactly was on offer to the Palestinians at Camp David. For example, by all accounts, at no point during or after did either the Israelis or the United States present the Palestinians with detailed maps of their proposal for a Palestinian state. Even the Israeli press expressed exasperation with Barak for continuously presenting the public with vague and ultimately meaningless descriptions of his Camp David proposals. And although generalized maps surfaced, they revealed anything but "generosity."

Reports leaked to the Israeli and American press confirm, moreover, that the proposal would have meant no territorial contiguity for the Palestinian state, no control of its external borders, limited control of its own water resources, and no full Israeli withdrawal from occupied territory as required by international law. In addition, the Barak plan would have included continued Israeli military control over large segments of the West Bank, including almost all of the Jordan Valley; the right of Israeli forces to be deployed in the Palestinian state at short notice; the continued presence of fortified Israeli settlements and settler-only roads in the heart of the Palestinian state; and would have required nearly 4 million Palestinian refugees to relinquish their fundamental human rights in exchange for compensation to be paid not by Israel but by the "international community." At best, Palestinians could expect a kind of super-autonomy, rather than independence, and the devolution of some municipal functions in the parts of Jerusalem inhabited by Palestinians, under continued overall Israeli control.

Given the Palestinian negotiators' recognition of Israel within the 1948 borders as well as their not contesting Israeli sovereignty over West Jerusalem, Palestinians could be forgiven for feeling that they had shown ample and even unparalleled willingness to compromise. From the perspective of the US media, however, Palestinian reluctance to accept further whittling away of their would-be state and embrace a future of permanent subordination to and dependency on Israel was presented as "intransigence" in the face of Israeli "concessions" of unthinkable magnanimity.

The *New York Times* spoke of Barak's government as one "willing to offer the most generous compromise terms possible under current political circumstances." Naturally, the only "political circumstances" under consideration were those of Israel. Thomas Friedman gave his blessing to Clinton's plan, saying the President had done "the Lord's work" by "clarifying what's a fair compromise."[31]

The Palestinians' resistance to the Barak plan was portrayed as a moral defect on the part of the Palestinians in general, and of Yasir Arafat in particular. "But the reality remains," declared the *Washington Post*, "Mr. Barak is prepared to make deep concessions for peace, while Mr. Arafat is not." Another explanation offered by the *Post* was simply that "Mr. Arafat does not want peace—at least not one that falls short of his maximalist demands." By "maximalist demands" the *Post* was referring to the Palestinian position that Israel should withdraw from occupied territory as required by international law.[32]

George Will of the *Post* explained it all thus: "Barak is a soldier who respects directness and thought he could make Arafat an offer he could not refuse. If Barak and all other Israelis who have allowed their wish for peace to father wishful thinking about Arafat now know that the only such offer is everything—the liquidation of Israel—the learning experience of recent weeks, although ghastly, has been useful." Will judged that "Barak may be the most calamitous leader any democracy has had," because through his offer to the Palestinians, "he risks forfeiting his nation's existence." Adding a note of moderation to what might be uncharitably seen as alarmist or hysterical rhetoric, Will compared Palestinians to Nazis in most of these columns.[33]

John Mearsheimer recognized the limitations of what Palestinians were being asked to accept as a final settlement, concluding that "it is hard to imagine the Palestinians accepting such a state. Certainly no other nation in the world has such curtailed sovereignty." Such sentiments were extremely rare, however, amid a near-total consensus on the editorial pages that the Palestinians had a moral obligation to accept whatever the Israelis put before them, and had "once again" missed an incredible opportunity to realize their national aspirations and would have only themselves to blame for whatever consequences ensued.[34]

The Fright of Return

One of the central issues underlying the breakdown of negotiations at Camp David and the subsequent uprising is the right of return for Palestinian refugees, those who were expelled from or fled their homes during the 1948 creation of Israel and their descendants. There are at least 3.7 million Palestinian refugees registered with the United Nations. The right of return is guaranteed to all refugees by the Universal Declaration of Human Rights and the Fourth Geneva Convention. Following their expulsion in 1948, it was specifically applied to the Palestinian refugees in UN Resolution 194, which demands that "the refugees wishing to return to their homes" should be permitted to do so. Central to both the Clinton and Barak plans was the demand that the Palestinian refugees should renounce or be stripped of their right to return. Palestinian insistence on upholding the right of return was commonly cited by newspaper commentators as a willful and irrational obstacle to reaching a final settlement with Israel, and as obstructionism for its own sake.

For many papers and pundits, not to mention the US government, their vehement stance against the right of Palestinian refugees to return to their homes constituted an extraordinary reversal of attitude on refugee rights. In 1999, the Clinton Administration led NATO into a war against Yugoslavia in the name of enforcing the right of return for the Kosovar refugees. The same American officials and media pundits who thundered then about the inviolability of refugee rights and the immorality of dispossession and forced exile demanded that Palestinians drop their "unrealistic demands" about refugee rights. These principles, which for Kosovars were held to be both sacred and a justification for international military intervention, in the case of Palestinians were dismissed as a fantasy, a ploy, and an insidious plot to destroy Israel.

During the Kosovo crisis, the *Washington Post* championed refugee rights and condemned any notion that ethnic cleansing in the Balkans "brought a welcome peace," because "as the people still pleading and petitioning to go back to their villages know well, 'ethnic cleansing' is no harsh but ultimately benign historical process. It is a violation of basic tenets of civilized society. It means that one family's house is taken away and given to another. To make it stick, the perpetrators will kill, rape, beat, rob and intimidate the rightful owners. This isn't 'cleansing,' nor do 'population transfer,' 'displacement,' 'dislocation,' 'mass migration' or any of the other impersonal terms often used to describe it quite suffice. Better to call it what it was and still is: murder, rapine, pillage, aggression and plunder."[35]

Palestinian refugees could well have been forgiven for feeling that no one had ever put their case as passionately and that they had found a staunch friend and ally in the *Washington Post*. They would therefore have been astonished and disappointed to read that, in the *Post*'s opinion, "the Palestinians would have to give up on any real implementation of the right of return." The *Post* lost interest in the "basic tenets of civilized society," instead developing a new appreciation for ethno-nationalism and arguing that "if taken seriously, after all, the right would obliterate Israel as a Jewish state, since there are several million Palestinians living outside the country, many of them still refugees." While the *Post* strongly condemned any suggestion that denying the rights of Kosovo refugees might be justified if this "brought a welcome peace" to the Balkans, Palestinian refugee rights became the principal obstacle to peace in the Middle East: "The question is whether Mr. Arafat means to compromise now at last or whether he will let the deal collapse over refugees."[36]

The *Post*'s astonishing double standard was matched and even outdone by *New York Times* columnist Thomas Friedman. Friedman was perhaps the most enthusiastic cheerleader for the Kosovo war, insisting that the noble purpose of ensuring the return of refugees justified massive use of force. "NATO's limited political objective is still the right one," he insisted, "a return of the Kosovar Albanian refugees under some form of international protection. We do not have the luxury of doing less." Friedman wrote that not ensuring the refugees' return would be "an unthinkable moral sellout" and "if the U.S. wants to return the Albanian refugees to Kosovo…NATO is going to have to intensify both its diplomacy and its bombing of Serbia, with no holds barred." Friedman was of the view that "the minimum diplomatic outcome we need" is "that the refugees be allowed to return to their homes in Kosovo, and run their own lives, protected by international peacekeepers." He even expressed a certain satisfaction at the bombing for its own sake, admitting "I'm glad we're punishing the Serbs now for their ethnic cleansing. It's barbaric."[37]

The champion of Kosovar refugee rights took a very different view when it came to Palestinians. Rather than being a bona fide justification for military intervention, as in the Balkans, assertion of Palestinian refugee rights became the equivalent of violence and a plot to destroy Israel: "It is becoming increasingly clear that Mr. Arafat and his colleagues cannot unequivocally accept Israel. Either they resort to violence when they don't like what they are offered at the table or they insist on things, such as the right of return for millions of Palestinian refugees to Israel, that would destroy the Jewish state demographically." Friedman thinks that while Serbs should be bombed to punish them for their ethnic cleansing, "Israel doesn't have to assume explicit responsibility" for the refugees. "But," he advises, "it should be generous in saying to Palestinians that they have suffered a historical injustice and have a moral right to return to their original homes." Lest anyone misunderstand, Friedman is quick to add that "as a practical matter Israel cannot allow more than a symbolic number to return to Israel proper, and the others will either have to reside in the West Bank or accept generous compensation." Uncharitable observers might conclude that Friedman's practical admonitions on the limitations of Palestinian refugee rights qualify, by his own standards, as "an unthinkable moral sellout."[38]

One of the most fascinating examples of moral inconsistency on refugee return was provided by Nobel Peace Prize laureate Elie Wiesel. A major proponent of the Kosovo war, Wiesel wrote poignantly about the plight and rights of the Kosovar refugees. In a much-publicized report to President Clinton, Wiesel recommended that "priority should be given the return of refugees to Kosovo—even if it means to the ruins of their homes." He told *Tikkun* magazine that not only must the Kosovars return home, but that "there has to be an international force to protect them."[39]

Wiesel does not feel the same way about Palestinian refugees. In the same *Tikkun* interview, he expressed the view that "there were reasons in the past to see some Palestinians as victims. There is no doubt about it. But now at this moment, after Oslo and after Barak's victory, we should not think in those terms." This probably made it easier for him to write in the *New York Times* that while "it is imperative that we resolve this problem [the plight of Palestinian refugees]…the solution of a mass return is unthinkable." This is because "to many Israelis, that would be tantamount to suicide." In a crude and ugly attempt to rationalize their eviction and exclusion, he repeats long-debunked fabrications: "incited by their leaders, 600,000 Palestinians left the country convinced that, once Israel was vanquished, they would be able to return home." As a man who spent the years surrounding the 1948 conflict and the expulsion of the Palestinians working for Menachem Begin's Irgun organization, a group that enthusiastically engaged in massacres and ethnic cleansing of Palestinians, Wiesel knows this is a grotesque distortion of the origins of the Palestinian refugee problem. He knows too, as does everyone with any grasp of the history of the conflict, that there never was any "incitement" by Arab leaders urging Palestinians to flee. A considerable degree of intellectual dishonesty is necessary to maintain such a glaring inconsistency on refugee rights.[40]

Jerusalem—Oh, My Withered Hand

Along with the refusal of Israel and the United States to seriously discuss the right of return for Palestinian refugees, the future of occupied East Jerusalem was widely cited as the main "sticking point" preventing an agreement. Following the Camp David talks and especially after the beginning of the new Palestinian uprising, a newspaper campaign was launched by ardent supporters of Israel seeking to denigrate Arab and Muslim (that is to say, Palestinian) links to Jerusalem, at the same time waxing lyrical about the undying Jewish love for the city. This false juxtaposition is supposed to justify a policy of exclusive Israeli control and Jewish domination of Jerusalem in defiance of UN Security Council resolutions such as 242 and 476.

Commentators such as Elie Wiesel, Daniel Pipes, Jeff Jacoby, and Marvin Hier, among others, presented variations of this argument. The centerpiece is always a contrast between the "real" Jewish connection to Jerusalem, which is presented as ancient and spiritual, even organic, as opposed to Arab/Muslim ties to Jerusalem, which are depicted as transitory and casual, almost accidental.

The argument generally begins with a stirring recitation of ancient Jewish ties to the city, including invocations of Abraham, Moses, and Solomon (all without acknowledging that these biblical figures are key elements of Islam as well as Judaism and Christianity). These are coupled with emotive references to "next year in Jerusalem" and right hands withering and so forth, as if anyone in the United States seriously calls into question the importance of Jerusalem to the Jewish people and faith.

The hint of desperation discernible in these passages becomes pronounced, however, in what inevitably follows: ugly and absurd attempts to dismiss Arab and Muslim historical and religious ties to the city. Ridiculous canards such as "Jerusalem is never even mentioned in the Koran," are supposed to demonstrate that a city, whose very name in Arabic is Al-Quds (The Holy), is of no special religious significance to Islam. The fact that it was never used by Arabs as a political capital is dredged up to suggest that the city whose skyline is dominated by one of the world's most important and beautiful mosques, not to mention the countless other Muslim and Christian holy sites throughout the Old City, was never of any real concern to the Arabs who built them.

These and other distortions are supposed to show that Arabs simply don't care about Jerusalem as much as Jews do, and, because of this, the Israeli occupation should continue in spite of the UN Security Council resolutions that demand its end. In the mind of *Boston Globe* columnist Jeff Jacoby "the Jewish and Muslim claims to Jerusalem are not remotely comparable. The bonds of loyalty and love that bind the Jews to Jerusalem are without parallel." Daniel Pipes made much the same point in the *Los Angeles Times*, claiming that while "Jerusalem has a unique importance to Jews…Jerusalem has a distinctly secondary place for Muslims," and further on the argument ends up with "Jerusalem being of minor importance to Islam." Pipes also describes the naming of the Al-Aqsa mosque as "tricky," as if Muslims had anticipated his arguments 1,300 years ago and sabotaged them with an insidious linguistic ploy.[41]

Elie Wiesel in the *New York Times* claimed that, unlike for Muslims, "for Jews, it [Jerusalem] remains the first. Not just the first; the only." As a result of this alleged superior connection, Israel, according to Wiesel, is entitled to the acquisition of territory by force and should ignore UN Security Council resolutions and international law: "Can one always say, 'Peace at any price'? To compromise on territory might seem, under certain conditions, imperative or at least politically expedient. But to compromise on history is impossible." This argument would appear to be little more than: "I think I want it more than you do, therefore it should be mine."[42]

It would be too simple and obvious to counter such nonsense by pointing out the concrete and historical realities that have made Jerusalem an Arab and a Muslim city for 1,500 years, all amply chronicled in the numerous books on its very well documented history. It would denigrate that unfathomably rich history with the same casual abuse to which Wiesel and company subject Jewish history in their reductive polemics. It also seems almost too obvious to have to point out that the Palestinian-Israeli conflict involves hundreds of thousands of Palestinian Christians and that it is a political struggle and not a battle over theology.

Instead of belaboring the obvious, we should ask what is really being said beneath this facade of distortions. The claims are simple: my religion is more true than yours, my history is more valid than yours, my feelings are more powerful and legitimate than yours, and I have the right to define not only my beliefs and feelings, but yours as well. It is chauvinism and fetishism run amok. Rabbi Hier's claim that "the Temple Mount doesn't belong to the government of Israel. It belongs to the Jewish people—

those no longer here and those yet to be born" serves as a useful illustration of this attitude.[43]

The truth is that Jerusalem is holy to three faiths and that religious sentiments are all equally valid. The truth also is that Jerusalem has grown in political significance for both Palestinian nationalism and Zionism in recent decades. Rhetoric about the fundamental and unchanging centrality of the Old City to Zionism requires a lapse of historical memory about what the founders of the State of Israel held most dear. In the late 1930s, the Zionist response to the Peel Commission's partition plan for Palestine demanded Jewish rule over West Jerusalem, but not East Jerusalem and the holy sites. At that time, the Jewish Agency simply did not consider the Old City a *sine qua non* for the realization of Zionism. Clearly, Zionist discourse has changed considerably since then, most notably since the conquest of East Jerusalem in 1967, after which one began to hear the now familiar dogma about an "eternal and undivided" capital.

This political evolution regarding Jerusalem and the holy places is mirrored on the Palestinian side by arguments that now implicitly or explicitly place more importance on control of holy sites than on the rights of millions of refugees, a position that could hardly have garnered any support among the displaced Palestinians in the 1960s and '70s.

Arguments holding that one faith or one history is more valid than another simply confirm what most people instinctively understand—that religious fanaticism and ethnic chauvinism are no grounds for sound political judgment. But, it seems, they make for welcome submissions to the opinion sections of major American newspapers.

Good Coverage

The patterns of bias and exclusion documented in this chapter should not be taken to imply that there was no good coverage of the conflict in the US press. Particularly praiseworthy were several reports for CBS News's *60 Minutes* and *60 Minutes II* by Bob Simon. Simon's reporting was a model of fairness, giving both Israelis and Palestinians a chance to air their views and scrupulously avoiding taking sides with either. Simon also never lost sight of the overall context of occupation in which the conflict was taking place, and what this meant for both sides.

In his October 24 report, "To Be Continued…," which focused mainly on the deaths of large numbers of Palestinian youths at the hands of Israeli troops, Simon allows Palestinians to explain that they were protesting because they lost all hope that the peace process would lead to the end of the occupation. But he notes that what he was told would be a peaceful protest "doesn't look very peaceful," since "I see stones going at the Israelis." Simon interviews Brigadier General Benny Gantz, commander of Israeli forces in Gaza, expressing the view that Palestinian children are being killed because Palestinians push their kids into harm's way in order to make Israel look cruel. For a Palestinian response to the charge, Simon turns to Hanan Ashrawi, who calls the accusations "the essence, the epitome of racism," and who says "I don't want to sink to the level of responding" to such allegations, "of proving I'm human."

Viewers of CNN were also provided with a broader perspective than that of most other American news media, in large part because of the work of Rula Amin, a CNN correspondent based mainly in Gaza. Amin's reporting allowed CNN's viewers access to stories from within the autonomous zones in the occupied territories and a better sense of what things looked like on the Palestinian side of the Israel-Palestine divide. The Israeli government is reported to have complained to CNN about Amin's coverage, and several pro-Israel groups objected that it was inappropriate for CNN to use the work of a Palestinian journalist, although no one has objected to the use of Jewish and Israeli reporters for American news organizations in Israel. Both CNN and the Israeli government denied these reports and Amin continues to report for the organization, providing a superior breadth of coverage to viewers.[44]

While the quality of reports on National Public Radio was erratic and inconsistent, some excellent pieces stood out, such as a report by Jennifer Ludden about the extreme marginalization experienced by Palestinian citizens of Israel and those by Anne Garrels from Hebron and Gaza. All of these reports successfully and directly conveyed to listeners the realities faced by Palestinians.[45]

Like a number of other major papers, the *New York Times* provided reporting that was often factual and straightforward. In a particularly good news analysis piece the *Times*'s Deborah Sontag delved into the many causes of Palestinian frustration that were fueling the intifada and took seriously Palestinian criticisms that the Oslo accords were simply a way to legitimize occupation by another name. This article, which cast serious doubt on the simplistic spin being served up by the *Times*'s editorial page, was buried deep on page eight.[46]

Some newspapers also made a conscientious effort to take the needs and concerns of both sides into account in their analysis. The *Chicago Tribune* stood out among major US dailies by taking an editorial line that expressed real understanding for Palestinian perspectives and experiences, as well as those of Israel. Generally, staff editorials consistently condemned Israel's excessive use of force against Palestinians, disapproved of Israel's construction of settlements in the occupied territories, and understood the harsh realities Palestinians face. The *Tribune* did sometimes lurch into territory well-trodden by others, such as the editorial on Sharon's election noted above and the claim that Arafat deliberately sent children out to provoke Israelis to shoot them,[47] but overall the newspaper attempted to take a sober, thoughtful, and balanced path, giving each side due consideration. The *Los Angeles Times* also deserves recognition for serious efforts to include a wide range of views in its commentary section, which offered its readers an outstanding range of opinion, almost certainly the most diverse in any major paper.

While the whole-hearted backing of Israel dominated the editorial sections of most major

American newspapers, a small number of columnists did take a pro-Palestinian stance. Most notable was Charley Reese, conservative columnist for the *Orlando Sentinel*, who has been an outspoken critic of Israel for many years. Reese consistently tried to explain that Palestinians were struggling for their liberation from occupation and that Israel's reaction to the uprising was brutal and unjustifiable. "You're probably wondering what it is these Palestinians over there want," Reese told his readers. "Well, even if you aren't wondering about it, I'll tell you anyway. They want the same thing the Founding Fathers of this country wanted: freedom." Citing the UN and human rights organizations' condemnations of Israeli brutality, Reese pointed out that "Madeleine Albright says, however, that Israel is a victim of aggression and is only defending itself. Now that lady is either nutty or evil. If she's so disconnected from reality that she thinks that people with no army, whose dead number 250 and whose wounded exceed 5,000, are a threat to the most powerful military state in the Middle East, she's nutty. If she's deliberately lying, she's evil."[48] Useful as his contributions no doubt are, the sad fact is that Reese is almost a lone pro-Palestinian voice among professional American columnists.

Another columnist who has taken a clearly pro-Palestinian position was attacked by her own newspaper. Amy Pagnozzi of the *Hartford Courant* argued in favor of Palestinian human and national rights throughout the intifada. She lambasted the US media for being a "palace court press" for Israel. She challenged her readers to test what most newspapers were telling them about the uprising, especially the myth of Palestinians sacrificing their own children: "Many Israelis have no choice but to see what some Americans still refuse to believe: that vast numbers of Palestinian children—many of them completely unarmed, holding neither stones nor guns nor bottle bombs—have been killed. But the controversy here is artificial. The occupied territories may be cut off from Israel, but anyone who wants to can still reach them by telephone. Wondering what's going on? Call the hospitals—the doctors will talk to you. Contact Physicians for Human Rights-Israel. Call Rabbis for Human Rights. Call Bat Shalom. My telephone carrier charged 22 cents a minute; how much could it cost you?" Given how heretical such a position is from the viewpoints that permeate the rest of the US media, Pagnozzi could have expected to be severely attacked by supporters of Israel. In her words she was "Flamed? Charbroiled is more like it." But the attacks on Pagnozzi's positions were not confined to legitimate criticism from readers. She was lambasted in a column by the *Courant*'s own "reader representative," associate editor Elissa Paprino.[49]

Holger Jensen's columns in the *Rocky Mountain News* occasionally took a pro-Palestinian stance but were generally in line with the conventional wisdom on the subject. They did, however, include a good deal of undisputed factual information about the conflict that supporters of Israel did not want to see in print. Jensen was forced to dedicate an entire column to "Israel's attempts at censorship." Jensen observed that questions about the uprising asked even in Israel were not being permitted into the American conversation.[50]

Conclusion

Even if he had been spending his days on long, multi-martini lunches and even longer siestas, Shmuel Sisso, the much-maligned Israeli consul-general in New York, can take considerable solace in the results of this survey. It strongly indicates that the American press's notorious pro-Israel bias is as pronounced as ever. If Israel's standing in US public opinion was being damaged by its crackdown on the intifada, this owed little to the tone and substance of much of the coverage and most of the commentary. It may be that the still and moving images of heavily armed Israeli troops opening fire on young demonstrators armed only with rocks and a will to be free simply could not be spun no matter what the journalists were saying. These images may well have managed to convey a fundamental truth about the nature of the confrontation between an oppressed population and an occupying army that no amount of misleading words could trump. But it would not have been for lack of trying. The results of this survey suggest that the day when the US press provides evenhanded coverage and balanced commentary to its readers, viewers, and listeners is still a long way off indeed.

Notes

1. "Tamir Asks for NY Consul-General Sisso's Recall," *Jerusalem Post*, October 17, 2000.

2. Natan Sharansky, "Don't Take It…" and Yossi Beilin, "A Chance for Peace…," December 31, 2000.

3. Avraham Burg, "I Was for Peace. Now What?" October 4, 2000; Amos Oz, "Let Palestinians Govern Palestinians—Now," January 6, 2001.

4. Rashid Khalidi, "The New Parameters of Reconciliation," December 27, 2000; Rami Khouri, "Israel's Deadly Errors," October 10, 2000.

5. Allegra Pacheco, "Israel's Doomed Peace," October 5, 2000; Meron Benvenisti, "Coexistence Is the Only Choice," October 27, 2000; David Grossman, "The Pain Israel Must Accept," November 8, 2000.

6. FAIR, "Muffled Coverage of U.N. Vote: Media Ignores Broad Mideast Consensus," October 16, 2000.

7. "No Peace, No Process," October 11; Charles Krauthammer, "Arafat's War," October 6, 2000.

8. Linda Gradstein, NPR, *Morning Edition*, October 11, 2000.

9. John Kifner, "Bethlehem, Dark and Quiet, Falls Victim to the Violence," December 25, 2000; Jennifer Ludden, "Israel's Now Tougher Stand on Peace Talks," February 8, 2001.

10. Jim Hoagland, "Peace Begins at Home," October 29, 2000; "Arafat Should Act Like Statesman," *Sun-Sentinel*, October 13, 2000; Krauthammer, "Realities of War," October 27, 2000.

11. Jessica Montell, "The Al-Aqsa Intifada; How Media Has Skewed Israel Conflict," *Tikkun*, January 1, 2001.

12. Thomas Friedman, "Ritual Sacrifice," October 31, 2000.

13. Montell, *op. cit.*

14. *Los Angeles Times*, June 3, 1985.

15. "Flash Points in West Bank and Gaza Ignite Again," *New York Times*, October 5, 2000.

16. Gradstein, *All Things Considered*, November 1, 2000; NPR, *Morning Edition*, November 2, 2000.

17. Addameer, Latest Developments No. 47—November 1, 2000, web posted 11:30 pm (GMT+2), Ramallah, West Bank.

18. Numerous wire reports, for example, "German Doctor Killed, 10 Palestinians Injured in Israeli Rocket Attacks," AP, November 16, 2000; Ludden, *All Things Considered*, November 16, 2000.

19. Ludden, *All Things Considered*, October 12, 2000.

20. *Oklahoman* editorial, "Thwarting Israel: Arafat, World Media," October 13, 2000; David Ivry, "Israel's Restraint," *Washington Post*, October 27, 2000.

21. "Dousing the Middle East Fire," *Times*, October 10, 2000; "Unacceptable Equilibrium," *Post*, November 18, 2000.

22. Physicians for Human Rights, *Evaluation of the Use of Force in Israel, Gaza and the West Bank, Medical and Forensic Investigation*, November 3, 2000; Human Rights Watch, *Investigation into Unlawful Use of Force in the West Bank, Gaza Strip, and Northern Israel*, Vol. 12, No. 3 3(E), October 2000; Amnesty International, *Israel/Occupied Territories: Findings of Amnesty International's Delegation*, October 19, 2000.

23. Michael Finkel, "Playing War," December 24, 2000.

24. Friedman, "Arafat's War," October 13, 2000; Meron Benvenisti, "Coexistence Is the Only Choice," October 27, 2000.

25. Friedman, "The Arabs' Road Map," October 20, 2000; Perlez, December 29, 2000.

26. Schorr, "Commentary," *All Things Considered*, November 29, 2000; "Israel's retreat on the peace front," *Chicago Tribune*, February 6, 2001.

27. Friedman, "Sharon, Arafat and Mao," February 8, 2001.

28. "Mr. Arafat's Silence," October 20, 2000.

29. Rod Dreher, "Naïve Hope Stuck in the Crossfire of Civilizations," October 17, 2000.

30. Reuel Marc Gerecht, "The Price of America's Naivete," October 14, 2000; Will, October 11, 2000.

31. "Contesting Jerusalem's Holy Sites," September 30, 2000; Friedman, "Win a Free Book," January 5, 2001.

32. "Unacceptable Equilibrium," November 18, 2000; "Mr. Arafat's Silence," October 20, 2000.

33. Will, "Talking Peace With Thugs," October 19, 2000; "A Feast of Retreats," October 11, 2000.

34. John Mearsheimer, "The Impossible Partition," *New York Times*, January 11, 2001.

35. "Another Word on 'Cleansing,' " May 1, 1999.

36. "Middle East Replay," December 23, 2000.

37. Friedman, "Steady as She Goes," May 11, 1999; "Bomb and Call in George Mitchell," April 2, 1999; "The Circular Firing Squad," April 9, 1999; "Bomb, Talk, Deal," March 30, 1999.

38. Friedman, "A Mideast Policy for Mr. Bush," January 19, 2001; "Give a Little, Get a Little," September 15, 2000.

39. Text of a report from Elie Wiesel to the President of the United States, M2 Presswire, June 11, 1999; "An interview with Elie Wiesel," *Tikkun*, July 1, 1999.

40. Wiesel, "Jerusalem in My Heart," January 24, 2001.

41. Jeff Jacoby, "Slice Up Jerusalem? Unthinkable," *Boston Globe*, January 4, 2001; Daniel Pipes, "Jerusalem Means More to Jews Than to Muslims," *Los Angeles Times*, July 21, 2000.

42. Wiesel, "Jerusalem in My Heart," January 24, 2001.

43. Marvin Hier, "Israel's Honor and Soul Should Not Be Up for Grabs," *Los Angeles Times*, January 10, 2001.

44. Amotz Asa-El and Dan Williams, "Back to Basics," *Jerusalem Post*, December 29, 2000.

45. Ludden, *All Things Considered*, November 21, 2000; Anne Garrels, *All Things Considered*, November 6, 2000, and *All Things Considered*, November 2, 2000.

46. "The Great Unraveling: End of Oslo Era, With a Bang," October 26, 2000.

47. "An Eye for an Eye in the Middle East," November 13, 2000.

48. Charley Reese, "What Is It Palestinians Really Want?" November 16, 2000; "The Right to Criticize Israel," December 7, 2000.

49. Amy Pagnozzi, "Territories Awash In Kids' Blood," November 28, 2000; "In Search of Truth, Not Dogma," December 19, 2000.

50. Holger Jensen, "Writers Protest Israel's Attempts at Censorship," *Rocky Mountain News*, December 19, 2000.

14. AMERICA'S LAST TABOO

EDWARD W. SAID

November/December 2000

The events of the past weeks in Palestine have been a near-total triumph for Zionism in the United States. Political and public discourse has so definitively transformed Israel into the victim during the recent clashes, that even though 140 Palestinian lives have been lost and close to 5,000 casualties reported, there is unanimity that "Palestinian violence" has disrupted the smooth and orderly flow of the "peace process." There is now a small litany of phrases that every editorial commentator either repeats verbatim or relies on as an unspoken assumption; these have been engraved in ears, minds, and memories as a guide for the perplexed. I can recite most of them by heart: Barak offered more concessions at Camp David than any Israeli prime minister before him (90 percent of the territories and partial sovereignty over East Jerusalem), Arafat was cowardly and lacked the necessary courage to accept Israeli offers to end the conflict, Palestinian violence has threatened the existence of Israel. There are all sorts of variations on this, including anti-Semitism, suicidal rage to get on television, sacrificing children as martyrs; an ancient "hatred" of the Jews burns in the West Bank and Gaza, where the PLO incites attacks against them by releasing terrorists and producing schoolbooks that deny Israel's existence.

The general picture is that Israel is so surrounded by rock-throwing barbarians that even the missiles, tanks, and helicopter gunships used to "defend" Israelis from them are warding off what is essentially an invasive force. Clinton's injunctions, dutifully parroted by Madeleine Albright, that Palestinians must "pull back" give us to understand that it is Palestinians who are encroaching on Israeli territory, not the other way around. In the US media, Zionization is so thorough that not a single map has been published or shown on television that would risk revealing to Americans the network of Israeli garrisons, settlements, routes, and barricades that criss-cross Gaza and the West Bank. Blotted out completely is the system of Areas A, B and C that perpetuates military occupation of 40 percent of Gaza and 60 percent of the West Bank, in keeping with the Oslo "accords." The censorship of geography, in this most geographical of conflicts, creates an imaginative void—once deliberately fostered, but now more or less automatic—in which all images of the conflict are decontextualized. The result is not just the preposterous belief that a Palestinian attack is under way on Israel, but a dehumanization of Palestinians to the level of beasts virtually without sentience or motive. Little wonder, then, that the figures of dead and wounded regularly omit any mention of

Left: Palestinians drive in the Mediterranean Sea to avoid an Israeli roadblock in Gaza

nationality—as if suffering were shared equally by the "warring parties." Nothing is said of house demolitions, land expropriations, illegal arrests, beatings and torture. Forgotten are the ethnic cleansing of 1948; the massacres of Qibya, Kafr Qassem, Sabra and Shatila; the defiance of UN resolutions and flouting of the Geneva Convention; the decades of military invigilation and discrimination against the Arab population within Israel. Ariel Sharon is at best "provocative," by no stretch of the imagination a war criminal; Ehud Barak is always a statesman, never the assassin of Beirut and Tunis. Terrorism is invariably on the Palestinian, defense on the Israeli, side of the moral ledger.

Ever since September 28 there have been an average of anywhere between one and three opinion articles a day in the *New York Times*, the *Washington Post*, the *Wall Street Journal*, the *Los Angeles Times* and the *Boston Globe*. With the exception of perhaps three pieces written with sympathy for the Palestinians in the *Los Angeles Times*, and two—one by an Israeli lawyer, Allegra Pacheco; the other by a Jordanian liberal who favors Oslo—in the *New York Times*, every such article—including the regular columns of Thomas Friedman, William Safire, Charles Krauthammer, et al.—has vociferously supported Israel and denounced Palestinian violence, Islamic fundamentalism and Arafat's back-sliding from the "peace process." The authors of this relentless tide of propaganda have been former US military officers and diplomats, Israeli functionaries and apologists, regional experts and think-tank specialists, lobbyists and front-men for Tel Aviv. The unspoken premise of this total blanketing of the mainstream press is that no Palestinian or Arab position on Israeli police terror, settler-colonialism, or military occupation is worth hearing from. In fine, American Zionism has made any serious public discussion of the past or future of Israel—by far the largest recipient ever of US foreign aid—a taboo. To call this quite literally the last taboo in American public life would not be an exaggeration. Abortion, homosexuality, the death penalty, even the sacrosanct military budget can be discussed with some freedom. The extermination of native Americans can be admitted, the morality of Hiroshima attacked, the national flag publicly committed to the flames. But the systematic continuity of Israel's fifty-two-year-old oppression and maltreatment of the Palestinians is virtually unmentionable, a narrative that has no permission to appear.

American Fanatics

What explains this state of affairs? The answer lies in the power of Zionist organizations in American politics, whose role throughout the "peace process" has never been sufficiently addressed— a neglect that is absolutely astonishing, given that the policy of the PLO has been in essence to throw our fate as a people into the lap of the United States, without any strategic awareness of how American policy is dominated by a small minority whose views about the Middle East are in some ways more extreme than those of Likud itself. A personal example can illustrate this contrast. Some time ago the Israeli newspaper *Ha'aretz* sent over a leading columnist, Ari Shavit, to spend several days talking with me. A good summary of this long conversation appeared as a question-and-answer interview in the August 18 issue of the newspaper's supplement, basically uncut and uncensored. I expressed myself candidly, emphasizing the expulsions and killings of 1948, the right of the refugees to return, and the record of Israel as an occupying power since 1967. My views were presented just as I voiced them, without the slightest editorializing by Shavit, whose questions were always courteous and unconfrontational. A week later, *Ha'aretz* published a reply by Meron Benvenisti, ex-deputy mayor of Jerusalem under Teddy Kollek. At a personal level, it was full of insults and slander against me and my family. But Benvenisti never denied that there was a Palestinian people, or that we were driven out in 1948. Certainly, he said, we conquered you—why should we feel guilty? I responded to Benvenisti a week later, reminding Israeli readers that Benvenisti was responsible for the destruction of Harit al-Magharibah in 1967, in which several hundred Palestinians lost their homes to Israeli bulldozers, and probably knew about the killing of several of them. But I did not have to remind Benvenisti or the readers of *Ha'aretz* that as a people we existed and could at least urge our right of return. That was taken for granted.

What is not so widely realized is that neither interview nor exchange could have appeared in any American newspaper, let alone any Jewish-American journal; and if, *per impossibile*, there had been such an interview, the questions would have been crude hectoring of the sort: why have you been involved in terrorism? why will you not recognize Israel? why was the Mufti of Jerusalem a Nazi? and so on. Whereas a right-wing Israeli Zionist like Benvenisti, no matter how much he may detest me, would never deny that there is a Palestinian people who were forced to leave in 1948, a typical American Zionist would for a long time maintain that no conquest took place or, as Joan Peters alleged in a now all but forgotten prize-winning book of 1984, *From Time Immemorial*, that there were no Palestinians with a life in Palestine before 1948. Every Israeli knows perfectly well that all of Israel was once Palestine, that—as Moshe Dayan said openly in 1976—every Israeli town or village once had an Arab name. American Zionist discourse is never capable of the same honesty. It must ceaselessly maunder about Israeli democracy that made the desert bloom, completely avoiding the essential facts about 1948, which every Israeli knows in his or her bones. So removed from realities are American-Jewish supporters of Israel, so caught between ideological guilt—after all, what does it mean to be a Zionist, and not immigrate to Israel?—and sociological swagger—is this not the most successful community in US history: supplying Secretary of State, Defense, Treasury, and successive heads of the National Security Council in the Clinton Administration?—that what often emerges is a frightening cocktail of vicarious violence against Arabs, which is the result of not having any sustained direct contact with them, unlike Israeli Jews.

For all too many American Zionists, Palestinians are not real beings, but demonized phantasms—fearsome embodiments of terrorism and anti-Semitism. A former student of mine, a product of the finest education available in the United States, recently wrote me a letter to ask why as a Palestinian I let a Nazi like the Mufti of Jerusalem still determine my political agenda. "Before Haj Amin," he informed me, "Jerusalem wasn't important to Arabs. Because he was so evil he made it an important issue for Arabs just in order to frustrate Zionist aspirations, which always held Jerusalem to be important." This is not the logic of someone who has lived with or has any personal experience of Arabs. It is no accident that Zionism, nurtured in the United States, has generated the most fanatical aberrations of all in Israel itself. Not for nothing were Dr. Baruch Goldstein, who murdered twenty-nine Palestinians quietly praying in the Hebron mosque, and Rabbi Meir Kahane, Americans. Far from being disavowed by their followers, both are revered to this day. Many of the most zealous far-right settlers in the West Bank and Gaza, clamoring that "the land of Israel" is theirs, hating and ignoring the Palestinian inhabitants all around them, also come from the States. To see them strutting contemptuously through the streets of Hebron as if the Arab city were already theirs is a frightening sight.

Policy Stranglehold

But the role of these immigrants is insignificant beside that of their sympathizers at home. There the American Israel Public Affairs Committee—AIPAC—has for years been the most powerful single lobby in Washington. Drawing on a well-organized, well-connected, highly visible and wealthy Jewish population, AIPAC inspires an awed fear and respect across the political spectrum. Who is going to stand up to this Moloch on behalf of the Palestinians, when they can offer nothing, and AIPAC can destroy a Congressional career at the drop of a checkbook? In the past, one or two members of Congress did resist AIPAC openly, but the many political action committees controlled by AIPAC made sure they were never re-elected. The only senator who once remotely tried to oppose AIPAC was James Abourezk of South Dakota, who resigned for his own reasons after a single term. Today, virtually the entire Senate can be marshaled in a matter of hours into signing a letter to the President on Israel's behalf. No one exemplifies the sway of AIPAC better than Hillary Clinton, outdoing even the most right-wing Zionists in fervor for Israel in her avid scramble for power in New York, where she went so far as to call for the transfer of the American embassy from Tel Aviv to Jerusalem and the grant of leniency for Jonathan Pollard, the Israeli spy serving a life sentence in the United States.

If such is the material of the legislature, what can be expected of the executive? In a little noticed but revealing episode, the US ambassador to Israel, Martin Indyk, was abruptly stripped of his security clearance by the State Department, supposedly for a lax use of his laptop that may have disclosed confidential information to "unauthorized persons." He is currently unable to enter or leave the State Department without an escort and is forbidden to return to Israel, pending a full investigation. It is not difficult to guess what happened. The originating scandal—naturally, never mentioned in the media—was Indyk's appointment in the first place. On the very eve of Clinton's inauguration in January 1993, it was announced that Indyk—an Australian national of Jewish origin, born in

London—had been sworn in as an American citizen at the express command of the President-elect, overriding all normal procedures in an act of peremptory executive privilege, to allow him to be parachuted immediately into the National Security Council, with responsibility for the Middle East. What had Indyk been or done to merit such extraordinary favor? He had been head of the Institute for Near East Policy, a Washington think tank that lobbies for Israel in tandem with AIPAC. Predictably enough, Dennis Ross—a State Department consultant who heads American superintendence of the "peace process"—is another former head of the same institute.

What, then, of civil society? Here the consensus that Israel is a model democracy, forming the one oasis of Western modernity in the political desert of the Middle East, is virtually impregnable. Should there be any sign of its slipping, an array of Zionist organizations, whose role it is to police the public realm for infractions, steps in. Rabbi Arthur Hertzberg, a respected American liberal cleric, once said that Zionism was the secular religion of the American Jewish community. Many Jewish organizations run hospitals, museums and research institutes for the good of the whole country. Alas, these noble public enterprises coexist with the meanest and most inhumane ones. To take a recent example, the Zionist Organization of America (ZOA), a small but vociferous group of zealots, paid for an advertisement in the *New York Times* on September 10 that addressed Barak as if he was their employee, reminding him that 6 million American Jews outnumber 5 million Israelis, should he decide to negotiate over Jerusalem. The language of the advertisement was positively minatory, upbraiding Israel's prime minister for contemplating actions anathema to American Jews. The ZOA feels it has the right to intervene in everybody's business. Its adherents routinely write or telephone the president of my university to ask him to dismiss or censure me for something I have said, as if universities were like kindergartens and professors to be treated as under-age delinquents. Last year they mounted a campaign to dismiss me from my elected post as president of the Modern Language Association, whose 30,000 members were lectured by the ZOA as so many morons.

In a similar vein, right-wing Jewish pundits like Norman Podhoretz, Charles Krauthammer and William Kristol—to mention only a few of the more strident propagandists—have not hesitated to express their displeasure at the prospect of any concessions, however faint or bogus, by Israel to the Palestinians. The tone of these self-appointed guardians of Zionism is a combination of brazen arrogance, moral sanctimony, and unctuous hypocrisy. Most sensible Israelis regard them with distaste. To describe their diatribes as curses from the Old Testament would be a slur on the prophets. But their relentless clamor, criminalizing support for Palestinian resistance against Israel, can rely on an ideological trump card in the United States. For a totalitarian Zionism, any criticism of Israel is proof of the rankest anti-Semitism. If you do not refrain from it, you will be hounded as an anti-Semite requiring the severest opprobrium. In the Orwellian logic of American Zionism, it is impermissible to speak of Jewish violence or Jewish terror when it comes to Israel, even though everything done by Israel is done in the name of the Jewish people, by and for a Jewish state. Of course, strictly speaking, this is a misnomer, since nearly a fifth of its population is not Jewish. These are the people the media call "Israeli Arabs," as if they were another species from "the Palestinians." What American reader or viewer would know they are the same people, divided only by decades of brutal Zionist policy, assigning apartheid to the former, occupation and expulsion to the latter?

Hapless Pleas

The worst of this implacable machinery of consensus in America, however, is Arab blindness to it. When the PLO opted after the Gulf War to follow the example of Egypt and Jordan, and work as closely as possible with the American government, it made its decision (as had the two Arab states before it) on the basis of vast ignorance and quite extraordinarily mistaken assumptions. The essence of its calculation was expressed to me shortly after 1967 by a senior Egyptian diplomat: we must surrender, and promise not to struggle any further—we will accept Israel and the determining role of the United States in our future. There is no doubt that continuing to fight as the Arabs had historically done would indeed have led to further defeat and disaster. But neither then nor today was it the case that the only alternative was to throw ourselves onto the mercy of America—saying, in effect, we will no longer resist you, let us join you, but please treat us well. The pathetic hope was that if Arabs cried long enough "we are not your enemies," they would be welcomed as friends. They forgot the disparity of power that remained. From the viewpoint of the powerful, what difference does it make to your own strategy if an enfeebled adversary gives up and declares, "I have nothing further to fight for, take me as your ally, just try to understand me a bit better and perhaps you will then be fairer"?

Such pleas are bound to fall on deaf ears in the American state. All peace arrangements undertaken in the illusion of an "alliance" with the United States can only confirm Zionist power. To submit supinely to American designs in the Middle East, as Arabs have done for almost a generation now, will bring neither peace and justice at home, nor equality abroad. Since the mid-1980s, I have tried to impress on the PLO leadership and every Palestinian or Arab I have met that the quest for a protector in the White House is a complete chimera, since all recent Presidents have been devoted to Zionist aims, and the only way to change US policy is through a mass campaign on behalf of Palestinian human rights, out-flanking the Zionist establishment and going straight to the American people. Uninformed and yet open to appeals for justice as they are, Americans are capable of reacting as they did to the ANC campaign against apartheid, which finally changed the balance of forces inside South Africa. James Zogby, then an energetic human rights activist, was one of the originators of the idea. Then he threw in his lot with Arafat, the US government and the Democratic Party, and abandoned it totally.

But it was soon clear that the PLO would never adopt this course anyway. There were several reasons for that. A strategy of this kind requires sustained and dedicated political work. It has to be based on democratic grassroots organization. It can only spring from a movement, not a personal initiative by this or that leader. Last but not least, it demands genuine knowledge of US society, rather than superficial pieties or clichés. The reality is that there exists inside America a vast body of opinion that is often bewildered by the lurid rhetoric of Zionism and would be capable of turning against it, were a mass campaign mobilized in America itself for Palestinian human, civil and political rights. The tragedy is that the Arabs have been too weak, too divided, too unorganized and ignorant to mount such a movement. But unless American Zionism is taken on in its homelands, all attempts to parley with the United States or Israel will lead to the same dismal and discrediting outcome.

The Oslo accords could scarcely have shown that more starkly. The Wye and Camp David talks have brought home the same truth once again. What has Barak's "unprecedented generosity" consisted of? The promise of a very limited military withdrawal made at Wye—from a mere 12 percent of the occupied territories—has never been kept, and is now forgotten. Instead, the Western media extol Barak's munificent offer of "90 percent" of the West Bank to the PLO, in exchange for its abandonment of the Palestinian refugees to their fate. The reality is that Israel has no intention of giving back Greater Jerusalem, which covers over 5 percent of the choicest West Bank land; or Jewish settlements, which amount to another 15 percent; not to speak of military roads or areas yet to be determined. The largesse of "90 percent" refers to what is left after all this is deducted. As for the grand gesture of considering shared authority over Haram al-Sharif, the breathtaking dishonesty of the matter is that all of West Jerusalem (principally Arab in 1948) has already been conceded by Arafat, plus most of a vastly expanded East Jerusalem.

The shameful charade of the "peace process" has now, at any rate temporarily, broken down amid the explosion of popular anger among Palestinians who were supposed to be grateful for it. The stones and slings of young men thoroughly tired of injustice and repression are now offering courageous resistance to a demeaning fate, meted out to them not just by Israeli soldiers armed by the United States but by a pact with Zionism designed to coop them up in reservations fit for animals, policed by Arafat's apparatus with US military and financial aid, openly collaborating with Shin Bet and the CIA. The function of the Oslo accords is to cage Palestinians in a remnant of their own lands, like inmates in an asylum or prison. What is astonishing is not the popular revolt against this diktat, but that it could ever have been passed off as peace instead of the desolation that it has really been all along. A dithering Palestinian leadership, unable either to retire or to go forward, has been caught on the wrong foot. But the signs are that a new generation will not be content with the miserable, denigrated place accorded them in the Zionist scheme of things, and will go on rebelling until it is finally changed.

This article was originally published in the November/December 2000 New Left Review.

PART III

REFUGEES, REMEMBRANCE, RETURN

15. BANISHMENT: THE PALESTINIAN REFUGEES OF LEBANON

JENNIFER LOEWENSTEIN

'We are lost, afflicted only this one way:
   That having no hope, we live in longing.' I heard
   These words with heartfelt grief that seized on me

Knowing how many worthy souls endured
   Suspension in that Limbo.

Dante's *Inferno*; Canto IV, 31–35

Summer 2000

On the way to Haifa Hospital each morning I walk through narrow passageways whose oppressive concrete walls are painted with pictures of Palestine and Jerusalem's Dome of the Rock. It is an attempt to prettify the dingy, labyrinthine paths through the Bourj al Barajneh refugee camp just south of Beirut. There is Arabic graffiti on the walls announcing God's greatness and His will to return the Palestinians to Palestine. I see the same word scrawled again and again on the windshields and doors of cars everywhere: *Filastin...Filastin...Filastin* ("Palestine").

Crumbling stone steps lead to a fruit market where the Palestinian flag hangs above the canvas awning. Every morning the proprietor greets me and offers me the best fruit he can find from the baskets at his stand. *Ahlan wa sahlan*, he always says, "welcome, welcome," when I embarrassingly thank him, sweat already dripping down my face. It is the hottest summer in years, and the Sahara wind will raise the temperature to 110 degrees by mid-afternoon. Intense humidity turns Beirut into a beastly hot metropolis, and so much the worse in the wretchedly constricted and overcrowded refugee camps.

The buildings at this end of the road are empty, grayish-brown cement blocks covered with bullet holes and dirt. They gape at me through their hollow, iron-rimmed windows as if conscious of their hopeless appearance and its inevitable reminder of war. The air about them is foul and heavy.

At the pharmacy across from the main hospital entrance two old men sit fingering their worry beads and look at me indifferently. I duck into the adjacent beverage store and pull out a strawberry banana juice and a bottle of water from the cooler. The storekeeper, Shadi, takes them from me and puts them back, carefully passing his hand over the other containers to see which are the coldest. Because of the daily power cuts the drinks are often lukewarm. Sometimes the ones from the back are still cold so he takes them from there, helps me figure out what I owe in Lebanese lira, and says thank you and good-bye in a quiet, pleased manner. The last time I said good-bye, before I returned home to Wisconsin and

Pages 266–67: Fatima Gate at the Lebanon-Israel border, with a poster of Hezbollah's Sheik Nasrallah
Left: Northern entrance to Bourj al Barajneh refugee camp, Beirut, with a poster of Syrian President Bashar Assad
Both photos: ©Jennifer Loewenstein

before the uprising began anew in Palestine, I did not know it would be forever. Shadi was shot in the head the day in early October that busloads of Palestinian refugees went down to the Lebanon-Israel border to throw stones at the Israeli army position just across the fence. He died instantly. His body was driven back to Haifa Hospital in Bourj just across from his beverage shop. Dr. Wassim wrote to tell me that he was their first hero; that the refugees who had gone to the border had bravely demonstrated their solidarity with their brothers and sisters in Palestine fighting the Zionist enemy and that there would be big demonstrations that day in the camps and in Beirut to protest Israel and America. I wrote back expressing my sadness and shock. "I am with you," I wrote twice. "I am with you." There is a sudden tightness in my chest when I remember Shadi's face. For me his death is a bitter waste.

Filastin Biladina, Al-Yahud Adou'ina

Little boys are singing this by the gate outside the hospital one afternoon while I am waiting for a friend. They sing it over and over and laugh and come up to me to talk and ask questions before an adult disperses them for "misbehaving." *Palestine is our land, the Jews are our enemy.* I love the children and tease them when they run up to me. What would they sing if they knew I was a *yahud*?

The forgotten people of the camps in Lebanon do not allow themselves to forget about Palestine. Two 10-year-old girls, Rajaa' and Samira, come to visit Andrea and me in our dismal camp apartment wanting to show us their "Jerusalem" dance, which they learned in school to a song about the city. It is a sad song—you can hear it in the voice of the singer. But they will return to Jerusalem and to all Palestine, she says. It is a hope that is desperately out of touch with current affairs. But the longing for Palestine, the insistence on Palestine, is relentless in this hellish limbo. The greater their abandonment by the outside world, the more ubiquitous "Palestine" becomes. It is a both a refuge from and a symptom of camp madness.

On an evening when the electricity is not out I listen to a BBC news report from Camp David, Maryland. The talks failed, a reporter says, over the "pivotal issue of Jerusalem." I pace my sweltering second-story cell and stop to look out the screenless open window near the kitchen. Here in Bourj, 20,000 people are crammed together in one square kilometer of land. There are people shouting in the apartment across the way. A baby is crying. Two young men are discussing something heatedly with their neighbors in the flat above mine. Someone is watching TV. Shops are closing. Footsteps shuffle along the winding paths below. The smell of sewage permeates the air. People are living on top of people in a teeming slum imploding from hopelessness and neglect. An abyss separates the "peace" talks from the lives that are closing in upon me.

What cruel folly makes our politicians think that solving the status of Jerusalem will bring peace to the region? The power in the camp goes out again and I fumble in the darkness for candles and matches.

Past

Laura sits across from me at the table in Pepe Abed's restaurant in Jbeil recounting her war stories. She is a remarkable woman, still beautiful in her mid-50s, who projects strength and defiance. In 1975, when the civil war in Lebanon started, she and her husband, Fuad, sent their four children (then aged 9, 11, 14, and 15) to America to live with her brother. Laura is a Maronite Christian and therefore likely to have been sympathetic to Israel when it invaded Lebanon in 1982 to destroy the PLO. Most Maronites, especially those who stayed in Lebanon throughout its bloody sixteen-year conflict (1975–91), still feel enormous antipathy for the Palestinians, whom they hold responsible for many of the catastrophes that befell their country. Indeed, it was violence between the Maronite Phalangist militiamen and the PLO led by Yasir Arafat that contributed directly to the outbreak of the civil war.

What made Laura unusual was her refusal to identify with the Phalangist movement both during and after the war and her ability to understand the plight of the Palestinian refugees in her land despite the horrors she blames them for. Like many other Maronites, she detested the presence of the PLO and its armed militias and cannot speak of them calmly when she reflects on the war. Her resentment is passionate. But unlike many, she understood the international dimensions of the conflict well enough to recognize that Israel and Syria exploited for their own interests the confessional and political factionalism that, even today, threatens the stability of Lebanon. Laura opposed the entrance of the Syrian army into Lebanon in 1976, but knows that it was the Maronite president, Suleiman Franjieh, who invited them in when it looked as though Palestinian forces would defeat the Phalangists. A look of vexation crosses her face when she thinks back on those times. "I am not a politician," she says, "but people knew that if the Syrians came in they would never leave. Now we are at the mercy of the Syrians." She tells me about the Syrian soldiers who took over her family's house one day. "They took everything valuable we owned. We lost all our wedding gifts—such beautiful china and silver. Then we had to move near Junieh, where the conflict was sometimes right outside our homes. I would yell at the [Phalangist] soldiers for their stupidity and brutality. They did not care whose lives they endangered." This was after she had sent her four children away so that they wouldn't grow up knowing only war.

Laura also understands only too well that the situation of the Palestinians in Lebanon is a direct result of the *Nakba*, or catastrophe, caused by the creation of Israel in 1948. The overwhelming majority of Palestinians living in Lebanese camps today never chose to live in Lebanon—they fled there during Israel's War of Independence, or following the Black September massacres in Jordan in 1970, which also trace their roots back to the 1948 expulsion and before. Corrupt and brutal as Arafat and his PLO were and are, they are the byproduct of a thwarted nationalist movement and of the militant, chauvinist brand of Zionism that took root in British Mandatory Palestine. Inexcusably ruthless in its earlier tactics, the PLO earned its violent reputation. It is nevertheless important to understand its genesis, just as it is necessary to understand the political climate of nineteenth- and twentieth-century Central and Eastern Europe in order to comprehend fully the ideology of contemporary racist Zionism. For Laura and many others, the Lebanon war was the end result of the disastrous and divisive policies of the European Great Powers and their superpower successors, primarily the United States, in pursuing selfish, imperialist aims in the Middle East. Laura has no love for the Palestinians in her country, but her antipathy extends well beyond Palestinian politics to Zionism and its principal supporters. "You can have peace or you can have a Jewish state," she almost yells. "You can't have both."

The first time I visited Lebanon, in July of 1999, my friend Robert took me through some of the refugee camps. In Shatila, the most notorious of them, a rush of children came up to us shouting and waving at me to take their pictures. Robert had to coax me away, or I'd have stayed with them the rest of the afternoon. He wanted me to hear people's stories and, quite deliberately, began asking older camp members about their lives. "Where are you from?" he'd ask. "Filastin" was the inevitable answer. "Where in Palestine?" he'd continue, and this would be followed by the name of a specific village, usually near Akka or Haifa, and a description of their former home. "Did you take your house key with you when you left?" he'd ask next, predicting an affirmative answer. "No," said an old woman probably in her mid-70s. "There was no time. My father was coming back from the fields and he said I must leave immediately with my oldest brother. My mother was still in the house when we left. They said they'd come after us shortly, but I never saw them again." I looked into this woman's eyes. They were filmy and tired-looking but she was smiling at us. "Do you think you will go back to Palestine?" Robert asked. In the past, he said, everyone would say yes even if they didn't believe it. Now the answers were mixed. The old woman sighed and said, "Me? I am too old now. But my grandchildren—they will go back." We continued in this routine for a while.

Turning the corner, we encountered a young couple. They couldn't tell us much because they had been young children here in Lebanon in the early 1980s and did not share the memories of the older people. They didn't want to talk about war, understandably. Mustering up my courage I asked them, "Where are you from?" The man answered for both of them. "We are Palestinian," he said. That is all.

As we are leaving, we pass two middle-aged women sitting on a broken stone stoop outside their home. We are about to move on but one of the women sitting outside is talkative and asks us if we aren't awfully hot walking around in the July sun. When she turns her face toward us, I notice a thick scar on her neck and shoulder. "What happened to you?" Robert asks, pointing out the scar. The woman stands up and turns around showing us the continuation of her scar into her upper back. "This happened in Tel el-Zaatar," she explains, naming a Palestinian camp that was besieged and destroyed in 1976 by Phalangist forces, who massacred about 3,000 of its civilians. "I was a young woman then. The Phalangists came into the camp and killed my whole family. They tried to kill me too, but I didn't die. I had nowhere to go after that so I came here."

Even then, however, I knew that I would return to Beirut. And now when I compare my impressions of that first trip with my experiences in the summer of 2000 in Bourj al Barajneh I am struck by the difference. The first time, I was an outside observer, watching parts of a story unfold. Now, when I wander the different streets of Beirut in my mind I feel the sultry air sticking to my face as if I have become inseparable from the landscape. Indeed, a part of me remains there, imprisoned.

Shatila camp is only a fifteen-minute walk from Bourj al Barajneh, but the feel of it is much different. Walls like those of a ghetto enclose Bourj. Shatila is rotting out in the open. Palestinians live here alongside poor Lebanese and Syrian day workers. The Syrians come looking for work in Lebanon because the Syrian economy is so weak. They come for a year or so to do menial jobs like construction and roadwork and take the income back home to their families. Their presence is a source of tension for the Palestinians, who are restricted by law to menial labor outside the camps. In the competition for jobs, Syrians are preferred. There is an invisible dividing line between Palestinian Shatila and the old Shatila where mostly Syrians live now.

We have been invited to lunch at Shatila's Najdeh elementary school. "We" are the camps' summer volunteers, all Canadians except for myself, the American. Many of us teach the younger children French and English during the week. As is true in all the camps, water and electricity are rationed. Nuhad, one of our hosts, takes us through the camp telling us bits of its history.

Since I've been to Shatila before, I know what we are coming to when we start "down that road" where the Syrian vendors are. An open, muddy, garbage-strewn lot lies behind the line of stalls in the street. This is Shatila's mass grave: the place where hundreds of bodies were buried after the massacres in the Sabra and Shatila camps in 1982. The Israeli army, stationed outside the perimeter of the camps, gave a green light and the necessary logistics to their allied Phalangist forces, who entered the camps and murdered everyone they found. This was in spite of a cease-fire and the departure of the PLO from Lebanon, and in spite of US guarantees to protect the Palestinians. Because most of the young men had had to flee the country or were in hiding, most of those murdered were old men, women, and children. Their bodies were later thrown together and buried in this lot. Today there is nothing that marks the site. The Lebanese government has prohibited it. But everyone knows what it is and no one is surprised to see us taking pictures. The dead are still there and haunt the camp even in the blazing August sun.

We walk away from the trash heaps at the entrance of the camp and head toward the busy main road. Bourj al Barajneh waits for us like a safe haven. I have to get out of Shatila and the swirling dementia that fills its streets. "I would go mad if I lived here," I remember my friend saying to me last summer. I've lived in Bourj for a while now. This is my first time back to Shatila this year. I forgot that it could be so much worse.

Present

People have different ways of coping with everyday hardships. Each one of the doctors I teach smokes one to two packs of cigarettes a day. I taunt them about this. "But you're *doctors*!" I say. They shrug their shoulders. Ahmad laughs sarcastically and says he would be in a mental hospital if he couldn't smoke. Safwat looks at me guiltily and says he knows it's unhealthy. Dr. Afghani asks casually what difference it makes if smoking kills him when he lives in these conditions. At least he enjoys it. The cardiologist is even more cynical. He puffs on his cigarette, smiles, and says it's people's smoking that keeps him in business.

The Marlboro Man and his competitors are ever-present on the billboards of Beirut. Outlawed by the US anti-tobacco lobby, they simply take up residence elsewhere. Alcohol has a harder time of it here because Lebanon is predominantly Muslim and Islam forbids its consumption. In the Christian areas of Beirut and in the downtown touristy areas, however, it is fairly easy to come by. More than once when I am out with friends from Bourj (which is all Muslim) we stop at little convenience stores far away from the camp, where they can purchase beer or liquor, which is then hidden in bags under car seats. More than half the doctors I work with received their medical training in Russia, where they became experts of varying degrees on vodka and lesser forms of alcohol. Drinking is not allowed in the camps, but behavior differs considerably on the outside. The doctors, especially, must behave like role models because of their status, so they take care not to be seen breaking the accepted social and religious codes at work or around their own neighborhoods. Those educated abroad tend to have the most difficult time trying to reconcile the different influences in their lives and appear to be the most unhappy about their physical surroundings and their personal prospects. Few have any hope of ever being able to leave and often express to me a gloomy and restless dissatisfaction with their conditions. All of my responses sound inadequate and foolish, so I learn just to listen instead.

Five times during the summer different doctors invite me to watch them perform operations. Once an aspiring nurse, I eagerly put on the sterile clothing, mask, shoes, and cap and prepare to watch. Haifa Hospital has three rooms for surgery. There are two computers in the building for record keeping but, as yet, no Internet access, no CT scanners, no MRI or mammography X-ray machines, no advanced life-support systems, no advanced cardiac-care unit, and no cancer treatment or chemotherapy programs. There is one out-of-date ultrasound machine, a small hospital pharmacy on the first floor, tall oxygen tanks in the surgical rooms, and some basic supplies (surgical instruments, gauze, sterile gloves, etc.) in the one supply closet.

I am not surprised to learn that when a patient is admitted to the hospital, his or her family members are responsible for bringing food and changes of clothing for the duration of the patient's stay. Most of the hospital is not air conditioned, although the patients' rooms have electric fans. Relatives sit on hard wooden benches in the hallways when a family member is being examined or operated on. There is no sitting room or cafeteria, no tables strewn with magazines for those seeking a distraction. There is no soda machine, water fountain, or public restroom. There are no receptionists to answer questions or provide information. Haifa Hospital is the second biggest and most well equipped of the camp hospitals in Lebanon.

When not engaged elsewhere, I sit in the tiny, one-room doctors' lounge on the third floor, breathing in the cigarette smoke of however many doctors happen to be on break or momentarily off duty and listening to the hum of the television in the background—usually tuned in to a news channel. This is the nicest room in the hospital because it is lightly air-conditioned and the atmosphere is congenial. There is a small refrigerator here for beverages and someone almost always brings in *manai'che*, pita with cheese or *zaatar* (a thyme and sesame-seed spice mix) for lunch. Here we can be more informal and talk or joke about various things.

It is here that the soft-spoken Dr. Hassan asks me one day, "So what do you think of all us terrorists?"

"It's clear you're a very dangerous bunch," I answer.

Politics is not the usual topic of conversation, but sometimes items in the news spark a few comments. Ehud Barak, Ariel Sharon, and Shimon Peres, all terrorist war criminals to Palestinians (and many others) in Lebanon, appear together during a segment of the news on Camp David and the "peace process"—words that few take seriously in the refugee camps—and someone observes aloud that Americans are unbelievably ignorant about the Middle East. I make no attempt to refute this statement, having for far too long experienced its reality. "America pays for Israel to kill us," someone mutters. "The problem isn't just that Americans don't know," Dr. Afghani remarks. "It is that *they don't care* that they don't know."

There isn't much time for uninterrupted conversation in the doctors' lounge, although once in a while there is a lull in the day's activities. According to facts compiled by the Institute for Palestine Studies in 1997, the patient-to-doctor ratio for the Palestinian population in Lebanon is approximately 1,100 to 1. This accounts for the scarcity of available rooms in the hospital and the generally miserable state of health care.[1] What galls me the most is that it is technically illegal for a Palestinian to practice medicine in Lebanon and, worse, that the camp hospitals are themselves illegal because the Lebanese government will not officially license and register them. (The camp doctors continue to practice and the hospitals and private clinics stay open, Dr. Hassan explains, because of the uproar that would follow if the doctors were jailed or had their foreign-bestowed licenses revoked or if the hospitals were shut down. This is small comfort to the practitioners and their staffs, however, who understand the arbitrariness with which their cases would be treated if they did something to offend a government official—or simply became "inconvenient.")

The PLO, through the Palestine Red Crescent Society branch in Beirut, pays general practitioners approximately $300 a month. Both the PLO and PRCS administrations are notoriously corrupt, and often the checks come in late and sometimes short of the expected amount. Nobody dependent on a salary from one of these organizations will complain openly about it, however, for obvious reasons, and $300 a month is a good living for a refugee.

There is approximately 40–50 percent unemployment in Bourj al Barajneh (a standard figure for the refugee camps), with an even higher underemployment rate. Palestinian refugees have no civil rights in Lebanon and are barred from practicing between seventy to eighty professions outside the camps. There is no right to travel freely in the country, and although laws governing departure and return to Lebanon have ostensibly been relaxed, everyone I spoke to said it was impossible to return (for example, to visit relatives) if you were lucky enough to leave the country permanently. But leaving is next to impossible: few countries will grant either permanent or temporary entrance visas to Palestinian refugees (although it sometimes helps to pay the correct officials exorbitant fees in attempting to get out). The camps, which the residents cannot by law rebuild or repair lest that suggest permanence, are holding pens for people with an undesirable identity. Many people I met had false foreign passports, which might let them get out of the country (being a citizen from almost anywhere else is preferable to being Palestinian). Without requisite working documents, however, a person who leaves with a false ID faces the prospect of illegal employment or vagrancy, in addition to other less pleasant possibilities.

The first and most illuminating operation I witnessed was a Caesarean section—for reasons not anticipated. The mother lay on her back awake (having been given a spinal anesthetic) as the gynecologist, Dr. Muhammad, cut open her belly. When he reached his hands inside her womb for the baby's head the power went out.

Unlike most of the rest of the camp buildings, Haifa Hospital has backup power generators for these occasions: the electricity is cut between eight and twelve hours a day not just in the camps but throughout Lebanon—compliments of the Israeli Air Force power-grid bombings three times the previous year (a war crime committed in order to punish the people of Lebanon for Hezbollah's legitimate resistance to the Israeli occupation of the south). The Lebanese call these power cuts brownouts, since many businesses in the downtown sections of cities have generators to compensate for the outages. The people in the camps are less fortunate. The hospital, however, could not function without backup generators. We nevertheless stand in pitch darkness for a suspenseful forty-five seconds or so until the reserve power dully kicks in.

Dr. Muhammad has got the baby in his hands and lifts him up carefully as the lights come on. I hear the infant's first cries and watch as a nurse takes him away. The baby's mother looks at me and asks, "Did you see my baby? Is my baby OK?"

"He is beautiful. He is healthy and beautiful." I am trying to smile because she looks anxious, but I feel off-balance. For the first time in my life I watch the birth of a baby, and he comes into the world in pitch-blackness. No one around me is the slightest bit unnerved; it is as if this is completely normal. I picture this happening in the hospital in my hometown; picture the flurry and hysteria of a hospital suddenly without any power—the blame and outrage of the staff and patients. "Do not worry, this happens frequently," says Dr. Muhammad reassuringly, seeing my face. He's not exaggerating. During each of the successive operations I am allowed to watch, the power goes out and then slowly, dimly, comes back on with the help of the generators. "These are our conditions," I remember Dr. Afghani saying to me once in the doctors' lounge, "What can we do?"

On September 16, 2000, there is a big march in Washington, DC, for the right of Palestinians to return to their homes in Israel, and 4,000 people turn out. It is an exhilarating event, even though most of the major media are notably absent.

Meanwhile, there have been demonstrations in Beirut. Palestinian refugees are protesting the lack of secondary schools for their children. A large number of Palestinian teens in Lebanon do not go to school, either because there aren't schools to attend, because they're tired of being in United Nations Relief and Works Agency classrooms of forty to sixty people where it is normal to have to share desks and textbooks, or because their parents cannot afford to send them to private Lebanese schools— which are more expensive for non-Lebanese. There are massive demonstrations in front of the UN building in Beirut, though again, they are unmentioned in the mainstream US press.

There is so much work to be done. Olfat Mahmoud, the volunteer coordinator in Bourj al Barajneh, head of the Women's Humanitarian Organization there, and herself a refugee, is interested in a project I suggest for the neediest of the camp. She tells me she does not expect Israel to grant the right of return any time soon, but that the situation of the refugees is not only political: the social problems in the camp are multiplying. There is domestic abuse, poverty, illiteracy, and crime. There are mental and physical illnesses and conditions for which there are no adequate remedies or supplies. There are social problems that confine the camp residents to a world apart.

"I took one hundred and fifty of the poorest children from the camp to a mall in Hamra [upscale Beirut] and they went wild. I could not control them. They had never seen an escalator before, or glitzy store windows with expensive items of clothing displayed in them. You must understand," she paused, "many of these children have never been outside of the camps before. No matter what happens in Palestine this is unacceptable. We may never return—*inshallah* [God willing] we will someday—but we cannot continue to live like this in these camps for another fifty-three years. How will these children grow up to be well-adjusted adults when they cannot integrate into the society across the street?

When they have no contact with the worlds that you and I are a part of? It is not just a question of money. They need human contact with the outside. They need people and families who will write to them and visit them and perhaps even bring them over to their countries to visit. They cannot continue to live life in such exile that they become incapable of dealing with the modern world." Her words ring in my ears. "We are always hearing about the need for and benefits of democracy. Well, nobody ever asks us what we want. Our fate is in the hands of arbitrary and unsympathetic powers."

Olfat is one of the reasons I will return to Beirut again. I am no longer at leisure to forget her words and move on with my own life. I begin to feel optimistic when I mention my ideas of a civic integration project to friends concerned with this issue. They would like to help. At times I am inspired just by the concern voiced by complete strangers over e-mail and by the slow but steady mobilization that is taking place. It makes me more hopeful.

This brief period of optimism is soon shattered by the outbreak of hostilities in Jerusalem. By the end of the fall the conflict degenerates into a war against the Palestinians in the occupied territories. All attention must be focused now on getting emergency food and medical supplies into the Gaza Strip and the West Bank, where murderously indignant IDF soldiers and armed Jewish settlers are killing hundreds and wounding thousands of Palestinians demanding a real peace —that is, one based not on the Oslo accords but on the Universal Declaration of Human Rights, to which Israel gave its willing signature, and on United Nations Resolutions 242 and 194, which demand the full withdrawal of Israel from the occupied territories, including East Jerusalem, and the right of the refugees to return to their homes. Those not involved directly in sending emergency supplies to the hospitals and elsewhere in the territories concentrate their efforts on undoing the distortion of US television and press reports, which portray Israel as being under siege by mobs of angry savages. The more brutal the IDF repression, the more homicidal and pernicious the reports in the press become until, a friend of mine argues, it is possible to rightly apportion blame for Palestinian deaths to the media for its complicity with the US/pro-Israel party line.

In Beirut in mid-October, a UPI press report quotes Selim al-Hoss, then Lebanese Prime Minister, as praising the "blessed intifada" in Palestine. "We sympathize with this struggling people and back them in their position regarding principal issues such as Jerusalem" and the right of return, he says. "This is a legitimate right and we back it."[2] His hypocrisy is disgusting—the Lebanese government is more repressive toward the Palestinian refugees than any other Arab regime and would not dream of allowing them basic civil rights or, God forbid, citizenship in Lebanon lest the dubious confessional balance be upset. (Most of the refugees are Sunni Muslim, and to grant them citizenship would mean challenging the myth—and the power structure based thereon—that the three primary religious groupings in Lebanon, Christian, Shiite Muslim, and Sunni Muslim, each represent about a third of the population.) While it is argued that few Palestinians would accept permanent repatriation in other

Arab countries, this does not excuse the indignities to which they are subject every day in countries such as Lebanon, above all.

The refugees are little more than a political card to be drawn by the Lebanese or Syrians on an appropriate occasion for the advancement of their own national self-interests. As the violence in the occupied territories escalates, the plight of the Palestinian refugees outside Palestine becomes a secondary issue. In leading political circles in the United States and Israel the right of return is no more seriously discussed than at any time in the past fifty-three years despite the attention that activist groups are increasingly drawing toward it. This fact highlights our leaders' willful refusal to seek a genuine way out of the unending conflict. I call friends in Bourj now who, after the initial excitement and anxiety caused by the new intifada, tell me that their conditions are unchanged and that life in the camps goes on as always. "Don't worry about coming to Beirut," they tell me. "It is quiet." The shunned continue to languish in unnamed despair.

Future

Hezbollah, or the Shiite Muslim Party of God, has gained enormous prestige throughout the Arab world for defeating the Israeli forces in south Lebanon. Thousands of Palestinians now watch its al-Manar TV station, which broadcasts information daily into the occupied territories on how to fight a guerrilla war against the Israelis effectively, a prospect that is unsettling—the Palestinian territories are not Lebanon, after all. Fighters cannot retreat into hills beyond Israeli control after an ambush of army vehicles, for example. Rather, they would remain trapped in an area surrounded by their adversaries, inviting wholesale slaughter and destruction, and no one should underestimate the willingness of the IDF to massacre its unwanted captive population, especially at a time when the fault can be cynically placed on the victims in the name of "security." There is nevertheless a clear need for leadership, discipline, organization, and, above all, hope among the Palestinians in the territories, which explains the appeal of al-Manar and its backers.

Only a small percentage of the refugees are Shiites. Two of the doctors at the hospital are Shiite; one was born into a Shiite family in Libya. Another, Safwat Iskandar, converted his entire family to Shiism. I was surprised to see a photograph of Hezbollah Sheik Nasrallah in the center of Safwat's living room wall. "We were Sunni," Safwat told me, "until I began to listen to Nasrallah. He is a very intelligent man, and his religious passion and ideas impressed me. Because my father died when I was only 16, I became the head of my family. After returning from my medical studies in Moscow [in the mid-1990s] I became interested in Hezbollah. They were the only ones trying to liberate Lebanon from Israeli occupation. They weren't corrupt and self-seeking like the [Lebanese and Syrian governments]." Did his co-workers know he was Shiite? I wondered. "I don't talk about religion at work," Safwat replied. "It is my business and I don't want to create tension. Here [in Lebanon] a person's faith is much more important than it is in America. People are very emotional about it and it is a central part of our lives. I think that's difficult for others to understand." I tell him I think I'm beginning to understand it better. I also note to myself how my own stereotypes are falling away: Safwat's sister is sitting next to him on the couch as he speaks. She is a bubbly, talkative girl of about 15 who is interested in fashions and boys and having fun with her friends. She is wearing a Gap T-shirt and pants. Neither she nor her well-made-up cousin, Salwa, wears a headscarf at home or in public. She and Safwat argue like true siblings over everything and we all end up laughing at the catty remarks they fling at each other over lunch. Safwat shows me photos of his days in medical school. He shows me the picture of his former Russian girlfriend, whom he looks at wistfully, and he plays melodious Russian folk songs for us on his guitar. There is nothing mysterious or sinister about him or his family, I catch myself thinking, remembering the one-sided images of Hezbollah portrayed in the US media.

Bourj al Barajneh borders the Shiite neighborhood of Haret Hreik. According to many of the people I spoke to, the Shiites of Lebanon are perhaps more sympathetic toward the Palestinian refugees than any other group in the country right now, something that has not always been the case. On one occasion when I ask my student Ahmad, who is Sunni Muslim, for his opinion of Hezbollah his response is quick: "The enemy of my enemy is my friend." I press him on this and he admits that he finds the sect too strictly Islamic for his tastes but that he is happy they finally forced the Israelis out of the south.

"I'm not so sure they are your friend," I say teasingly as I watch him pour himself a second glass of vodka. We sit in Ahmad's seventh-floor apartment overlooking the poor Shiite neighborhoods beyond the camp. His wife, Rajaa', is listening to us. Her English is not so good but she understands the gist of the conversation. Rajaa' is a lab technician, and a heavy smoker like her husband. They have three children, two girls and a boy. The whole family is Sunni Muslim but not strictly so. Ahmad rarely goes to the mosque on Fridays and heeds religious restrictions only when necessary. His is as nontraditional a family as I have met since coming to Lebanon. I doubt they'd feel much at home in an Islamist-controlled land. Then again, it is unlikely Hezbollah or any other Islamist group will ever take full power in Lebanon. This hasn't diminished its status in the country since its liberation of the south, however. Even some Christians celebrated its victory. The Lebanese government has, for the time being, decided to let Hezbollah deal with the Israelis at the border for cynical, self-serving purposes undoubtedly determined by Syria. The prospects for a stable future in Lebanon are as uncertain as ever. Fundamentalist groups such as Hezbollah in Lebanon and Hamas and Islamic Jihad in Palestine are gaining popularity for a variety of reasons, including the US refusal to deal justly with the Palestinian crisis.

When I get back to my apartment, there is the familiar smell of backed-up sewage coming from the bathroom and the stale, overpowering heat. With the candles lit I sink into a broken armchair and sit without moving until I stop sweating. There's no point in going to the kitchen for something to drink.

Everything will be warm by now and cockroaches have made their way into the vegetable drawer, where they're helping themselves to a moldy feast.

"I think I'm going insane," I tell Robert over coffee one afternoon. "It's all starting to feel normal." I've been telling him about my living conditions. "Oh you're not insane, you're fine," he says to me. He has lived in Beirut almost twenty-four years now. "It's time to worry when you start naming the cockroaches Charlie and Buster and calling them to come get their food in the morning," he says cajolingly. Coming from a man who has seen every misery that war and hatred can bring to a country, I feel both amused and chastised. A sense of humor is mandatory here.

This helps explain why so many of my friends in Bourj are always making jokes and laughing with each other. One of them, Dr. Hamurabi, looks at me in between laughs one morning. "We have to laugh because we are depressed," he says and then laughs again. "We need some full-time psychiatrists on our staff here." He looks at me and smiles apologetically. "Speak for yourself," someone else retorts. Hamurabi just laughs again, this time pretending to be mad. He is a Christian from Dbayeh camp in East Beirut. He is materially slightly better off than those in Bourj al Barajneh, and later in the fall he obtains a visa for the Emirates. Hamurabi is the one who, one morning when I arrive at the hospital, says "Shalom" in front of some of the other staff, who all look at each other and then at me. I ignore the remark but I don't forget it. I am not hiding my identity, but then I'm not publicizing it either. Despite the awkwardness I feel after that, I sense no malice from anyone, and in fact later that day Hamurabi asks me to come to a picnic in Damour the following Sunday. It will be a festive occasion honoring a surgeon who is retiring from practice. I am happy to be invited, because soon I will be leaving and I want to enjoy a day in the country with all the people I've come to know this summer.

A picnic in Damour nevertheless strikes me as somehow incongruous with what I know of the place. In 1976, shortly after the massacre of Palestinians at the Karantina refugee camp in East Beirut by the Phalangists, PLO fighters brutally murdered nearly 150 Christian civilians living near the seaside village of Damour. The response to this by the Phalangists was the massacre of about 3,000 Palestinians at the Tel el-Zaatar refugee camp. Many of the survivors were brought to Damour, where they lived in desperate poverty. When Arafat came to visit them he was pelted with rotten vegetables and called "traitor" by those who understood that by asking the fighters at Tel el-Zaatar to stand their ground against hopeless odds he was using them to acquire "martyrs" for his cause.[3] In 1982, before its invasion of Lebanon, and again in 1984 the Israel Defense Forces bombed Damour. It seemed odd to be looking forward to a picnic in Damour. Then again, where in Lebanon could one go to enjoy oneself without being haunted by the ghosts of recent history?

At the picnic the children climb down a grassy bank to swim in the shallow river waters and the others set the food out on tables or play backgammon or cards. People talk together in small groups and relax. When my student Khalil arrives, his wife and their 8-week-old daughter are with him. I offer to hold the baby so Khalil's wife can have some time to socialize freely. I rock the baby in my lap and then turn her to face me. She is cooing and I tickle her toes. Later Khalil comes over to see his daughter and thanks me for watching her. "We will miss you when you leave," he says to me, and a sudden sadness comes over me. "I wish I could stay longer; I'm not ready to go back yet." It has been a long time since I enjoyed myself so well as with the friends I have made here. Dr. Wassim winks at me and tells me to watch him beat Dr. Bahjat at backgammon. Hala offers me plate after plate of fresh salad, hummous, pita, kibbeh and grape leaves. She is making sarcastic remarks about the men flirting with her. "They are all the same," she says rolling her eyes, "naughty little boys with men's bodies." We have a good laugh at that.

The older men are sitting together at one of the picnic tables talking animatedly and the women are greeting each other and talking as though it has been a long time since they've seen one another. Khalil's wife comes to take her baby back and thanks me for watching her. Over at the river the children are swimming in their underclothes. The water is uninviting because it is strewn with paper trash. Someone has started playing music from a portable radio and the atmosphere is livelier than ever.

A chair moves up beside me and Ahmad sits down and takes out a cigarette. "Do you like to take a walk?" I look at him uncertainly. "Away from the noise and the people? It is quiet over there," he says pointing toward a field lined with trees. "I guess," I say with just as much uncertainty. "Just to walk and talk," he says. "I am married and you are married, and you are a foreign woman so nobody will be upset if we leave for a while."

We get up and walk together up some stone steps past a small waterfall. Ahmad lights another cigarette and is quiet for a while. "You are thinking about something," he finally says—almost as if it is a question.

"I'm just being reflective. It's my nature to be quiet and to ponder things."

"Yes, I know. I like your nature," he says, looking kindly into my eyes. "But I think you have a secret."

"A secret?" I'm surprised by this comment. "Do I have a secret?" Now I am asking myself more than him.

"Yes, I think you have a secret, because I've seen it in your face." We stop in front of a brook away from the picnicking crowds. The sound of the water is refreshing and neither of us speaks for a moment.

"You want to say it?" he asks. It occurs to me then that he is asking me something very specific, and I search his face for an advance reaction.

"I suppose it is a secret but not in the way you think," I finally answer. He says nothing, just stands there smoking his cigarette. "I am Jewish," I say. "Does this bother you?" Without answering my question he says simply, "We know."

"You know? How do you know? I didn't tell anyone here."

"OK, then, we suspect."

"Why?" I ask. He doesn't really have an answer to this question, so he just mentions my being here for the summer to teach, the only American, older than the other volunteers; always talking about politics…his voice trails off.

"Some say maybe you are with the CIA," he ventures. This makes me laugh out loud. "Me? With the CIA? You must be kidding." He shrugs his shoulders.

"I don't think this," he says.

"I can't stand the CIA and I can't stand my government's policies in the Middle East—including and especially in Israel. I am not a Zionist, if that's what you're wondering. I am against Zionism. Maybe I am here because I am so angry at what my country is responsible for." There is intensity in my voice that was absent only a few moments before. It surprises even me. "It's not your fault," Ahmad replies, but I'm shaking my head no. "In a genuine democracy we are all responsible for what our government does. I have to care or I am a bad citizen. Besides that, it bothers my conscience."

"Look," Ahmad goes on, "We have many problems here—just in Lebanon. It is not just the Zionists or just the Americans who are responsible." We are walking toward a grove of citrus trees and sit down in the shade of a lime tree. Ahmad reaches up and plucks a ripe lime off the tree and hands it to me. "A souvenir," he says with a grin. The fresh green fruit lies in my palm like a treasure.

"I don't care that you are Jewish," Ahmad says at last. "It is not Jews who are our enemy. It is Zionists and their supporters we must struggle against." Ahmad looks 45, but he's only 34. He was born and raised in the refugee camps of Lebanon. In 1980, at 13, he was in uniform carrying a gun and fighting with the PLO. During the Israeli siege of Beirut, Ahmad fought against the Phalangists and the Israelis in the streets near where he lives today. There is a bullet wound that goes clear through his left leg and a deep scar on his right hand. He led a youth brigade of the PLO and helped train new recruits. For a time, he brought orphaned children he found in the streets home with him until his family found them a place to go. When the PLO evacuated Lebanon he was left behind. Knowing he would be killed if found, Ahmad appealed to a Bulgarian journalist, Evon Garuloff, for help—a man he'd met by chance when different foreign journalists were interviewing the "children of war." In an act of remarkable courage, Garuloff hid Ahmad in the back of his car and smuggled him past the border guards in the north and out of Lebanon. This is how Ahmad came to receive his medical training in Bulgaria. There he also met his wife and had his first daughter, Eva—named after the man who saved his life. He returned to Beirut and to his family near the end of the war and began practicing as a doctor in Bourj al Barajneh. He helps support his mother and sister as well as his own wife and children. His siblings are scattered about, some in the West Bank, some as far away as Amsterdam. He cannot visit them.

"My whole life has been a war. I don't want the same for my children." We have been sitting under the lime tree for almost an hour. No doubt the rumors have already begun. It's time to return to the picnic and mingle with the others. "I hope we will stay in touch after you return to America. Will you visit Beirut again?" Ahmad looks at me with a mark of sadness in his eyes.

"Yes," I answer. "I don't know when but I know I will come back."

By mid-December the new intifada has been raging for more than two months, with the death toll for the Palestinians already past 300 and rising daily. Syria, Lebanon, and Israel cynically play their war games, with the Palestinians at the center of the conflict yet again. There is no end in sight; on the contrary, various groups are urging the Palestinians to step up their resistance while Israel responds with disproportionate and indiscriminate violence against them and rejects, with full US backing, all of their most basic, concrete demands: no viable Palestinian state, with its capital in East Jerusalem; no removal of the illegal settlements or even a halt to their continued expansion; no attempts to disarm the settlers; no return to the 1967 borders. No right of return or compensation for the 3–4 million Palestinian refugees living unrecognized lives. What "peace" can come about under these terms?

It seems unlikely to me that Ahmad's children and the other refugee children will grow up not knowing war, as their parents so desire. I hear from people in the camps that there are regular demonstrations in support of the intifada and that they will continue to demand their right to return home. To give up is to succumb to perpetual and state-sanctioned wretchedness. To fight on is to invite more disappointment and disaster. But at least struggling rekindles some hope.

I make plans to return to Beirut but wonder about the wisdom of returning at a time like this. Just how welcome will I be again in Bourj al Barajneh? In a letter to my former supervisor, I ask him if it is safe for me to return right now. His letter allays my fears, but its message is bittersweet.

Dear Jennifer,

How are you? I received your message.… Thank you for your support. If you decide to come, welcome to you any time.… Here in the camp in general it is quiet. Periodically we [have] demonstrations in support of ours in [the] West Bank and Gaza.… I know you [are] following the intifada…[and] because of that I will not talk about politics.

Jennifer, if you wish to come do not [be] afraid. All the camp will guard you as one of us, and we will keep you [safe]. [You have] nothing to be afraid of even [though] you [are] American.… People here are not hating Americans as Americans but we hate the American policy.… Welcome to you any time. You can consider yourself Palestinian.

Dr. Wassim

Notes

1. "Health and Education," *Palestinian Refugees in Lebanon* (Institute for Palestine Studies brochure on the refugees in Lebanon, 1997), p. 10.

2. Abdel Mawla Khaled, "Palestinian Refugees Denounce Mideast Summit," UPI, October 16, 2000.

3. Robert Fisk, *Pity the Nation* (New York, 1990), pp. 101–2.

16. LIFE IN THE CAMPS
MAYSSOUN SUKARIEH

Mayssoun Sukarieh, a volunteer teacher in Shatila refugee camp in Beirut, asked some of her students to write about their experiences, which she translated from the Arabic.

No Land, No Honor

Farah Obeid
14 years old

"Who doesn't have a land, does not have honor." That was what the elderly in the camp always used to say, but I never comprehended its meaning until I joined a Lebanese school.

When I reached the elementary level my father put me in a Lebanese school thinking that the educational standard at UNRWA [United Nations Relief and Works Agency] schools was not good enough; he and my mother had been educated there without benefiting much. When I joined the Lebanese school I met a lot of friends, but as the days passed I started to lose them as a result of my being Palestinian. And because my accent was so different from theirs, they would leave me and go play with the others. Once the teacher asked me, "What does your father do?" When I told her that he was a garbage collector, she changed and stopped loving me, while my friends not only mocked and despised me but also called me "daughter of the garbage collector." This was a great source of pain for me and for my brothers and sisters. As a result of our daily weeping and complaining, my father quit his job.

When I reached the intermediate level I moved to another Lebanese school. At the beginning, I used to talk to most of my classmates, who, as soon as they found out that I lived in Shatila and that I walked to the school next to the Makassed Hospital, started to mock me, saying that I had a "complex." Once a classmate told me she did not talk to me because I was Palestinian, and Palestinians were the cause of the Lebanese civil war, and because we were refugees with no land or identity.

I always beg my father to let me join UNRWA schools with the Palestinian students, but he says that I have to bear the difficulties in order to learn and return to Palestine. That is why I concede and bear people's harsh words. But when I thought that they might naturalize us, I was afraid that I would become like my friends at school.

I want to return to Palestine to have a land and an identity. Then nobody would dare mock me and say I am a refugee.

Left: Family in the tent where they live in Khan Yunis, Gaza

Muhammad al-Durra and Me

Mona Zaaroura
13 years old
Saffouri-Nazareth-Palestine

Every day, I watch Muhammad al-Durra's photo being slowly downloaded on the Internet. Through his photo, I see my life and the lives of all the refugee children in the camps. What I see first in Muhammad's face are scared eyes, in which I feel my fear and the fear of all the refugee children of our present lives, future and destiny.

In his head, tucked between his shoulders like a turtle's, I see the bent heads of the refugee children—bent by the tough life they are leading, where poverty, loss and oppression are the dominating themes. Then emerges an open mouth crying for help. In his cry I hear my cry to the world: "Enough, enough of what you are doing to us!" But I know that my cry, like Muhammad's, won't reach anywhere. In his cry I also hear our cry for return to our homeland, Palestine. Then I see him dying in his father's lap, as he is engulfed by fear. This is what I feel upon closely observing his face covered by his small hands. At this point a question I've often asked comes to my mind: "Is death our redemption?" The photo of the dead Muhammad al-Durra says, "No, even death won't protect us from fear and insecurity." On the wall behind his body are bullet holes that show the Zionists' ruthlessness. I knew they were ruthless, but I did not imagine they could kill a child in cold blood.

When the photo is completely downloaded, I get to see Muhammad al-Durra hiding behind his father's back and held by him so tight. Then, I envy him. At least he had a father who could protect him and hold him tight. My father and most of my friends' fathers in Shatila died in massacres and wars. And those who are still alive are dying from poverty and oppression, and thus are left too helpless to support and protect their children.

Muhammad al-Durra resembles me and all other refugee children. We die every day, just as he did. But at least he died in his homeland, not as a refugee in the diaspora. We won't forget you, Muhammad al-Durra. You will always be in our hearts.

Eyewitness from Shatila

Walid Balkis
15 years old
October 7, 2000

As we watched the news in Palestine, sitting in the refugee camp, we wished we could go to Palestine to confront our enemy. But all we could do was demonstrate every day in the camp, and twice outside in

Beirut. The biggest demonstration in Beirut was after the death of Rami. When I saw Rami killed I felt angry and outraged. I knew the Israelis were cruel, but not to that extent. How could they kill a child in cold blood?

I dreamt that night that all the Palestinians are one person who was lost in a forest, surrounded by frightening monsters. So I started to think we should do something, and we all started to talk about going to the south [to the Israel/Lebanon border].

I woke up early in the morning, I prayed, and I told my mother that I might become a martyr or I might come back wounded. What made me go is the feeling that this should be the end: Either we all die—as Palestinians—or we live together free and with dignity in our land. I felt I should participate in the liberation of Palestine.

I kissed my mother and went to the south. Most of those who went did not have their parents' approval. "We are young, but we are strong, and we can fight for Palestine!" we thought. All of us are fed up with living in Shatila; if we die, we thought, at least we will be dying for Palestine.

On the way we were chanting for Palestine and for return. We shouted, "With blood, with soul, we will sacrifice for you, Palestine!" When we got to the border we saw that only a wire fence separates us from our people.

I can't tell you how beautiful Palestine is. How can we be Palestinians and have such a beautiful country, and yet live in Shatila? Is it fair that other people are enjoying the beauty of Palestine while we live in humiliating conditions in the camp? Damn you, Shatila, and damn you, Israel!

Then we saw Zarit [an Israeli settlement], where the Israelis have many outposts. We could see them so clearly behind the fence. We were only about twenty meters from them. We started to throw stones. While I was throwing stones, I was thinking of my friends in Dheisheh refugee camp [in the West Bank], and all the children of Palestine. I threw stones for my friends in Shatila who could not come with us.

Then they started to fire tear gas at us. I fainted, and so did many others, but we got up and started to throw stones at them again. Around 1 o'clock, Hasan Hassanein threw Molotov cocktails at the Israelis. He threw five of them, and while he was throwing the last one, two helicopters flew over us. They fired tear gas, and we couldn't see each other. The Israeli soldiers fired two shots at him. He was hit in the chest and stomach. He was carried away while making a victory sign and chanting for Palestine.

We continued throwing stones. The bosses were telling us to throw stones while they were sitting up the hill, each with his camera and some of them with videocameras. For a while I thought it would be good to throw stones at them, but this was not the time. I had the Israelis in front of me.

Half an hour later, the leaders ordered us to tear the fence down. Since we were outraged, some of us started to. When we were almost done, Shadi Anas from Bourj al Barajneh camp threw a Molotov at the Israelis, burning one of their vehicles and a watchtower. Then they shot him and fired more tear gas at us.

We went on throwing stones until 3 o'clock, and then we heard that Hasan and Shadi had died. We started to chant for them and sing the songs that Palestinians sing for grooms. We headed back to Shatila. We were so sad, until we heard the news that Hezbollah had captured three Israeli soldiers and fired fifty Katyushas from Fatma Gate in retaliation for Hasan and Shadi and the twenty-two injured. We were jubilant and started to sing.

When I got back to the camp, my mother and friends were waiting for me. They all hugged and kissed me. I was so happy because I had lived what our people in Palestine are living. We should all be living there. I wished I had come back to Shatila a martyr for Palestine. But unfortunately, I came back alive and had to go back to my previous jail in Shatila. Oh how I love Palestine! I love it now more than ever.

17. "THIS IS A PLACE OF FILTH AND BLOOD WHICH WILL FOREVER BE ASSOCIATED WITH ARIEL SHARON"

ROBERT FISK

February 6, 2001

Even when I walk these fetid streets today, more than eighteen years after what was—by Israel's own definition of that much-misused phrase—the worst single act of terrorism in modern Middle East history, the ghosts haunt me still. Over there, on the side of the road leading to the Sabra mosque, lay Mr. Nouri, 90 years old, gray-bearded, in pajamas with a small woollen hat still on his head and a stick by his side. I found him on a pile of garbage, on his back, fly-encrusted eyes staring at the blazing sun. Just up the lane, I came across two women sitting upright with their brains blown out, next to a cooking pot and a dead horse. One of the women appeared to have had her stomach slit open. A few meters away, I discovered the first babies, already black with decomposition, scattered across the road like rubbish.

Yes, those of us who got into Sabra and Shatila before the murderers left have our memories. The flies racing between the reeking bodies and our faces, between dried blood and reporter's notebook, the hands of watches still ticking on dead wrists. I clambered up a rampart of earth—an abandoned bulldozer stood guiltily nearby—only to find, once I was atop the mound, that it swayed beneath me. And I looked down to find faces, elbows, mouths, a woman's legs protruding through the soil. I had to hold on to these body parts to climb down the other side. Then there was the pretty girl, her head surrounded by a halo of clothes pegs, her blood still running from a hole in her back. We had burst into the yard of her home, desperate to avoid the Israeli-uniformed militiamen who still roamed the camp; coming in by the back door, we had found her body as the murderers left by the front door.

And as I walked through the carnage on September 18—the last day of the three-day massacre—with Loren Jenkins of the *Washington Post*, a fierce, tough, Colorado reporter, I remember how he stopped in shock and disgust. And then, with as much energy as his lungs could summon in the sweet, foul air, he shouted, "SHARON!" so loudly that the name echoed off the crumpled walls above the bodies. "He's responsible for this fucking mess," Jenkins roared. And that, just over four months later—in more diplomatic words and in a report in which the murderers were called "soldiers"—was what the Israeli commission of inquiry decided. Sharon, who was minister of defense, bore "personal responsibility," the Kahan commission stated, and recommended his removal from office. Sharon resigned.

And so today, in this fetid, awful place, where Lebanese Muslim militiamen were—three years later—to kill hundreds more Palestinians in a war that produced no official inquiries, where scarcely 20 percent of the survivors still live, where brown mud and rubbish now covers the mass grave of 600

Left: Ariel Sharon, surrounded by bodyguards, on the Haram al-Sharif/Temple Mount, September 28, 2000
Photo © Khaled Zighari, Source: Reuters News Picture Service

of the 1982 victims, the Palestinians wait to see if their tormentor will hold the highest office in the state of Israel.

"Ariel Sharon was responsible," a well-dressed young man shouted at us from an apartment balcony yesterday morning. And who could disagree? Israel had invaded Lebanon on June 6, 1982, with a plan—known to Sharon but not vouchsafed to his Likud prime minister, Menachem Begin—to advance all the way to Beirut and surround Yasir Arafat's Palestine Liberation Organization guerrillas in the Lebanese capital. Officially named "Operation Peace for Galilee" (the real Israeli military code name was "Snowball"), the invasion was supposedly a response to PLO rocket attacks across the Israeli border.

But the rocket attacks had followed a series of Israeli air raids on Lebanon that had ended a UN-brokered cease-fire and that were supposedly in "retaliation" for the attempted murder of the Israeli ambassador to London—though his would-be killers came from the Abu Nidal group, which had nothing to do with the PLO and hated Arafat. But Sharon had anyway received an earlier American "green light" for his operation from Alexander Haig in the spring of 1982. After two months and almost 17,000 deaths, most of them civilians—the majority killed by Israeli gunfire and air attack—the PLO withdrew from Beirut under international protection, leaving their unarmed families behind. At which point Sharon announced that 2,000 "terrorists" remained in the Sabra and Shatila camps. These mythical "terrorists" prompted a small advance by Israeli tanks—contrary to an agreement with Washington—toward the Palestinian camps. A French UN officer who tried to photograph the advance was shot dead by an "unknown" sniper. Sharon repeated his extraordinary claim that "terrorists" remained in the camps. And it was then that the Christian Lebanese president-elect, Bashir Gemayel— the leader of the Phalange militia, which had already murdered thousands of surrendering Palestinians in the Tel el-Zaatar camp in 1976—was assassinated.

Sharon paid his condolences to Gemayel's father, Pierre. He must have known the old man's history. Pierre Gemayel had founded his party after being inspired by the Olympics in Nazi Germany in 1936 ("I liked their idea of order," he once confided to me). Not for nothing did Israel's militia allies use the fascist "Phalange" as their name. As the Christians prepared to bury their hero, Sharon—again contrary to assurances he had given the Americans—ordered the Israeli army into West Beirut to "restore order." The Israelis then asked the Christian Phalange—armed and uniformed by Israel and allied to Israel since 1976—to enter the Israeli-surrounded camps to "liquidate" the "terrorists." Which is why, on Thursday, September 16, guided by signposts that the Israelis had laid across a Beirut airport runway, the Christian gunmen walked through the southern entrance of Shatila, some of them drunk, a number on drugs—all under the eyes of the Israelis—and embarked on a war crime.

Today, much scarred by later wars, the lanes of Shatila still follow the same paths I walked down eighteen years ago. There are always survivors who have never told their stories to us before. Yesterday I wandered up an alleyway—rippling with water pipes and running with rain and sewage—to find a middle-aged woman buying tomatoes from a stall. I was thirty meters from the road where I discovered Mr. Nouri's body almost two decades ago. She took me to her family home and introduced me to her daughter, Nadia Salameh. Nadia was only 12 when Ariel Sharon's soldiers watched the Phalangist militia slaughter their way through the camps.

"At the end of this alleyway outside our home, we were all shocked by what we saw," she told me, her voice slowly rising with the memory of horror. "I saw corpses there, seven deep, some decapitated, others with their throats slit. One of our neighbours was lying there, Um Ahmed Saad, and her body had grown big with the heat. Her hands had been chopped off at the wrists. She used to wear a lot of bracelets, a lot of gold. The Phalange obviously wanted the gold."

Each house I enter contains the faded photographs of young men killed in the war, some by Israel's allies, others by Shia Muslim gunmen in the later 1985 camps war. But their memories have not faded. Old Abdullah—he is 78 and pleaded with us not to use his family name—talks without looking at me, eyes staring at the wall. The ghosts are returning again. "The Phalange were led by Elie Hobeika," he said, "but who sent them into the camps? The Israelis. And who was the defense minister? Sharon. They put their tanks round the camp. I was part of a delegation that tried to negotiate with them. We carried a white flag. When we got near, there was a man's voice on a loudspeaker telling us to have our identity cards ready. But I didn't have my ID. So I went back home. And it turned out the loudspeaker was being used by a Phalangist. And they murdered all the men in the delegation. I was the only one to survive."

There was no doubt that the Israelis could see what the Lebanese Christian Phalange were doing. The Kahan commission was later to quote Lieutenant Avi Grabovski, deputy commander of an Israeli tank unit that was helping to encircle the camp: he watched the murder of five women and children and wanted to protest, but his battalion commander had replied to another soldier who complained that "we know, it's not to our liking, and don't interfere." Up to 2,000 Palestinians were murdered—two mass graves remain unexhumed in Beirut—and Sharon's reputation, already besmirched by the much earlier slaughter of more than fifty Palestinian civilians by his Commando Unit 101, seemed as buried as the Palestinian victims.

But like the garbage that has collected over the only known mass grave, the historical narrative—save for that of the survivors—has become overgrown. History moves on. Arafat recognized Israel and found himself trapped by an agreement that would give him neither a real "Palestine" nor secure the return of the refugees—including those in Sabra and Shatila—to what is now Israel. And the new leader of Israel is, within hours, likely to be the man who allowed the killers into the Beirut camps more than eighteen years ago.

With power, of course, comes respect. CNN now calls Sharon "a barrel-framed veteran general who has built a reputation for flattening obstacles and reshaping Israel's landscape," while the BBC World

Service on Sunday managed to avoid the fateful words Sabra and Shatila by referring only to his "checkered military career." As for Nadia Salameh, "Sharon's role here shows what he is capable of. If Sharon is elected, the whole peace process falls by the wayside, because he doesn't want peace." It's a relief to recall that up to a million Israelis demonstrated their moral integrity in 1982 by protesting in Tel Aviv against the massacre. And equally chilling to reflect that some of those one million—if the polls are accurate—may well be voting for Mr. Sharon today.

This article originally appeared in The Independent *on February 6, 2001. Reprinted by permission of The Independent/Syndication, London.*

18. THE IMPLEMENTATION OF THE RIGHT OF RETURN
SALMAN ABU SITTA

One of the most important lessons we have learned from the fifty-three-year Palestinian-Israeli conflict is that the essence of the struggle is the expulsion of the people of Palestine from their homes and the confiscation of their land. Another term for this is "ethnic cleansing." A foreign minority descended upon the shores of Palestine, expelled the national majority, denied its existence and rights, and created a state on its soil.

This cataclysm caused havoc in the area: regimes were toppled, leaders were assassinated, five major wars were fought, and hundreds of smaller attacks were carried out. The result was that all of British Mandate Palestine was conquered, in addition to territories in the four neighboring countries.

Yet the refugees, dispersed as they are, many of them living in deplorable conditions in exile, others suffering under occupation or virtual siege, harassed by friend and foe, still survive. They are the largest popular force to shape the modern history of the Middle East. The implementation of their inalienable rights is the key to a permanent peace. All else, including a Palestinian state, so-called regional cooperation or other contrived devices to obscure this fundamental issue, is peripheral.

The surprised reaction in the West to the Al-Aqsa Intifada is an indication of the distorted image ("the irrational Middle East") built up over the years by pro-Israel bias. The current surge of articles in the Israeli and American press about the right of return points more to surprise than recognition, to fear about, rather than interest in, Palestinian rights. By all sensible measures, the refugees are still the main problem to contend with.

Ethnic Cleansing Plan

Getting rid of the native inhabitants of Palestine has long been one of the tenets of Zionism.[1] It was clearly spelled out by Yosef Weitz, the head of the Transfer Committee and the chief of land-confiscation operations. As early as 1940, he proposed an ethnic cleansing plan: "The only solution is to transfer the Arabs from here to neighbouring countries. Not a single village or a single tribe must be left."[2]

Plan Dalet was designed to "occupy" and to "expel"[3] the Palestinian people. It was David Ben-Gurion's doctrine that the destruction of the Palestinian people and their cultural and physical landscape was the precondition for creating the state of Israel on its ruins.[4] The systematic elimination of the Palestinians in 1948 took the following forms:

Left: Carrying flour back to al-Mawasi, part of Khan Yunis

(1) Military Plans for Jewish Settlement

As early as January 1948, four months before the official war began, the Zionists prepared plans for the settlement of 1.5 million new immigrants over and above the existing 600,000 Jews, two-thirds of whom were themselves recent immigrants under the British Mandate. During the Jewish military operations that followed the UN partition resolution of November 1947 and before the end of the British Mandate, more than half the Palestinian population was expelled. The settlement agencies headed by the Jewish National Fund (JNF) directed the military attacks to acquire coveted land, such as the villages of Indur, Qumiya, Ma'lul, Mujaidil and Buteimat in Galilee, which were destroyed primarily to grab their land.[5]

(2) Physical Elimination of the Refugees

Almost every one of the thirty-odd Zionist/Israeli military operations was accompanied by a massacre of civilians. There were at least thirty-five reported massacres,[6] half of which took place before any Arab regular soldier set foot in Palestine. The most infamous of these massacres is Deir Yassin, the largest is Dawayma, and the latest disclosed by an Israeli researcher, Teddy Katz, but known to Palestinians all along, is Tantoura.

Shooting of civilians was not restricted to wartime. After the fighting ceased, some of the refugees tried to return home to rescue civilians left behind, to retrieve some belongings or to attend to crops or cattle. These returnees were shot on the spot as "infiltrators." The UN truce observers reported hundreds of such cases.[7]

(3) Plunder and Destruction of Property

Plunder took place in the immediate aftermath of military assaults, especially in cities such as Haifa, Jaffa, Lydda, and Jerusalem. The looters included nearby kibbutzniks, Israel Defense Forces (IDF) brigade commanders and the high-ranking political figures of the ruling Mapai (Labor) party.[8] There followed a massive campaign of destruction, which lasted over fifteen years and in which 53 percent of the 418 villages surveyed were totally destroyed, 32 percent were substantially destroyed, and 12 percent partially destroyed (3 percent were inaccessible to the survey).[9] The clear aim of this destruction was to prevent the return of the refugees.

(4) Political Action

Soon after the state of Israel was declared (May 14, 1948) and following the protest of UN mediator Count Folke Bernadotte, who witnessed, by June 1948, the expulsion of about 500,000 refugees, the Provisional Government of Israel said it could not allow any refugees to return before a peace treaty was signed, on the pretext that these refugees would be a "security threat." Even after the fighting stopped, Israel refused to re-admit the refugees, and it maintains this position in the international arena to this day. It does so even though Israel's admission to the UN in May 1949 was unique in that it is the only UN member whose admittance is "conditional" upon return of refugees (Resolution 194) and withdrawal to the lines of the partition plan (Resolution 181).[10]

(5) Creation of a Fictitious Legal Web to Mask Illegal Confiscation

Before, during and after the 1948 war, Israel resorted to many legal devices to organize and justify the confiscation of 18,700 square kilometers (92 percent of Israel) of Palestinian land, in addition to the property found in 530 depopulated towns and villages. The property was held by the Custodian of the Absentee (i.e., refugee) Property and transferred later to the Development Authority. All such land, as well as JNF holdings, is now administered by the Israel Land Administration (ILA). In simple terms, the "Absentee" is a Palestinian refugee unable to return. The term also applies to Palestinian citizens of Israel, who are not "Absent," hence dubbed "Present Absentees"; much of their land has also been confiscated.[11]

(6) Importing of Jewish Immigrants to Fill the Depopulated Villages

Immediately upon the invasion of Palestinian villages, Israel activated its program of sending Mossad agents to transport Jews in Arab countries to Israel. The immigrants were persuaded by a mixture of rosy promises, incentives, and, for the reluctant ones, various acts of coercion, including sabotage and bombings.[12] About 700,000 arrived in the period 1949–52. Many of them were unhappy about the discriminatory treatment they received at the hands of the ruling Ashkenazi. Their resentment is still strong today.

All these actions were designed to prevent the return of refugees to their homes. While Israel was successful in preventing return, the refugees remained adamant. They could often see their old homes across the barbed wire of the armistice line; indeed, most refugees still reside within a two-hour bus ride of these homes. The problem for Israel thus became how to get rid of the refugees themselves, wherever they were.

Resettlement Plans

Today, 88 percent of the refugees live in Palestine and environs: 46 percent in British Mandate Palestine, 42 percent in Jordan, Syria, and Lebanon, within a 100-mile radius of Israel. Only 12 percent reside further afield, equally divided between Arab and other countries. Their total number, according to 1998 figures, is 4.9 million, of which only 3.6 million are registered with the United Nations Relief and Works Agency, the official body set up to care for the refugees.[13] More than two-thirds of the Palestinian people are refugees. This situation is unique in modern history.

The proximity of the refugees and their unquenched desire to return explains the feverish Israeli attempts to bring in as many immigrants as possible from such diverse places as Ethiopia and Russia, just to fill the depopulated Palestinian locations. There are over three dozen such schemes[14] (over a hundred if we consider minor variations). They are all Israeli-inspired and are based on one or several of the following premises: that the Palestinians are not a distinct "people," that they could and should live anywhere else, that they have no rights to qualify them for return, that their return is not physically possible, or that their return is not desirable because it would threaten the "Jewish character" of Israel.

The latest edition of these schemes is a proposal made by Donna Arzt.[15] Although dressed in humanitarian garb, it is essentially a continuation of the ethnic-cleansing plan executed by Ben-Gurion, Weitz and Ariel Sharon. The plan calls for the transfer of 1.5 million refugees to various parts of the world and the forced exile of several million others under a scheme of threats, coercion and bribery.[16]

Former US President Bill Clinton's proposals, "bridging" or otherwise, at the final-status talks at Camp David in the summer of 2000 play the same theme with minor variations. All such schemes have failed, and they will continue to fail. Therefore, it becomes increasingly necessary to go back to basics and find creative solutions. First we must refute the Israeli taboo that the right of return is not possible.

Why Should the Refugees Return?

First, it is perfectly legal in accordance with international law.[17] The well-known UN Resolution 194 has been affirmed by the international community 135 times in the period 1948–2000. There is nothing like it in UN history. This universal consensus elevates the weight of this resolution from a "recommendation" to an expression of the determined will of the international community. International law also prohibits mass denationalization of a people if the territory in which they live undergoes a change of sovereignty.[18] Thus the refugees are entitled to return to the homes they lost and to a restoration of their nationality as well. The right of return is supported by the Universal Declaration of Human Rights and the many regional conventions based on human rights law. It is also derived from the sanctity of private ownership, which is not diminished by change of sovereignty, occupation or passage of time.

Second, the right of return is sacred to all Palestinians. It has remained their fundamental objective since 1948. Their determination on the return issue has endured despite warfare, suffering, and enormous social and political changes. In this, the refugee from Iqrit, who is an Israeli citizen, the refugee from Lydda, who is a Jordanian citizen, the refugee from Haifa, who is stateless in Syria or Lebanon, and the refugee from Jaffa, who is a US citizen, have the same determination.

Third, there is no acceptable reason why they should not return. The Israelis oppose return on the grounds that it will pollute the "Jewish character" of Israel and cause outward emigration of Jews. They say it is impossible because the refugees' villages have been largely destroyed and property boundaries lost. None of these claims stand serious scrutiny.

The Demographic Case

It is often claimed that there is no room in Israel for the refugees' return. Even if this were true, it would not diminish this fundamental right. In fact, it's not true. Previous studies on the subject19 can be summarized as follows:

It is possible to divide Israel's forty-six natural regions into 3 groups (see Figure I on page 305). Group A, 1,628 square kilometers, has a Jewish population of just over 3 million (67 percent of Israel's total Jewish population).[20] This area is, roughly, the land acquired by Jews during the period of the British Mandate. Most Jewish settlement after the creation of the state centered around this earlier domicile.

Group B, 1,508 square kilometers, is almost the same size but not the same location of the land owned by the Palestinians who remained in Israel after the 1948 war (since 1948, Israel has confiscated two-thirds of the property of its Palestinian citizens). In group B there are 436,000 Jews, or 9.6 percent of all the Jews in Israel, along with 92,000 of Israel's Palestinian citizens. Thus, 77 percent of Jews live in 15 percent of Israel's area.

That leaves group C, 17,381 square kilometers, located in two large blocks, corresponding roughly to the Northern and Southern Districts as per Palestine and Israel's administrative divisions. This is the land and heritage of about 5 million refugees who were expelled from their homes in 1948 and their descendants. About a million Jews live in group C, but 80 percent of them live either in cities that were originally Palestinian and are now mixed, or in a number of small new "development towns." These development towns, heavily populated by Sephardic Jews, or Mizrahi, are generally impoverished, with the highest unemployment rates and the lowest annual incomes in Israel; they are living proof of the country's ethnic segregation and discriminatory policies.

This leaves 200,000 rural Jews who exploit vast areas of refugee land (the remainder of the land is used for military purposes and afforestation). Most of these rural Jews (160,000) are residents of the moshavim (cooperative farms) and kibbutzim (collective farms). The kibbutz, which used to be the flagship of Zionism, is now dying out. Today only 8,600 kibbutzniks live on agriculture, assisted by tens of thousands of hired laborers from Thailand, an ironic subversion of Zionist doctrine, which prohibited the employment of non-Jewish (especially Palestinian) labor.

Thus, the rights of 5 million refugees are pitted against the prejudices of 8,600 kibbutzniks.

To illustrate the point further, consider this scenario: If/when the registered refugees in Lebanon (362,000) return to their homes in Galilee (still largely Arab) and the registered refugees in Gaza (759,000) return to their homes in the Southern District (now largely empty; rural Jewish density is 6 persons per square kilometer, compared with 5,500 persons per square kilometer in Gaza), there will be negligible effect on Jewish density in group A, and Jews will retain numerical majority in A, B, and C.

The number of Russian immigrants is equal to the number of refugees from Lebanon and Gaza combined. If the Russians had not immigrated and these 1 million refugees had been allowed to return home, Israel would have its present density. Instead, immigrants were admitted to Israel while the rightful owners of the land have not been allowed to return to their homes.

Restoration of Palestinian Villages

Another Israeli claim is that all village traces are lost and have been built over by housing for new immigrants. Again, even if this were true, it would not undermine the right of return: property robbery does not grant a title deed. However, the claim is false.

In Figures II and III on pages 306–7, all the existing built-up areas in Israel today have been plotted, and superimposed on them are the sites of 530 towns and villages depopulated by the Israelis in 1948. The striking result is that the sites of the absolute majority of such villages are still vacant. All village sites, except one each in the subdistricts of Safad, Acre, Tiberias and Nazareth, are vacant. Naturally, the area most affected is the coastal strip, especially in the Tel Aviv suburbs. There, a dozen village sites have been built over as a result of the expansion of the city. The displaced refugees from these built-over areas now number 110,000, or only 3 percent of all registered refugees. The largest displaced villages are Salama, Yazur, and Beit Dajan, with a combined population of 75,000. A number of village sites west of Jerusalem, and north and south of Tel Aviv, have been built over.

However, well over 90 percent of the refugees could return to empty sites. Of the small number of affected village sites, 75 percent are located on land totally owned by Arabs and 25 percent on Palestinian land in which Jews have a share. Only 27 percent of the villages affected by new Israeli construction have a present population of more than 10,000. The rest are much smaller.

The accommodation of the returning refugees from the affected villages is fairly simple, at least from an operational point of view: they could retain the property rights and grant a forty-nine-year lease to existing occupants, most of which are institutions. Meanwhile, they could rent or build housing for themselves in the vicinity.

We are, however, left with the comfortable prospect that the overwhelming majority of the refugees would be able to return to currently empty sites. Their housing should not be an insurmountable problem. In addition to Israel's tenfold increase (through both natural increase and immigration) of its 1948 Jewish population of 600,000, we can cite the examples of Amman's expansion (ten times), Beirut's (six times), and Kuwait's (thirty-three times), in which the Palestinian refugees themselves played a key role.

What Is the Profit and Loss Account?

If a historical conflict is solved by the return of 5 million refugees to their homes in accordance with international law, what is the price of this huge achievement?

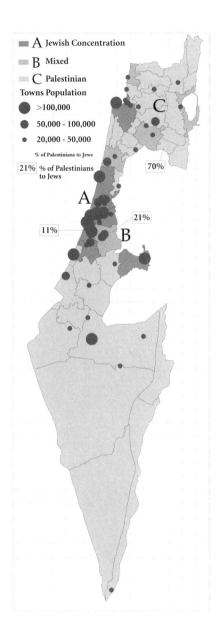

A Jewish Concentration

B Mixed

C Palestinian

Towns Population

● >100,000

● 50,000 - 100,000

• 20,000 - 50,000

% of Palestinians to Jews

21% % of Palestinians to Jews

Figure I: Jewish and Palestinian Concentration in Israel

Area A, with two-thirds of Israel's Jewish population, is essentially the same land in which Jews lived in pre-1948 Palestine. Area B is mixed, where Palestinians and Jews live. Almost 80 percent of the country's Jews live in Areas A and B. Area C represents largely the land and heritage of 5 million refugees who are denied the right to return home. Only 160,000 rural Jews live there, in addition to 863,000 urban Jews who live in cities that were originally Palestinian.

Northern District

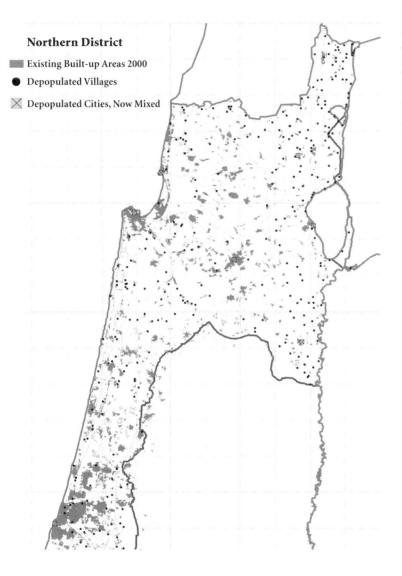

Existing Built-up Areas 2000

Depopulated Villages

Depopulated Cities, Now Mixed

Figure II: Existing Built-Up Areas in 2000—Northern District

The central part of Israel's Galilee is densely populated by Palestinians. When the refugees return, they will find the majority of their old village sites vacant. They will live among their relatives, and Jews in Area A will hardly feel the difference.

Figure III: Existing Built-Up Areas in 2000—Southern District

When the refugees return to the south, they will find it almost empty, except for a few towns. All rural Jews, in 14,000 square kilometers, would fill only a single refugee camp; while the density in Gaza is 5,500 persons per square kilometer, Jewish rural density is 6 persons per square kilometer. Return of the refugees will hardly be felt at the center.

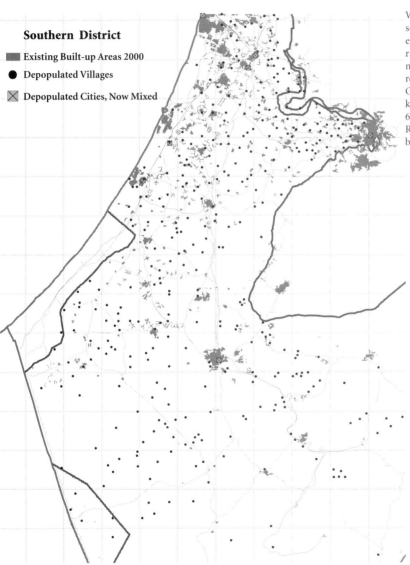

Southern District

▨ Existing Built-up Areas 2000

● Depopulated Villages

⊠ Depopulated Cities, Now Mixed

The 160,000 moshav and kibbutz residents who would be affected may decide to stay and rent land (this time from the owner, not from the ILA, by a simple change in the lease contract), or they may decide to relocate. The kibbutzniks have always been considered the pioneers of Zionism and the elite of Israeli society. A high proportion of army generals and Knesset members are kibbutzniks. They were usually granted the most fertile (Palestinian) land. However, this has dramatically changed. While 90 percent of Jewish immigrants joined a kibbutz in 1917, today only 3 percent of Israelis live on a kibbutz. There are constant desertions and very few new recruits. Most of the kibbutzim are near bankruptcy, with only 26 percent of them producing 75 percent of total kibbutz agricultural output.[21]

The area of irrigated fields cultivated by the kibbutzim decreased from 213,628 acres in 1987 to 189,564 acres in 1991.[22] The economic return of these vast resources is meager and diminishing. Out of $5 billion of accumulated debt borne by the kibbutzim, the government has written off $2 billion, rescheduled $2 billion and encouraged the private sector to contribute $1 billion.

Recently a major change in government policy affecting kibbutz and moshav land further undermines the rights of the Palestinian owners. Until recently this land was officially held by the ILA and leased to the kibbutzim and moshavim. In the early 1990s Ariel Sharon, as Minister of Infrastructure, and Raphael Eitan, as Minister of Agriculture, introduced regulations permitting the rezoning of this agricultural land for residential construction to accommodate Russian immigrants and to build commercial outlets, shopping malls and private apartments. The kibbutzniks would then be compensated for this transaction at 51 percent of its value. This made the bankrupt farmers very rich overnight by allowing them to pocket the value of (Palestinian) land they never owned in the first place. This angered urban taxpayers, the vast majority of Israel's population. Two committees, one in 1997 and another in 2000, reduced the compensation to 25 percent of the land value. Thus has "sacred spiritual property" been transformed into commercial real estate.

In 1997 the ILA started to sell refugees' land. Its average contribution to the treasury amounted to $1 billion a year, excluding compensation to the kibbutzniks. One dunam (one-quarter of an acre) in the center of the country sells for $1 million.[23] In 1998, 110 kibbutzim were allowed to expand their residential area (that is, change the zoning from agricultural to residential), which can be sold to others, by 115 percent. "Others" may include any Jew living anywhere in the world. Out of a general plan for 500,000 residential units, 150,000 were planned in the kibbutz.

Sharon, who expropriated for himself a farm of several thousand dunams near Iraq Al Manshiya (Qiryat Gat), said: "The only way to absorb the immigrants was by taking land from the Kibbutz.… I knew the [economic] hardship they are experiencing.… It is better they build on the land and sell houses."[24]

In June 2000, fifty-two members of the Knesset submitted a bill to rezone 4 million dunams, or 80 percent of the land registered with the UN Conciliation Commission on Palestine, from agricultural to residential land—in other words, to transfer the UN registry of Palestinian refugees' land from that of land leased to the kibbutz to land sold to a developer in order to build and sell apartments to Israelis and Jews of any nationality.

An interesting intervention was made by the impoverished Sephardic community, who did not share in the extravagant benefits showered on the kibbutzim. The Sephardim formed a group, Hakeshet Hamizrahit, which petitioned the High Court against sale of kibbutz land, stating that "the land in question was largely expropriated from Palestinians and thus transferring property rights to the inhabitants of the rural communities means negating forever the Palestinian refugees' right of return."[25] Thus, the return of 5 million refugees and the end of the historical conflict is weighed against the livelihood of 8,600 kibbutzim, an economically bankrupt movement now mostly abandoned by the Israelis themselves.

Water and Agriculture

Water can be a cause of war in the Middle East. It has been widely reported that Israel's invasion of the West Bank and Syria in 1967 was designed to control the headwaters of the Jordan River and the tributaries and aquifers of the West Bank. Israel's desire to maintain control of these water sources is one of the main reasons for its refusal to seal an agreement with Syria and the Palestinians. Each of these resources, diverted from Syrian and West Bank waters, amounts to 500 million cubic meters per year (500 mm3/y), much of which is wasted, as will be demonstrated.

Water resources in the territory of Palestine on which the State of Israel was declared in 1948 are 350 mm3/y. This amount was increased before 1967 by Israeli drilling under the West Bank and by full control of Palestinian and Syrian sources after the 1967 war. It reached 2,020 in 1990, of which 1,471 mm3/y is taken from sources located in Arab territory.[26]

Where does this water go? In 1995, 594 mm3/y went to municipal (domestic) purposes, 133 to industrial use and 1,300 to agricultural use. As Peter Beaumont has shown,[27] this works out to be a constant 100 m3/y/person for municipal purposes for every year since the creation of the state in 1948. This is higher than the consumption of Jordan (60), and much higher than the impoverished West Bank (37.5), which has lost 90 percent of its water resources to Israel. And the overcrowded Gaza Strip has a critical water deficit with dangerously increased salinity.

Israel has maintained the use of 1,200–1,400 mm3/y for agriculture. The more extravagant use of 860 m3/dunam (1 hectare = 10 dunams) in the 1950s has now been reduced to 600 m3/d. These precious resources are provided to the farmers at 70 percent of the cost at 19¢/m3, while the cost to domestic user is $1–$1.76/m3.[28] Thus domestic users underwrite vast water subsidies to farmers, who raise water-intensive crops like potatoes, corn, cotton and watermelon.

Following the expulsion of the Palestinians and confiscation of their land in 1948, the amount of land under irrigation increased rapidly, from about 300,000 dunams in the early 1950s to 2 million dunams in the late 1970s, the difference between the figures being Palestinian property. By 1999 this figure had shrunk to 1.1 million dunams because of general lack of interest in agriculture.[29] The total amount of land under cultivation has grown from about 1 million dunams in 1950 to 4.2 million dunams in 1997, shrinking from a maximum of 4.4 million dunams in 1990,[30] the difference between 1 million dunams and the other figures being confiscated Palestinian property.

Who utilizes this vast land? In 1998 there were 72,500 agricultural employees,[31] of which 36,800 were Jews. Of those Jews, only 8,600 were kibbutzniks. These vast land resources, with their generous water subsidies, account for only 1.8 percent of Israel's GDP.[32] To produce this meager contribution, Israel has had to import 24,300 foreign workers (mostly from Thailand) while denying the right of the Palestinian farmers to till their own land. (Some of the Palestinian workers allowed in Israel actually work their own land, as hired laborers, for the benefit of Israelis.)

The waste in water has been noted by other authors. Some advocate reducing agricultural activity or changing it to more profitable crops, which would free water for other uses. One study notes that "the evidence strongly suggests that Israel's water quantity crisis is more a result of misallocation than absolute scarcity."[33] Another recommends that the wasted water could be "sold" to Jordan and the West Bank in a peace deal. Apart from the irony that Israel would be selling illegally confiscated water back to its rightful owners, the fact is that Israel's enormous water and land resources are exploited by so few to produce so little. If this land and water were turned over to the lawful owners, there would be little loss to Israel—despite common claims to the contrary—and tremendous gain in the nation's political legitimacy, with a real chance for genuine peace in the region.

Professor Fadle Naqib, an expert on the Palestinian economy formerly with the UN Conference on Trade and Development, says that although it is common for developing countries to reduce the agricultural share of their economy, it is necessary for Palestine to develop its agricultural sector.[34] Capital requirements at this stage would be small, an ideal situation for a recovering economy. The vast majority of the refugees are farmers, and agriculture has been their occupation from time immemorial. When they recover their land, they will no doubt greatly enhance the value of the agricultural product. The refugees in Gaza already do so. With scarce and saline water, they produce better and cheaper vegetables than the neighboring kibbutzim. That is why Israel refuses to admit their products to its market.[35] I am not of course suggesting that all refugees should revert to agriculture or that agriculture is their only occupation. Palestinians are one of the most highly educated peoples in the Arab world and have flourished in a number of skilled occupations. The point here is simply that Palestinians have a deep attachment to their land and will be able to cultivate it more economically than the Israelis. With their education, they will be able to meet the challenge of industrialized agriculture when this economic threshold is reached.

Another area of Palestinian excellence is Jaffa oranges, known for centuries. After the Israelis conquered the Jaffa environs in 1948, "the overwhelming majority of the 150,000 dunams of citrus trees remained unattended.... Roughly one-fifth of the abandoned citrus groves in the whole country were still being cultivated."[36] The Israelis looted the pumps and pipelines and earmarked large tracts for housing construction. The remainder of citrus groves, which produced 950,000 tons in 1975, deteriorated to the extent that only 340,000 tons were produced in 1997 and 250,000 tons in the drought year of 1991.[37] The famous Jaffa oranges could be revived by the Palestinian farmers who originally planted these citrus groves.

To be sure, there are problems to solve. Many refugees would have to change their present occupation (mostly in construction) and revert back to agriculture. Tighter controls on water consumption will have to be applied. At some cut-off point, say a maximum of 1,300 mm3/y, agriculture has to be industrialized. New and improved crops will have to be grown. In all this, Israeli research may be useful. Certainly the Palestinians would be enthusiastic workers, since they would be returning to land cultivated by their families for centuries. All in all, the return to peace and a stable region far outweighs any application problems.

The "Jewish Character" Syndrome

Considering the European Jews' history of being oppressed, Jewish fear of gentiles is understandable. But when this fear is forged into active policy, it is dangerous and bloody, as the case has been in Palestine. The expulsion and expropriation of the Palestinians, as a precondition for establishing the state of Israel, was a result of this paranoia. That was Ben-Gurion's doctrine, now fully documented by historians. This doctrine is still being followed. It calls for committing an actual murder for fear that the victim, if he lived, might harm the murderer.

The claim that the "Jewish character" of Israel would be threatened is commonly recited to justify the denial of fundamental right of Palestinians to their land and property. But what is the meaning of "Jewish character"? If it entails policies that deny the return of refugees and allow unlimited numbers of Jewish immigrants in their place, this is best described by the noted jurists Thomas and Sally Mallison, who pointed out that "the term, 'the Jewish character', is really a euphemism for the Zionist discriminatory statutes of the State of Israel which violate the human rights provisions of the Partition Resolution.... The United Nations is under no more of a legal obligation to maintain Zionism in Israel than it is to maintain *apartheid* in the Republic of South Africa."[38] The US State Department rejected any special meaning for the Jewish citizens of Israel by stating that it "does not recognize the legal-political relationship based on the religious identification of American citizens.... Accordingly it should be clear that the Department of State does not regard the 'Jewish people' concept as a concept of international law."[39]

This is not an isolated view. In 1998 the UN Treaty-based Committee on Economic, Social and Cultural Rights said that Israel's "excessive emphasis upon the State as a 'Jewish State' encourages discrimination and accords a second-class status to its non-Jewish citizens.… The Committee notes with grave concern that the Status Law of 1952 authorizes the World Zionist Organization/Jewish Agency and its subsidiaries including the Jewish National Fund to control most of the land in Israel, since these institutions are chartered to benefit Jews exclusively.… The Committee takes the view that large-scale and systematic confiscation of Palestinian land and property by the State and transfer of that property to these agencies constitute an institutionalized form of discrimination because these agencies by definition would deny the use of these properties by non-Jews."[40] Israel cannot maintain this position for long. The moral and legal weight of human rights will catch up with it one day. How can this concept of "Jewish character" be an acceptable basis for peaceful relations?

Some mean by the "Jewish character" a society in which Jews are a numerical majority. But in what territory? In the whole of British Mandate Palestine? Today, 47 percent of the population of Palestine are Arabs and 53 percent Jews. In fact, the percentage would be reversed if we take account of the fact that about half of the Russian immigrants are not really Jews.

In Israel itself, if we extrapolate from the natural population growth from 1948 to 1999 of Jews (1.6 percent) and Palestinians in Israel (4 percent), the two ethnic groups will be equal in about 2050.[41] Are the Israelis buying time? If we narrow the territory in question to the 15 percent of Israel where almost 80 percent of the Jews live, and where the Palestinians are only 11 percent of the Jewish population, the future date in which the Palestinians become a significant minority will recede considerably.

All these examples indicate that the notion of the numerical superiority of Jews is a cruel time game in which the refugees rot in their camps until the Israelis realize, or admit, that this contention is a horrible hoax, intended to keep the conquered land empty until its owners give up or are gotten rid of by a "final solution" of the Palestinian problem.

The most incredible notion is the claim that the "Jewish character" means a socially homogeneous society in which Jews speak one language, dress and behave similarly, and uphold the same values such that the presence of one national group, the Palestinians, will pollute this uniformity. It is hard to imagine that very many Israelis really believe that, since there are no dominant common features between the Russians and Moroccans, the Mizrahi and Ashkenazi or the Haredim and the secular. There are thirty-two spoken languages in Israel and about two dozen political groups with an equivalent number of newspapers for a Jewish population a little larger than Los Angeles. The problem of a fractured society is a serious one, and it is already causing internal conflict in Israel, now tenuously held together by the drummed-up Arab danger. Considerable research has already been devoted to this question.[42] But the return of Palestinians to their ancestral homes would not substantially exacerbate these problems. Already, the Palestinian citizens of Israel are (Fig 1) 11 percent of the population in group A, 21 percent in group B and 70 percent in group C.

If "Jewish character" refers to religious practice, this has rarely been a problem in the Arab and Islamic world. Numerous historians have demonstrated that Islamic and Arab societies have treated Jewish minorities far better than Christian societies have.

There is no ethical or legal justification for the maintenance of a "Jewish character" that denies human rights or violates international law. The real reason for Israel's racist practices is to maintain its hold on Palestinian land and keep it as a reserve for future Jewish immigration. On March 1, 2001, the Israeli media reported that Prime Minister–elect Ariel Sharon told the Jewish Agency board that his plan is to bring 1 million immigrants from Russia, Mexico and Ethiopia, and that Israel must bring all of the world's Jews to Israel by 2020.

The Logistics of Return

Assuming that the force of international law will be exercised, as it eventually was, with varying degrees of success and consistency, in Kosovo, Bosnia, East Timor, and Kuwait, the actual process of return is fairly straightforward.

First, locating the refugees: The refugees from 530 depopulated towns and villages, in addition to 662 secondary localities, are registered with UNRWA.[43] A typical village consists of four to five large and related families who know one another quite well. A record of 3.6 million (1998) registered refugees is kept by UNRWA with full names of all individuals, their birth date, their origin (the depopulated village) and where they reside today in each of the five UNRWA areas: Gaza Strip, West Bank, Jordan, Syria, and Lebanon. The unregistered refugees (1.3 million) are mostly previous inhabitants of Palestinian cities. Again, they belong to well-knit families and can be found in Arab and foreign capitals without much difficulty.

Second, locating their land: Palestine was divided into administrative units where village boundaries and town-planning boundaries are well marked on about 130 British maps. Thus village and town properties are well defined within their respective units, both in terms of area and location. For individual ownership within the village or town limit, the UN Conciliation Commission on Palestine keeps about half a million owner index cards defining the land owned and the parcel and block for each owner in a village or town. This index can be related to a map reference. To define Palestinian land, it is much easier to identify Jewish land and subtract same from the area of Palestine, since Jewish colonists before 1948 were keen to keep records to prove ownership and residence in Palestine.

Third, transfer of ownership from the ILA. As explained above, the Palestinian land together with JNF land has been administered by the ILA. All such land is leased to users by means of forty-nine-year leases (now renewed, possibly to longer periods) to Jewish entities only: kibbutzim, moshavim, cooperatives, the IDF (airports, bases, firing ranges), and various government ministries (forestry, mining, fishing). Upon return of the refugees, either the lease contract can be terminated or reduced to cover only the surplus land. There are many creative ideas here. One of them was suggested by the Israelis themselves: in 1948 the Mapam party, which worked briefly for Arab-Jewish coexistence, proposed that with compensation paid to the refugees they could improve productivity of their land such that there would be enough "surplus" land to lease to the neighboring kibbutzim.[44]

Fourth, phasing of return: The most depressing hardship cases are in the Gaza Strip and Lebanon. The return of the Gaza refugees to their villages in group C of the Southern District should be straight-forward. The rural area is empty, save for a total of 78,000 rural Jews in an area of 14,231 square kilo-meters. Their number is smaller than a single refugee camp in Gaza. As indicated before, almost all village sites are vacant. The Jewish inhabitants of cities like Beersheva, Majdal-Ashkelon and Isdud (Ashdod) could continue to pursue their occupations without hindrance.

Most of the refugees living in Lebanon would be returning to Galilee (Northern District of C). Here there are about 90,000 affected rural Jews, or about the same number as one large refugee camp in Lebanon. The adjustment should not be that difficult because many of the refugees would be reunited with long-separated family members in their old villages. They would find few social difficulties in an Arab environment where Palestinians today outnumber Jews by one and a half times.

After the Gaza and Lebanon refugees are absorbed, refugees could return to groups A and B, which have a sizable Jewish population. Group B would be easier, as most village sites are still vacant. In group A, about a dozen villages in Tel Aviv suburbs and four in West Jerusalem have been encroached upon by new construction, although there are gaps and still-standing houses left. Here, the transfer of lease contract to the rightful owner and the compensation he receives will enable him to build or rent a house/apartment nearby unless or until another arrangement with the present occupant is made. This problem and its solution are common. It has already been encountered by refugees who returned with PA officials to the West Bank.

Fifth, housing construction: This is a major project but definitely manageable. The huge housing schemes constructed in Amman, Kuwait and Saudi Arabia, in which many of the engineers were Palestinian, are good examples. Because Palestinian society is relatively homogeneous and the refugees would be returning to their ancestral villages, there is little chance of repeating Israel's mistakes in the construction of its dysfunctional "development towns," in which there is a great deal of friction between the diverse ethnic groups involved.[45] The funds for construction would come partly from compensation paid by Israel for (a) material and psychological damages to refugees in accordance with international law and similar precedents, and (b) the accrued revenue from their property exploited by Israel for fifty-three years in accordance with UN General Assembly Resolution 53/51 of December 3, 1998, paragraph 1.

There is a wealth of information regarding large housing projects. As an instrument of execution,

UNRWA could turn itself into an organ of the UN Development Program. It already has 21,000 Palestinian staff members, although most of them work in educational and medical services. But the technical and labor force is readily available inside and outside Palestine, even on a volunteer basis. In short, the technical aspects of the return are solvable.

Sixth, the legal aspects: to start with, the UN Security Council should act to implement Resolution 194, first passed in December 1948, by all possible means at its disposal, acknowledging meanwhile that "the earliest practicable date" specified in the resolution should have been July 1949, when the last armistice agreement between the 1948 belligerents was signed. If a choice is offered to the refugees for return or resettlement, this should be done only after the Security Council's decision to implement Resolution 194. Compensation should then be offered, but not as a substitute for return, and should be paid to individual refugees, each according to his losses, "under principles of international law or in equity," as stipulated in the resolution, by "the governments or authorities responsible."

Resolution 194 already created the mechanism for implementing the return. This is the Conciliation Commission for Palestine (CCP), which still exists at the UN. Its early failure to carry out its functions was a result of Ben-Gurion's intransigence. He believed, rightly, that if peace treaties were signed at the time, this would mean the return of refugees and return of territories Israel had occupied in excess of the 1947 Partition Plan (24 percent of Palestine). However, it is clear now that no return means no peace. The UN CCP should have its mandate bolstered to deal with the present situation. It should also take up the role of protecting the returning refugees physically, ensuring their peaceful repatriation, building infrastructure and monitoring provisions for their protection against discrimination of any kind in line with provisions of Resolution 181 (II) of November 29, 1947. This resolution covers all necessary aspects of the rights and duties of returning refugees as citizens in one of the two envisaged states. Their minority rights are protected by this resolution as well. While returning refugees retain their national identity as Palestinians, they can take up citizenship in Israel in accordance with Chapter 3 of the resolution. According to international law, the territory and people go together; whoever holds the territory must keep the population. They cannot be expelled and disfranchised, as Israel has done to the Palestinians.

The attempts to dissolve UNRWA prematurely—that is, before the full repatriation of the refugees—and to disregard the CCP are obviously means to circumvent and marginalize international law. This will not work, nor will the attempts to replace the CCP with the UN's High Commissioner for Refugees, which would treat the Palestinian refugees in the same manner as victims of flood, famine or coups d'état. The UNHCR is prohibited from extending protection to the Palestinian refugees under paragraph (1D) of its charter. This paragraph excludes from its mandate any group of refugees who are already covered by another UN agency, thus acknowledging the unique position of the Palestinians, who are covered by the UNRWA for welfare and relief and by the CCP for conflict resolution, both in accordance with Resolution 194. Another Israeli attempt to evade its responsibility is its proposal to create an international fund for the refugees' compensation in which Israel contributes very little money but has a great deal of control. Israel, as the beneficiary of Palestinian property for fifty-three years and the responsible party for the *Nakba*, must solely pay the compensation according to Resolution 194 and customary international law, which combines the body of applicable laws, including the Universal Declaration of Human Rights and the Fourth Geneva Convention. Compensation is not meant for sale of homes and land; these are not for sale. Compensation is owed because of psychological suffering, loss and damage to property, and for exploitation of property for fifty-three years.

Conclusions

Both Israelis and Palestinians agree that there can be no peace without a resolution of the refugee problem, but they differ on the method of resolution. Israelis believe they can extend and legalize their original ethnic-cleansing operation. This is an illusion. The fact that all of their so-called resettlement schemes have been nipped in the bud, by governments and people alike, is proof enough of that.

In spite of the misfortunes they have endured, Palestinians continue to shape the political events of the Middle East, and they are supported not only by millions of Arabs but by an increasing number of Europeans and Americans. The refugees' plight will be debated domestically in many countries in the near future. Nobody will be far enough from the Middle East to ignore its problems.

I have demonstrated that the Israelis have no legal, ethical, practical, demographic or economic reason to persist in denying the refugees' rights. Israel's position is solely derived from racist policies, the only one left in the world and thus condemned by the rest of the world. That this odd situation has prevailed for half a century was made possible primarily by the military, financial and political support of the United States. The price of maintaining this position will be high, the more so when the people of the region force their rulers to adopt policies toward the United States and Israel that are strictly consistent with international law and human rights.

The price Israel has to pay for permanent peace is far less than imagined. In a land that is relatively underpopulated today, in which half its citizens are, on average, outside the country at any one time[46] and where the appetite of its young people for war has waned considerably, peace—especially a peace that guarantees the rights of Jews and Palestinians under international law—should be highly desired. All Israel has to do is become a truly democratic country for all its citizens and interpret its Law of Return on a legal, not a racist, basis. In its absorption capacity, it should give priority to those who are lawfully qualified to return, not those who bring seeds of conflict and war. Priority should be given to those who own, not those who conquer.

If Israel fails to take this opportunity, it will commit the Middle East to at least fifty more years of bloodshed. The refugees have paid more than their share of the cost.

Notes

1. Nur Masalha, *Expulsion of the Palestinians: The Concept of 'Transfer' in Zionist Political Thought, 1882–1948* (Washington, DC, 1992).

2. Central Zionist Archives, Weitz Diary, A 246/7 entry for December 20, 1940, pp 1090–91. More explicit statements are found in the unedited manuscript of the Weitz Diary. Cited in Nur Masalha, "An Israeli Plan to Transfer Galilee's Christians to South America: Yosef Weitz and 'Operation Yohanan' 1949–1953," Center for Middle Eastern and Islamic Studies, University of Durham, Occasional Paper No. 55, 1996.

3. W. Khalidi, "Plan Dalet: Master Plan for the Conquest of Palestine," in *Journal of Palestine Studies*, Vol. 18, No. 1, Autumn 1988, pp. 3–70. Benny Morris, *The Birth of the Palestinian Refugee Problem 1947–1949* (Cambridge, 1987). Michael Palumbo, *The Palestinian Catastrophe* (London, 1987).

4. Nur Masalha, *A Land without People: Israel, Transfer and the Palestinians 1949–1996* (London, 1997).

5. For various instances of ethnic cleansing, destruction of villages and land confiscation, see Meron Benvenisti, *Sacred Landscape: The Buried History of the Holy Land* (Berkeley, 2000), pp. 102–209.

6. S. Abu Sitta, "The Palestinian Nakba 1948: The Register of Depopulated Localities in Palestine," The Palestinian Return Center, London, 2nd edition, 2000, pp. 16–20.

7. UN Archives 13/3.3.1 Box 11, Atrocities; S. Abu Sitta, "Jewish Carnage Policy Aimed to Evacuate the Galilee Palestinians as Mentioned in the UN Truce Observers Reports in 1948," *al Hayat* (London), February 6, 2000, p. 10.

8. Ben-Gurion War Diary, entries for February 10, May 1, June 17 and July 15, 1948. Tom Segev, *The First Israelis-1949* (Arabic trans.), Institute for Palestine Studies, 1986, pp. 86–88, 98. Benvenisti, *Sacred Landscape*, p. 165.

9. Ghazi Falah, "The 1948 Israeli-Palestinian War and Its Aftermath: The Transformation and De-Signification of Palestine's Cultural Landscape," *Annals of the Association of American Geographers*, June 1996, Vol. 86, No. 2.

10. UN Resolution No. 273 (III) of May 11, 1949 states: "Recalling its resolution of 29 November 1947 [No. 181, the Partition Plan] and 11 December 1948 [No. 194, the refugees' repatriation] and taking note of the [Israeli] declarations … in respect of the implementations of the said resolutions…," Israel was admitted to the UN. See detailed discussion of UN resolution regarding the right of return in W. Thomas Mallison and Sally V. Mallison, "The Right of Return," *Journal of Palestine Studies*, Vol. 9, No. 125, Spring 1980, pp. 125–36. See the full version of the paper in: "An International Law Analysis of the Major UN Resolutions Concerning the Palestine Question," UN Doc. ST/SG/SER.F/4, UN Sales #E. 79.I.19 (1979). See also Kathleen Lawand, "The Right of Return of Palestinians in International Law," *International Journal of Refugee Law* 4 (1996).

11. S. Abu Sitta, "Confiscation of the Palestinian Refugees' Property and the Denial of Access to Private Property," Memorandum submitted to the UN Social, Economic and Cultural Rights Committee, BADIL submission, November 14, 2000, Geneva. See John Quigley, *Palestine and Israel: A Challenge to Justice* (Durham, 1990) and George E. Bisharat, "Land, Law and Legitimacy in Israel and the Occupied Territories," *The American University Law Review*, Vol. 43, pp. 467–591.

12. See Wilbur Crane Eveland, *Ropes of Sand: America's Failure in the Middle East* (New York, 1980), pp. 48–49; Marion Woolfson, *Prophets in Babylon: Jews in the Arab World* (London and Boston, 1980), pp. 186–90; Naeim Giladi, *The Link*, Vol. 31, No. 2, April-May 1998.

13. S. Abu Sitta, "The Palestinian Nakba 1948," *op. cit.*, p. 22.

14. Elia Zureik, *The Palestinian Refugees and the Peace Process* (Washington, DC, 1996).

15. Donna Arzt, *Refugees Into Citizens: Palestinians and the End of the Arab-Israeli Conflict* (New York, 1997).

16. S. Abu Sitta, "The Return of the Refugees Is the Realistic Solution," UN International Conference on Palestine Refugees, Paris, April 26–27, 2000; S. Abu Sitta, "Between Domestication and Resettlement: The Battle of Spurious Scholarship," *al Hayat* (London), August 6, 1997, p. 7.

17. Quigley, *Palestine and Israel*; Quigley, "Displaced Palestinians and a Right of Return," *Harvard International Law Journal*, Vol. 39, No. 1 (Winter 1998). See also footnote 10.

18. Quigley, "Mass Displacement and the Individual Right of Return," *British Yearbook of International Law*, Vol. 68 (1997).

19. S. Abu Sitta, "The Feasibility of the Right of Return" in *The Palestinian Exodus*, Chapter 7, edited by Ghada Karmi and Eugene Cotran (Ithaca, London, 1999), pp. 171–96, and www.arts.mcgill.ca/mepp/prrn/papers/abusitta.html. See also Abu Sitta, "The Return of the Refugees: the Key to Peace," at www.arts.mcgill.ca/mepp/prrn/papers/abu-sitta, and the Palestinian Refugee Research Net, Articles and Research papers, at www.prrn.org.

20. All figures in this section are from Israel Statistical Abstracts, No. 49, 1998, Chapter 2.

21. Yair Aharoni, *The Israeli Economy: Dreams and Realities* (London, 1991), pp. 134, 200, 208–13.

22. Eliezer Ben-Rafael, *Crisis and Transformation: The Kibbutz at Century's End* (Albany, 1997), p. 240, Table 19 and p. 237, Table 10.

23. S. Abu Sitta, "The Great Israel Land Grab," *Jordan Times* (Amman), March 2, 1998, p. 6; Hanna Kim, "A Liquidation Sale of Public Lands," *Ha'aretz*, June 20, 2000; Nehemia Strasler, "The Great Land Robbery," *Ha'aretz*, July 21, 2000.

24. Benvenisti, *Sacred Landscape*, p. 191.

25. Yair Sheleg, "The Big Sellout," *Ha'aretz*, June 23, 2000.

26. S. Abu Sitta, in *Palestinian Exodus*, Karmi and Cotran, ed., p. 187.

27. Peter Beaumont, "Water for Peace in the Middle East: The Sacrifice of Irrigated Agriculture in Israel?" *The Arab World Geographer*, Vol. 3, No. 2, 2000, pp 97–112.

28. Nehemia Strasler, "Farms Are the Water Wasters," *Ha'aretz*, March 10, 2000.

29. Amiram Cohen, "Water Commission Fails to Check Land Usage" and "Incompetent, Negligent, Lazy," *Ha'aretz*, April 30, 2001.

30. Israel's Statistical Abstracts No. 50 (1999), Table 13.1.

31. Israel's Statistical Abstracts No. 50 (1999), Table 13.8.

32. Central Intelligence Agency, *The World Fact Book*, 2000.

33. S.C. Lonegran and D.B. Brooks, *Watershed: The Role of Fresh Water in the Israeli-Palestinian Conflict* (Ottawa, 1994), pp. 76–79.

34. Fadle Naqib, *Palestinian Economy in West Bank and Gaza: Problems of Transition and Future Policies* (Beirut, 1997, in Arabic), pp. 107–13.

35. For the effect of closure on agriculture and other aspects of the economy, see for example, the report of the UN Office of the Special Coordinator in the Occupied Territories (UNSCO) and the World Bank, "Closure on the West Bank and Gaza," at www.arts.mcgill.ca/mepp/unsco/unfront.html.

36. Benvenisti, *Sacred Landscape*, pp. 164–65.

37. Cited by Beaumont, *op. cit.*, p. 105.

38. W. Thomas Mallison and Sally V. Mallison, "The Right of Return," *Journal of Palestine Studies*, Vol. 9, No. 125, Spring 1980, pp 125–36.

39. Letter from Assistant Secretary of State Talbot to Dr. Elmer Berger, American Council for Judaism, April 20, 1964, in 8 *Whiteman Digest of International Law* 35 (1967). Cited by W.T. Mallison, "The Legal Problems Concerning the Judicial Status and Political Activities of the Zionist Organization/Jewish Agency," Institute for Palestine Studies, Monograph No. 14, Beirut 1968.

40. "Concluding Observations of the Committee on Economic, Social and Cultural Rights," December 4, 1998, E/C.12/1/Add.27. See the www.unchr.ch website.

41. "UN Report: Palestinians in Israel Will Outnumber Israelis in 2050," *Jerusalem Post*, March 1, 2001. The full report may be found at www.un.org/esa/population/wpp2000h.pdf.

42. There is a growing body of literature on the nonhomogeneous and fractured Israeli society. See, for example, Akiva Orr, *Israel: Politics, Myths and Identity Crises* (London, 1994), and A. Cohen and B. Susser, *Israel and the Politics of Jewish Identity* (Baltimore and London, 2000).

43. S. Abu Sitta, "The Palestinian Nakba 1948," p. 21.

44. Benvenisti, *Sacred Landscape*, p. 175.

45. David Newman, "The Palestinian Refugee Settlement: Learning from the Israeli Development Town and Mass Experience of 1950's and the 1990's" *PRRN*, July 2000, at www.arts.mcgill.ca/mepp/prrn/newman.html.

46. Israel's Statistical Abstracts No. 50 (1999), Table 4.2.

PART IV

ACTIVISM AWAKENED

סגר

أغلق!

closure

19. THE ISRAELI PEACE MOVEMENT SINCE THE AL-AQSA INTIFADA

GILA SVIRSKY

When a society considers itself embattled—as Israeli society does, whether justified or not, in the face of the Palestinian intifada—the work of peacemakers becomes much more difficult. I will review here how the peace movements in Israel responded to this new reality and, in particular, to look at some changes that have emerged, particularly in strategy.

The State of the Movement When the Intifada Broke Out

When the Al-Aqsa Intifada broke out in late September 2000, the peace movement in Israel consisted of two general camps: (a) the large, consensus-oriented Peace Now organization; and (b) the many small progressive groups whose platforms all revolved around ending the Israeli occupation from virtually all parts of the West Bank, Gaza, and East Jerusalem, with little concern for how this was regarded as extremist by most Israelis.

Constituents of both camps were faced with a public opinion that was rapidly shifting to the right. This shift had begun in the summer prior to the intifada, when Israelis began to believe that a negotiated peace was impossible, after hearing Ehud Barak's version of events at Camp David. Public opinion continued to move to the right over the course of the intifada, during which the Israeli leadership, with the Israeli media in tow, depicted the Palestinians as the aggressors, and Israel as merely defending itself and its citizens in the territories, and that with great restraint. The most recent shift rightward came as the arena of violence moved into Israel proper—not only Palestinian car- and suicide-bombers in Jerusalem, Netanya, Kfar Saba, and who knows where else by the time this is published, but the firing of mortars from within the area under autonomous control of the Palestinian Authority into Israel proper, on this side of the Green Line. Many more Israelis than ever before now believe Israel is the defender, not the attacker, that Arafat is "not a partner" for peace, and that Israel's iron-fist policy in the territories is the correct response.[1]

The reaction of the Israeli peace camp to the Al-Aqsa Intifada falls into the two categories described above: The progressive camp rejects this shift to the right and staunchly demands an end to the occupation, while Peace Now has remained virtually silent during this period, with the exception of its monitoring of settlement expansion in the territories. Peace Now has always been centrist and close to the Labor and Meretz parties; when these parties are in power, it avoids public criticism of government policies and actions. Peace Now was silent when the Israeli government spun Camp David as evidence of Arafat's intransigence, and it remained silent during Ehud Barak's overheated response to Palestinian demonstrations and riots. It held its tongue even after the February election of the Likud party's Ariel Sharon, in the face of increasing Israeli demonization of Palestinians and escalating violence on both sides.

From my personal familiarity with some of the Peace Now leadership, I know their views are more progressive, but for reasons they define as strategic, they choose not to express them publicly at this time. "More than anything else, Peace Now feared running ahead of its constituency and criticized tendencies in the left to hold small, unimpressive activities," wrote Reuven Kaminer in his analysis of the peace movement during the first intifada. This holds today as well.[2]

The Progressive Camp Begins to Respond

The "progressive camp," as I shall call it, did respond, but only sporadically during the first three months. Two weeks after the Al-Aqsa Intifada erupted, both the Hadash (mostly Communist) Party and the Gush Shalom (Peace Bloc) movement held demonstrations in Tel Aviv and Haifa, calling for an end to the occupation. There was also a noteworthy women's demonstration on November 21, called by the New Profile Movement, a women's anti-militaristic group, to condemn the killing of thirteen Israeli Arabs by the Israeli police during intifada-solidarity demonstrations inside Israel. But with these two exceptions, no large-scale protest was waged during the first three months.

This changed with the emergence of a united women's peace movement (founded on November 8), which brought together eight different women's peace organizations as the Coalition of Women for a Just Peace. The largest and most active members of this Coalition were Bat Shalom, the Israeli side of an Israeli-Palestinian partnership; New Profile, which addresses issues of militarism and supports conscientious objectors; Tandi, mostly Arab women associated with Israel's Communist Party; Women and Mothers for Peace, the regrouped Four Mothers movement, which was instrumental in bringing an end to the Israeli occupation of Lebanon; and Women in Black, who have stood in weekly, one-hour vigils since the beginning of the previous intifada—thirteen years ago—calling for an end to the occupation.

Despite the political differences among the constituent organizations, a sense of urgency impelled the women to hammer out a set of political principles under which everyone agreed to operate. These included ending the occupation, establishing a Palestinian state side by side with Israel based on the 1967 borders, recognizing Jerusalem as the shared capital of both states, calling upon Israel to recognize its share of responsibility for the results of the 1948 war, finding a just solution for the Palestinian refugees, and demanding that women participate fully in negotiations for peace. The first major action, held December 29, seemed to break the paralysis that had set in, even among progressive organizations. The following description, which I wrote and sent by Internet to thousands of supporters internationally, captures some of the excitement and enthusiasm of those who attended:

Yesterday, Israel saw the largest rally for a just peace that has been held since the outbreak of the intifada three months ago…and it was a joint Israeli-Palestinian event.

The day began in a conference center where we had hung two huge banners in Hebrew and Arabic on the walls: "Women Demand: No to Occupation—Yes to a Just Peace!" Women took the podium one by one, Palestinian and Israeli alternately, to speak movingly and passionately of both the suffering as well as the determination to end the bloodshed between our peoples. I will just quote two: Michal Pundak-Sagie, activist in New Profile, called upon soldiers to refuse orders that their conscience does not allow. And Zahira Kamal, a leading grassroots spokesperson for Palestinian women in the occupied territories, declared that the principles of the Coalition of Women for a Just Peace provide a sound basis for peace between our peoples.

After the conference, waiting buses moved the entire crowd to the Women in Black vigil, and an estimated 2,000 women filled the entire plaza and spilled over onto the side streets wearing black and carrying the traditional black hand signs with "End the Occupation" painted in Hebrew, Arabic, and English. This silent one-hour vigil was an even more dramatic sight than usual. The extreme right wing did its best to infiltrate the ranks, to provoke us and draw attention to themselves, and finally ended up exchanging blows with the police, but they were overcome and moved behind barriers—out of sight, mind, and media.

At 2 pm, the crowd poured out of the plaza and from every corner and side street, we began our march toward East Jerusalem. Men and women who had joined us from other organizations—Gush Shalom brought its own busload of activists—held aloft their own collection of banners and signs for peace. The sight was overwhelming, as the street filled with marchers and voices. Nabila Espanioli, a Palestinian from Nazareth, grabbed a megaphone and led responsive chanting: "Peace?" "YES!" "Occupation?" "NO!" doing renditions in Hebrew, Arabic, English, and even Italian for the delegation of thirty-five who had flown in for the action. Flying high were signs and banners saying "Palestine Side by Side With Israel—On the '67 Borders," "Jerusalem—2 Capitals for 2 States," "The Age of Generals Is Over," "Fund the Poor, Not Settlers," and "We Refuse to Be Enemies."

It was breathtaking to be part of that march. Finally, we reached the ancient walls of the Old City of Jerusalem and spread out in their shadow on the grass, exhilarated and awaiting the closing ceremony. Because of the traffic jams we had caused, the sound system had not yet arrived, but the crowd waited patiently. Meanwhile, four brave young women took banners and actually managed to climb to the top of the wall from inside the Old City—some by stairs, but also by one quite daring leap—and made their way to the top of the wall just over our gathering, beside two armed soldiers "protecting" us. From here, they unfurled four banners down the height of the wall saying "Shalom, Salaam, Peace," and "End the Occupation" in the three languages. The crowd roared its approval and the Old City was crowned the city of peace for one brief moment—until the soldiers overpowered two of the women and took their banners. But that was a great moment.

Finally, the sound system was set up, and Halla Espanioli [Nabila's sister] spoke movingly of our longing for peace. A minute of silence was held in memory of all those who had been killed in recent months, and the stillness in the crowd was palpable. Following this, I made a slightly modified Jewish prayer: "May the Divine Presence give strength to all her peoples, and may she bless all her peoples with peace." And we all ended by singing "We Shall Overcome."

This event seemed to answer the question in the progressive camp about whether large numbers of Israelis could be recruited for anti-occupation demonstrations.

From Demonstrating to Active Resistance

The above event emboldened the Coalition of Women to explore more daring tactics. This decision was reinforced by the fact that the foreign and local media had virtually ignored this dramatic Israeli-Palestinian march, despite the best efforts of a professional PR agent.

The Coalition then launched a series of civil disobedience actions against Israel's "closure" of the territories—the IDF's virtual siege of towns and villages. At the first action, on February 4, seventeen people were arrested—mostly women—for lying down on the road to prevent the entry of cars to Israel's Defense Ministry in Tel Aviv. Although some journalists took photos of the violent conduct of the police in dragging away the women demonstrators, neither the newspapers nor the television stations reported on it at all. In a second action on February 24, Coalition women sought to push past the checkpoint in Bethlehem, again with little coverage.

At this point, mixed-gender organizations resumed their initiatives, and now a pattern emerged of "joint sponsorships," something that had been rare in peace work during the previous intifada. Again, the cooperative spirit was the product of a sense of urgency in the face of escalating violence and a brutal closure. The usual partners for these actions were Gush Shalom, Rabbis for Human Rights, the Israeli Committee Against House Demolitions, and the Coalition of Women for a Just Peace. It was agreed by all that nonviolent resistance to the occupation was the strategy of choice, and the first joint action was held on March 23 to resist the closure in Rantis, a small Palestinian town. I circulated the following description on the Internet:

> Together we were about 300 activists who set out on buses this morning. Most of us were Israelis, but there was a significant presence of internationals, too. When we reached the perimeter of the village, we began to march with our shovels and hoes toward the trench, now being blocked by a line of soldiers. But we were many more activists than soldiers, they didn't open fire, and we easily passed through. As soon as we reached the trench, we swarmed all over, shoveling rocks and dirt into it, trying to fill it up. It seemed an impossible task, as we had so few tools and the trench gouged out the road quite deeply from one side to the other. What's worse, the ground was very hard, studded with rocks, and it was very difficult to loosen earth for use as fill.
>
> Soon after we began work, someone found a second trench about fifty meters (roughly 160 feet) further along. Half the group broke away to work on filling up that trench, and we realized it would be twice the work to break the siege on Rantis. But then, suddenly, soldiers swooped down on those of us holding tools, and grabbed them out of our hands. We began to chant "Dai LaKibbush," which means "End the Occupation." Some struggled not to release their shovels, others less. Soon, the soldiers had confiscated every tool we had brought, and arrested four of us.
>
> In my recollection, there was no pause at that point and no discussion about what to do. We just all got down and with our bare hands began to scratch out handfuls of dirt and rocks, and throw them into the trenches. Some of us used rocks to loosen the ground, others tried sticks. Some held posters (that read "Dismantle the Settlements") on the ground like big dustpans, and others pushed pebbles and dirt onto them, for transfer

into the trench. Some of the children from Rantis came out and joined us, and we worked together like that in the hot sun for over two hours. And when it was over, everyone was amazed to see that we had actually filled in both trenches, and made the road passable.

And now at home, freshly showered and sitting down to tell you about this small victory, I get a call from Dina, who made friends with one of the villagers. The army returned, the Palestinian told her, and used their heavy machinery to dig out fresh trenches. We expected that. And now, he said, they also placed large concrete slabs in front of the trenches, which could never be moved by bare hands and grit alone. And the truck that had brought these slabs had driven off the road, deliberately destroying crops in the fields. And one villager had been beaten and his car window smashed.

These are more than just reprisals against the Palestinians. They are a message from the army to us: this will happen every time you do something like this.

Tomorrow, five women will go to Rantis to document the new damage and talk to the villagers. We'll also be thinking about how to continue to subvert the oppression without jeopardizing the Palestinians themselves.

This concept of resistance had its first significant expression on the Israeli side in 1998, when the Israeli Committee Against House Demolitions began to rebuild homes that had been destroyed by the Israeli army. These rebuildings effectively drew international attention to this issue, especially when rebuilt homes were subsequently demolished. Now, resistance has also become an integral component of actions planned by other progressive Israeli organizations—those mentioned above and others. Moreover, a few individuals—young women, in particular—have pushed resistance one step further by lying down in front of army bulldozers and chaining themselves to olive trees, in an effort to prevent further destruction of Palestinian homes and property, ending invariably in arrests. Protest has clearly entered the stage of civil disobedience for many.

Other Arenas of Occupation Protest

Three other significant genres of peace activity can be delineated.

First, there are the street-theater protests of small groups of young people in their 20s and 30s. A group called Direct Action drove two cars through Tel Aviv while they broadcast, "A curfew has been imposed on Tel Aviv. Residents must enter their homes. People seen on the streets after 7:30 pm risk responses according to the usual procedures." This, of course, is the same announcement used by the IDF to impose curfews on Palestinian areas. Three of the activists were arrested for "terrorizing the public."

In the same vein, the so-called Passover Closure Group "lay siege" to Kokhav Ya'ir, an upscale Israeli community where many army generals reside. The announcement of that action read: "Kokhav Ya'ir is a place inhabited by several army generals who endanger both our security and the security of the whole region. Therefore, for security reasons, tomorrow, Thursday April 11, we will put a siege on this town to prevent these dangerous people from leaving it to go about their harmful business." Again, a takeoff on IDF tactics.

And a group called ReFrame staged a march through Jerusalem carrying signs saying "Restore the British Mandate!" Perhaps they confused some onlookers, but the message was clear: British colonial rule of Palestine was in many ways more benign than the Israeli occupation. This defiance of the Israeli occupation by the young—often daring, often with humor—helps expose the absurdities of the occupation and subvert the self-righteousness of its perpetrators.

Second, groups of Israelis have organized convoys of aid to Palestinian villages—food, medicine, supplies. This kind of action is useful for several reasons: It brings material support that is much needed, it draws attention to the plight of Palestinians under the closure, and it defies Israeli army regulations that forbid Israelis to enter areas under siege. Understanding that these are acts of protest, the Israeli army often impedes them and sometimes arrests participants, drawing important media attention. Organizations pursuing this kind of activity include Ta'ayush (Arab-Jewish Partnership) and Windows—Channels for Communication. Several individuals have also organized such convoys.

Third, resistance to army service is another kind of peace activity, even though it is unclear how much of it has to do with ideology. An article in the London *Daily Telegraph* by Inigo Gilmore (April 1, 2001) reported that "Israel has jailed 600 reserve soldiers in an attempt to halt a growing rebellion against military service in the West Bank and Gaza Strip…. At least 2,500 reservists have gone absent without leave, while thousands of others have become 'grey conscientious objectors', meaning that they have fabricated medical or personal reasons why they should not be called up for duty."

The IDF conceals these statistics, but there is clear evidence of the reluctance of Israeli men to show up for army reserve duty. In a series of demonstrations in recent months, Israeli reserve-duty soldiers have demanded better pay, increased medical insurance, and other perks for service; and Knesset members are hurrying to enact laws to satisfy them. This suggests that the lawmakers, who know the statistics, are deeply concerned. While shirking duty may, to some extent, be motivated by personal rather than ideological reasons, in a sense this "postideology" orientation—the chipping away at the heroic image of the army—is itself encouraging. And whatever the numbers of those in jail, organizations that offer support to conscientious objectors (New Profile) and even encourage young men not to serve in the occupied territories (Yesh Gvul) report increased numbers of calls from men asking for help. This is certainly a source of optimism.

Cooperative Efforts With Palestinians

Finally, a word about cooperation between Israeli and Palestinian peace activists. The injunction among Palestinians against "normalizing" relations with Israelis—in effect for years, but ratcheted up to higher levels since the Al-Aqsa Intifada—has certainly taken a toll on cooperative activities. Most joint activity—dialogue, academic projects, school programs, peace work, and other—has simply stopped. While individual Palestinians continue to be helpful to the Israeli peace camp (their help is essential in setting up some of the actions on the Palestinian side), on an institutional level, this cooperation no longer exists, or only partially exists. For example, in late 2000, Palestinian women staged two small protest demonstrations at the checkpoints and invited Israeli women from Bat Shalom to demonstrate "in parallel, but separately."

The first major event that was fully cooperative took place on April 14 and was a particularly moving occasion, which I described as follows:

> Today was a great day for peace in the Middle East. Palestinian, Israeli, and international activists for peace managed to break through the barriers separating us, push through cordon after cordon of Israeli soldiers, and meet together to pledge ourselves to end the occupation and make a just peace between our peoples.
>
> The event was initiated and sponsored by the Center for Rapprochement, a Palestinian peace organization based in the town of Beit Sahour, not far from Bethlehem. On the Israeli side, the sponsors were the Coalition of Women for a Just Peace, Gush Shalom, Rapprochement, and the Committee Against House Demolitions. The internationals—split between both sides—included people from Italy, Germany, the US, England, France, and probably many other countries. We were about 200 on each side.
>
> As agreed, the Palestinians started out from the Hotel Paradise in Bethlehem, which has suffered so much severe shelling in recent weeks. Israelis started from the Mar Elias Monastery on the Israeli side. At the pre-arranged time, both groups walked simultaneously toward the checkpoint separating Bethlehem from Jerusalem, the barrier between Israel and Palestine-to-be. Many of our signs said, "End the Occupation" and "Stop the Siege of Palestinian Towns," but primarily our message was the medium—the meeting of Palestinian and Israeli allies for peace. We had not expected to actually get closer than waving distance, and that's how it started.
>
> Soldiers prevented the Palestinians from continuing along the main road, but they took side streets and were finally brought to a halt about 100 meters from the checkpoint. The Israelis took the main road and walked right up to the checkpoint, where the soldiers formed a cordon to block us from going through. They presented an order that the area was a "closed military zone." After some negotiation, they agreed to allow in a "small delegation." Our "small delegation" turned into thirty, as more and more people slipped through the soldiers and became delegates. The delegation walked down the road and we could see the Palestinians at the other end waiting for us, and we began to chant, "Peace—Yes! Occupation—No!" When we reached the Palestinians, we fell into each other's arms and embraced, even though most of us barely knew each other.
>
> Moved by the moment, the group spontaneously turned to walk together to the checkpoint, even though the soldiers now formed a solid wall of armed men to block us. We interlocked arms and walked right up to them and began to push through. They fortunately did not draw their weapons, but locked their arms against us. But how could they possibly win, with no moral strength on their side? And we were infused with a burning sense of doing the right thing. We pushed and they pushed back, and there seemed to be a standoff, and the soldier pushing me said, "You don't have a chance against us," and I heard myself say, "You have no idea how powerful a moral purpose can be," and one of us was apparently right, because soon I felt them giving way, and our group was pushing them backwards, and we were moving forward. They dropped back and regrouped, and again we had our pushing game, and this went on for nearly half an hour, until they could not

contain this powerful group, and we pushed through their entire cordon and broke through to the group of Israelis cheering us on and waiting at the checkpoint.

The meeting of both groups was as inspired a moment as can be. People were clapping and whistling and hugging and shaking each other's hands and slapping backs. There were meetings of old friends, and making of new friends. The moment felt so sweet. There were speeches, but nobody could hear us, and who cares what we said. The very fact of our presence together, united in our yearning for peace, for justice, for a state of Palestine side by side with a state of Israel, was all that really mattered.

This sort of activity is of great importance in motivating Israelis to openly oppose the occupation. It is also of inestimable value in the symbolic impact that it conveys to the rest of the world: that significant numbers of Israelis and Palestinians are struggling together for peace. From such a common platform, joint messages about the specifics of the peace agreement would be even more powerful. This format was used for years by the Jerusalem Link—a joint Israeli and Palestinian women's peace movement—but the Palestinian side of the Link withdrew from cooperation when the Al-Aqsa Intifada broke out. Although Arafat himself has recently eased the injunction against cooperating with Israeli NGOs, provided they meet certain criteria, cooperative ventures are sometimes thwarted by Islamist or nationalist groups on the ground, and even by moderate Palestinians at times when violence by either side is exacerbated.

In Closing

The only visible movement for peace in Israel since the Al-Aqsa Intifada began has been the progressive voice. But that is not enough. When the leadership of Peace Now and the Meretz Party become convinced that they can be one step ahead of their constituencies, helping them develop a more nuanced understanding of the conflict, this will mark a sea change in restoring support for a negotiated peace inside Israel. Historically, it has always been the role of the progressive peace movement in Israel to nip at the heels of the liberals and shift them leftward; this task continues.

Notes

1. See "Peace Index—March 2001," conducted by E. Yaar and T. Hermann, Tami Steinmetz Center for Peace Research, Tel Aviv University, www.tau.ac.il/peace; and "Israeli Attitudes Toward Peace," conducted by Mina Zemach for *Yediot Ahronot*, March 30, 2001.

2. Reuven Kaminer, *The Politics of Protest: The Israeli Peace Movement and the Palestinian Intifada* (Brighton, England, 1996), p. 98.

20. REBUILDING OUR ACTIVISM

WHAT WE CAN LEARN FROM THE EXAMPLE OF SOUTH AFRICA AND THE CIVIL RIGHTS MOVEMENT

NANCY MURRAY

"If there is no struggle, there is no progress. Those who profess to favor freedom, and yet deprecate agitation…want crops without plowing up the ground…. Power concedes nothing without a demand. It never did and never will."

—Frederick Douglass, 1857

These words could serve as an epitaph for the Oslo process, officially declared dead in February 2001 by both Prime Minister Ariel Sharon and President George W. Bush. They stand as an indictment of the behind-the-scenes deal-making initiated at Oslo, which turned legitimate Palestinian resistance into illegitimate anti-Israel "incitement" and eviscerated the demands of the first intifada—the demand for an end to the Israeli occupation and colonization of Palestinian land, for meaningful self-determination, for human rights, for the implementation of UN resolutions and international law.

The prime demand of Oslo was that the Palestinian Authority (PA) serve as watchdog for Israeli security, not its own people's interests. Under Oslo, Israel has quite literally, and vigorously, plowed up the ground to expand settlements and "Jewish only" bypass roads, doubling the number of settlers. Palestinians have been forced to harvest the bitter fruit of closure, of steep economic decline, of repeated human rights violations by both the occupier of thirty-four years and its "peace partner." As the term "occupied" morphed into "disputed," and "two states" into one dominant power and several fragmented enclaves, it seemed just a matter of time before international law and UN resolutions would be evicted altogether from final-status talks, leaving the discredited Palestinian leadership to sign on to whatever Israel, backed by the world's superpower, was prepared to concede at the negotiating table.

The September Uprising

The Al-Aqsa Intifada has succeeded in laying Oslo to rest, but at a human cost that may prove too much for its population to endure. Israel's resort to economic strangulation and blockades, and its use of sharpshooters, undercover death squads, US-made Apache and Cobra attack helicopters, tanks and other military armaments against Palestinian villages and towns, have paralyzed life to such an extent that, in the words of *Ha'aretz* journalist Amira Hass, "every car trip is a minor uprising."[1] The lack of an overall Palestinian strategy and effective leadership, the failure to mobilize all the segments of civil society, and the opening that the militarization of struggle has given to the most intense repression are

Left: Office of the Palestinian newspaper Al Hayat al-Jadidah, sandbagged to protect from Israeli gunfire

sounding alarm bells within the occupied territories and diaspora. Citing as examples the struggle against South African apartheid and the American civil rights movement, Edward Said deplored the lack of leadership and vision in the pages of *Al-Ahram Weekly* and reminded readers that "only a mass movement employing tactics and strategy that maximize the popular element has ever made any difference on the occupier and/or oppressor."[2]

The limitations of the Al-Aqsa Intifada are compounded by the weakness of the international solidarity movement—another casualty of the Oslo process, especially in the United States, where it is most needed. Shortly after the signing of the 1993 Declaration of Principles, the blueprint for the torturous agreements and disagreements that transfixed the media over the next seven years, I wrote as follows in *Breaking the Siege*, the newsletter of the Middle East Justice Network: "A solution that consigns the Palestinians to be Israel's wards in entities amounting, at most, to bantustans is no solution at all. As the system of apartheid is dismantled in South Africa, we must not stand by to see it erected in the West Bank and Gaza Strip, complete with the stamp of international legitimacy."[3]

At the time, this point of view brought us considerable criticism. We were seen to be anti-peace diehards, unwilling to admit that the Israeli-Palestinian conflict was at long last approaching a "solution," and woefully out of step with Arafat's diplomatic offensive. Within a few years, there was no organized way of alerting the broad public to the reality rapidly taking shape on the ground. "Even at its worst," wrote Professor Israel Shahak on May 12, 1995, "South African apartheid was not as all-inclusive as what is planned for the West Bank and what already exists in the Gaza." In the United States, who knew?

By October 2000, while American pundits were castigating the Palestinians for their refusal to embrace Israel's "generous" offer of a state, an editorial in the (UK) *Observer* saw things very differently:

> If Palestinians were black, Israel would now be a pariah state subject to economic sanctions led by the United States. Its development and settlement of the West Bank would be seen as a system of apartheid, in which the 'indigenous' population was allowed to live in a tiny fraction of its own country, in self-administered 'bantustans,' with 'whites' monopolising the supply of water and electricity. And just as the black population was allowed into South Africa's white areas in disgracefully under-resourced townships, so Israel's treatment of Israeli Arabs—flagrantly discriminating against them in housing and education spending—would be recognized as scandalous too.… Israel's indefensible policy of apartheid must be condemned for what it is. Until then there can be only more distrust, hatred and violence.[4]

Unfortunately, practically until the demise of the Oslo process, both Yasir Arafat and the South African government viewed it as "the only way to reach lasting peace in the region."[5] After five years of frustrating talks, with settlements rapidly expanding and conditions worsening on the ground, Arafat finally turned in desperation to the international community. During his August 1998 state visit to

South Africa he called for the United States, the European Union, and the global community to exert on Israel "the same kind of international pressure that was put on the apartheid regime in its last years. No one can deny the role international economic sanctions played against the apartheid regime in forcing it to enter negotiations and reach a permanent settlement."[6]

Arafat's appeal for government-to-government intervention showed little understanding of the grassroots nature of the anti-apartheid movement that pressured governments into adopting sanctions. Neither did he appear to recognize the role played by the mass mobilization in South Africa and the international community in bringing South African Prime Minister de Klerk to the negotiating table and keeping him there. Such mobilization made it possible for the African National Congress (ANC), in Nelson Mandela's words, "to use the negotiations process to capture beach-heads within the power equation, and then proceed to strengthen our forces from a new vantage point."[7]

Whatever criticisms one may have of the compromises made by the ANC, especially of its capitulation to economic neoliberalism, one must admit that the successive "beach-heads" it captured, culminating in the April 1994 elections and the ratification of a new Constitution, represent significantly greater gains for the South African people than the circumscribed territorial toe-holds established by the PA. The ANC did not simply conduct behind-the-scenes negotiations, PLO-style. As Mandela reported to the 49th ANC Conference in December 1994, it was concerned "to pursue negotiations combined with mass actions, as well as strengthening our organizational and military capacity.... We also had to adopt a new approach to our own relations with the international community, to ensure that the world supported change in a manner that strengthened the forces of democracy in our country."

Can anything sound further removed from the way Arafat chose to play what one PLO official termed "the only game in town"? For years the nascent forces of democracy within Palestinian society had been stifled by a corrupt PA and Arafat's authoritarian leadership, with occasional "mass actions" orchestrated by one or other of the more than ten Palestinian security forces. The Fatah-led Al-Aqsa Intifada has been a genuinely popular uprising spearheaded by refugees, but it has not engaged all sectors of the society in the manner of the first intifada, and its goals have never been clearly articulated. Given the apartheid realities on the ground, what hopes were left for a two-state solution?

By 2001 despair about where things were heading was intensified by the spectacle of the PA collaborating with the Barak government and CIA to keep the Oslo process alive even as it executed Palestinians for the crime of collaboration and arrested Islamic activists in a Gaza refugee camp on the pretext of targeting collaborators. In the words of the Gaza Strip's *Ramattan Daily*, the arrests "raised many questions about the relationship between the PNA [Palestine National Authority] and the people, and that of opposition parties and PNA institutions."[8] Popular disillusion with the leadership grew as the Israeli occupation forces throttled the economy; seized more land; razed homes, greenhouses and olive trees; blockaded roads used by Palestinians and built new roads to service settlements; and killed and injured Palestinian civilians at will. Under these circumstances it is not surprising that the people of the northern Gaza Strip refused to heed the call to make Israeli election day a "day of rage."[9]

It is also hardly surprising that US supporters of Palestinian rights are finding it difficult to surmount the confusion surrounding current developments. There have been robust local pro-Palestinian demonstrations since late September, teach-ins and other forums, and significant Internet organizing is being done around the refugees' right of return and against media bias. But the absence of a well-organized, nationwide solidarity movement has meant that while the repression of Palestinians is being underwritten by US tax dollars and carried out with US military weapons, the US mainstream media and elected representatives are able to ignore these facts and to exonerate Israel from responsibility for the rising toll of dead and injured.

What kind of resistance must be developed within Palestine and the international community—especially the United States—if we are to maximize the potential for a just solution to the Israeli-Palestinian conflict? The indigenous and international movement against South African apartheid offers valuable lessons and a constituency that could well be the source of fruitful alliances in the work ahead.

The South African Example

We often forget that the indigenous resistance to European colonization in southern Africa was hundreds of years in the making. The ANC was founded as long ago as 1912. This was a year before the Native Lands Act set aside just 13.6 percent of the land of South Africa for African peoples, who made up 75 percent of the population. After apartheid was made official government policy in 1948, the land set aside for Africans was divided into ten separate and noncontiguous bantustans, or "national states." Some 4 million Africans were forcibly removed from "white areas" (often with only a day's notice) and dumped into bleak bantustans, where they would supposedly exercise their "citizenship" rights. The South African government declared four of these bantustans to be "independent nations" and carried out forced removals to the very brink of negotiations—in 1987 nearly 48,000 Africans were forcibly resettled.

There is a tendency today to think that the South African bantustan policy was so preposterous that it never would have been acceptable to the international community. But in the absence of unrelenting resistance within South Africa and the development of a significant international solidarity movement, would this still have been the case? In the eyes of the West, apartheid South Africa was both a source of mineral wealth and a pivotal ally in the cold war. As Israeli Professor Benjamin Beit-Hallahmi has documented, the United States long colluded in the "unique alliance" between Israel and South Africa, seeing it as a way of strengthening bulwarks against both the Soviet Union and national liberation movements.[10] It took sustained public education and pressure on government elites to make the international recognition of bantustans unthinkable. This may seem to be stating the obvious, but it bears repeating, given the failure to mount a similar campaign of education and agitation against the legitimation of apartheid in Palestine.

President Arafat, for example, did not seem to realize that the kind of international pressure he called for during his 1998 visit to South Africa was the *culmination* of the resistance that was mounted in various sectors of South African society after the banning of the ANC, through such channels as the Black Consciousness movement, the student movement, the United Democratic Front (comprising over 700 organizations and 2 million members), the trade union movement COSATU, and finally the Mass Democratic Movement.

We should also remind ourselves of the magnitude of the international struggle—beginning in the late 1950s and 1960s anti-apartheid groups were established in most European countries, and soon in the United States. In response to an appeal from the ANC, these groups initiated a boycott of South African goods, raised money for the Treason Trials defendants (1956–61), disseminated information about apartheid through articles, films, buttons, songs, T-shirts, skits, plays, murals, posters, demonstrations, school curricula and cultural events, pressured their governments and sent material aid to the liberation movement. Activists campaigned for divestment, for sanctions legislation, for a trade embargo and a people's boycott of South African products, and for the release of Nelson Mandela and all political prisoners. Members of the US Congressional Black Caucus demonstrated in front of the South African Embassy (in striking contrast to the support that twenty-one members of the CBC gave House Resolution 426 on October 24, 2000, absolving Israel from blame for violence in the West Bank and Gaza). A UN-initiated mandatory arms embargo, voluntary oil embargo, cultural boycott, sports boycott and attempt to isolate South Africa economically intensified the pressure. School kids boycotted Coca-Cola and the Kellogg Corporation because of their ties with South Africa. Longshoremen in some seaports refused to unload ships from South Africa, and airport workers refused to unload planes. As negotiations got under way, this international solidarity apparatus was not abandoned. Instead, the heat was kept up through a call for comprehensive sanctions, and a "Vote for Democracy" campaign pushed for the main demand of the 1955 Freedom Charter—one person, one vote in a unified, nonracial South Africa.

It is often assumed that it is impossible to build this kind of a grassroots movement for Palestinian rights because of the strength of the pro-Israel lobby and the hardball tactics that are used to silence other voices. Granted, the Afrikaners could not invoke the Holocaust to justify their deeds (although they could claim to be victims of concentration camps, erected by the British during the Boer War). However, anyone who has done Palestinian solidarity work in the United States knows how profoundly compelling the Palestinian story can be, and how relatively easy it is to move audiences beyond the pro-Israel propaganda they usually hear. During the 1970s and early 1980s, some public opinion polls showed that by a 2-1 margin Americans opposed increasing military assistance to Israel and supported the idea of a separate Palestinian state. By the late 1980s, images of the intifada had created a groundswell of sympathy for Palestinians around the world, including in the United States. Regrettably, the opportunity of telling the story, of activating the latent empathy for the Palestinian cause, was largely squandered by the PLO.

Writing in 1984, the British journalist James Adams stated that "the campaigns against South Africa and Israel in the United Nations and elsewhere grow more fierce every day. In many people's minds, apartheid and Israel's policies against the Palestinians have become synonymous."[11] Adams's observations were based on what was happening in Europe. The level of understanding in the United States was, as ever, considerably more stunted. The Massachusetts-based Middle East Justice Network held international conferences in 1989 and 1991 to highlight the parallels and connections between Israel and South Africa, and it took anti-apartheid activists on delegations to the West Bank and Gaza. Familiar as they were with conditions in South Africa under the State of Emergency, they were invariably shocked by the intensity of repression in the territories.

But this was isolated activity. As apartheid was being dismantled in South Africa, only to be reinforced in Palestine, there were no "fierce campaigns" in evidence, and barely a glimmer of recognition about the obvious parallels.

Edward Said has suggested why this was the case in several of his essays, including "Decolonizing the Mind" (1994) and "Strategies of Hope" (1997).[12] Said contrasts the ANC's recognition of the crucial importance of cultivating international grassroots support with the approach of Palestinian activist-intellectuals and PLO officials. They preferred cultivating the "experts" and influential policy-makers rather than "wasting time" trying to create a grassroots movement. To them, nothing mattered outside Washington. This egregious short-sightedness and ignorance about the functioning of civil society in the West, especially in the United States, has permitted Israel to violate Palestinian rights, confiscate Palestinian land, expand settlements and bypass roads, and carve up the territories into bantustans with virtual impunity.

As for the solidarity work that did exist a decade ago in the United States, it was underfunded and underdeveloped, and sometimes undermined by the factional fault line (Fatah versus Popular Front for the Liberation of Palestine) that ran through Palestinian-American society. For the most part it was isolated both in its impact and its reach. Except during the buildup to the Gulf War, little effort was made to create working alliances with groups not exclusively focused on Israel/Palestine.

What lessons can we now take from the case of South Africa, as we seek to rebuild our activism? I would argue that late as it is, it is not too late to build on what has already been achieved by the progressive movement, which has created everywhere potential allies opposed to apartheid, bantustans, forced removals, house demolitions, racism, torture, and other human rights violations. We need to form new working alliances and draw upon the strategies of the anti-apartheid movement to assess what can work in the Palestinian context. A first step in this process was taken at the University of California at Berkeley in early February 2001, when a teach-in titled "Apartheid Then, Apartheid Now" discussed divestment as a tool against human rights violations in Palestine. Organizers pointed out that the anti-apartheid campaign in the 1980s induced the University of California Regents to sign a declaration of principles agreeing to withhold investments from all countries that violate international human rights laws, yet today, 7 percent of the University of California's $50 billion endowment is invested in the Israeli economy.

The South African example shows the importance of knowing where you want to go, and of clearly and insistently articulating not just a goal or goals of struggle but a vision of a new society that can engage the population and form the basis for international solidarity work. The South African Freedom Charter enabled anti-apartheid activists to seize the high moral ground. The goal was one person, one vote, in a nonracial South Africa. On this there could be absolutely no compromise. Articulating a vision of what the society could look like when it was no longer deformed by apartheid culminated in the extraordinary effort of soliciting over a million submissions to the Constitutional Assembly, which then distributed for comment in the country's eleven official languages some 4 million copies of the working draft of the new Constitution, accompanied by explanations for both literate and illiterate audiences.

Contrast this with Israeli-Palestinian negotiations, a "process" that led to no discernible destination and no popular involvement, but to the opportunity for endless compromise and surrender, and to plenty of wishful thinking about a Palestinian state, with no analysis about what that state would look like and what powers it would possess. In the absence of democratic structures and fully mobilized support, both inside and outside Palestine, any "state" Israel might agree to will fail the aspirations of the Palestinian people.

The Example of the US Civil Rights Movement

How can Palestinians and their international supporters together shake off Oslo-induced defeatism and nurture a resistance that speaks truth to power? We can draw certain lessons from the struggle of African-Americans in the 1950s and 1960s. Each summer I take a group of young people on a civil rights tour of the South to learn about the successes and "unfinished business" of the Movement, in both its civil rights and Black Power phase. We get an understanding of the strengths and limitations of the techniques of civil disobedience, economic boycott, and other forms of nonviolent direct action used by the protesters. We discover the short-sighted nature of the goals put forward in the civil rights phase of the Movement, which did indeed end legal segregation and give African-Americans the vote—but also left the racial hierarchy in place and economic power undisturbed. What good is it, Dr. King finally asked, to be able to sit at a lunch counter if you can't afford the price of a hamburger? In South Africa today the same question is being asked.

The Movement broke apart before it could make significant strides toward the kind of economic restructuring that both King and Malcolm X sought in the last years of their lives. Student Nonviolent Coordinating Committee veteran Hollis Watkins, who accompanied us to South Africa in 1996, explained the failure to make the sort of lasting changes that would transform the US socioeconomic order in the following way: "We mobilized, but we didn't organize."

There is more to organizing than bringing people into the streets. Organizing involves a careful match of tactics and strategy. It requires thorough investigation of the problem and the planning of successive actions that can consolidate gains and enable a step-by-step movement toward long-term goals. It necessitates weighing up the costs of particular actions, so that the population is not forced to make more sacrifices than it can reasonably bear.

Israeli repression of both intifadas teaches us that the tactics of nonviolent direct action that worked in the United States in the 1950s and 1960s will not necessarily work in the same way in the occupied territories. Tear gas and clubs were used against the men, women and children who attempted to march from Selma to Montgomery in 1965. But bullets were used against the students of Soweto protesting Bantu education, and against the Children of the Stones demonstrating against the occupation. Civil disobedience in the West Bank and Gaza has little chance of being effective if we in the international community fail to organize. We must use all the resources at our command to focus world attention on the situation in the territories and maximize the pressure on Israel and the US government—not just with one grand action, but day in and day out, and if necessary, year after year.

As we get started, we can draw some encouragement from the Civil Rights Movement: apparently, mass meetings back then were not so "mass." They often involved fewer than ten people. Nor was the grassroots leadership particularly numerous. During its five-year lifetime, SNCC only had a few hundred organizers and field workers. We were told that the work often seemed incredibly slow and discouraging, with little to show for months of door-to-door attempts to get people to overcome their fear and get involved. But a handful of activists persevered, working with the situation at hand in the face of pervasive fear, violence and intimidation, and they finally managed to achieve their immediate goals.

Moving Forward

We in the international community who are committed to the Palestinian cause can take comfort from the movement example. We must not allow ourselves to be paralyzed by our scattered numbers, by Arafat's authoritarianism and the confusion surrounding the Al-Aqsa Intifada, but we should work with the situation at hand, taking advantage of all available opportunities to plow up the ground.

Building a new movement requires knowledge of the lies, mistakes and traps that other struggles can illuminate. It also requires the kind of truth-telling Mandela had in mind when, on February 27, 1990, shortly after his release from prison, he embraced Arafat at the airport in Lusaka, Zambia. At a press conference Mandela stressed the similarities between the struggles of the ANC and PLO and added, "If the truth alienates the powerful Jewish community in South Africa, that's too bad.... We expect everybody who is exploring the possibility of lasting solutions to be able to face the truth squarely."

We must organize for the long haul—and make up for lost time. No matter how unclear the signals from the West Bank and Gaza, there are certain things we do know that can be the basis of our renewed activism.

First, we know that there will be no lasting peace without a recognition of the Palestinian Right of Return and restitution. Four million people, international law and UN resolutions cannot be made to disappear because Israel refuses to acknowledge them. The case of the refugees was not insistently articulated as a "demand" during the first intifada. We must now make the refugee cause an integral part of all our organizing work, using the excellent material produced by Salman Abu Sitta and others. We must also find ways to forge links with Palestinians in the camps, so their voices can be heard more powerfully in the West.

Second, we know that as US taxpayers we have a direct responsibility for the ongoing Israeli occupation of Palestinian land and violation of Palestinian rights. Back in May 1989, the 700 delegates of the World Council of Churches conference on World Mission and Evangelism, meeting in San Antonio, Texas, called the first intifada "a liberation struggle which is transforming the Palestinians from victims to controllers and builders of their own destiny." They then adopted a resolution requesting the churches of the United States to "demand of their government that all forms of military and economic aid to the state of Israel be withheld until the legitimate rights of the Palestinians are achieved." Instead, our aid has been used over the past decade to perpetuate a terrible injustice and our weapons have killed and maimed thousands. We must inform Americans across the country about what they are paying for—and encourage them to join the campaign to end it.

Finally, we must learn from the example of South Africa how to create a powerful grassroots anti-apartheid movement. Did we fight to dismantle South African apartheid only to stand by while a new apartheid system is erected in Israel/Palestine? If the Palestinians can re-invigorate their uprising with a vision and set of concrete goals that proclaim to the world they will not trade meaningful sovereignty for disconnected bantustans, if they can embrace democracy as a strategy for liberation, both personal and national, if international supporters can carry out the grassroots work of education and agitation, then a "demand" will be created that Israel will be unable to resist. That is the task before us.

An earlier version of this article was delivered as a talk at the Center for Policy Analysis on Palestine in September 1998.

Notes

1. *Ha'aretz*, January 28, 2001.

2. December 7–13, 2000.

3. October-November 1993.

4. *Guardian Weekly*, October 19–25, 2000.

5. South Africa Foreign Affairs Department, August 10, 1998, quoted in *This Week in South Africa: News Highlights from the South African Media*, August 11–17, 1998.

6. Ibid.

7. Political report by President Nelson Mandela to the 49th African National Congress National Conference, December 1994.

8. *Ramattan Daily—The Daily News Update Direct from Gaza*, February 4, 2001.

9. *Ramattan Daily*, February 7, 2001.

10. Benjamin Beit-Hallahmi, *The Israeli Connection: Who Israel Arms and Why* (New York, 1987).

11. James Adams, *The Unnatural Alliance: Israel and South Africa* (Quartet Books, 1984), p. 18.

12. Edward W. Said, "Decolonizing the Mind," *Peace and Its Discontents: Essays on Palestine in the Middle East Peace Process* (New York, 1996); "Strategies of Hope," *The End of the Peace Process: Oslo and After* (New York, 2000).

ABOUT THE AUTHORS

Ali Abunimah, vice president of the Arab-American Action Network, a Chicago-based social service and advocacy organization, is a coordinator of the website *The Electronic Intifada* and a contributor to *Iraq Under Siege: The Deadly Impact of Sanctions and War.*

Salman Abu Sitta, the author of more than fifty articles on the Palestinian refugees, is a former member of the Palestine National Council. He is president of the Palestine Land Society.

Ghassan Andoni is president of the Palestinian Center for Rapprochement between People, based in Beit Sahour, occupied West Bank (www.rapprochement.org).

Omar Barghouti, a doctoral candidate in philosophy (ethics) at Tel Aviv University, is a regular contributor to Palestine Media Watch (www.pmwatch.org/pmw/index.asp).

Nidal Barham lives in Beit Sahour and teaches English at the Talitha Kumi Lutheran School in Beit Jala, both in the occupied West Bank.

Dr. Azmi Bishara is a Palestinian Member of Israel's Knesset representing the National Democratic Alliance (Tajammu).

Noam Chomsky, Institute Professor in the department of linguistics and philosophy at the Massachusetts Institute of Technology, is the author of many books, including *Fateful Triangle: The United States, Israel, and the Palestinians*; *Deterring Democracy*; *World Orders Old and New*; and *A New Generation Draws the Line: Kosovo, East Timor and the Standards of the West.*

Robert Fisk, a seven-time winner of the British International Journalist of the Year Award, is Middle East correspondent for *The Independent* of London. He is the author of several books, including *Pity the Nation: The Abduction of Lebanon.*

Muna Hamzeh was born in Jerusalem, educated in Jordan and the United States, and lived for over ten years in the refugee camp of Dheisheh in the occupied West Bank. She has written for *Ha'aretz, The Economist,* and the *Christian Science Monitor* and is the author of *Refugees in Our Own Land: Chronicles from a Palestinian Refugee Camp in Bethlehem.*

Hussein Ibish is national media director of the American-Arab Anti-Discrimination Committee.

Jennifer Loewenstein, who has spoken and written extensively on the Israel/Palestine conflict and on the role of the United States in the Middle East, works with Palestinian refugees in Beirut, Lebanon, and in the occupied Gaza Strip. She also teaches English in the School of Business at the University of Wisconsin, Madison.

Nancy Murray is the former director of the Middle East Justice Network and a member of the Boston Coalition for Palestinian Rights. She is the author of *Palestinians: Life Under Occupation*.

Allegra Pacheco, a licensed American and Israeli human rights attorney, represents Palestinians in the occupied territories in Israeli military courts and the Israeli Supreme Court. Her practice includes house demolitions, land confiscations, torture, prisoners' rights, freedom of movement, and administrative detention. In 1999 Pacheco, along with several other Israeli attorneys, won a seminal case in the Israeli Supreme Court banning the use of certain torture methods in Israel.

Mouin Rabbani is director of the Palestinian American Research Center in the West Bank town of Ramallah.

Glenn E. Robinson, the author of *Building a Palestinian State: The Incomplete Revolution*, is an associate professor in the School of International Graduate Studies at the Naval Postgraduate School in Monterey, California, and a research fellow at the Center for Middle Eastern Studies at the University of California, Berkeley.

Sara Roy is a research associate at the Center for Middle Eastern Studies, Harvard University. She is the author of *The Gaza Strip: The Political Economy of De-Development*.

Edward W. Said is University Professor of English and comparative literature at Columbia Unversity. He is the author of many books, including *The Question of Palestine*, *Orientalism*, *The Politics of Dispossession*, *The End of the Peace Process* and, most recently, *Reflections on Exile*.

Ahdaf Soueif was born in Egypt and now lives between London and Cairo. Her novels include *In the Eye of the Sun* and *The Map of Love*, which was shortlisted for Britain's Booker Prize in 1999.

Mayssoun Sukarieh is a volunteer teacher in Shatila refugee camp in Beirut.

Gila Svirsky is a veteran peace and human rights activist in Israel. For many years, she was director in Israel of the New Israel Fund, and subsequently director of Bat Shalom—the Israeli side of The Jerusalem Link: A Women's Joint Venture for Peace. She has also served as chairperson of the Israeli human rights organization B'tselem. After the Al-Aqsa Intifada broke out in September 2000, she cofounded and coordinates the Coalition of Women for a Just Peace, a coalition of nine peace organizations.

Alison Weir, who was most recently the editor of *Marin Scope* newspaper in Sausalito, California, reported from the Palestinian territories as a freelancer.

RESOURCE GUIDE

Media Organizations

Al-Ahram Weekly Online
www.ahram.org.eg/weekly
This Cairo journal features regular dispatches from Edward Said, Graham Usher, and others.

The Alternative Information Center
www.alternativenews.org
This Palestinian-Israeli information and research organization publishes *News From Within*.

Between the Lines
P.O. Box 681, Jerusalem
E-mail: tikva20@zahav.net.il & toufic_haddad@hotmail.com
An indispensable new journal.

The Birzeit Complete Guide to Palestine's Websites
www.birzeit.edu/links
Brought to you by Palestine's flagship university.

The Electronic Intifada
www.electronicintifada.net
"A Resource for Countering Myth, Distortion and Spin from the Israeli Media War Machine."

Ha'aretz English Edition
www3.haaretz.co.il/eng/htmls/1_1.htm
Israel's leading daily.

The Independent Media Center, Israel
www.indymedia.org.il/imc/israel/webcast/index.php3
An independent media collective "offering grassroots, non-corporate coverage of major protests."

Middle East Research & Information Project (MERIP)
www.merip.org
Publishes the invaluable quarterly *Middle East Report*, as well as regular Press Information Notes on its website.

Palestine Information Clearinghouse

www.palestinemonitor.org

Set up by the Palestinian NGO Network as a "gateway to Palestinian civil society."

The Palestine Report and The Palestine Report Online

http://mail.jmcc.org/media/reportonline

"Palestine's Only Independent News Digest," a project of the Jerusalem Media and Communications Center.

ZNet's Mideast Watch

www.zmag.org/meastwatch/meastwat.htm

Articles by top analysts from all over the world, with a superb list of links.

Research Organizations

Applied Research Institute Jerusalem

www.arij.org

Founded in 1990, this nonprofit, originally set up as an aid to the agricultural community, offers a wealth of information and publications, including maps and photographs, on water, land use and other environmental issues in the occupied territories.

BADIL Resource Center for Palestinian Residency & Refugee Rights

www.badil.org

This community organization, based in Bethlehem and registered with the Palestinian Authority, offers information on the refugee issue.

Foundation for Middle East Peace

www.fmep.org

Publisher of the bimonthly Report on Israeli Settlement in the Occupied Territories.

Institute for Palestine Studies

www.ipsjps.org

This nonprofit research and publication center publishes the indispensable quarterly *Journal of Palestine Studies.*

MIFTAH: The Palestinian Initiative for the Promotion of Global Dialogue & Democracy

www.miftah.org

Established in 1999, this Jerusalem-based institution is "committed to fostering the principles of democracy and effective dialogue based on the free and candid exchange of information and ideas."

Palestinian Refugee Research Net

www.arts.mcgill.ca/mepp/prrn/prfront.html

This site, maintained by the Inter-University Consortium for Arab Studies in Montreal, offers scholarly research papers and documents on the refugee issue as well as links to other sites.

Union of Palestinian Medical Relief Committees

www.upmrc.org

Founded in 1979 by Palestinian doctors and health professionals, this group offers detailed statistics on intifada casualties.

Human Rights Organizations

Adalah: The Legal Center for Arab Minority Rights in Israel

www.adalah.org

This nonprofit was established in 1996.

Addameer (conscience): Prisoners Support and Human Rights Association

www.addameer.org

Established in 1992, Addameer focuses on support for Palestinian prisoners and campaigns against torture.

Al-Haq

www.alhaq.org

Founded in 1979, Al-Haq is the West Bank affiliate of the Geneva-based International Commission of Jurists.

Al Mezan Center for Human Rights

www.mezan.org

Founded in 1999 and based in the Jabalia refugee camp in the Gaza Strip, this NGO concentrates on economic, social, and cultural rights.

Amnesty International

www.amnesty.org

AI has issued several important policy statements on human rights violations since the outbreak of the intifada, including *Israel and the Occupied Territories: Excessive Use of Lethal Force.*

B'tselem: The Israeli Information Center for Human Rights in the Occupied Territories

www.btselem.org

The premier Israeli human rights organization, founded in 1989, has issued several major reports on the new

intifada, including *Illusions of Restraint* and *Civilians Under Siege*.

Center for Economic and Social Rights

www.cesr.org/index.html

This Brooklyn, New York–based organization, founded in 1993, has issued several detailed reports on social and economic human rights violations during the Oslo period.

Human Rights Watch

www.hrw.org

HRW has issued several major reports on the new intifada; see especially *Center of the Storm: A Case Study of Human Rights Abuses in Hebron District*.

LAW: The Palestinian Society for the Protection of Human Rights and the Environment

www.lawsociety.org

The LAW Society provides daily updates on human rights violations in the territories.

Palestinian Center for Human Rights

www.pchrgaza.org

Founded in 1995, this Gaza City–based NGO, affiliated with the International Commission of Jurists and the International Federation for Human Rights, investigates both Israeli and Palestinian Authority human rights violations.

Palestinian Human Rights Monitoring Group

www.phrmg.org

Founded in 1996, this group has done extensive work on human rights violations by the Palestinian Authority.

Physicians for Human Rights—Israel

www.derechos.net/ngo/phr

This Tel Aviv–based NGO was founded in 1988, during the first intifada.

United Nations Commission on Human Rights

www.unhchr.ch

Pursuant to an October 19, 2000, resolution of the commission, a Human Rights Inquiry Commission traveled to Israel and the territories and issued its important report, *Question of the Violation of Human Rights in the Occupied Arab Territories, Including Palestine,* on March 16, 2001.

Activist Groups

Al-Awda: The Palestine Right to Return Coalition

http://al-awda.org

Founded in April 2000 in the United States, Al-Awda has been conducting a vigorous grassroots campaign, especially in America, for Palestinian rights, including the right of refugees to return to their homes.

American-Arab Anti-Discrimination Committee

www.adc.org

Founded in 1980, this Washington, DC–based civil rights organization has long been active in the Palestinian cause.

Bat Shalom

www.batshalom.org

This Israeli feminist peace organization, based in West Jerusalem, has, with the Jerusalem Center for Women in East Jerusalem, formed the Jerusalem Link, a coalition of Israeli and Palestinian women working together for peace and cooperation between the two peoples.

Christian Peacemaker Teams

www.prairienet.org/cpt

The Christian Peacemaker Teams, composed of Mennonite, Church of the Brethren, the Friends United Meeting, and other groups, has maintained a presence in Hebron since 1995, in keeping with their mission of "'Getting in the Way'—challenging systems of domination and exploitation as Jesus Christ did in the first century."

Gush Shalom

www.gush-shalom.org

Established in 1992, Gush Shalom—the "Peace Bloc"—is an Israeli grassroots group that supports full Israeli withdrawal from the territories occupied in 1967 and a Palestinian state with East Jerusalem as its capital.

Ittijah: Union of Arab Community Based Organizations

www.ittijah.org

Founded in 1995, this umbrella group works "to end political, legal, social, economic and cultural discrimination against Palestinians in Israel."

Jewish Unity for a Just Peace

www.junity.org

An international grassroots activist group that supports "a complete end to Israel's Occupation of the West Bank, East Jerusalem and the Gaza Strip."

Jews for Justice in the Middle East

P.O. Box 14561

Berkeley, CA 94712

Publisher of *The Origin of the Israel-Palestine Conflict* (see www.cactus48.com).

Not in My Name

www.nimn.org

A loose coalition of Jewish American peace activists, Not in My Name is based on the principle that "peace can only be achieved when Israel withdraws from its settlements in the Palestinian territories and addresses the legitimate national and human rights of the Palestinian people."

Palestinian Center for Rapprochement Between People

www.rapprochement.org

Established in 1988, this nonreligious organization based in Beit Sahour in the occupied West Bank is formally registered under the auspices of the Mennonite Central Committee in Jerusalem. PCR's "main objective is to encourage peaceful solutions to the Palestinian cause through disabling existing stereotypes and prejudice."